2—

The Charleston, Savannah & Coastal Islands Book

The South of Broad neighborhood has its share of historic plaques but it never feels like a recreated and restored environment like Williamsburg.   Credit: Peter Loftus

6TH EDITION

THE CHARLESTON, SAVANNAH & COASTAL ISLANDS BOOK

Cecily
McMillan

The Countryman Press
Woodstock, Vermont

ISBN 978-1-58157-100-4
ISSN 1550-252X

Front cover photo © Quang-Tuan Luong, Terra Galleria Photography
Interior photos by the author unless otherwise specified
Book design by Bodenweber Design
Composition by Christine Cantera Design
Maps by Mapping Specialists Ltd., Madison, WI © The Countryman Press

Published by The Countryman Press, P.O. Box 748, Woodstock, Vermont 05091

Distributed by W. W. Norton & Company, Inc., 500 Fifth Avenue, New York, NY 10110

Manufactured in the United States of America

10 9 8 7 6 5 4 3 2 1

GREAT DESTINATIONS TRAVEL GUIDEBOOK SERIES

Recommended by *National Geographic Traveler* and *Travel + Leisure* magazines

[A] crisp and critical approach, for travelers who want to live like locals.
—*USA Today*

Great Destinations™ guidebooks are known for their comprehensive, critical coverage of regions of extraordinary cultural interest and natural beauty. The authors in this series are professional travel writers who have lived for many years in the regions they describe. Each title in this series is continuously updated with each printing to ensure accurate and timely information. All the books contain more than one hundred photographs and maps.

Current titles available:

THE ADIRONDACK BOOK

ATLANTA

AUSTIN, SAN ANTONIO
& THE TEXAS HILL COUNTRY

THE BERKSHIRE BOOK

BERMUDA

BIG SUR, MONTEREY BAY & GOLD COAST WINE
COUNTRY

CAPE CANAVERAL, COCOA BEACH
& FLORIDA'S SPACE COAST

THE CHARLESTON, SAVANNAH
& COASTAL ISLANDS BOOK

THE CHESAPEAKE BAY BOOK

THE COAST OF MAINE BOOK

COLORADO'S CLASSIC MOUNTAIN TOWNS

COSTA RICA: GREAT DESTINATIONS CENTRAL
AMERICA

THE FINGER LAKES BOOK

THE FOUR CORNERS REGION

GALVESTON, SOUTH PADRE ISLAND
& THE TEXAS GULF COAST

THE HAMPTONS BOOK

HAWAII'S BIG ISLAND

HONOLULU & OAHU: GREAT DESTINATIONS
HAWAII

THE JERSEY SHORE: ATLANTIC CITY TO CAPE MAY

KAUAI: GREAT DESTINATIONS HAWAII

LAKE TAHOE & RENO

LOS CABOS & BAJA CALIFORNIA SUR:
GREAT DESTINATIONS MEXICO

MAUI: GREAT DESTINATIONS HAWAII

MICHIGAN'S UPPER PENINSULA

MONTREAL & QUEBEC CITY:
GREAT DESTINATIONS CANADA

THE NANTUCKET BOOK

THE NAPA & SONOMA BOOK

NORTH CAROLINA'S OUTER BANKS
& THE CRYSTAL COAST

PALM BEACH, FORT LAUDERDALE, MIAMI & THE
FLORIDA KEYS

PALM SPRINGS & DESERT RESORTS

PHOENIX, SCOTTSDALE, SEDONA
& CENTRAL ARIZONA

PLAYA DEL CARMEN, TULUM & THE RIVIERA MAYA:
GREAT DESTINATIONS MEXICO

SALT LAKE CITY, PARK CITY, PROVO
& UTAH'S HIGH COUNTRY RESORTS

SAN DIEGO & TIJUANA

SAN JUAN, VIEQUES & CULEBRA:
GREAT DESTINATIONS PUERTO RICO

SAN MIGUEL DE ALLENDE & GUANAJUATO:
GREAT DESTINATIONS MEXICO

THE SANTA FE & TAOS BOOK

THE SARASOTA, SANIBEL ISLAND & NAPLES BOOK

THE SEATTLE & VANCOUVER BOOK

THE SHENANDOAH VALLEY BOOK

TOURING EAST COAST WINE COUNTRY

WASHINGTON, D.C., AND NORTHERN VIRGINIA

YELLOWSTONE & GRAND TETON NATIONAL PARKS AND
JACKSON HOLE

YOSEMITE & THE SOUTHERN SIERRA NEVADA

If you are traveling to, moving to, residing in, or just interested in any (or all!) of these enchanting regions, a Great Destinations guidebook is a superior companion. Honest and painstakingly critical, full of information only a local can provide, Great Destinations guidebooks give you all the practical knowledge you need to enjoy the best of each region. Why not own them all?

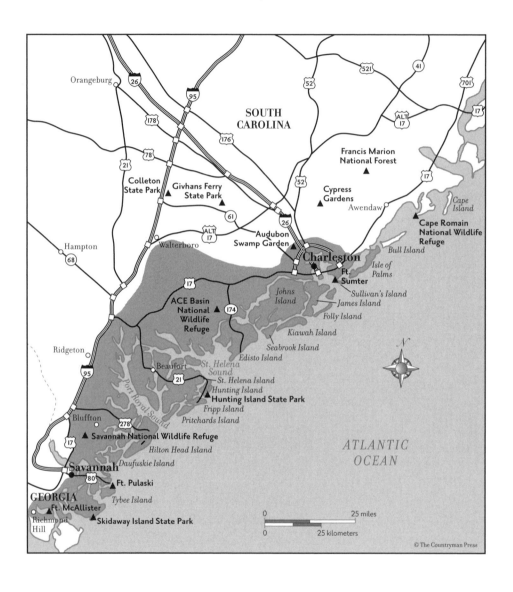

Orangeburg

SOUTH
CAROLINA

Francis Marion
National Forest

Colleton
State Park
Givhans Ferry
State Park

Cypress
Gardens

Awendaw

Cape
Island

Cape Romain
National Wildlife
Refuge

Hampton

Walterboro

Audubon
Swamp Garden

Charleston

Ft.
Sumter

Bull Island

Isle of
Palms

Johns
Island

Sullivan's Island
James Island

ACE Basin
National
Wildlife
Refuge

Folly Island

Kiawah Island

Ridgeton

Beaufort

St. Helena
Sound

Seabrook Island

Edisto Island

St. Helena Island

Hunting Island
Hunting Island State Park

Fripp Island
Pritchards Island

Bluffton

Savannah National Wildlife Refuge

Hilton Head Island

ATLANTIC
OCEAN

Daufuskie Island

Savannah

Ft. Pulaski

GEORGIA

Tybee Island

Richmond
Hill

Ft. McAllister

Skidaway Island State Park

0   25 miles

0   25 kilometers

© The Countryman Press

Contents

Map: The Lowcountry 6

Acknowledgments 9

Introduction 10

The Way This Book Works 11

1
History
"No Fayrer or Fytter Place"
15

2
Charleston
A City of Stories
37

3
Savannah
An Old City, A Modern City
99

4
Beaufort, Edisto & Bluffton
Sea Island Gems
141

5
Hilton Head
Courts, Courses, Sails & Sand
179

6

INFORMATION
Practical Matters & Seasonal Events
211

IF TIME IS SHORT   236

GENERAL INDEX   240

LODGING BY PRICE   253

DINING BY PRICE   254

DINING BY CUISINE   255

MAPS
      THE LOWCOUNTRY   6
      CHARLESTON   38
      SAVANNAH   100
      BEAUFORT   142
      HILTON HEAD   180

Acknowledgments

Many longtime friends in Charleston, Beaufort, and Savannah have helped improve this book in every edition. This updated version is particularly enhanced with the addition of many new photographs by Peter Loftus, who on his first visit to the area captured its essence. He, like Wade Spees, showed me the Lowcountry in a new light. I am also grateful to the professional staffs at regional visitor bureaus and chambers of commerce, especially Erica Backus in Savannah, Erin Coy in Charleston, Dan Carter on Edisto, and Brenda Wells at the Lowcountry and Resort Islands Tourism Commission. In Beaufort I have relied on Cheryl Steele and others to provide recommendations. Thanks to Philip Rich for many years of helpful editing and Jennifer Thompson at The Countryman Press. Also especially to Priscilla Johnson McMillan who continues to nurture my Lowcountry life.

INTRODUCTION

There are some places about which we have such strong impressions that when we finally go there they seem familiar. The Lowcountry seems to have lodged itself so securely in so many imaginations that I often find, when I am asked about it, that what I have to say matters less than the opportunity I may be giving someone to fine-tune the picture they already have.

Where these clustered impressions come from, whether learned in a history lesson on the Civil War, gathered from a friend, understood in a novel, or viewed on a movie screen, seems less important than the fact that they feel fully conceived. This isn't surprising: The Lowcountry has earned our permanent attention. It is a compelling world. Like other places that have witnessed tremendous historic upheavals and whose residents have had to adjust to changed circumstances, it evokes a natural sympathy in us for its stories.

I first visited the Lowcountry in the summer of 1979, and have been listening in on its history ever since. I return to where I feel the presence and rituals of the past: the shores of St. Helena Sound, where I catch crabs on a string or dig for oysters much as Native Americans might have done; Drayton Hall, where beds of lilies bloom, as they did in Jefferson's Monticello garden; Penn Center, where descendants of slaves honor their heritage and the strength of their forebears in song; the squares of Savannah, laid out more than 250 years ago and still possessing a power of geometry that untangles nature and orders the pace of urban life.

The region's physical beauty is just as evocative. The landscape is soft, uninterrupted by hills on land, carpeted with marsh grass and flowing waters at its edges. The air itself seems to press down, weighted by all the humidity, wrapping the Lowcountry like a package. There are distinctive seasons here, which bring their own changes in color and light, in bird migrations and blossoms. Every day the shoreline is redefined by the tides.

This book is intended to both introduce you to some of the long-standing pleasures and pastimes found in the Lowcountry and point you to where you might discover ones of your own. Individual chapter openings lay out a broad context into which you may place yourself, as a traveler looking to plan a day or as a reader adjusting the imaginary pictures you arrived with to those you observed first-hand. Sometimes, your efforts may be studious—admiring architecture, exploring sites of historic and cultural significance. At other times, you will be content to satisfy your senses: to feel the beach between your toes, smell the salt marsh, watch a pelican dive, taste fresh shrimp. Don't neglect to listen for old stories, either.

It may turn out that, having come to the Lowcountry for a vacation, you end up joining the ranks of those who return for good. The glossy residential resorts on the developed islands like Kiawah and Hilton Head have drawn national attention to the area; Beaufort has appeared on so many "Best Small Town" lists and attracted so many new visitors that it is possible to walk down its main street and see only unfamiliar faces. The Spoleto Festival has put Charleston on an international map.

Yet the inexorable need in many of us for community, for a sense of continuity that comes from bringing the past forward, keeps the Lowcountry alive; keeps it from resting solely on the life of its past for vitality. Today, restaurants, bookstores, jazz and blues clubs, clothing shops, art galleries, and B&Bs are embedding themselves in the old Lowcountry places. They are enlarging the remnant world, just as spats fasten on oyster banks and make them grow.

Cecily McMillan
St. Helena Island, South Carolina

THE WAY THIS BOOK WORKS

This book is divided into six chapters. Several of them cover specific regions of the Lowcountry. But, like a shelf of individual volumes, it encourages browsing: You may want to thumb through the opening sections of individual chapters, for example, to get an overview of the subject. Or you may want to start with the Chapter One, *History,* then pick and choose among the others as your visit unfolds and your needs become apparent.

If you're interested in finding a place to eat or sleep—and during the high season in spring you're encouraged to consider advance planning—look over the restaurant and lodging charts in the Index (organized by area and price); then turn to the pages in the general index and read the specific entries for the places that most interest you.

Some entries, most notably those in the Lodging and Dining sections of chapters, include specific information (telephone, address, hours, etc.) organized for easy reference at the beginning of each listing. All such information has been checked for accuracy as close to the time of publication as possible, but details change so it's best to call ahead. Wherever possible I have included Web sites for planning and reference. For year-round tourist information see the sources listed in Chapter Six, *Information.*

Prices

Prices change, too, and for that reason we've avoided listing specific prices in favor of noting their range. Lodging price codes are based on a per-room rate, double-occupancy in the high season months. Low season rates, which generally apply in December and January, are usually about 20 percent less. In the high season many places, small and large, require a minimum two-night stay and may also have specific rules regarding adequate notice and refunds in the event of cancellation. Check ahead.

You might also confirm information that we've provided about policies in effect concerning such things as handicapped access and smoking.

Restaurant prices indicate the cost of a meal including appetizer, entrée, and dessert, but not bar beverages, tax, or tip. Prix-fixe menus are noted. Here again, the season of your visit may bring on special conditions: When there are crowds, most restaurants extend their hours of operation, serving meals both earlier and later. In the winter, they may shut down for a day or two.

Price Codes

	Lodging	*Dining*
Inexpensive	Up to $60	Up to $15
Moderate	$60 to $120	$15 to $30
Expensive	$120 to $200	$30 to $50
Very Expensive	Over $200	Over $50

Credit cards are abbreviated as follows:

AE—American Express	DC—Diner's Club
CB—Carte Blanche	MC—MasterCard
D—Discover Card	V—Visa

To the memory of George McMillan, who first brought
me to the Lowcountry and turned my eyes to its subtleties,
and to our son, Tom, with whom I continue to love it.

The Charleston, Savannah & Coastal Islands Book

Washed up or discarded oyster shells created the ingredients for "tabby," which when burned (into lime) and mixed with sand resulted in a building material used for foundation walls for many of the earliest Lowcountry structures. Peter Loftus

History

"No Fayrer or Fytter Place"

Toward the middle of the 16th century, European adventurers were spreading across the Atlantic Ocean in a wild burst of exploring, hoping to claim for their sovereigns and sponsors vast territories of land and the riches they believed to flourish there. Aboard what now seem to be preposterously small ships and guided by hopeless maps (few of these expeditions ever landed where they intended), they arrived, established forts, and set to their business. One of the places they landed—Spanish, French, and English in succession—was the region we now know as the Lowcountry of South Carolina and Georgia.

The next 150 years was a period of settling and retreating, of establishing colonies and defending them—from one another, from the Native Americans who lived there, and from the twin scourges of disease and deprivation. Motivated by religious zeal and political unrest at home, as well as by the drive to acquire real estate, slaves, or converts to Christianity, the Europeans kept returning to build, to trade, to map, to start life over in new places on which they imposed Old World order. In the end, it was the English who dominated the Lowcountry.

While the accounts of these years outdo one another in their use of superlatives to describe God and king, they contain even richer praise for the new country. Captain Jean Ribaut, a Frenchman who led 150 Huguenot colonists to the Lowcountry in 1562, claimed in a report (translated into English the following year) that there was "no fayrer or fytter place" than the area of Port Royal Sound, near present-day Beaufort, one of the "goodlyest, best and frutfullest countres that ever was sene"; where egrets were so plentiful bushes "be all white covered with them"; where there were "so many sortes of fishes that ye may take them without net or angle."

On a site now at the edge of a golf course at the Marine Corps Recruit Depot on Parris Island, Ribaut and his settlers built Charlesfort. It was a basic defensive structure measuring 96 feet by 78 feet, barricaded with palisades, and surrounded by a moat. There were gun platforms at its corners and, inside, a rude house with a straw roof. Modest though it may have been, Charlesfort represented the first attempt by the French to establish a colony in what is now the United States. The effort took place three years before the founding of St. Augustine by the Spanish, and 45 years before the English settled Jamestown.

Impressed with the Lowcountry and confident of its potential, Ribaut quickly returned to France, intending to return with supplies and recruits. He never made it back; the colony itself collapsed soon afterwards. The well-situated site did not lie fallow for long, however. In 1566 the Spanish expanded their reach north from St. Augustine and constructed Fort San Felipe on the ruins of Charlesfort. It seemed inevitable that a place so plentifully endowed would not go begging.

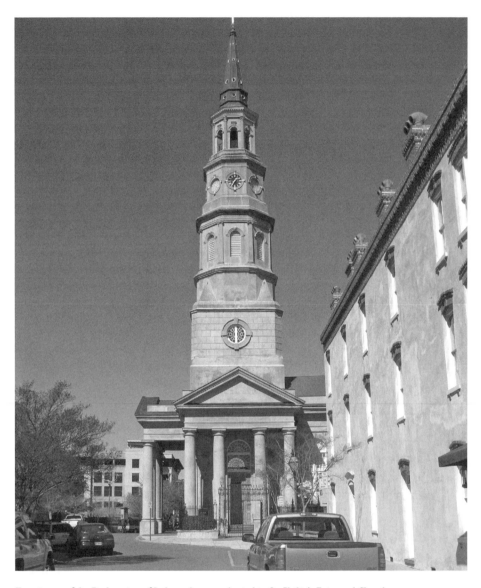

Two signers of the Declaration of Independence are buried in St. Philip's Episcopal Church west cemetery.
Peter Loftus

To a modern traveler who chances upon a rookery in Hunting Island State Park, or to the youngster throwing a cast net and needing the strength of two to draw it in, perhaps nothing has changed. Today, as centuries ago, the natural resources of the Lowcountry are breathtakingly impressive wherever you go. There will be schools of dolphin by your boat off Hilton Head, dozens of shrimp from casting your net in Edisto Island's creeks, hundreds of eggs in the loggerhead turtle's nest on Pritchard's Island, and thousands of terns, which—when they rise all at once off a sandbar in St. Helena Sound—appear as a cloud of smoke on the horizon. There will be late-afternoon light so intense and golden it makes the dun bark of the grayest sycamore shimmer.

And remember: When Ribaut called the Lowcountry a place "where nothing lacketh," Charleston, Beaufort, and Savannah had not even been invented.

By 1740, each of these towns had developed the intense self-consciousness—the spirit of place—that is apparent here today. You can find it in the watercolors of a native artist, in the concert of an African American chorus, in the words of a docent, in then tales of a fisherman. Before the first roads were laid, the wharves constructed, or the means of governance fully conceived, the continuity of culture that characterizes all the Lowcountry was begun. It is the rare American place to have evolved intact, with its monuments and houses and symbols of achievement still pointing to a documented and recognized past.

So overwhelming is the sense of place in the Lowcountry I have often felt of people I know that if they ever left the city limits of Charleston or Savannah they would vaporize.

There's no doubt, to read from their accounts, that visitors from the earliest days of settlement have shared the feeling that the Lowcountry is a special place, a dramatic place apart. Looking backward, it is hard to pinpoint precisely when the term "Lowcountry"—or even, as it is sometimes spelled, "Low Country"—became widely used. It is certainly an apt geographical description for an area that is hill-less and hardly above sea level. But to accurately define the Lowcountry, to comprehend it at its broadest, you must consider that it is many things: a place of dozens of distinctive, interconnected natural communities and ecosystems; a site where historical forces have been converging, sometimes with disastrous consequences, for 400 years; a region whose tiny society influenced national culture; a self-conscious political subdivision of the United States.

Technically, the Lowcountry is divided from what is known as the South Carolina Upcountry by the fall line, that feature of geography which bisects the state from the Georgia border at Augusta, approximately 90 miles from the coast, to North Carolina. Upland of the fall line the soil is red clay, and it is hilly; downward the land flattens and spreads, creating broad alluvial plains, which meet the sea.

As for other defining attributes, the Lowcountry that stretches from Charleston to Savannah and the Sea Islands in between seems to enjoy an enduring sense of pride: Old families, old houses, old customs, and old loyalties remain, if not as guiding principles, then ones whose legacy is passed on, as one might give a quilt to the next generation. As the writers of the classic WPA Guide, *South Carolina, A Guide to the Palmetto State*, wrote in 1941, the Lowcountry inhabitant "may live in Charleston, a city that competes with the New Jerusalem in his dreams; or he may live in a drafty Georgian country house" but he "recalls his past glory with a pride that surpasses his ability to appreciate thoroughly the good things of the present."

Today residents do appreciate the present but they are aware they must protect what they have, even at a price. Lowcountry residents were willing to pay it once, to take the drastic measure of firing on Fort Sumter, and they are continuing that commitment. Maintaining Historic Districts, scenic vistas, two-lane island roads, Gullah communities, marine sanctuaries comprising tens of thousands of acres—these are among the accomplishments of present-day preservationists who seek to insure the presence of the past in everyday life. Their victories are for you to savor, too.

NATURAL HISTORY

The coastline that defines the Lowcountry was, until about 245 million years ago, still more or less attached to the eastern rim of what became present-day Europe and Africa. The shifting of geologic plates that caused the movement of the landmass and created the

Sand Hills

I continued through this forest nearly in a direct line towards the sea coast, five or six miles, when the land became uneven, with ridges of sand hills, mixed with sea shells, and covered by almost impenetrable thickets, consisting of Live Oaks, Sweet-bay, Myrica, Ilex, . . . The dark labyrinth is succeeded by a great extent of salt plains, beyond which the boundless ocean is seen. Betwixt the dark forest and the salt plains, I crossed a rivulet of fresh water, where I sat down a while to rest myself, under the shadow of sweet Bays and Oaks; the lively breezes were perfumed by the fragrant breath of the superb Crinum, called by the inhabitants, White Lily. This admirable beauty of the sea-coast islands dwells in the humid shady groves, where the soil is made fertile and mellow by the admixture of sea shells . . . and the texture and whiteness of its flowers at once charmed me.

—From *Travels of William Bartram*
(New York: Viking Penguin, 1988. First published in 1791.)

southern Appalachians, among other mountain ranges, led to the formation of the Atlantic Ocean and the Lowcountry coastal plain.

In the geologic history of the southeast region, the coastal plain is a rather new development. Long before the present-day coastline obtained its shape (toward the end of the Miocene—third epoch of the Cenozoic Era) the upcountry regions already were well established. They were formed in an earlier era, the Mesozoic (220–70 million years ago, the time when the dinosaurs came and went), and their ancient mineral formations contrast sharply with those of the coast.

Over time, a cycle was begun. Eroded material from these highland ridges was carried by streams draining the Blue Ridge and Piedmont uplands and deposited, again and again, to the south and east. This Cretaceous material extended the landmass. Periodic inundation by the sea followed, covering the sediment and creating distinctive geologic layers of clay, sand, and gravel. At least seven such terraces have been identified, ranging in elevation from 25 feet to 270 feet. Mining activity near Charleston has unearthed fossils of shark teeth and mammoth vertebrae.

In short, millions of years ago much of the present-day Lowcountry was under water, while as recently as thousands of years ago, the Native Americans who lived here probably collected oysters and shellfish from beds that, were we to locate them today, would lie some 95 miles out to sea.

Today, well beneath the sandy soil, ranging in thickness from 1,000 to 3,000 feet, lie the sandstone, siltstones, shale, and limestone that were dumped there. They undergird the land and stretch well beyond it into the ocean to form the continental shelf and the upper slope. The oldest rocks of the coastal plain lie in scattered sections under these layers and it is activity in their faults that can, and has, caused earthquakes, such as the one that damaged Charleston in 1886.

The geologic history of the Lowcountry has given its farmers, residents, and for a time its phosphate-mining industry, some unique advantages. Unlike northern coastal areas such as New England, the area is free of surface rocks. Preparing a field never required the building of a stone wall beside it. The nature of subterranean rock formations has provided some especially good soils for timber cultivation. More important, the deeper layers of rocks serve as aquifers to provide potable water for agriculture, industry, and homes—not an idle resource given the near sea-level elevation of the Lowcountry.

Finally, if the Lowcountry were without the plentiful deposits of easily eroded rock that tumbled from the highlands over the years, the region would have no beaches. The sand you traverse, across miles of coastal and barrier beach, is their legacy.

The phenomenon of rocks-into-sand is one piece of the Lowcountry's geologic history. Another is the transformation of one massive ocean into a landscape of sculptured sounds, estuaries, and marshes. Their evolution has defined the Lowcountry as the site of one of the nation's most productive fisheries, a home to dozens of species of native and migratory birds, and a habitat for mammals small and large. Even the trees and plants of the coast flourish in direct response to these various bodies of water.

The Marine Environment

The Lowcountry marine environment includes several distinctive parts: swamps, estuaries, marshes, maritime forests, dunes and interdune meadows, tidal creeks and sounds, alluvial and blackwater rivers. Their functions are interdependent; to all, tidal action—about 6 to 9 feet throughout the region—is significant. Evidence of the complexity of the marine ecosystem is best seen at any number of points where the land meets the sea, for it is here that some of the most dynamic and subtle dramas of nature are played out. To witness them, a traveler need do no more than lean over a bridge or pier at low tide, step out of the car by a rural creek, or walk the beach.

Perhaps the most common sight of the Lowcountry is the field of smooth cordgrass (*Spartina alterniflora*) that makes up the salt marsh and the muddy banks and flats that cut through it. Rimmed by wax myrtle, nandina, and Carolina cherry laurel on its banks, overshadowed by huge live oaks whose limbs are draped with Spanish moss (an air plant, member of the pineapple family) and dotted with resurrection fern, the salt marsh is nature's most productive nursery.

What you will see here is this: filter-feeders such as snails, crabs, oysters, shrimp, and mullet ingesting the detritus—a potent mixture of decomposed marsh grass, animal matter, algae, and fungi. Or something larger, a heron, say, or a bottlenose dolphin, or a raccoon eating its smaller prey. The fiddler crabs with their lopsided claws will gather and disperse by the hundreds, a muddy cavalry. Look up and there are the shrimp boats, nets dragging at their sides. Behind them flock the gulls scavenging for cast-off fish. As the tide recedes, you will hear the marsh release oxygen and pop like 100 pricked balloons. The earthy, slightly sweet, slightly sulfurous smell of "pluff mud" will fill the air. Locals call that smell "puffy." If you venture to the edge of the marsh and get your sneakers wet, when they dry you'll see it's not mud at all, rather gray material that's finer and lighter than sand and shakes off like dust.

A Pleasing Music

A beautiful green frog inhabits the grassy, marshy shores of these large rivers. They are very numerous, and their noise exactly resembles the barking of little dogs, or the yelping of puppies: these likewise make a great clamour, but as their notes are fine, and uttered in chorus, by separate bands or communities, far and near, rising and falling with the gentle breezes, affords a pleasing kind of music.

—From *Travels of William Bartram*
(New York: Viking Penguin, 1988. First published in 1791.)

In brackish marshes slightly farther inland, along the tidal rivers, there will be more sediment, flushed from the upland, and greater plant diversity. In the shelter of the vegetation lie the nests of waterfowl; in the highest trees is, perhaps, the nest of a bald eagle. Three of the state's most significant rivers, the Ashepoo, Combahee, and Edisto, form one of the largest estuarine systems on the East Coast— the ACE Basin, located in and around US 17 south of Charleston. Protection and expansion of the basin is assured by a consortium of federal, state, nonprofit, and private interests. Farther south, the Savannah Wildlife Refuge offers another opportunity to see these natural forces at work.

The Worlds of Islands and Cities

The barrier islands offer another view of the marine ecosystem. Developed or not, they maintain a sense of isolation and fragility at "the edge of the world." Even as they appear solid, they are in fact changing shape all the time: their dunes migrating, growing, eroding, their forests shaped by the unforgiving winds and salt spray. The lives of the birds and mammals that make their homes here are impacted daily by the elements. If the beach has suffered from erosion, oak-tree roots and upended palmettos will obstruct your path. As if to mock this rough beauty, dozens of sanderlings play at the water's edge, while overhead the big brown pelicans impose an order of their own as they fly in unerring formation.

Voluptuous Charm

Picket life was of course the place to feel the charm of the natural beauty on the Sea Islands. We had a world of profuse and tangled vegetation around us, such as would have been a dream of delight to me, but for the constant sense of responsibility and care which came between. Amid this preoccupation, Nature seemed but a mirage, and not the close and intimate associate I had before known. I pressed no flowers, collected no insects or birds' eggs, made no notes on natural objects, reversing in these respects all previous habits. Yet now, in the retrospect, there seems to have been infused into me through every pore the voluptuous charm of the season and the place; and the slightest corresponding sound or odor now calls back the memory of those delicious days.

—From *Army Life in a Black Regiment*
by Thomas Wentworth Higginson
(New York: W. W. Norton, 1984. First published in 1869.)

You may be lucky enough to participate in a late-night "turtle watch" when groups of residents observe the 300-pound loggerhead sea turtles drag themselves up the beach, dig holes, and lay eggs. On several barrier islands, including the resort islands where you may be staying, teams of volunteers are charged with marking the nests and moving the eggs to a secure hatchery, away from predators, poachers, and high tides. At the time of release, the hatchlings make their way to the ocean in groups of two and three, and then somehow, miraculously, paddle with their tiny fins to the open sea.

Precisely where these turtles go is not known. From Lowcountry marinas, it takes a big fishing boat several hours to reach the Gulf Stream, where, as every fisherman knows, the

The Mock-Bird

This ancient sublime forest, frequently intersected with extensive avenues, vistas and green lawns, opening to extensive savannas and far distant Rice plantations, agreeably employs the imagination, and captivates the senses by scenes of magnificence and grandeur. The gay mock-bird, vocal and joyous, mounts aloft on silvered wings, rolls over and over, then gently descends, and presides in the choir of the tuneful tribes.

—From *Travels of William Bartram*
(New York: Viking Penguin, 1988. First published in 1791.)

big, fighting fish swim—creatures that might eat a turtle in a second. And there are other giants in this marine wildness—the right whales and the manatees.

Coastal refuges show life in abundance; but even in the cities, away from the water's edge, you will be surrounded by natural beauty. In downtown Savannah, the parkways are filled to bursting with azaleas and flowering dogwood in the spring. Honeysuckle, jessamine, wisteria, and trumpet vine tumble wildly over garden walls or race up tree trunks. And then there are the birds: the tiny Carolina wren, practically domesticated as it makes its nest in a flower box; mourning doves cooing on telephone wires, chuck will's widows repeating their chants at dusk, and the ever-present mockingbird.

Mark Catesby, the naturalist who "discovered" the mockingbird in this region more than 250 years ago, noted its fantastic ability to mimic. Today it is said that the bird can imitate 39 songs and 50 call notes, not to mention the cackling of hens, the creak of old gates, and the croaking of frogs. Given the diversity and abundance of Lowcountry life, the mockingbird has songs enough for a lifetime.

SOCIAL HISTORY

Early Human Inhabitants

The Native Americans who ranged along the coast from the earliest days—as far back as 10,000 B.C.—have left the merest impression of their lives in patterned pottery shards, woven reed baskets, huge shell middens and rings, cypress-log canoes, and the remains of burial or religious sites scattered throughout the region. They also left their names, now anglicized in common usage, to confirm their presence in a dozen Lowcountry places. Some of the most prominent archaeological remains have been found on coastal islands—Hilton Head, Callawassie—suggesting that these early inhabitants possessed both geographic agility and a sense of territorial significance. Their population is thought to have numbered 50,000 at its peak.

Their society in the Lowcountry was divided into loose tribal confederations, each of which may have communicated in its own tongue. Summers were spent along the coast and on the coastal islands, farming and harvesting fish and shellfish; in winter they retreated inland, where they hunted deer and small game. An apparently abundant food supply and an absence of harshness in the climate or geography seem to have helped insure the stability of these native societies. Communal farming produced several crops a year of corn and bounteous harvests of beans, peas, pumpkin, and watermelon. The forests yielded wild fruits, nuts, berries, and other plants for food; roots and barks for medicinal drinks.

Well-fortified towns, rimmed with circular stockades and enclosing an ever-burning cere-
monial fire, established their home base.

Houses had the appearance of Quonset huts, long and domed. They were constructed of wooden frames over which mats, woven from palmetto fronds, could be
draped, or, during hot weather, removed. Inside, the walls were lined with benches for
sleeping. Some houses were grander than others, featuring rooms and pillared platforms usually reserved for a chief or tribe member believed to have unusual wisdom or
healing powers.

A larger structure, perhaps 200 feet in diameter, served as a community center for religious and social activities. Early European observers noted devout attention to ritual celebrations in praise of the harvest, accompanied by singing, dancing, and playing of
instruments—cane flutes, drums, and rattles made from shells and seed pods. Some Native
American games included forms of bowling and lacrosse. They laid their dead to rest,
wrapped like swaddled babies, atop high scaffoldings.

Encounters with Europeans

By the time of their first encounters with white men, the coastal Native Americans had
sorted themselves into various confederacies. From Charleston to the Savannah River lived
a group of tribes known collectively as the Cusabo, including the Combahee, Ashepoo,
Edisto, Stono, Wando, Kiawah, and Etiwan.

Their responses to the incursion of Europeans were mixed: Some were generous and
open to trade, teaching the newcomers how to fish and make secure shelter, and in so
doing probably saved their lives. Some Native Americans also shared farming techniques.
One white settler told of his success in cultivating with one tribe such crops as grape vines,
pomegranates, orange and fig trees, barley, onions, and garlic. Some Native Americans and
their chiefs, known as *caciques,* helped the Frenchmen of Charlesfort build a ship, caulked
with moss, for a return voyage to Europe. Some delivered to English explorers the prime
high-bluff settings on which the newcomers laid the cities of Charles Town and Savannah.
Some boarded ships and went abroad, or to Barbados.

Other accounts, however, report canoe flotillas fleeing in shock, the villagers hiding for
days in the woods. Fighting and massacres were not unknown. Among the Europeans, the
toll was largely on French and Spanish settlers, who were the first to land.

If the settlers faced an uneasy alliance with the Cusabo, the Cusabo themselves knew an
even stronger enemy in the Westo, a vigorous inland tribe. Over time, the Westo dominated until they in turn were swept out by stronger tribes and the English settlers of early
Charles Town.

By the time of persistent English colonization, toward the end of the 17th century, another
tribe, the Yemassee, had gained prominence in the region. Once friendly with the Spanish
explorers to the south and educated in their ways of civilization, this group shifted its alle-
giance to the English as its members migrated north. They proved to be loyal supporters of
Colonel "Tuscarora Jack" Barnwell, a flamboyant Irishman who had recently come to the
Lowcountry, in a campaign to subdue hostile North Carolina tribes. Barnwell, who is buried
in St. Helena's Episcopal Churchyard in Beaufort, proved to be a diplomat, as well: In 1719, he
was called on by the settlers of Charles Town to represent their grievances to the Lords
Proprietors, an action that resulted in the formal establishment of a royal colony.

The Yemassee carried on a healthy deerskin trade with the new Europeans, and there
developed over time a far-ranging network of agents, outposts, and agreements. Yet,

finally, the very success of the enterprise and the pressure of increased migration onto native lands proved to be the colonists' undoing. Long-simmering resentment of unscrupulous traders, unfair taking of land, and abuse of their people led to a gathering of 15 Native American nations, who directed an assault from the Yemassee town at Pocotaligo. They attacked on Easter Sunday, 1715, killing as many traders as they could and sending the residents of Beaufort to their ships. The bloody Yemassee War lasted two years. At times, hundreds of warriors were dangerously close to Charles Town, reminding its residents of their isolation and pitiful protection under the crown. Eventually, the Yemassee forces disbanded and moved out of the region for good. By the middle of the 18th century, the last remnant tribes near Savannah had left the area.

The Settling of Charles Town

Carolina was originally known to Europeans as "Carolana," and it was the dream of the kings of Spain and France to have it. Their struggle for domination, played out on lands far distant from their own among native inhabitants who had been there for thousands of years, marked the earliest days of settlement.

The Spanish arrived first, in 1521, under the leadership of Francisco Gordillo: He named the Sea Island area Santa Elena. Further colonization was planned for but never materialized. Five years later, another Spaniard, Vasquez de Ayllon, having heard marvelous stories of the rich, vast land of Santa Elena, gathered 500 settlers and established his party at a point farther north along the coast. Their hopes, too, were to be dashed—by illness, a revolt among the slaves they had brought, attacks by Native Americans, and unusually harsh winter weather.

In 1562, Captain Jean Ribaut established Charlesfort, the first Protestant colony in North America, in the area he named Port Royal. Charlesfort, too, soon petered out and by 1566 the area belonged to the Spanish, who commenced to build a string of forts along the coast. In 1629, Charles I of England announced his intentions of ownership. In the end, it was the English claim that stuck, although the early residents of Charles Town faced Spanish, French, and Native forces several times before they were secure.

Time passed, however, before the English pursued their claim by actually settling. It took a monarch pressed to return favors—and a group of men with means, entrepreneurial spirit, and a keen sense of the market—to reap the benefits imagined for so long by so many. The monarch was Charles II, king of England during the Restoration. The group of men was Carolina's Lords Proprietors: Sir John Colleton, the Duke of Albermarle (George Monk), Lord Craven, Lord Berkeley, Sir William Berkeley, Sir George Carteret, the Earl of Clarendon, and Lord Ashley (Anthony Ashley Cooper).

The familiar nursery rhyme that calls Old King Cole a "merry old soul" might aptly have applied to Charles II. By 1663, restored to the throne after the dispatch of Cromwell, Charles found himself short of cash and facing obligations to those who had helped him in the late civil war. As a token of his appreciation, he gave to his loyal friends the territory "described in the parts of America not yet cultivated or planted, and only inhabited by some barbarous people who have no knowledge of Almighty God." This was to be the Carolina Province. Its development, particularly along the lower coast, was to define a society that exists today.

Planning for colonization began immediately. Sir John Colleton, who had lived among the planters in Barbados, convinced his associates of the need for expansion of the society there (already nearly 40 years old) and of the profits to be made in overseeing its relocation.

In the summer of 1663, Captain William Hilton sailed the ship *Adventure* into Port Royal Sound, and their project began in earnest.

Hilton's successful foray and contact with friendly natives led to another exploratory trip three years later under the leadership of Captain Robert Sandford. This time, the English left behind Henry Woodward, a surgeon whose interest in the culture, language, and habits of the Native Americans was to ease the way, several years hence, for the first settlement at Charles Town. That day finally came in 1670 with the arrival of the ship Carolina, the only one of three ships to complete the voyage from England via Barbados.

It was at first unclear precisely where to settle—whether in the vicinity of Port Royal Sound, which Hilton had explored, or farther north, along the North Edisto River, where Sandford had ventured. Finally, after further viewing of both sites under the piloting and careful guidance of the *cacique,* or chief, of the Kiawah tribe, the colonists established a fort at Albermarle Point in the lands of the Kiawah, at Old Towne Creek up the Ashley River from present-day Charleston.

The earliest years of this colony have been brought to life at Charles Towne Landing which today offers a true sense of the importance of siting—high on a bluff from which unfriendly Spanish ships might be seen—and evidence of agricultural successes and failures. Small-scale farming worked; large cash crops, upon which rested the hopes of the Barbadian planters, didn't as yet.

In 1671, another shipload of colonists arrived, including more from Barbados, accompanied by their slaves; by the following year the colony consisted of 30 houses and 200 people.

The colonists prospered and gained confidence, such that by 1680 they had removed themselves from Albermarle Point to a site on the peninsula at the mouth of the harbor, where they laid out their city. From this time forward, the development of Charles Town— indeed of the entire Lowcountry of which it was the capital—proceeded rapidly.

Early Growth and Prosperity

Between 1690 and 1720, according to the historian Carl Bridenbaugh, the population of Charles Town tripled. New immigrants included French Huguenots and Irish, who established themselves in business and government. Wharves, churches, protective sea walls, defensive bastions, and homes were built. Streets were named (Church, Broad, Meeting, Tradd, and Queen are among those you can see today) and some of them were paved with oyster shells. Recent archaeological excavations related to new construction in downtown Charleston have provided evidence of this early town-building. Trade with the Native Americans was lively, and exports thrived: Deerskins and fur were shipped to England; pork, corn, naval stores, and lumber went to Barbados and the southern islands. The vast natural networks of creeks and rivers opened up the countryside to planters who raised beef and pork, cultivated cotton, rice, and indigo, and harvested lumber. And of course the waterways were crucial to transporting all these goods to Charles Town.

In governance, the influence of the Barbados colony continued to be felt in the key areas of law and representation by parish, and in the adoption of the slave code. The settlers from Barbados also imposed their architecture—the classic design with its raised basement and upstairs piazzas—and their intent to develop plantations outside the city limits. The increasing importation of slaves followed, an absolute essential in making large-scale agriculture a success.

Thus, from the very beginning, Charles Town was a society in which profitability and expansion—not to mention ease of living, even among the less grand—were inextricably

Charleston single houses that are one room deep began to be built before the Revolution. Often an office was on the first floor. Peter Loftus

tied to slaves and their management by law and custom. The historian Peter Wood estimates that by 1715 the slave population exceeded the European population.

Prosperity did not guarantee security, though. Charles Town faced threats from outsiders: There were skirmishes with Native Americans, Spanish soldiers, even pirates such as Blackbeard (Edward Teach) and Stede Bonnet. In 1718 alone, 49 pirates were hanged.

Success in trade and a growing, more diverse population did, however, embolden the citizens to improve their lot. Prompted by resentment toward England (which refused to help pay for the defense of the city, attempted to enact trade restrictions, and raised the colonists' quitrents, among other heavy-handed actions), the citizens challenged the very form of proprietorship under which their colony had been established. In 1721, after much to-and-fro with England, the Carolina Province became a royal colony. By the 1730s, it was referred to by its new name, Charlestown. Only after the Revolution, when incorporated as the new state of South Carolina's first city, would it finally adopt the now-familiar spelling, as Charleston.

Expansion in Colonial Lowcountry

Once people were settled, once they were safe, once they had established their markets and their means of production—and their slave workforce—the Lowcountry around colonial Charlestown started its meteoric climb to achieve what it eventually became: person for person, the wealthiest region in the colonies. It started with rice, continued with indigo, and finally came cotton. The fact that all these crops were suited to Lowcountry cultivation, that there was land to support them and slaves to work them, that there was desire abroad for their harvest (in some cases a bounty paid for it), and hefty profit to be made on it, left only a need for a class of men to seize the opportunity to grow rich. As was the case in other colonies, there were plenty of them, and they promptly did so.

The world they began to establish, the ways they embellished it, the physical and social order they imposed on it, and the choices they made to keep it alive defined Lowcountry culture right up to the Civil War. Even after that, even today, the echoes of those efforts resound in Lowcountry political, social, and economic life. In the deepest way, they form the basis of the stories people tell themselves about who they are.

As planters and their families spread out—and as new colonists continued to arrive from Barbados—they ventured across the Ashley River to Magnolia Plantation, Drayton Hall, and Middleton Plantation; they went to Goose Creek and points inland; across the Sea Islands of Kiawah, Seabrook, John's, and Edisto; and south to Beaufort and its islands of St. Helena, Lady's, and Hilton Head. In addition to their main house in the city, planters might establish a "big house" on one plantation which served as their base, while overseers and slaves worked additional acreage nearby, living in rude dwellings. Profits were turned to acquire new land and more slaves. A merchant, having amassed a fortune in town, would follow a path similar to the one taken by this newly landed gentry. Planters were businessmen, and vice versa.

Thus emerged a small society that was at once far-flung across the Lowcountry but glued together by shared aspirations, tastes, assumptions about plantation life and the treatment of blacks, and very strongly, by marriage.

The relation between city and country was intimate. Charlestown, already the throbbing commercial heart of this society, came to display all its wealth. There were theatrical per-

The Circular Congregational Church was a favorite of the New England merchants who came to Charleston after the American Revolution. Its cemetery has many elaborately carved headstones.   Peter Loftus

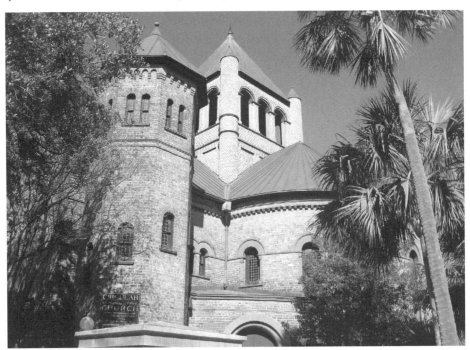

formances, clubs of every variety, subscription concerts followed by elaborate balls, race-tracks, even a "season" that included "Race Week" in February. Some refinement had been brought to the wilderness. In fact, there was still a lot of wilderness: To the south, it was just being tamed. By 1742, when there were nearly 7,000 people living in Charlestown, Savannah's population numbered only in the hundreds.

The Founding of Savannah

By comparison with the settling of Charlestown, the founding of Savannah in 1733 was seen as a far less ambitious enterprise—and perhaps a morally loftier one. The colony began as the idea of a group of 20 Englishmen, who petitioned the Crown for a grant of land. They were known as the Trustees, and they had idealistic, philanthropic goals: Land would be held communally, settlers would be selected from "impoverished classes;" Trustees would pay for passage of settlers; there would be no liquor, slavery, or land specu-lation. The Trustees were given executive and legislative powers for 21 years. They could distribute land to settlers, but land was held in the Trustees' name.

The 114 or so settlers who arrived under the flag of King George were mostly of modest means, and their goal—as outlined by the Trustees—was the development of exports, including wine and silk. They were also supposed to defend the colony from the Spanish, and thus provide a buffer for prosperous Charlestown.

They were led by General James Oglethorpe, a high-minded Englishman with a care-taker's concern for his flock, many of whom addressed him as "Father." Such was his sense of mission that when the ship *Ann* arrived in Charlestown harbor for consultations with the royal governor, the passengers were required to remain aboard and fish for their sup-per, so as not to have their heads turned by the glamorous city.

Continuing south, the *Ann* stopped at tiny Beaufort. Here passengers were allowed to fraternize with the residents, whose standard of living probably appeared to be more in line with what the newcomers, in the best of circumstances, might hope to accomplish. General Oglethorpe chose as his site for Savannah a place where "the river forms a half-moon, along the south side of which the banks are about 40 feet high, and on the top a flat, which they call a bluff." He was assisted by Colonel William Bull, a engineer from Charlestown with local surveying experience, and guided by Tomochichi, a friendly Yamacraw chief. The site was about 18 miles from the river's mouth on the Atlantic, on water sufficiently deep for ships drawing up to 12 feet to navigate within 10 yards of the shore.

Oglethorpe and Bull immediately addressed the task of planning the city, and it is the legacy of their inspired effort that distinguishes Savannah today. The city was, and is, a meticulously planned urban environment stretching back from the river in a series of squares and boulevards, which, then as now, are landscaped focal points. The basic form consisted of blocks of five symmetrical 60- by 90-foot lots encompassing 21 squares. Space was designated for public buildings and market areas, as well as for secure retreats, where settlers living outside the city limits could take cover in the event of Native American upris-ings. The plan has been designated a National Historic Civil Engineering Landmark.

As things turned out, relations with the Native Americans remained friendly. Tomochichi supported the colonists' work throughout his life and was instrumental in winning the trust of tribes in the area. He was also willing to support Oglethorpe in battles with the Spanish, which were to occur sporadically over the next 10 years. The existence of a trading post nearby—run by John Musgrove, from South Carolina, and his wife, Mary, who was part Creek—also smoothed the way for natural contact.

Given such a propitious start, it was up to the settlers to clear and build, hunt and farm, and establish the Trustees' Garden. This they did, on the grants of 50 acres received by heads of families (5 acres in the city, 45 outside it for farming). The settlers were also the beneficiaries of hundreds of head of livestock from their South Carolina neighbors, as well as rice and horses. For quite some time, even after Savannah got on its feet, South Carolina, and the port of Charlestown in particular, was to dominate the commercial life of the southern coast.

More settlers, including Irish, Scots, Swiss, Germans, and Italians, came very quickly. Jews and Protestant Salzburgers from the German-Austrian border area sought refuge from religious persecution. By 1741, there were 142 houses, a courthouse, jail, storehouse, market building, and a 10-acre, fenced public garden. By 1742, the liquor ban was repealed by popular demand.

Soon enough the settlers found that some of the original restrictions intended to guide development were hampering it. By 1749, the ban on slavery was repealed because settlers felt they could not compete with South Carolina's productivity and overseas trade. In 1750, the Trustees relinquished their hold on land (again, by popular demand): Private property ownership ensued.

In 1752, when the original Trustee Charter was up for review, Parliament refused further aid. As a result, in 1754, the colony became a royal province with governance by a royal council appointed by the king. As such, the province was subject to all the taxes, levies, duties, etc. that the other American colonies endured.

Thus in a sense released from Oglethorpe's idealism, the colonists proceeded to develop plantations as their neighbors had. However, it took until the close of the French and Indian War in 1763 (when Florida was ceded to England) for Savannah to begin to flourish as a colonial city and primary port serving the Georgia backcountry. By the time of the Revolution, the South Carolina and Georgia colonies had settled lingering border disputes, were engaging freely in trade, and were communicating through four Lowcountry newspapers. The region had pulled together, united by shared commercial and social goals, and a culture deeply affected by slavery.

In 1775, a Provincial Congress was called because Savannah residents were as fed up with English governance and taxation as the rest of the colonies. In a show of solidarity and goodwill, the colony joined the Revolution.

The American Revolution

Ten years before reports of the battles of Lexington and Concord reached the Lowcountry, its residents were taking independent action to defy British rule, especially its methods of colonial governance and taxation. By the time of the Stamp Act in 1765, they had become wealthy, self-confident, and better organized in their own military defense. Having built their cities from scratch, they were in no mood to be further subjugated, and their responses were violent. In Charlestown, long-festering political disagreements between the colonists and the royal governor burst to the surface. They bitterly resented his order to move the Assembly and center of government to Beaufort, a day's journey by boat. In Savannah, where relations between colonists and governor had been more cordial, groups of Liberty Boys nevertheless were openly challenging loyalists and destroying British property.

By 1774, many colonists had become defiant. The merchants of Charlestown refused to buy tea that had been taxed, preferring to let it mold in the Exchange Building (which you

Sea Island cotton planters also kept homes in Beaufort to use during the hot summer months.   Peter Loftus

can see today at the foot of Broad Street). British products were boycotted. Five delegates were sent to the First Continental Congress. In Savannah, leaders gathered at Tondee's Tavern to sign a petition denouncing the acts Parliament had passed in response to the Boston Tea Party (the Intolerable Acts) and insisting on their independent rights.

At this point, war seemed inevitable, even though there were loyalists throughout the Lowcountry who urged negotiation and reconsideration of non-importation policies. In 1776, four South Carolinians and three Georgians signed the Declaration of Independence. Colonial rule was over, but the fighting had just begun.

In the first significant victory of the Revolution (June 28, 1776, a day that is still celebrated in Charleston), General William Moultrie, outnumbered and outgunned, defeated an invading fleet of 50 British warships from his position on Sullivan's Island, in a fort built of palmetto logs. Visitors to the site today are impressed by the degree of risk and bravery that battle entailed.

But the Lowcountry was not yet secure. In December 1778, the British captured Savannah, and in May 1780, after a one-month siege, they finally subdued Charlestown. The British avenged the colonists by imprisoning and executing patriots. When they finally left the Lowcountry, in 1782, they were loaded down with war booty.

The American Revolution had a profound effect on stable Lowcountry society. It was nothing less than a civil war dividing families and generations. Robert Rosen points out in his book, *A Short History of Charleston,* that William Bull was for the king but his nephews for the revolutionaries. Daniel Heyward was a Tory, but his son Thomas signed the Declaration of Independence. Similar clashes of ideals and politics occurred in other prominent Lowcountry families such as the Draytons, Pinckneys, Manigaults, Horrys, and Hugers.

The political questions raised by the conflict sensitized new classes of people to their own self-interest. The governments that came into place afterwards reflected these diverse new motivations. No longer were mechanics and other artisans—"the little people"—satisfied with government dominated by the planter class, especially when planters' slaves soaked up most of the available work. As for the wealthy, they were forced to read the writing on the wall; fortunately, some of the Lowcountry's planters were themselves ardent patriots, and they adjusted to democratic government, though their influence remained out of proportion to their numbers.

The years following the Revolution saw a boom in population, in building, and in commerce. Many of the houses of the Lowcountry date from this Federal period, when new fortunes were made and old ones even further enhanced. If the architecture of the Lowcountry can be read as a book, this is its first great chapter.

Entrepreneurs, ship captains, military people, and merchants from New England came to the cities and Sea Islands to build their plantations. While the bounty on indigo was a casualty of war and led to a decline in that crop, the invention in 1793 of the cotton gin, on a plantation near Savannah, meant that the process of removing seeds from cotton could occur with greater ease and speed. Slaves working in the ginhouses still plucked seeds by hand from the most highly prized strain then being grown: Sea Island cotton, whose long, silky fibers would be broken by the action of the gin. These seeds were saved, analyzed, compared, and the best of them used for the following crop. Despite ups and downs in the cotton market and competition from the rest of the new American republic developing to the west along the Mississippi, for most of the next 60 years the Lowcountry flourished.

Plantation Life and Gullah Culture

The first African American slave came to the Lowcountry to stay, in 1670. Ever since then, slaves, freedmen, and their heirs have defined in the most essential way imaginable the politics, growth, lifestyle, culture, language, and habits of the Lowcountry. The complexity of relations between blacks and whites—who, in city or country, lived in close quarters and experienced daily contact but were governed by strict social codes enforced by penalties—has informed all Lowcountry history. Fear of black uprising, especially after the ill-fated Denmark Vesey rebellion in 1822, made for a regulation of life unknown outside the South.

For the best overview of slave life, visit The Charleston Museum. Or drive to Middleton Place, another site that, with its landscaped gardens and farmyard, offers splendid evidence of the world the slaves built. Imagine the daily bustle of slaves around what is now Charleston's Market Area, or in Savannah's waterfront warehouses, now restored.

When out and about in the Lowcountry and thinking about its past, probably the two most significant things to recognize are the immense enterprise that characterized plantations (where they now may be silent and grand, they were once fantastically busy places, with dozens of buildings) and the isolation the slaves endured there.

The world of the plantation was self-sufficient, marked by dozens of specific activities taking place according to the season: gathering marsh hay for fertilizer; harvesting, clearing, and burning the fields; building and repairing; growing food crops and raising cows and hogs for slaughter; moting and ginning cotton, packing it in the cotton house, taking it to the landing to be shipped on barges. Within that world of action, and responding to its often-crushing demands, there arose a culture among slaves, now generally called the Gullah culture, which included elements of their African past. Scholars have identified these remnant "Africanisms" in religious and mythical beliefs; in patterns of speech and dress; in basketry, art, dance, and song. In its totality, Gullah is a way of life that informed—and still informs—the manner in which slaves and their descendants managed their relationship toward white people and kept intact some expression of their own identity.

From the earliest days, black slaves from certain rice-growing regions of the West African coast were prized for their knowledge of that crop's cultivation. Rice-growing is a delicate business. It requires periodic flooding of fields; the design, building, and maintenance of a dike-and-gate system; and hundreds of people, including children, to protect the rice plants from birds, gather it in, separate the grain from the chaff by means of seagrass "fanner baskets," and clean it with mortar and pestle. In all of these areas, black people were experienced, and they taught what they knew.

Built in the style of a Greek temple, and destroyed during the American Revolution and again during the Civil War, only the ruins of the Old Sheldon Church remain today.

Indigo and cotton crops demanded other kinds of hard labor—in preparing the fields with usually nothing more than a hoe and a plow-dragging ox; in building pits to soak the indigo or in chopping weeds to free the cotton plants; in extracting the dye or in picking tufts from spiky bolls. Labor was apportioned by "tasks" of land, a task being about a quarter of an acre, for which slaves were responsible. Plantation ledgers were organized around work completed according to this system. In addition, slaves were used as carpenters, blacksmiths, cooks, loggers, boat-builders, butchers, and house-servants. While planters left at the onset of "the sickly season" to escape malaria, blacks were somewhat resistant to this fever and worked through the miasmic heat of summer.

A caste system grew up within the population that served the needs of the plantation master: Slaves associated with domestic life were at the top and field hands were at the bottom. Becoming a black "driver" meant that a slave would work with an overseer to direct crews; it also meant meting out punishment and whippings to fellow slaves. With blacks outnumbering whites by vast majorities, keeping order through work and brutality was essential to the plantation system.

The treatment of slaves varied widely in the Lowcountry. It is important to remember that while the majority of white people in the city and the country owned slaves, only a very small portion of them owned more than a dozen. Some planters bought and sold families; some kept them together, some did not. Some allowed friendships or marriage to occur between plantations; some took skilled slaves to the city and hired them out. Some planters allowed slaves to hunt and fish, keep gardens, raise fowl, and sell eggs. Some gave them staples—molasses, cloth, tobacco, shoes—on a periodic basis.

Slaves lived in cabins or slave rows that shared a common wall and had dirt floors. On the plantations they worshiped at praise houses—usually small, clapboard buildings lined with benches—where services were marked by recitations of the gospel, praying, and the singing of spirituals in which an elder "deaconed out" a line and the worshippers responded in unison. They buried their dead in separate slave cemeteries, dozens of which are in still in use today.

Whatever the specific case, a slave's identity (and that of his family) was tied to one place, which he might never leave during his lifetime. If ever he did travel, it was under a strict pass or ticket system. His fortunes were often tied to one white family, and his heirs to its heirs. Education of slaves was either haphazard or strictly forbidden.

It is not possible to overestimate the way in which the Civil War disrupted the order imposed by the plantation world and the society it held in check. When recovery was to come to the Lowcountry, it would come to the countryside last.

The Civil War and the Years of Poverty

If the Lowcountry is seen by visitors as a place rich in references to the Civil War, both physical and cultural, perhaps it is because there was such a difference in the "before" and

Secession is the fashion here. Young ladies sing for it; old ladies pray for it; young men are dying to fight for it; old men are ready to demonstrate it.

—From a dispatch to the London *Times*, April 1861, sent from Charleston by English journalist William Howard Russell

Born into slavery, Robert Smalls was a Civil War hero and prominent Reconstruction-era congressman from Beaufort.

"after." The cataclysmic changes wrought by that great conflict are well known.

Perhaps less well known is the fact that even before the Civil War, the Lowcountry already had been undergoing a slow transformation. Historians point to a definite drift of the Lowcountry after the 1820s, from occupying a place at the center of colonial and post-Revolutionary commerce to becoming just one of many prosperous regions in the South.

The Lowcountry's golden age was, in fact, the now-distant time of relative innocence and optimism long before the antebellum era, a time of cosmopolitan outlook and quiet accommodation with the rest of the country that was lost during the overheated days immediately prior to the Civil War. (It was only in the later years of the 20th century— as recently as the great resort booms, the "second Yankee invasion"—that the Lowcountry has been able to consider itself as reentering the mainstream of American culture.) The nostalgia for long-lost days, which most every visitor to the Lowcountry feels, is probably for a time more nearly 200 years ago than 140.

By the 1850s, due to a number of factors, including the price and availability of cotton elsewhere, protective tariffs for new industries in the north, and the emergence of the abolitionist movement, the Lowcountry had lost its position of national preeminence. As a result, its outlook became more narrowly regional. Political positions hardened; tolerance for a national view of things receded. The institution of slavery was viewed less as a necessary evil—possibly temporary—and more as a positive benefit, one from which Southerners could not turn back. And there were politicians, like John C. Calhoun, who made an eloquent case for this vision. As Mary Boykin Chesnut wrote in her diary at the time of secession: "South Carolina had been rampant for years. She was the torment of herself and everyone else. Nobody could live in this state unless he were a fire-eater."

Of course, life did go on, populations increased, profits were made. Charleston and Savannah grew, with the addition of magnificent mansions in the Greek Revival style—such as Charleston's Edmondston-Alston House—or in the Regency style—such as the William Scarbrough House in Savannah. Small towns like Beaufort raised their own gentry. Nonetheless, planters' societies that might, in the past, have discussed nothing more ominous than crop yields, seed types, and the accounting practices of their agents and cotton factors, now found their attentions turned to defensive matters concerning their slaves, their fortunes, and their state's rights. Some on St. Helena Island loaned their slaves to build defensive earthworks.

In December 1860, led by Lowcountry secessionists, South Carolina separated itself from the Union. The following year, Georgia followed suit. Soon, the harbor forts that watched over both cities—Fort Sumter and Fort Pulaski—were battle sites. Both of the forts can be visited today, and the story of their defense is a dramatic one.

Additional glimpses of the Civil War period are poignantly on display at the Confederate Museum in Charleston, with its frayed uniforms and flags, and in the Green-Meldrim House in Savannah, headquarters of General Sherman, who, having completed his victorious March to the Sea in 1864, not only celebrated Christmas in Savannah but also offered the city itself as a gift to President Lincoln.

A less well known chapter of Civil War history, having Beaufort as its center, concerns the efforts of Northern abolitionists to live among the newly freed slaves and prepare them for full "citizenship." The enterprise followed by several months the Union invasion of Port Royal in November 1861. Over the next several years, a hundred or so men and women took up residence in the abandoned plantation houses on Beaufort's outskirts—Lady's Island and St. Helena—and managed the plantations for the government, which looked to cotton crops for revenue. They set up schools for slaves young and old, in front parlors and cotton houses. Beaufort itself was home to the central command of the Union Army in the region; houses and public buildings were converted to hospitals, dwellings, and offices.

After the Civil War, the Lowcountry, now impoverished, turned in upon itself. It was as if people simply went home and stayed there, hoarding their gentility in their city homes as they might their last pennies, taking in sewing, teaching, and boarding guests. In the country, they concentrated on making a living, albeit a far more modest one. People were thrown back on their resources—fishing, hunting, and farming—and they made do. Only small numbers of freedmen actually received, and were able to hang on to, land they had been promised. Often families banded together to buy land from Northern speculators, giving rise in the 20th century to extremely complicated efforts to unwind ownership of "heir's property" in which descendants own fractional claims.

Although phosphate mining, timbering, and shipyards emerged as centers of postwar activity, the economy was slow to repair itself. An idea of just how poor conditions were, right up until World War II, can be glimpsed in the work of Walker Evans, Marion Post Wolcott, and other photographers sent by the Farm Security Administration to document Lowcountry life. Many of these images can be accessed online in the records of the Library of Congress.

As it turns out, the legacy of poverty was just as crucial in preserving the built environment of the Lowcountry as prosperity had been, in the early years, for bringing it to life. As early as the 1920s, Charlestonians were organizing to save their old buildings. In 1931, the city passed the nation's first Historic District zoning ordinances; some 20 years later, the Historic Savannah Foundation was founded to oppose the demolition of the Isaiah Davenport House.

Ever since, these cities' Historic Districts and properties in the country nearby have been central attractions to generations of tourists. They have provided architects, landscape gardeners, historians—even novelists—with material for inspiration. It is a remarkable testament to the Lowcountry's enduring legacy and powers of regeneration that, despite all this scholarly trawling, the region doesn't seem fished out.

The Lowcountry Legacy

Through all its changes, the Lowcountry landscape has retained its immense allure for those who have lived and traveled here, from roving early settlers to today's nomads of the bus tour. Perhaps this is because a sense of history and a sense of place intersect at so many points in the Lowcountry. There is no high ground here. History itself provides the only vantage point, the only way to detach oneself from an insular sense of place that is always responding to forces—of wind and tide, of society and war—greater than itself.

It was and is a place to be desired. Whether your quest is satisfied by filling a bucket with oysters, paddling a canoe in the marsh, or visiting an old home accompanied by nothing more than your imagination, the Lowcountry offers a rare chance to enact and to observe the subtle rituals of the past, and to take from them, for yourself, the pleasures they've delivered for so long to so many.

To describe our growing up in the lowcountry of South Carolina, I would have to take you to the marsh on a spring day, flush the great blue heron from its silent occupation, scatter marsh hens as we sink to our knees in the mud, open you an oyster with a pocketknife and feed it to you from the shell and say, "There. That taste. That's the taste of my childhood." I would say, "Breathe deeply," and you would breathe and remember that smell for the rest of your life, the bold, fecund aroma of the tidal marsh, exquisite and sensual, the smell of the South in heat, a smell like new milk, semen, and spilled wine, all perfumed with seawater.

—From *The Prince of Tides* by Pat Conroy
(Boston: Houghton Mifflin Company)
©1986 by Pat Conroy

Market Hall defined the head of the city market area where every commodity, including slaves, was bought and sold. Peter Loftus

2

CHARLESTON

A City of Stories

Charleston is one of the nation's oldest urban environments. It has been the site of some of the most dramatic and significant events in American history, and it has an architectural inventory that is more varied and abundant than any other city in America. As a colonial city, and then as a regional capital for nearly 350 years, it has a continuity of culture.

To a visitor, awareness of this cultural legacy may seem quaint or idiosyncratic. It is in fact a meaningful and pervasive sentiment, one that informs the smallest turn of phrase and the largest civic hopes of people who have long viewed their city as a place apart, a place with values so closely held that residents would, and did, die for them. In such a world (Charlestonians have called their home "The Holy City" with only a trace of irony) it is not surprising that when residents talk with visitors about Charleston's history—about its essence—they begin by talking about relationships: those between the races, between and among individuals and families, between the region and the rest of the country.

Compounding this sense of intimacy with the past is its indisputable physical expression in the city's manmade and natural landscape. For while it is one thing to tell a story of times gone by, it is quite another to be able to locate that narrative, and to read it, in an urban setting that still exists and reverberates with meaning. This quality is at the core of the city's cultural identity, more important than buildings or objects, although there are plenty of them, too. Charleston is a city of culture because people believe that a sense of history and of place distinguishes their lives.

Charleston has stayed small—some might say defiantly so—in a way different from any other region in the United States. Unlike many American places, it was not compelled to reinvent itself over time. The traditional cultural pleasures to be had in dress balls, small concerts, the cultivation of gardens, card playing, church picnics, and literary societies continued for generations. The life of the plantation, in which families would be absent from the city except in seasonal bursts, heightened the importance of domestic culture: It has been said that without the plantations, set at some distance from each other, there would have been no tradition of Southern hospitality, nor the development of the domestic art of "visiting," so significant to this day.

Most obviously, Charleston stayed the same for so long because it liked what it was. It preferred its provincial insularity to what it perceived as vulgarity elsewhere. And, especially in the early years of this century, it was too worn down to do much but carry on in the old ways, its people too habituated to the familiar social roles they inherited long after the society which had assigned those roles had been wiped out.

TO:
The Citadel
(located on
Moultrie St.)

TO:
Cypress Gardens,
Francis Beidler State Park

TO:
Angel Oak,
Beaufort,
Charles Towne
Landing,
Drayton Hall,
Edisto Island,
Folly Beach,
Kiawah Island,
Magnolia Gardens
Middleton Place

TO:
Boone Hall,
Fort Moultrie,
Isle of Palms,
Palmetto Islands
County Park,
Patriots Point,
Sullivan's Island

CONGRESS ST.
HAGOOD AVE.
PRESIDENT ST.
ASHLEY AVE.
HUGAR ST.
STUART ST.
JOHNSON ST.
HARRIS ST.
JACKSON ST.
LEE ST.
FISHBURNE ST.
CAROLINA ST.
HANOVER ST.
LINE ST.
NORMAN ST.
ASHTON ST.
LINE ST.
BOGARD RD.
BLAKE ST.
COLUMBUS ST.
SPRING ST.
CANNON ST.
BEE ST.
COURTENAY DR.
PRESIDENT ST.
MORRIS ST.
RADCLIFFE ST.
WARREN ST.
VANDERHORST ST.
WOOLFE ST.
AMHERST ST.
MARY ST.
ANN ST.
AIKEN ST.
NASSAU ST.
AMERICA ST.
EAST BAY ST.
CONCORD ST.
Roper
Hospital
ASHLEY AVE.
RUTLEDGE AVE.
CALHOUN ST.
HALSEY BLVD.
Bon Secours
St. Francis Xavier
Hospital
JOHN ST.
Visitor
Center
CHAPEL ST.
ELIZABETH ST.
City
Marina
LOCKWOOD DR.
HUTSON ST.
CHARLOTTE ST.
ALEXANDER ST.
WASHINGTON ST.
BULL ST.
SMITH ST.
PITT ST.
COMING ST.
SAINT PHILIP ST.
KING ST.
CALHOUN ST.
MONTAGUE ST.
AVE.
GEORGE ST.
MEETING ST.
ANSON ST.
WENTWORTH ST.
LAURENS ST.
BEAUFAIN ST.
BARRE ST.
SOCIETY ST.
WENTWORTH ST.
HASELL ST.
RUTLEDGE ST.
QUEEN ST.
FRANKLIN ST.
ARCHDALE ST.
PINCKNEY ST.
N. MARKET ST.
S. MARKET ST.
CUMBERLAND ST.
CONCORD ST.
CHISHOLM ST.
BROAD ST.
NEW ST.
LOGAN ST.
S. BATTERY
MURRAY BLVD.
COUNCIL ST.
TRADD ST.
LENWOOD ST.
LEGARE ST.
KING ST.
MEETING ST.
CHURCH ST.
STATE ST.
PRIOLEAU ST.
CHURCH ST.
WATER ST.
E. BATTERY
White Point Gardens

0   0.5 miles
0   0.5 kilometers

CHARLESTON

© The Countryman Press

King Street house, Charleston.

But when the time came, in the 1920s, to protect the life they knew and valued, Charlestonians acted. They did not do so violently, as in the case of Fort Sumter, but by using political talent, hard work, and a potent sense of what mattered, residents enacted the country's first historic preservation ordinance, protecting buildings and sites that otherwise might have been destroyed in the name of "progress."

The success of preservation efforts in the ensuing 85 years has meant that the past has been brought forward for all to see: in individual houses, neighborhoods, and districts. The city has become a magnificent backdrop for all sorts of cultural activities.

Like the historic sections of the city, cultural activities keep brushing themselves up, reinvestigating the old, and cultivating the new. For every historic house there seems to be an art gallery; for every plantation house tour, a deeper study of slave life. Where gardens were once celebrated informally, now programs and walks guide a visitor. The spirituals of the praise houses and the blues of the cotton fields are performed for bigger audiences. Modest sailing regattas have become Water Festivals.

Perhaps no event showcases Charleston like the annual Spoleto Festival, held for several weeks in May and June (for information see the Spoleto entry in the Culture section). Dozens of operatic, theatrical, dance, and musical performances transform the city. Fine art exhibits and lecture series proliferate. Performers and artists with international reputations take up residence and flock to restaurants and parks. The city itself sponsors a companion arts festival, Piccolo Spoleto, made up of free events at outdoor sites.

Putting aside all of the activity that enlivens Charleston, it is enough to say that it is a marvelous city because it has escaped the trend that architectural critic Ada Louise Huxtable called the "theming of America" in which "authentic reproductions" of the past are constructed from selected remnants: Charleston has no need to be replaced by a neater version of itself, to be understood.

GETTING THERE

Charleston International Airport (www.chs-airport.com) is your destination, served by major airlines (AirTran, American, Continental, Delta, Northwest, US Airways, and United Express) with direct flights from cities across the United States. It's an easy place to negotiate, well designed, with few of those anonymous spaces and corridors that make traveling tiresome. Rental cars from several agencies are available; when returning your car, there's convenient, no-waiting, parking-lot check-in. Expect to pay $12 per person for shuttle service to peninsular Charleston, about $25–$30 for a cab (for two passengers; $12 extra for a third.) The larger hotels offer their own shuttle service—ask when you book your rooms. **Greyhound** (843-744-4247; www.greyhound.com; North Charleston) serves the area with a depot about 20 minutes from downtown. **Amtrak** (843-744-8264 or 1-800-872-7245; www.amtrak.com; 4565 Gaynor Ave.) travels the north-south corridor, making daily stops at North Charleston about 25 minutes from downtown. By car, Charleston is located at exits off I-95 via I-26 heading east, about 30 minutes to downtown. Parking downtown may be nonexistent, difficult, or costly. Check with your B&B, inn, or hotel about locations of municipal lots.

The distance from Washington to Charleston is 512 miles; from Jacksonville to Charleston is 241 miles; from Asheville via I-40 to I-26 is 265 miles. From Charlotte, take I-77 south to I-20 at Columbia; follow I-20 for a few exits to link up with I-26 east. Distance to Charleston: 200 miles. From Atlanta take I-75 to I-16. When it crosses I-95 go north for Charleston, 286 miles.

LODGING

When President George Washington toured the states of the new nation in 1791, he was determined to observe life at all levels of society. In the Lowcountry, he accepted the enthusiastic hospitality of the planters—he was rowed in their barges by slaves dressed in finery, and took meals in their mansions—but he preferred to spend the night in the "public houses" that existed along the main highways, in the simple places frequented by messengers and mail carriers, small farmers and merchants. He even paid his own way when permitted.

The public houses of Washington's day are long gone, but the modest style of overnight lodging they offered, of clean rooms, shared bathrooms, and communal meals, existed well into the 20th century. It was a custom, like most, that had its roots in necessity: During the years of poverty following the Civil War, taking in guests provided income for families or Confederate widows who still lived in the commodious old houses.

These days, if you stay in an old home that has been transformed into a glossy bed & breakfast—and they are among the most romantic lodging options—the only Confederate widow in evidence will be in a portrait on the wall. They are elegant places, with Jacuzzi tubs and fireplaces: You are likely to hang your clothes in an antique armoire or view from your window, walled gardens rimmed with flower beds and dense with camellias and azaleas.

Charleston also has first-rate luxury hotels; several inns and hotels renovated from larger commercial buildings; modest chain hotels; and, on its outskirts, dazzling beach resorts. The lodgings included here represent a sampling of offerings in all of these categories. The list is by no means complete because building and remodeling go on apace. Places at the beach—a house in

Hidden gardens thrive in the city's microclimates that mimic Mediterranean conditions. Peter Loftus

a neighborhood or a villa in a gated resort—are plentiful, and generally handled by agents or through individual resorts.

Each option carries with it unique possibilities. Although the distance between Charleston and the beach is not great, if you intend to spend most of your time in the city, to shop and eat out and take part in cultural life, you may not want to travel 25 to 35 minutes to the beach for a night's sleep. Alternatively, if golf, tennis, boating, and being on the ocean are at the center of your vacation, or especially if you're traveling with children, it might be wise to make a resort or rental home your base, and travel to Charleston by day. Of course, for trips lasting several days, many combinations of lodging are possible.

The hospitality industry is highly evolved here: More than 3 million people visit the area each year. The large hotels provide every amenity you'd expect. The luxury inns outdo each other in finishing

touches: Afternoon tea and stronger brews are served gratis in gardens, parlors, or courtyards. Even the B&B units, where a home's owner is your host, offer helpful extras like jogger's maps, a selection of restaurant menus, tips on neighborhood sights, even history lessons from the house-proud.

If you're traveling with children, some hotels and inns can recommend on-site babysitting services. You should inquire and make specific arrangements in advance. Some places discourage guests traveling with children; others have rules as to minimum ages and the placement and cost of extra beds in the room. At the resorts, well-staffed activity programs occupy the younger set.

If you have special needs, ask to see if they can be accommodated. Pets, for example, are sometimes allowed; smoking is always regulated, often allowed only on balconies or in courtyards, sometimes

Fountain at Charleston Place.

forbidden. Wheelchair access, by ramps or elevators, in bathrooms or bedrooms does vary. Off-street parking is usually provided by larger establishments. Confirm the arrangement or fee with smaller ones and private-home accommodations. Respect deposit/cancellation policies, as they are strictly followed in smaller inns and B&Bs. For more information, Web site addresses have been included and are a good source for online discounts.

Rates

Inexpensive	Up to $80
Moderate	$80 to $140
Expensive	$140 to $200
Very Expensive	$200 and up

These rates do not include room taxes or special service charges that might apply during your stay.

Credit cards

AE—American Express
CB—Carte Blanche
D—Discover Card
DC—Diner's Club
MC—MasterCard
V—Visa

Hotels and Larger Inns

Charleston Place

843-722-4900 or 1-800-611-5545 (within US). www.charlestonplacehotel.com. 205 Meeting St., Charleston, SC 29401. Price Expensive to Very Expensive. Credit Cards: AE, D, DC, MC, V.

The construction of this luxury hotel some 25 years ago, with its own elegant shops and the cachet to draw brand-name stores to the neighborhood, signaled a fateful change. It's a microclimate now, with Saks, Talbot's, and the like, a part of but slightly apart from, the old downtown. It hums by day and night with well-dressed tourists and conventioneers, and offers a premium and convenient Charleston address. There are two restaurants, a popular bar with evening jazz, a sensational pool and spa. Its dramatic decorations—a grand curved staircase, a huge chandelier, massive pots of flowers, shiny marble floors, and rooms of polished furniture—make it a destination. Special rate packages, which include tickets to Spoleto performances, and very reasonable off-season rates, are worth looking into.

Embassy Suites—Historic District
843-723-6900 or 1-800-362-2779.
www.historiccharleston.embassysuites.com.
337 Meeting St., Charleston, SC 29403.
Price: Moderate to Expensive.
Credit Cards: AE, D, DC, MC, V.

This large chain has managed a fine makeover of the 19th-century Citadel building where generations of Southern boys attended military school. It still looks formidable, with massive, theatrical palm trees, a courtyard, and crenellated turrets, but the outdoor pool and sundeck soften the institutional edges. The two-room suites allow for flexibility (the living rooms have a sleeper sofa) if you're traveling with children or need a workspace, and also convenience, with mini-kitchens and televisions. Located near the Visitor Center where many tours and trolley service originate.

Francis Marion Hotel
843-722-0600 or 1-877-756-2121.
www.francismarioncharleston.com.
387 King St., Charleston, SC 29403.
Price: Expensive to Very Expensive.
Credit Cards: AE, D, DC, MC, V.
Handicap Access: Some rooms.

Overhauled and redecorated and awarded membership in the Historic Hotels of America (affiliated with the National Trust for Historic Preservation), this was a solid 1920s hotel to begin with: wide stairs and hallways, wood paneling, plaster moldings covered in gold-leaf, a lobby with big windows and club chairs, and high ceilings. Today there are 230 guest rooms, including suites of various configurations for extended families. It overlooks Marion

Square (with great views of Charleston from rooms on the upper floors), and from the coffee bar you can watch the goings on in the upbeat College of Charleston neighborhood.

Harbour View Inn
843-853-8439 or 1-888-853-8439.
www.harbourviewcharleston.com.
2 Vendue Range, Charleston, SC 29401.
Price: Expensive to Very Expensive.
Credit Cards: AE, D, DC, MC, V.

Just steps from the Waterfront Park and featuring many rooms with stunning views and harbor breezes, this new hotel has the right mix of elegance and understatement. The minimalist feel to the rooms emphasizes volume and light over decoration: sea grass/rush carpeting, cream-colored walls, big windows (some with broad slatted "plantation" shutters), perhaps one framed print, and an armoire made by a local woodworking company. Many of the rooms have fireplaces, some have balconies, some have whirlpool baths. A good deal of attention is paid to details here, even in the choice, framing, and hanging of art in the hallways, and it really shows.

King Charles Inn
843-723-7451 or 1-866-546-4700.
www.kingcharlesinn.com.
237 Meeting St., Charleston, SC 29401.
Price: Moderate to Expensive.
Credit Cards: AE, D, DC, MC, V.

A Best Western choice for visitors on a budget. An outdoor pool is located on an elevated, screened terrace, affording good privacy for an establishment that's in the heart of downtown. It may be modest but the service is attentive, there's free parking, and the location is unbeatable.

The Mills House
843-577-2400 or 1-800-874-9600.
www.millshouse.com.
115 Meeting St., Charleston, SC 29401.

Price: Expensive to Very Expensive.
Credit Cards: AE, D, DC, MC, V.

This is a big Holiday Inn hotel with a metropolitan feel that was completely renovated in 2007 to better recall its 1853 origin. Its marble floors, glittering chandeliers, and period reproductions create an atmosphere of hushed activity where you can people watch from a lobby banquette or in the piano bar. Great central location. There are 214 guest rooms and 19 suites, with three handicapped-accessible rooms. After a day of walking, or in the early evening before you head out to dinner, the pool and deck are particularly inviting.

Renaissance Charleston Hotel
843-534-0300 or 1-800-468-3571.
www.renaissancehotels.com.
68 Wentworth St., Charleston, SC 29401.
Price: Expensive.
Credit Cards: AE, D, MC, V.

A large hotel (166 rooms) with an outdoor heated pool and fitness center, in a good location just north of Market St. and the hipper location of upper King Street. Luxury, yes, with granite counters, wireless Internet, two-line phones, and décor a little more mainstream than other hotels (more colors, valances, and dust ruffles), but locals send their business here—management is well known to be thoughtful about its small-business neighbors and has recommendations for shopping and dining that are not obvious.

Smaller Luxury Inns
Ansonborough Inn
843-723-1655 or 1-800-522-2073.
www.ansonboroughinn.com.
21 Hasell St., Charleston, SC 29401.
Price: Moderate to Expensive.
Credit Cards: AE, D, MC, V.

This circa-1900 stationer's warehouse two blocks from the City Market was given new life as an all-suite inn, but reminders of its past use—including huge beams, plank

floors, and walls of exposed brick—remain to good effect. Each of the 37 suites has a wet bar including microwave and mini-refrigerator, modem hookups, and varieties of bed sizes so that your suite can comfortably accommodate everyone in your party.

Battery Carriage House Inn
843-727-3100 or 1-800-775-5575.
www.batterycarriagehouse.com.
20 S. Battery, Charleston, SC 29401.
Price: Expensive.
Credit Cards: AE, MC, V.

The main house at Number 20 South Battery was built in 1843, and today's visitors stay in rooms beneath and behind it, in the old carriage house. South Battery defines the edge of the historic residential district known as "South of Broad." This is the neighborhood that comes to mind when most people think of Charleston, a place of iron gates entwined with jasmine, houses with massive columns set on high foundations, narrow streets, and families like your innkeepers, the Hasties, to whom the house has belonged for several generations. There is one suite and 10 rooms, whose small dimensions are alleviated by access to a narrow piazza and a lovely back garden. Continental breakfast and the newspaper arrive at your door, or you can start your day under the rose arbor.

Fulton Lane Inn
843-720-2600 or 1-800-720-2688.
www.charminginns.com.
202 King St., Charleston, SC 29401.
Price: Expensive to Very Expensive.
Credit Cards: AE, D, DC, MC, V.
Handicap Access: Two rooms.
A non-smoking inn.

This inn is located between King and Meeting Streets amid the downtown antique and gallery district. The 27 rooms have a refreshing, airy, look: sisal, wicker, and muslin decorating accents; louvered shutters; wall-coverings and paint in soft, liquid colors like celadon, pale peach, and lemon. The feel is summer in the Lowcountry—all year long. You can go simple or go deluxe, with canopied beds and fireplaces, kitchens, and cathedral ceilings; all rooms have either one king-sized bed or two queen-sized beds. Passes for an offsite health club are available for $10. Part of a local consortium of inns with good service and referrals.

Governor's House Inn
843-720-2070 or 1-800-720-9812.
www.governorshouse.com.
117 Broad St., Charleston, SC 29401.
Price: Expensive to Very Expensive.
Credit Cards: AE, MC, V.

The governor who lived in the Governor's House was Edward Rutledge, who at 26 signed the Declaration of Independence and at 30 was a patriot under arrest. He may have suffered at the hands of the British, but the stunning restoration of this grand home suggests he appreciated the finer things in life. There are 11 guest rooms—the nicest among them have 12-foot ceilings and their own verandah access, with rooftop views of the South of Broad neighborhood. Two of the rooms are suites, one on each floor of a kitchen house dependency, featuring its original 1760 fireplace, now converted to gas. With over-the-top marble bathrooms, it's an excellent spot for an indulge-yourself weekend.

John Rutledge House Inn
843-723-7999 or 1-800-476-9741.
www.johnrutledgehouseinn.com.
116 Broad St., Charleston, SC 29401.
Price: Expensive to Very Expensive.
Credit Cards: AE, D, MC, V.

Tradition has it that John Rutledge (who later signed the U.S. Constitution) built this imposing house around 1763 for his bride, Elizabeth Grimke. The antique furnishings, parquet floors, high ceilings, carved mantelpieces, and rich fabrics that characterize the house today suggest its original opulence, such as might have impressed President George Washington when he visited. Nineteen rooms are offered to guests, either in the main house or in two carriage houses. Suites in the main house include an additional sitting room and fireplace; some have Jacuzzi tubs. Continental breakfast is included and full breakfast is available. A big plus to staying here is the use of a charming courtyard, sheltered from the street, where you may gather to relax, eat, or have a cocktail or late-night snack. Like its neighbor the Governor's House across the street, it's just a minute's walk from the South of Broad neighborhood.

Planters Inn
843-722-2345 or 1-800-845-7082.
www.plantersinn.com.
112 N. Market St., Charleston, SC 29401.
Price: Expensive to Very Expensive.
Credit Cards: AE, D, DC, MC, V.
Handicap Access: Some rooms.

A location at the intersection of North Market Street and Meeting Street makes this 62-room inn superbly convenient to nightlife, shopping, the Gibbes Museum, and the historic residential areas. You can walk in any direction and find something going on—the closest Charleston comes to having a "big city" feel. The service is superior and the rooms elegant, many with fireplaces and four-poster beds. The acclaimed Peninsula Grill restaurant is located here (see the review below, under Dining).

Two Meeting Street Inn
843-723-7322 or 1-888-723-7322.
www.twomeetingstreetinn.com.
2 Meeting St., Charleston, SC 29401.
Price: Very Expensive.
Credit Cards: None.
A non-smoking inn.

This Queen Anne mansion, with its wrap-around porches and rocking chairs, has passed the age of 100 but may never have looked better. (Given Charleston, it's young almost to the point of new.) Its oak-paneled sitting rooms and guest rooms are filled with Oriental rugs and period accessories, and highlighted by fabrics and wall coverings in rich, deep colors. There are nine rooms on three floors, all with private baths (some with Victorian-style tubs), some with private balcony access. This is the place for honeymooners and celebrating couples who often book a year in advance—especially for those rooms with canopied four-posters needing a special set of stairs to reach. Continental breakfast is served, and there is an elaborate afternoon tea. Minimum stays are required on holidays and weekends, and cancellations must be three weeks in advance. Children over 12 are welcomed.

Wentworth Mansion
843-853-1886 or 1-888-466-1886.
www.wentworthmansion.com.
149 Wentworth St., Charleston, SC 29401.
Price: Very Expensive.
Credit Cards: AE, D, DC, MC, V.
Handicap Access: Some rooms.

Visitors worship Charleston's 18th-century and antebellum architecture, but this Second Empire–style mansion (built in 1886 for a cotton baron) will turn your head. For sheer per-square-foot, Gilded Age extravagance, it has no peer: carved plasterwork ceilings, marble fireplaces, Tiffany glass, mahogany paneling, intricately tiled floors, and a cupola accessed by a stairway for the brave, which yields a panoramic view of the city. And that's what was there before millions were spent on deluxe renovation, antiques, and a spa. Today there are 21 sumptuous guest rooms and suites, many with separate Jacuzzis and walk-in showers, some with private porches, almost all with fireplaces. A continental breakfast buffet is set on a sun

porch; a classic gentleman's library is a late-night refuge. Complimentary parking and health club passes are available. One of Charleston's best restaurants, Circa 1886, is in the Carriage House (see the review below, under Dining).

Bed & Breakfast Lodgings in Private Homes and Gardens
A central reservation service, Historic **Charleston Bed and Breakfast** (843-722-6606 or 1-800-743-3583; www.historic charlestonbedandbreakfast.com; 57 Broad St., Charleston, SC 29401) offers some 50 listings of rooms with private baths in homes or their garden dependencies in Charleston's historic neighborhoods. Their phone lines are open weekdays from 9–5. Credit cards (MC, V) can be used to book a deposit, but the balance is usually cash or check only. Other useful sources of information are provided by the **South Carolina Bed & Breakfast Association** (1-888-599-1234; www.southcarolinabedandbreakfast.com), whose online listings provide the information necessary to make a choice, and www.bbonline.com, a national listing service. There are bargains, especially if you're willing to leave the South of Broad/Market neighborhood, but flexibility and adventure might be the real draw—the chance to feel like a local, sit in a courtyard and read, or bring a picnic home at midday. Some accommodations are well suited to larger parties, families, or couples traveling together, and they may also have their own kitchen facilities, gardens, and bicycles for you to use. The service makes a good match if you have some sense of what you want. You may also contact individuals directly or book lodgings that are not owner-occupied but not exactly commercial, either. Places of this sort may be as large as four rooms and quite private. Credit cards that are accepted are noted. Otherwise, cash, personal check, or traveler's check is acceptable.

Broad Street Guest House (843-577-5965; www.charlestonkosherbedandbreakfast .com; 133 Broad St., Charleston, SC 29401) Accommodations in three suites and a cottage in a kosher home built in 1884. Enjoy Shabbat dinner, walk to Shul, and linger over kosher meals served in an elegant dining room or large piazza. Expensive. Many holiday packages are available for longer stays. AE, D, MC, V.

1837 Bed and Breakfast (843-723-7166; 1-877-723-1837; www.1837bb.com; 126 Wentworth St., Charleston, SC 29401) Nine guest rooms, porches with rockers, full breakfast. Located a few blocks north and west of Charleston Place. Moderate. AE, D, MC, V.

Fantasia B&B (843-853-0201; 1-800-852-4466; www.fantasiabb.com; 11 George St., Charleston, SC 29401) Rooms in a carriage house or the main house, with kitchenettes, private baths, balcony access, and cable. Internet available in main house living room. In the Ansonborough neighborhood, about a 10-minute walk to Broad Street. Moderate to Expensive. AE, D, MC, V.

4 Unity Alley (843-577-6660; www.uni tybb.com; 4 Unity Alley, Charleston, SC 29401) Three suites with bedroom and sitting room, and communal dining area, located just off East Bay Street in the French Quarter neighborhood, a mix of commercial (galleries, fancy restaurants) and residential uses. Expensive. AE, MC, V to hold your reservation, but payment due in cash or by check.

Hayne House (843-577-2633; www.hayne house.com; 30 King St., Charleston, SC 29401) A native Charlestonian familiar with the world of historic preservation and his family are your hosts: six rooms in both a kitchen house and a main house, private baths, and the use of garden and piazza; full Southern breakfast in the main house. No television, great location, kids welcome. Expensive. MC, V.

Merhaven Bed No Breakfast (843-577-3053; 16 Halsey St., Charleston, SC 29401) Two non-smoking rooms with shared bath in a recently renovated Arts & Crafts style bungalow. Off-street parking in the Medical University/College of Charleston neighborhood. Moderate.

Phoebe Pember House (843-722-4186; www.phoebepemberhouse.com; 26 Society St., Charleston, SC 29401) The walled meditation garden and a studio which offers yoga classes, meditation instruction, and massage, send a message of healing to guests. Rooms are available in the 1807 main house or in a carriage house. Expensive. MC, V.

36 Meeting Street Bed and Breakfast (843-722-1034; www.36meetingstreet .com; 36 Meeting St., Charleston, SC 29401) Three suites with cooking areas and private baths—one in an 18th-century home and two in an adjacent carriage house. Children welcome. Moderate to Expensive. D, MC, V.

Thomas Lamboll House (843-723-3212 or 1-888-794-0793; www.lambollhouse.com; 19 King St., Charleston, SC 29401) Open the French doors from your bedroom onto the piazza of this pre-Revolutionary house located steps from the Battery. Two rooms with private baths and fireplaces. Expensive. MC, V.

21 East Battery Bed & Breakfast (843-556-0500 or 1-800-543-4774; www.21eastbattery.com; 21 E. Battery, Charleston, SC 29401) A newly renovated carriage house and adjacent two-story former slave quarters form a private residence that can accommodate 10, tucked in the historic Edmonston-Alston House museum complex. A complimentary tour of that property is included. Very Expensive. Reservations by phone only.

27 State Street (843-722-4243;
www.charleston-bb.com; 27 State St.,
Charleston, SC 29401) Enter your private
suite (with kitchenette) through the courtyard of a foursquare, circa-1800 house in
Charleston's "French Quarter," a block off
East Bay Street and the harbor. Expensive
to Very Expensive. MC, V.

Charleston Environs

If you prefer to stay outside Charleston,
near a plantation or one of the Sea Islands,
you'll find plenty to choose from. Here are
some possibilities, arranged by location,
with separate sections on resort and rental
accommodations and beach rental agents.

The Inn at Middleton Place (843-556-
0500 or 1-800-543-4774. www.theinnat
middletonplace.com. 4290 Ashley River Rd.,
Charleston, SC 29414)
Price: Expensive to Very Expensive.
Credit Cards: AE, MC, V.

The Middleton Inn, located on a bluff adjacent to the beautiful gardens at Middleton
Place, is about 25 minutes from downtown
Charleston. For serenity and privacy, for
long walks along the Ashley River or at
Middleton Place (admission waived for inn
guests), for kayaking and horseback riding,
come here. Ask about weekend packages.
Designed by W. G. Clark about 25 years ago
and winner of architectural awards, it's
handsomely modern on the outside, splen-
didly understated on the inside. There are
53 rooms in four buildings, each with
working log fireplaces, custom-made furniture, soft colors, and large bathrooms.
Some are handicapped accessible. Floor-
to-ceiling windows with louvered shutters
filter the light and air in the woodland setting. The restaurant at Middleton Place
serves lunch and dinner daily.

Folly Beach

Charleston on the Beach (843-588-6464
or 1-800-465-4329; www.charlestonon

thebeach.com; 1 Center St., Folly Beach, SC
29439) A 132-room oceanfront Holiday Inn
hotel, with game room, pool, fishing pier,
restaurant, and bar. Handicap access and
non-smoking rooms available. Moderate to
Expensive. AE, D, DC, MC, V.

Holliday Inn of Folly Beach (843-588-2191
or 1-800-792-5270; www.hollidayinnfolly
beach.com; 116 W. Ashley Ave., Folly Beach,
SC 29439) This modest motel, one block
from the beach, is as reliable as the chain
hotel with the similar name, but it's much
more inviting. Moderate to Expensive. AE,
D, MC, V.

Isle of Palms

The Palms Hotel (843-886-3003 or 1-
888-484-9004; www.thepalmshotel.us;
1126 Ocean Blvd., Isle of Palms, SC 29451)
There are 69 rooms, including 18 suites,
situated in a great location with all the
beach amenities—including microwaves
and mini-refrigerators. Moderate to
Expensive. AE, MC, V.

Seaside Inn (843-886-7000 or 1-888-
999-6516; www.seasideinniop.com; 1004
Ocean Blvd., Isle of Palms, SC 29451) A 51-
room hotel, basic but all you need, located
next to the Windjammer, the beach area's
most popular bar/restaurant.

Resorts and Rentals— Charleston Area Sea Islands

The Sea Island resort areas around
Charleston are 25 to 35 minutes from
downtown. They are self-contained destinations from which you can travel to the
city by day to sightsee and shop, and to
which you can return for recreation, dining,
and relaxation. You can play golf and tennis
and walk on the beach twelve months a year,
and swim in the ocean from May to
November. Each resort has a well-super-
vised children's activity program.

What follows is a list of the resorts and
an outline of their lodgings. If you are

interested in longer stays of a week or more, you may also want to contact some of the rental agents who specialize in private beach properties, including villas and houses located both within the resorts and outside of them. Note that rental rates for some especially fancy private homes within the resorts can be as much as twice the average rates quoted below.

Rental accommodations are fully furnished, including washer and dryer, but you should check to see if you need to bring anything, if there are special features like handicap access, or if a fee for cleaning after your departure is included. Deposits are necessary, and if you need to cancel, you must often do so up to three weeks in advance to have your deposit returned. During summer months, minimum stays of three days (in a villa) to a week (in a house) are usually required.

Typical summer rental prices for a two-bedroom, oceanfront house ranged from $1,300 to $2,900 per week. The farther you are from the beach—by a lagoon or in the woods—the less expensive the rate. November through February are low-season months and rentals are priced accordingly. The resorts offer numerous packages covering a long-weekend or week's stay to attract golfers, honeymooners, Thanksgiving get-togethers, and visitors coming for the tours of historic homes in the fall and spring. There may be bargains, such as there would not be in downtown Charleston, for larger family reunion groups.

Kiawah Island Golf Resort and The Sanctuary

843-768-2121 or 1-800-654-2924 for the Golf Resort. 843-768-6000 or 1-877-683-1234 for The Sanctuary. www.kiawahresort.com.
12 Kiawah Beach Dr., Kiawah Island, SC 29455.
Price: Expensive to Very Expensive.
Credit Cards: AE, D, DC, MC, V.

There are many ways to enjoy Kiawah: in the original 150-room inn, a rambling building with decks, breezeways, ceiling fans, and plenty of places to sit in the shade; in one of some 300 villa accommodations, fully furnished with kitchens, which come in several sizes; or in a private, architect-designed "beach house" that is not anything like the faded house on stilts where you played board games in your bathing suit as a kid. The beach is private and 10 miles long. Thirty miles of paved bike trails wind around five golf courses and recreational areas, ultimately linking two distinct resort villages. The latest addition to the resort and residential layout is The Sanctuary, a self-enclosed luxury hotel complex which features 255 guest rooms, a luxurious spa, and two oceanfront restaurants that are favorably rated by local gourmets.

Seabrook Island Resort

843-768-0880 or 1-800-742-2532.
www.seabrookislandlodging.com.
115 Freshfields Dr., Johns Island, SC 29455.
Price: Expensive to Very Expensive.
Credit Cards: AE, D, MC, V.

Seabrook is a 2,200-acre private country club community that's low key and means to stay that way. Visitors rent cottages, villas, or homes. Its unique asset is its equestrian center and miles of riding trails, but it also provides resort amenities like golf (two courses), tennis (15 Har-Tru courts), a beach and beach club, pool, and fitness center.

Wild Dunes Resort

843-886-6000 or 1-888-778-1861.
www.wilddunes.com.
5757 Palm Blvd., Isle of Palms, SC 29451.
Price: Expensive to Very Expensive.
Credit Cards: AE, D, MC, V.

Wild Dunes is just 15 miles north of Charleston, a small resort located on the northeast end of the modest Isle of Palms. It's the place to stay if you want beach resort life (two golf courses, tennis, pools, water sports, kids' recreation program, beach club) and the advantage of the city an easy ride away. Sullivan's Island is close by, too. Guests choose accommodations in the 93-room Boardwalk Inn or in fully outfitted villas, townhouses, and cottages.

Beach Rental Agents

Beachwalker Rentals (843-768-1777 or 1-800-334-6308; www.beachwalker.com; Freshfields Village, Johns Island, SC 29455) Accommodations on Kiawah and Seabrook Islands with many family-friendly properties.

Carroll Realty (843-886-9600 or 1-800-845-7718; www.carrollrealtyinc.com; 103 Palm Blvd., Isle of Palms, SC 29451) Homes and villas by the week, month, or year on Isle of Palms, Wild Dunes, and Sullivan's Island.

Great Beach Vacations (Kiawah: 1-800-870-4059; www.kiawahinfo.com; Seabrook: 1-800-845-2233; www.seabrookinfo.com; Wild Dunes, Isle of Palms: 1-800-346-0606; www.isleofpalmsinfo.com) A clearinghouse of information with a deep inventory of investment/rental properties.

Island Realty (843-886-8144 or 1-800-905-6290; www.islandrealty.com; 1304 Palm Blvd., Isle of Palms, SC 29451) Wide selection of rentals and golf packages on Sullivan's Island, Isle of Palms, and the more remote Dewees Island.

Pam Harrington Exclusives, Inc. (843-768-0273 or 1-800-845-6966; www.kiawah exclusives.com; 3690 Bohicket Rd., Suite 2-C, Johns Island, SC 29455) Homes and villas on Kiawah.

Seabrook Exclusives (843-768-0808 or 1-888-718-7949; www.seabrookexclusives.com; 3690 Bohicket Rd., Johns Island, SC 29455).

DINING

Dining is one Lowcountry ritual that remained important, even through hard times. Schoolchildren released for an hour from class and fathers home from the office gathered daily at the midday meal. It honored family, tradition, the art of conversation, and the resourcefulness of the cook. As the extraordinary Southern chef Edna Lewis said: "The birds are just the beginning. In the South you put everything you have on the table."

Indeed, accounts tell of hunting and fishing parties that delivered marsh hen, dove, quail, and crab by the dozens; that brought in pigeon and deer hunted by torchlight; that landed huge drum, a beast of a fish that pulled at hook and line and dragged a *bâteau*, or boat, as a whale might. Add to these hunters' trophies the harvest from garden and field—okra, corn, peas and beans, turnips, beets, greens, and, of course, rice, first introduced to the Lowcountry in the late 1600s—and you had, and have to this day, a traditional Southern meal, flavored as always with meat marked by "a streak of lean and a streak of fat."

It was not only the natural bounty of the land and the availability of labor for several harvests that led to a Lowcountry dining tradition. The plantation operation and its physical layout—including detached kitchens and smokehouses—gave rise to a separate world of cooking. Slaves were in charge here and they contributed their own sense of spicing, texture, ingredients, and method. The influence of their African and West Indian heritage, combined with European preferences, produced a distinctive regional style that today is being self-consciously redefined at restaurants like Cypress Lowcountry Grille and Circa 1886, and examined by acclaimed food writers like John Martin Taylor and the brothers Matt and Ted Lee. Taylor gave up his signature store in Charleston to sell his books, food products, and other food-related items online (www.hoppinjohns.com), and to launch a great blog. The Lee brothers (www.mattleeandtedlee.com) published a fat cookbook in 2007, have a thriving boiled peanut business, and tour and write extensively about Southern cuisine from their Charleston base.

The proliferation of restaurants and a stable, creative food culture has come recently to Charleston, but reflects its roots. High-end meals are served everywhere, but there are still plenty of modest places that serve specials and are best known to local people. A former food critic for the *Charleston Post and Courier* posts her thoughts about the local scene at www.charlestonchow.blogspot.com. The list below reflects a range of prices and styles; more and smaller places are listed at the end of the **Food Purveyor** section under "Pizza, Sandwiches, and Faster Food."

Here are some suggestions. Many of them have online sites where you can check menus and make reservations. The general price range we list is meant to reflect the cost of a single meal, usually dinner, featuring an appetizer, entrée, dessert, and coffee. Cocktails, beer, wine, gratuity, and tax are not included in the estimated price. Lunches are generally less expensive, and in some cases, noted as a bargain.

Dining Price Code

Inexpensive	Up to $10
Moderate	$10 to $30
Expensive	$30 to $50
Very Expensive	$50 or more

Credit Cards
AE—American Express
CB—Carte Blanche
D—Discover Card
DC—Diner's Club
MC—MasterCard
V—Visa

During Spoleto, most Charleston restaurants relax their hours, serving lunch as late as 3 PM, early supper at 5:30, and full meals at midnight. The crowds pile up, so make reservations. If you're rushing between performances, picnic in the open-air pavilions at the Waterfront Park at the foot of Queen Street, in the shady grove of Washington Square, or on a bench at the Battery.

Anson
843-577-0551.
www.ansonrestaurant.com.
12 Anson St.
Open: Daily.
Price: Expensive.
Cuisine: American.
Serving: D.
Credit Cards: AE, D, MC, V.

The cooking technique here is last-minute sautéing: The dish arrives at your table sizzling hot, with crispy vegetables, meat, fish from that morning's catch, or fowl glistening with juice. The produce comes from local farms growing Charleston "heirloom" vegetables that were cultivated in the 19th century; the rice is "Carolina Gold," growing again after a 100-year hiatus; the lamb, duck, quail, and squab are free-range. There are comfy banquettes and lots of smaller tables for four or six, done up in heavy linens. The Market area in which Anson used to stand out as an attractive oasis is a little more care-worn and Anson less a local favorite, but still full of brio.

Basil
843-724-3490.
www.basilthairestaurant.com
460 King St.
Closed: Sun.
Price: Moderate.
Cuisine: Thai. Serving: L (Mon.–Fri.); D (daily).
Credit Cards: MC, V.

Downtown merchants, professionals, gallery owners, and professors flock to this corner restaurant on the booming section of King Street north of Calhoun. Sometimes there's a line; no reservations are taken, but Charlestonians have been waiting for an excellent Thai restaurant for a while: now they have it. Standards like crispy duck and spicy noodle soups, dishes with peanuts and coconut and curries. The grill is open, with seating at the chef's counter, or at tables, in booths, or at a tiny bar. Lunch is a bargain. A welcomed place, simple and elegant.

Boathouse on East Bay

843-577-7171.
www.boathouserestaurants.com.
549 E. Bay St.
Open: Daily.
Price: Expensive.
Cuisine: Seafood.
Serving: D and Sun. Brunch.
Credit Cards: AE, D, MC, V.

A big space whose teak and mahogany paneling and nautical décor recall the small craft and "mosquito fleet" heritage of the harbor. The staples of Lowcountry kitchens plain and fancy—like coleslaw, shrimp and grits, fresh catch, or fried green tomatoes are here, as are sushi and oysters from far above the Mason-Dixon Line. There's a happy-hour scene around the raw seafood bar. It gets full—make reservations.

Charleston Grill

843-577-4522.
www.charlestongrill.com.
224 King St., at Charleston Place.
Open: Daily.
Price: Expensive to Very Expensive.
Cuisine: New Southern.
Serving: D.
Credit Cards: AE, D, MC, V.

Astonishing menu, or manifesto? Acclaimed chef Bob Waggoner makes his convincing case for a Lowcountry cuisine

(with some French guidance) that reaches beyond homegrown ingredients and local imaginations. He stuffs the homely hushpuppy with caramelized figs and gives it self-confidence. He marries escargot to truffled grits. The entrées are good, but you can make a meal of appetizers and salads. The atmosphere is relaxed—a broad, generous clubroom feel, with live jazz every night.

Circa 1886

843-853-7828.
www.circa1886.com.
149 Wentworth St.
Closed: Sun.
Price: Expensive to Very Expensive.
Cuisine: American.
Serving: D.
Credit Cards: AE, D, MC, V.

The Wentworth Mansion and its carriage house were built in the late 19th century and Circa 1886 resurrects all of the opulence of that time with contemporary flair. Once common local ingredients like conch, quail, and fresh beets turn up with fruit and sweet accents, and spicing inspired by the West Indies. There's a vegetarian entrée, but big servings of beef tenderloin and lamb chops, too. Set in a quiet garden corner, with the garden itself off the beaten track, the lovely building is set up with two rooms (about 50 seats), handsomely decorated with remnant beadboard, heart pine, and original stall-door details.

Cypress Lowcountry Grille

843-727-0111.
www.magnolias-blossom-cypress.com.
167 E. Bay St.
Open: Daily.
Price: Expensive to Very Expensive.
Cuisine: American with Asian accent.
Serving: D.
Credit Cards: AE, MC, V.

The makeover of this once typical exposed-brick, warehouse-style place is nothing short of awesome. It includes soft lights that change colors like a mood ring and a three-story glass wall behind which are stored thousands of bottles of wine lined up in perfect rows of black racks (actually, they look like they're in jail). You can eat downstairs at huge banquettes or beautifully dressed tables, or in the upstairs bar. The idea is sumptuous elegance with a surprising light, lively, minimalist feel. The food is superb, ranging from a sampler of sushi, benne-seed shrimp, and oysters, to filet of hickory-smoked beef and braised leeks.

Fish

843-722-3474.
www.fishrestaurant.net.
442 King St.
Closed: Sun.
Price: Moderate to Expensive.
Cuisine: Southern.
Serving: L (Mon.–Fri.); D (Mon.–Sat.)
Credit Cards: AE, MC, V.

Located in an 1837 single-house with its side-to-the-street entryway used for outdoor dining, this is an intimate place full of customers who live in the Upper King Street neighborhood or who choose it for an off-the-beaten-path feel. The owners have cultivated relationships with local growers and fishermen so that the menu, in winter, may be full of root vegetables, and when shad are running in the Edisto River, sweet roe. Near the Visitor Center, so it's a good lunch stop (more of a bargain) before or after a tour.

Fulton Five

843-853-5555.
5 Fulton St.
Closed: Sun.
Price: Moderate to Expensive.
Cuisine: Northern Italian.
Serving: D.
Credit Cards: AE, DC, MC, V.

It's said Gian Carlo Menotti chose Charleston for his Spoleto Festival USA because it had a Mediterranean feel, a serene charm as easy to appreciate and as softly worn as stucco walls. Fulton Five wasn't open then, but its romantic setting fits the description. This restaurant, which seats perhaps 40, inside or on a patio, exudes quiet confidence and lack of pretension, both in the menu and in the décor: green walls that seem murky and lustrous, recessed windows set off by dark brown shutters, brocade fabrics that are velvety to the touch. It's comfortable to eat here alone. The Northern Italian menu includes clams with Tuscan beans, carpaccio, paper-thin veal, risotto dishes, and osso buco.

Gaulart & Maliclet

843-577-9797.
98 Broad St.
Closed: Sun. no dinner Mon.
Price: Inexpensive to Moderate.
Cuisine: French.
Serving: B, L, D.
Credit Cards: AE, D, MC, V.

Known by its nickname "Fast and French," this bistro is the most popular, enduring little place in the Historic District. Seated on high chairs at a counter that juts out into tiny bays, and at communal tables, your neighbors are likely to be Broad Street lawyers, Legare Street dowagers, and Queen Street artists (in Charleston, that may describe one family). You'll find platters of pâté, sausages, selections of cheeses, and French bread; hearty soups; fondues; excellent wine. Vegetarian options. Open late after house tours and Spoleto performances.

Hank's

843-723-3474.
www.hanksseafood.com.
10 Hayne St.
Open: Daily.

Price: Moderate to Expensive.
Cuisine: American; Seafood.
Serving: D.
Credit Cards: AE, D, MC, V.

This warehouse in the Market area used to
be an eccentric "club" (if you needed to
ask you didn't belong); now it houses
Hank's Seafood, a handsome, self-conscious (the building has been properly
"aged" with faux details), good-natured
throwback to family seafood houses of the
1950s. Except in this incarnation, the
shrimp cocktail actually tastes like
shrimp, there's not sawdust on the floor,
and the grilled fish entrées could come
with beurre blanc. Were there rare seared
tuna plates with lemon soy broth back in
the day at the Clam Box I loved? The communal table draws its own crowd and is
another way to be a part of a local scene.

High Cotton
843-724-3815.
www.mavericksouthernkitchens.com.
199 E. Bay St.
Open: Daily.
Price: Expensive to Very Expensive.
Cuisine: New American.
Serving: D; Sat. and Sun. Brunch.
Credit Cards: AE, D, MC, V.

Prosperity's high tide of restaurants
surged on East Bay Street, and this is one
remarkable piece of sea glass it left
behind. It's glossy, unabashed, and high
energy: Its intent, apparent in every detail
from the smoked meat and home-brewed
sauces to the paintings and potted palms,
is to make you look good and feel good.
And who are you? You are looking for quail
or red meat or encrusted fish. On Saturday
you'll go for eggs and barbecue duck hash.
Come here for a robust dinner (in-house
smoking and searing a specialty) and
share a dessert soufflé with your friends.
Jazz and entertainment nightly and at
brunch.

Hominy Grill
843-937-0930.
www.hominygrill.com.
207 Rutledge Ave.
Open: Daily.
Price: Inexpensive to Moderate.
Cuisine: Southern.
Serving: B, L, D; Sat. and Sun. Brunch.
Credit Cards: AE, MC, V.

What is it about Charleston that an old bar-
bershop with a tin ceiling in an offbeat
neighborhood can be redone so simply,
come alive as a full-service restaurant,
serve terrific food, and not seem to break a
sweat? Or burst into irony? The answer is
probably the city's deep reserves of youth,
and its appreciation of pleasure, gardens,
nice weather, and frame buildings. There is
still modesty and grace amidst the excess. A
day that starts with butcher-paper tablecloths, thick mugs of coffee, biscuits, and
bacon can proceed seamlessly to a turkey
club or pimento spread sandwich, then
move on to linens, catfish, and starlight in
the walled garden. Hominy Grill deserves
every iota of its national praise as a
Charleston institution; so does its celebrated buttermilk pie.

Il Cortile de Re
843-853-1888.
193 King St.
Closed: Sun., Mon.
Price: Inexpensive to Moderate.
Cuisine: Italian.
Serving: L (Thurs.–Sat.), D (Tues.–Sat.)
Credit Cards: MC, V.

A storefront Italian bistro with an outdoor
garden in the midst of the King Street
antique district, an easy walk to the
Gibbes Museum, the Nathaniel Russell
House, and Church Street galleries. The
lunch menu is small, maybe three salads,
three panini sandwiches, three pastas;
dinner is far more elaborate and features
Italian entrées like boar, veal, and

sausage. Local people who know food consider it a favorite, because it still feels like a neighborhood spot, but the details, such as the balsamic dressings and amazing cheese selections, are not left to chance. A lunchtime bargain.

Jestine's Kitchen
843-722-7224.
251 Meeting St.
Closed: Mon.
Price: Inexpensive to Moderate.
Cuisine: Homestyle Southern.
Serving: L.
Credit Cards: MC, V.

Plain and simple Southern food, with lots of fried entrées (chicken, oysters, tomatoes, pork) and greens and grits on the side. Unpretentious room right on Meeting Street where, if you get nothing else, you can come for pie and the best sweet tea in town.

Magnolia's Uptown/Down South
843-577-7771.
www.magnolias-blossom-cypress.com.
185 E. Bay St.
Open: Daily.
Price: Moderate to Expensive.
Cuisine: "Nouvelle" Southern.
Serving: L, D.
Credit Cards: AE, MC, V.

This big and breezy place epitomizes the willing-to-please personality of the New South. It's energetic, with a menu that sticks to basic Southern foodstuffs—greens, black-eyed peas, grits, and shrimp—and dresses them up in unusual ways. It's very popular, with more visitors than locals during the high season, but has kept its touch and still delivers. Sunday brunch lasts past 3 PM for you late risers. Reservations required due to national popularity.

McCrady's
843-577-0025.
www.mccradysrestaurant.com.
2 Unity Alley (off E. Bay St.).
Open: Daily.
Price: Expensive to Very Expensive.
Cuisine: New American.
Serving: D.
Credit Cards: AE, MC, V.

Award-winning for wine and food, expanded to include both a wine bar and lounge (entrance on East Bay Street), and with its original space in a beautifully redone 18th-century tavern, McCrady's is an understated, excellent restaurant. The menu features local fish, though more than the usual—tuna, grouper, and skate, for example—as well as local vegetables that are imaginatively paired and dressed up with sauce reductions. The cooking has classic French underpinnings with art-world presentation. Prix fixe options are sometimes available, and the wine bar serves house specials in smaller portions.

Peninsula Grill
843-723-0700.
www.peninsulagrill.com.
112 N. Market St.
Open: Daily.
Price: Expensive to Very Expensive.
Cuisine: American with Southern accents.
Serving: D.
Credit Cards: AE, D, DC, MC, V.

An elegant dining room, sometimes a bit noisy, never overbearing. The room has a great geometry, a square place punctuated by pillars and further softened by walls of dark velvet dressed with 19th-century paintings. The light is suffused with soft gold overtones, as if the color had been rubbed on the air. Jell-O would taste good here. You may order "simple" entrées like strip steak, veal chops, or grouper and choose your sauces and sides; or go for the house specials (pan-roasted breast of duck is one). Champagne is always on the menu here. You may also eat in the courtyard. Reservations are essential.

Relaxing at Vickery's café.

Sermet's Corner

843-853-7775.
276 King St.
Open: Daily.
Price: Moderate.
Cuisine: North African, Mediterranean.
Serving: L, D.
Credit Cards: AE, D, MC, V.

This restaurant looks and acts like a real bistro, where students, children, grandparents, couples, and solo types feel at home. It's simple and open: big plate-glass windows open onto a busy intersection just north of Saks. The salads are imaginative, many garnished with fruit relish, and there are plain choices for kids and the less adventurous: paninis, pasta, soups, and many vegetarian entrées. Live music at night.

Vickery's

843-577-5300.
15 Beaufain St.
Open: Daily.
Price: Inexpensive to Moderate.
Cuisine: American; Cuban.
Serving: L, D.
Credit Cards: AE, D, MC, V.

A popular place for young locals and College of Charleston students, with tables and banquettes surrounding a horseshoe-shaped bar, and walls decorated with . . . stuff. Outdoor dining under the umbrellas is the place to be on a Friday afternoon in spring; inside it's noisy and friendly. Cuban and Caribbean spices warm up burgers, chicken, and pork; black beans and rice, with hot sausage, is the choice of regulars; three dozen varieties of beer wash it all down.

Vintage Restaurant and Wine Bar

843-577-0090.
14 N. Market St.
Open: Daily.
Price: Expensive.
Cuisine: New American.
Serving: D; Sun. Brunch.
Credit Cards: AE, D, MC, V.

A restaurant and wine bar in a wonderful minimalist space (located via passageway) at the foot of the Market, across East Bay Street. It has the feel and menu of a bistro for the new millennium—imaginative, pristine, not too fussy. A simple mix of textures, as in monkfish with foie gras emulsion and a root vegetable, is all you want. There are some 400 wines available, 70 by the glass; on Sunday nights several varieties are paired with offerings on a special, multi-course menu. It's probably a tad too expensive to become a weekly habit, but its intimate, fresh feeling would encourage one.

Virginia's on King

843-735-5800.
www.virginiasonking.com.

412 King St.
Open: Daily.
Price: Moderate to Expensive.
Cuisine: Southern.
Serving: L; D (not on Sun.); Sun. Brunch.
Credit Cards: D, MC, V.

The menu reflects years of passed-down family favorites and the temperament of Charleston Sunday after-church dinner. It's a place where taste bud sentiment meets the 21st century. You will find Frogmore Stew, fried okra, she-crab soup, and the extras you're greedy for: mashed potatoes and fried tomatoes. A beautiful renovation/restoration retained the exposed soft brick walls and modern stylists added the bistro look. Located a block north of the intersection with Calhoun Street, it's a great destination after shopping on King Street.

Charleston Area and the Sea Islands

If you are staying at a Sea Island resort, you will find a variety of dining choices offered in a range of prices and styles. Bohicket Marina Village at Seabrook Island boasts very attractive, informal restaurants on the marina's edge. The best are at Kiawah—Jasmine Porch and the Ocean Room. If you are more adventurous and want to eat with local people, you might try some of the following restaurants.

Bowen's Island Restaurant

843-795-2757.
1870 Bowen's Island Rd., 2 miles before Folly Beach.
Open: Mon.–Sat.
Price: Inexpensive to Moderate.
Cuisine: Lowcountry seafood.
Serving: D.
Credit Cards: None.

Charleston's Vintage Restaurant and Wine Bar.

If Huck Finn lived in the Lowcountry, this is where he'd eat. It's really, really basic: screen doors slamming, beat-up wooden tables engraved with initials, great breeze; offering hushpuppies, shrimp, roasted oysters cooked the old-fashioned way (throw them across a piece of metal sheeting above an open fire and cover with wet rags until they steam open). A local tradition some 60-years old that has resisted any attempts at self-improvement. Service is definitely lackadaisical and a new mop might be in order, but Charleston wasn't always as fancy as it is today.

Gullah Cuisine
843-881-9076.
www.gullahcuisine.com.
1717 SC 17, Mount Pleasant, about 2 miles from the Ravenel Bridge.
Open: Mon.–Sat.
Price: Inexpensive.
Cuisine: Lowcountry homestyle.
Serving: L,D.
Credit Cards: V.

Owner and caterer Charlotte Jenkins has made a roadside restaurant into a destination for locals and newcomers who love their comfort food of the Lowcountry served without affectation, and in its delicious incarnation: fried chicken and fish, dirty rice, boiled greens with hocks, conch stew, and field peas.

Mustard Seed
843-849-0050.
1220 Ben Sawyer Blvd., Mt. Pleasant.
Closed: Sun.
Price: Inexpensive to Moderate.
Cuisine: New American.
Serving: L, D.
Credit Cards: AE, MC, V.

A casual, very popular local restaurant, often packed, but with a nice bar and a simple, robust menu. A hippie feel for a new century. Lots of pastas, seafood with light sauces, grilled portobello mushrooms, vegetarian specials. Other locations, equally charming, in Summerville and James Island.

Food Purveyors

Bakeries/Coffee Houses
Baker's Café (843-577-2694; 214 King St.) A busy place, especially for Sunday brunch, but ideal for lunch or a snack. Located at the head of the King Street antique district.

Café Café (843-723-3622; 177 Meeting St.) Opens at 7 AM, so just the place for a croissant and coffee after a morning run in the Waterfront Park.

Joseph's (843-958-8500; 129 Meeting St.) A local favorite for breakfast, homemade soups at lunch, and courtyard dining.

Saffron (843-722-5588; 333 E. Bay St.) The glass cases filled with daily specials like chocolate-chip scones and pastries, and the racks of fresh bread, could lead to a gourmet picnic if you don't want to eat here.

Candy and Ice Cream
Charleston Chocolates (843-577-4491; www.charlestonchocolates.com; 190 East Bay St.) It's Valentine's Day year-round here, with hand-dipped chocolates and fancy trimmings.

Häagen-Dazs (843-723-9326; 43 S. Market St.) Sometimes it's far too hot in the Lowcountry for ice cream—it's a melted mess after a few licks—but this old favorite stays open after the sun goes down.

Lucas Neuhaus (843-722-0461; 73 State St.) If you're in the Market area and overwhelmed by all the shops and all the merchandise for sale, drop in for one fabulous Belgian chocolate or confection.

Maggie Moo's Ice Cream and Treatery (843-722-6667; 159 Church St.) Ice cream made fresh daily and sculpted with your add-ins.

Pizza, Sandwiches, and Faster Food

Andolini's (843-722-7437; 82 Wentworth St.) The place for pizza in Charleston. Order as you enter, eat in a high-backed booth or on the back patio.

Juanita Greenberg's Nacho Royale (843-723-6224; 439 King St.) The four food groups are represented here—all hot, fresh, simple. Big burritos, handmade nachos in portions made for two. You can start with a margarita at 4 PM.

Kennedy's Market and Bakery (843-723-2026; 60 Calhoun St.) Hearty gourmet sandwiches, fresh bakery goods, soup, and wine.

The Kickin' Chicken (843-805-5020; 337 King St.) Fifteen flavors of wings so take plenty of napkins. Salads and sandwiches.

TOURING IN THE HISTORIC DISTRICT AND BEYOND

As in Savannah, opportunities for tours are plentiful and varied, including by carriage, bus, van, on foot, and by boat. Practically everyone has a special angle. Tour operators are licensed and amazingly patient with questions; they really know their stuff. Tours range from one to two-and-one-half hours, longer for out-of-town sites and scheduled stops at house museums, with prices in town starting at about $13 for children and $18 for adults and escalating quickly according to the length of the trip. Check the Web sites, and reserve there if one suits your interests. Tours that cover areas in the Sea Islands are more plentiful these days, with an emphasis on Gullah culture. Reservations are highly recommended for all tours and pay attention to departure times. Note that some tours with a nature emphasis are described more fully in the **Recreation** section later in this chapter.

If you're a generalist, start your day (and park your car) at the **Charleston Visitor Center** (375 Meeting St.) where there are lots of maps, helpful docents, and an audio-visual presentation that presents an excellent introduction to the city. Carriage tours, city shuttle buses, minivan tours, and walking-tour guides often collect and discharge passengers at this site. Sometimes a motorized tour is the most efficient way to review the city's deep inventory of houses—from the famous "single house" (one room wide, standing endways with its door to the street) to double-piazza mansions dominating their harborside sites. Or you may head out on your own. Any way you choose, you won't be disappointed. Only at the Visitor Center may you purchase a Heritage Passport (www.heritagefederation.org) which costs $39.95 and permits entry to nine of Charleston's most popular sites, including Drayton Hall, Middleton Place, the Gibbes

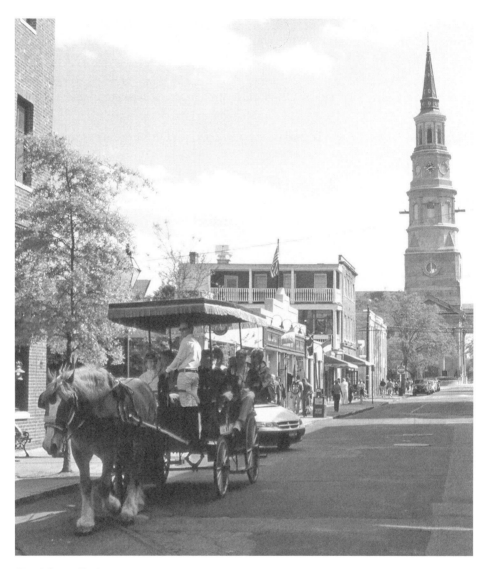

Church Street, Charleston.

Museum of Art, and five renowned historic houses in Charleston. It is a terrific bargain. Water-based tours generally depart from the Aquarium Wharf Dock (360 Concord St.)

By Bus or Minivan

The emergence of the "New South" has as much to do with economics and enlightenment as with air-conditioning. There's no doubt that the comfort and cool of a minivan or bus tour—in which the guide is like your favorite classroom teacher and the atmosphere as fresh as a fine hotel room—has its virtues. The audio is high quality, the video on a laser disc, and the extra-large windows offer great views. These tours also travel to sites out of the city limits, such as historic forts and plantations. But remember that comfort comes at a sacrifice—larger vehicles may not be able to navigate the old, sometimes alley-width streets of Historic Districts, and the pace is swiftly modern. They are a good choice for handicapped passengers, the eager visitor who wants to cover a lot of ground in a day, and groups of six or more.

Motorized tours generally pick up and deliver passengers from major downtown hotels and the Visitor Center.

Charleston Tours, Inc. (843-571-0049; www.charleston-tours.com).

Doin' The Charleston (843-763-1233 or 1-800-647-4487; www.dointhecharlestontours.com).

Sites and Insight Tours by Al Miller (843-762-0051; www.sitesandinsightstours.com) Emphasize African American history and the Gullah culture.

Talk of the Towne (843-795-8199 or 1-888-795-8199; wwwtalkofthetowne.com)

Taylored Tours (843-832-3321; www.toursofcharleston.com).

By Boat

Sandlapper Water Tours (843-849-8687; www.sandlappertours.com).

Schooner Pride (84-foot tall ship) (843-772-1112 or 1-800-344-4483; www.schooner pride.com).

Spiritline Harbor Tour (843-722-2628; www.spiritlinecruises.com).

By Bicycle or on Foot

Discovering the nooks and crannies of the Historic Districts under your own steam is an intimate way to imagine the past. Furthermore, even though homes, churches, and ballast-stone streets have been preserved impeccably, they are still neighborhoods, not museums. Getting out from under the windshield or behind the tinted glass will help you understand the real, living context of these places, in which so much has occurred over time. Besides, it's probably dangerous to smell the jasmine and make a left turn at the same time.

The typical daily rate is $20 for a bicycle, $45 for a tandem, and $15 for child trailer. Higher-end touring bikes for longer rides are $40; it's suggested you bring your own pedals and reserve in advance. Shop staff has maps and ideas for longer rides. Helmets, baby-seats, and locks are provided at low or no cost. These downtown shops can help you further:

The Bicycle Shoppe (843-722-8168; www.thebicycleshoppecharleston.com; 280 Meeting St.).

Bike The Bridge (843-853-2453;www.bikethebridgerentals.com; 6 Vendue Range).

Walking tours are a Lowcountry art form. Extolling the virtues of one's city in lacy prose comes naturally. There are many stories to tell, and an abundance of people to tell them.

As guiding has evolved, so have tours tailored to specific interests: architecture, gardening, the Civil War, African American culture, religious heritage, ghosts, even sites of films or novels set in the Lowcountry. With sufficient advance notice, some private guides will craft a unique tour for your group, or offer bilingual service.

Walking tours generally last up to two hours and are scheduled in both morning and afternoon. Ask how large the group can get—smaller is better. Reservations are recommended, in some cases required. In the summer, wear a hat and sunscreen, and carry water. Prices start at about $19 per person. Self-guided walking tours, with a cassette and headphones, can be rented at the Visitor Center for 24 hours ($17).

Architectural Walking Tours (1-800-931-7761; www.architecturalwalkingtoursof charleston.com).

Charleston Walks (1-800-729-3420; www.charlestonwalks.com).

Civil War Walking Tour (843-722-7033; www.civilwarwalk.com).

Culinary Tours of Charleston (843-856-3833 or 1-800-979-3370; www.culinarytoursof charleston.com).

Ghosts of Charleston (843-723-1670 or 1-800-854-1670; www.tourcharleston.com).

Gullah Tours (843-763-7551; www.gullahtours.com).

By Carriage

Carriages drawn by horses or mules pull you into the past while your guide tells colorful tales. The companies listed below are some among many. Tours generally last one hour and are scheduled throughout the day and evening. Prices per person are about $20 for adults; $12 for children. Customized or private tours are often available if you inquire in advance. Tours depart from either the company stables or from pre-arranged pick-up sites.

Carolina Polo & Carriage Co. (843-577-6767; www.cpcc.com).

Old South Carriage Co. (843-723-9712; www.oldsouthcarriagetours.com).

Olde Towne Carriage Co. (843-722-1315; www.oldetownecarriage.com).

Palmetto Carriage Works (843-723-8145; www.carriagetour.com).

CULTURE

Architecture

Whether you have a serious or a layman's interest in architecture, you should approach the riches of Charleston and its environs with a game plan. Is it small rooms and thickly carved mantels of the Colonial period you like? The fine lightness of touch and classical decoration introduced by the Adam brothers? Do open-air living spaces afforded by piazzas and walled gardens appeal? Ironwork? Brick or clapboard? Small country churches or city steeples? Interiors or exteriors? Grand plantations or modest row houses? Rooms adorned with 18th-century furniture or ones that remain bare? For suggestions on buildings that express these aesthetic considerations, see the "Historic Homes" listing later in this chapter. Don't overlook the marvelous decorative ironwork that adorns buildings and streetscapes throughout the city. The most revered practitioner in Charleston is Philip Simmons, whose work has been recognized by the National Museum of American History at the Smithsonian Institution. Find out more about Simmons and get directions to two sites where you can see his work at www.philip simmons.org or through the Philip Simmons Foundation, 843-728-8018, 91 Anson St., Charleston, SC 29401.

The Calhoun Mansion is considered one of the most significant Victorian houses in the South.   Peter Loftus

Art

Gibbes Museum of Art (843-722-2706; www.gibbesmuseum.org; 135 Meeting St.) The permanent collection presents Charleston from the 18th century to the present. Not to be missed are Charles Fraser's exquisite miniatures of prominent citizens during the city's early days, interpretations of 20th-century plantation and rural life, including Alice Ravenel Huger Smith's watercolors, or sketches and woodcuts by Alfred Hutty and Anna Heyward Taylor. Also, a very fine museum shop. Open Tuesday through Saturday 10–5; Sun. 1–5. Closed Monday and holidays. Adults $9; children $7.

Dance

Dance performances take place through most of the year, but are especially frequent during the Spoleto Festival. Call ahead for schedules and ticket information.

Charleston Ballet Theatre (843-723-7334; www.charlestonballet.org; 477 King St.)

Robert Ivey Ballet (843-556-1343; www.robertiveyballet.com; 1910 Savannah Hwy.)

Film

First-run movie houses tend to be located in malls away from downtown, and they account for most of the region's audiences. In Charleston, the American Cinema Grill is a gem, where you can order a simple meal and glass of wine and watch the movie from your table. Locally organized film festivals presenting documentaries or foreign films occur once a year. Check local newspaper listings or look for handbills posted around town.

American Cinema Grill (843-853-0246; 446 King St.).

Charleston Film Festival (843-722-1947).

Citadel Mall 6 (843-763-7052; 2072 Sam Rittenberg Blvd.).

Carmike James Island (843-795-9499; 1743 Central Park Rd.).

Northwoods Mall Cinema (843-569-6794; 2181 Northwoods Blvd.).

Galleries

The Charleston Fine Art Dealers Association (www.cfada.com) is a force for appreciation of both the work of the Charleston Renaissance artists of the 20th-century and of the New Renaissance artists in the Charleston of the 21st. Their Fine Art Annual each November, held in association with the Gibbes Museum, consists of lectures, demonstrations, and gallery receptions designed to educate and celebrate the enduring work of local and regional artists.

There are also galleries for contemporary art from national artists, as well as places where the collections are more intimate reflections of Lowcountry light and life. The French Quarter of Charleston, from South Market to Tradd Street, from the waterfront to Meeting Street, is a thriving place for artists and galleries, too. An association of artists (www.french quarterarts.com; 843-577-7100) holds quarterly walks there on the first Friday evening of March, May, October, and December.

Here are some of the notable art galleries in the city.

Carolina Galleries (843-720-8622; www.carolinagalleries.com; 106-A Church St.) The best place to see the paintings, etchings, pastels, drawings, and more, of the artists who made up the Charleston Renaissance: Alice Ravenel Huger Smith, Anna Heyward Taylor, Alfred Hutty, and others.

The Charleston Renaissance Gallery (843-723-0025; www. fineartsouth.com; 103 Church St.) Located in a beautifully restored post-Revolutionary brick building, Robert Hicklin's gallery is at the forefront of renewed interest in Charleston's 20th-century art history—and it's worth going to for the education it offers. West Fraser's city scenes and Lowcountry landscapes, some in oil, some in watercolor, are showcased, as are 19th-century paintings and sculptures.

Coleman Fine Art (843-853-7000; www.colemanfineart.com; 79 Church St.) Members of the gallery include a number of artists working in a realistic style in oils and watercolors as well as the paintings of portraitist and illustrator Mary Whyte. Smith Coleman III, who owns the gallery, also restores damaged works of art and makes lovely frames. The gallery is located in the former studio of Elizabeth O'Neill Verner.

Eva Carter Gallery (843-722-0506; www.evacartergallery.com; 132 East Bay St.) Abstract oils, works on paper, and sculpture.

Gaye Sanders Fisher Gallery (843-958-0010; www.gayesandersfisher.com; 124 Church St.)
Located in an 18th-century single house, featuring watercolors that burst with the feeling
of Lowcountry landscape and architecture.

John Carroll Doyle Art Gallery (843-577-7344; www.johncdoyle.com; 54 Broad St.)
A Charleston native, Doyle is one of the painters in the "new" Charleston Renaissance,
capturing people in intense moments (like blues harmonica players) and teasing that
intensity out of landscapes and animals.

Margaret Petterson Gallery (843-722-8094; www.margaretpetterson.com; 125 Church
St.) Vibrant oil paintings of the city and its flora, as well as monotypes.

Martin Gallery (843-723-7378; 18 Broad St.) Contemporary art and elegant craft work,
including jewelry incorporating precious stones and sculpted gold.

Nina Liu and Friends (843-722-2724; 24 State St.) Wonderful contemporary art in media
such as fabric, collage, ceramic, paper and glass—it can be startling, magical, and strong.
The owner is an artist with a fine eye.

Sculpture by Darrell Davis in the Smith-Killian Gallery, in the French Quarter.

Smith-Killian Fine Art (843-853-0708;
www.smithkillian.com; 9 Queen St.)
Representing well-known painter Betty
Anglin Smith and her accomplished
triplets—painters Jennifer Smith Rogers
and Shannon Smith, and photographer
Tripp Smith. The best place to see the
Lowcountry and Charleston itself being
represented at this moment in time.

The Sylvan Gallery (843-722-2172;
www.thesylvangallery.com; 171 King St.)
Representing more than 30 artists, the
gallery features sculpture and 20th- and
21st-century representational art.

Wells Gallery (843-853-3233; www.wells
gallery.com; 125 Meeting St.) Contemporary
art of nationally recognized artists such as
Susan Mayfield West, John Carroll Doyle,
and Rhett Thurman. A good stop to see how
the Lowcountry experience is being realisti-
cally brought to life.

Historic Homes, Gardens & Religious Sites

It's hard to avoid historic sites in
Charleston, but whether or not you visit
one, and how much time you spend there,
will, of course, depend on your interest and

schedule, whether you're traveling with children, and whether you have your own car. It may be preferable, for example, to do just one big thing in a day (a boat ride to Fort Sumter, a visit to a plantation garden) plus two smaller ones (see a house museum or church, take a walking tour, picnic in a park).

Distances are not great: to gardens and lighthouses and island sites from Charleston takes about 30 minutes. The sites in the following list are open all year, unless otherwise noted. Admission fees and hours are as of 2008; reduced admission generally applies to children 12 and under, seniors, students, and military personnel. Combination tickets offer savings at historic houses, sites, and museums, so ask at the venue or at the Visitor Center. If time is short, consult a new Web site, www.charlestonmuseummile.org, which simplifies touring along a section of Meeting Street through the heart of the Historic District.

Keep in mind that the last tours of the day start approximately 30 minutes before closing time. Visitors generally are welcome to enter religious sites, but are asked to observe the worship schedule and related courtesies of visitation, as few of the sites offer regular tour services. Handicapped access is sometimes limited in the old buildings, and there are usually rules regarding strollers.

Aiken-Rhett House
843-723-1159.
www.historiccharleston.org.
48 Elizabeth St.
Mon. through Sat. 10–5; Sun. 2–5.
Admission: Adults 10; reduced admission with combination tickets to selected historic properties.

Built in 1817, representing high-style Greek Revival and Rococo interiors, the Aiken-Rhett House is preserved in a somewhat less formal way than other houses. It's full of atmosphere, a little worn at the edges. During the fiercest shelling of Charleston in the Civil War, it was the headquarters of Confederate General P. G. T. Beauregard, a purpose for which it was well suited by virtue of its scale, design, and location off the Battery. The intact work yard is a compelling example of African American urban life.

Audubon Swamp Garden
See "Nature Preserves" in the **Recreation** section below.

Boone Hall Plantation
843-884-4371.
www.boonehallplantation.com.
P.O. Box 1554, Mt. Pleasant.
Mon. through Sat. 9–5; Sun. 1–4.
Admission: Adults $14.50; children $7.

Of particular interest are the nine mid-18th–century brick slave cabins (these housed house slaves and skilled craftsmen, not the field hands); the Gin House, used for processing cotton; and the magnificent avenue of oaks, which runs three-quarters of a mile.

Congregation Beth Elohim
843-723-1090.

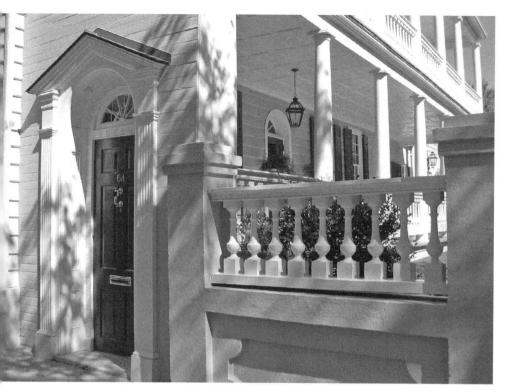

A classic single house with the side-facing piazza, decorative gouge work on the door surround, and coffered soffit display the epitome of 19th century architecture.   Peter Loftus

www.kkbe.org.
90 Hasell St.
Mon. through Fri. 10–12 (tours).

The country's oldest synagogue in continuous use, built in 1840 to replace an earlier building that was destroyed by fire, it is a superb example of Greek Revival architecture.

Cypress Gardens
See "Nature Preserves" in the **Recreation** section.

Drayton Hall
843-769-2600.
www.draytonhall.org.
3380 Ashley River Rd. (SC 61, 9 miles NW of Charleston).
Mar. through Oct., 8:30–5; Nov. through Feb., 8:30–4.
Admission: Adults $14; children $8.

It's a measure of the greatness of this 18th-century Georgian-Palladian dwelling that even as it remains unfurnished, unrestored, unchanged (just stabilized), it exists in a class by itself. Built between 1738 and 1742, and set on a lovely Ashley River site, it is one of the most architecturally significant dwellings in America. House tours start on the hour (written tours in French, German, English, and Spanish available). A tour focusing on African American history occurs three times daily. You are welcome to take self-guided walking tours of the grounds and marsh areas. A new DVD produced by The History Channel is available for rent on a simple player: It greatly enhances individual interpretation. Not to be missed even if it's raining.

Edmonston-Alston House

843-722-7171.
www.middletonplace.org.
21 E. Battery.
Tues. through Sat. 10–4:30; Sun. & Mon. 1:30–4:30.
Admission: Adults $10; reduced admission with combination tickets to selected historic properties.

First built in 1825 by one wealthy man, later enlarged by another, it reveals—in structure, lavish decoration, documents, family furnishings, silver, and china—the best of what money could buy. You get a sense that this was the life and lifestyle Southerners fought the Civil War, in part, to protect.

Emmanuel A. M. E. Church

843-722-2561.
110 Calhoun St.

The Free African Society, composed of free blacks and slaves, was formed in 1791, and by 1818, under the leadership of Morris Brown, this independent congregation built a small church for their services. Denmark Vesey planned his slave insurrection there; when the rebellion failed, the church was shut for 43 years. Reorganization came after the Civil War; the present church was built in 1891.

Exchange Building/Provost Dungeon

843-727-2165.
www.oldexchange.com.
122 E. Bay St.
Daily: 9–5.
Admission: Adults $7; children $3.50.

Before this building was completed in 1771, the site was used for a variety of public purposes in the young colony. Its commanding location, at the foot of Broad Street, defined both an end boundary for the city, and also, from the water, its point of arrival. In terms of sheer geography it looms large. It's the kind of outsized place that was, and still is, used for huge receptions. During the Revolution the British held political and military prisoners in the basement.

French Protestant (Huguenot) Church

843-722-4385.
136 Church St.

French Huguenots fleeing religious persecution worshipped in Charleston as early as 1687. This church, built on the site of earlier ones, dates from 1845.

Heyward-Washington House

843-722-2996.
www.charlestonmuseum.org.
87 Church St.
Mon. through Sat. 10–5; Sun. 1–5. Last tour at 4:30.
Admission: Adults $10; children $5. Discounted admission with combination ticket to other Charleston Museum properties.

Built in 1772 by a rice planter whose son, Thomas Heyward Jr., signed the Declaration of Independence, this house was also the headquarters of George Washington in 1791. Its furniture collection, including several 18th-century Charleston-made pieces and the magnificent Holmes bookcase, is unmatched.

Joseph Manigault House

843-723-2926.
www.charlestonmuseum.org.
350 Meeting St.
Mon. through Sat. 10–5; Sun. 1–5. Last tour at 4:30.
Admission: Adults $10; children $5. Discounted admission with a combination ticket to other Charleston Museum properties.

The outside of this structure is three stories of brick; the inside is something like shaped light. Designed by native son Gabriel Manigault for his brother and completed in 1803, this house, exuding both formality of plan and spontaneity of gesture, shows the nature of beauty and taste favored by elite planters who may have been, as Gabriel Manigault was, educated in Europe and exposed there to sophisticated design ideas and decorating schemes. The furniture is of the period: English, American, and French.

Magnolia Plantation and Gardens

843-571-1266.
www.magnoliaplantation.com.
3550 Ashley River Rd. (SC 61, 10 miles NW of Charleston).
Daily: 8–5:30; shorter hours in winter.
Admission to the Plantation and Gardens: Adults $15, with additional costs for tours of the house and rides on the Nature Preserve train.

The current building was floated here by barge in 1873, but the entire tract dates back to the time of the Barbadian planters who relocated on the Ashley River. The legacy here is gardens, acres of them, reflecting (in layout and specimen planting) two centuries of horticulture. The gardens include 250 varieties of Azalea indica and 900 varieties of *Camellia japonica;* there are bike and walking paths, a petting zoo, a canoe trail, and picnic areas. You may access an adjacent nature preserve by small train. This is also the site to enter the Audubon Swamp Garden (see "Nature Preserves" in the **Recreation** section).

Middleton Place

843-556-6020 or 1-800-782-3608.
www.middletonplace.org.
4300 Ashley River Rd. (SC 61, 14 miles NW of Charleston).

Daily: 9–5.
Admission: Adults $25; children $5; house tours always cost an additional $10 per person.

The formal gardens, laid out in 1741 and constructed by 100 slaves over a decade, feature terraces, camellia allées, butterfly lakes, hillside drifts of azalea, and acres of landscaped paths. The site is so grand that it can be appreciated even when little is in bloom: The geometry of the original plan itself is breathtaking. The adjacent stables and farmyard area evoke the self-sufficiency of the plantation era, with demonstrations by a potter, weaver, blacksmith, and carpenter. (The animals just hang around on their own.) The main house was sacked by Union forces; tours of a remaining wing honor the Middletons, but the real reason to come here is what's outside. Nice restaurant for lunch and dinner.

Nathaniel Russell House
843-724-8481.
www.historiccharleston.org.
51 Meeting St.
Mon. through Sat. 10–5; Sun. 2–5.
Admission: $10.

Nathaniel Russell House.

People have no doubt been admiring this brick townhouse and its garden from the day it was completed (ca. 1808), and with good reason. It represents the high point of the Adam style in the city—its stairway appears to float, a lovely combination of function and fantasy—and it is one of the most thoroughly conceived and exquisitely executed neoclassical dwellings in the nation. The interpretation (it belongs to the Historic Charleston Foundation) is rich and thorough, from the look of table settings, to the lives of slaves who made such a household run smoothly.

St. Michael's Episcopal Church
843-723-0603.
Meeting St. at Broad St.
Daily: 9–4:30.

This church is still the center of many Charlestonians' lives, as it has been since 1761. Research suggests that its stunning white steeple is a close match to the one at St. Martin-in-the-Fields in London, and may have been designed by James Gibbs. It is part of the famous "Four Corners of Law" in downtown Charleston, an intersection that represents, in reli-

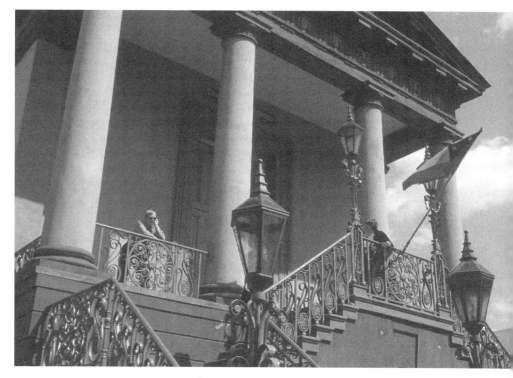

The Confederate Museum, Charleston.

gious, civic, judicial, and federal buildings, the order imposed on society. There is a tranquil walled graveyard to explore.

St. Philip's Episcopal Church
843-722-7734.
146 Church St.

Constructed in 1835–38, facing a central park, and flanked by its graveyard, St. Philip's seems out of the Old World of Europe. The building is sheathed in a mottled, tan, stucco material that reflects the gradual shifting in light over the course of a day. The church is open for services Sundays, Wednesdays, and selected Fridays.

Thomas Elfe Workshop
843-722-2142.
54 Queen St.
Tours Mon. through Fri. 10–12.
Admission: $5.

A meticulously restored Charleston "single house," this dwelling was built before 1760 by the renowned cabinetmaker, who came to Charleston from England in the mid-18th century and left his mark in homes and furniture throughout the city. The carved fretwork that embellishes mahogany tables, chairs, and bookcases makes his work artistically distinctive; his abundant record keeping has enabled historians to understand his life and times. The small house, paneled in cypress, showcases his artistry.

Military Sites

The presence of the military—invaders and defenders—has enriched the history of the Lowcountry since the time of the American Revolution, and it is still felt today. You needn't be a veteran, or even a Civil War buff, to enjoy the forts, military museums, and rural sites that are so plentiful in the region. Children—with their innate appreciation of danger and adventure and their love of costume—especially seem to twig these sites and installations.

The Citadel Museum
843-953-6726.
www.citadel.edu.
171 Moultrie St.
Sun. through Fri. 2–5; Sat. 12–5.
Free admission.

Located on the campus of the Military College of South Carolina, founded in 1842, it tells the history of the school and the Corps of Cadets through documents, photographs, and uniforms. Dress parades take place most Fridays at 3:45 during the academic year.

The Confederate Museum
843-723-1541.
188 Meeting St.
Tues. through Sat. 11–3:30.
Adults $5; children $3.
Handicapped accessible.

There's a Gullah expression in the Lowcountry that sums up this museum: When you ask someone on the telephone "Is that you?" the person may reply, in a weary tone laced with irony, "That's what's leff' of me." This may be what's left of the old Confederacy: uniforms, tattered flags, documents, artifacts, and a fragrant sense of the Lost Cause.

Fort Lamar Heritage Preserve
803-734-3893.
www.dnr.sc.gov/managed/heritage.
(SC Dept. of Natural Resources/Heritage Trust Program).
Fort Lamar Rd., James Island (Take SC 171 to Battery Island Rd. Left for approx. 8 miles to Fort Lamar Rd. Right for approx. 5 miles to small parking lot on left).
Open: Daily dawn to dusk.
Self-guided tour; maps available on site.

The site of the Battle of Secessionville, waged in the predawn darkness of June 16, 1862, when Federal troops attacked this Confederate earthwork fort. The battle, involving some 1,400 men, was over in three hours. The walking tour directs you across what was an open field rimmed by marsh and woods, around the simple "M"-shaped field fortification, by the magazines, dry moat, earthworks, and the likely mass grave of Federal wounded. Off the beaten track: For information call the number listed above which oversees the rustic site.

Fort Moultrie

843-883-3123 (National Park Service local office).
www.nps.gov/fomo.
1214 Middle St., Sullivan's Island; 10 miles E. of Charleston.
Daily: 9–5.
Admission: Adults $3; $5 per family.

The primary site of Charleston's seacoast defense system, from its first test in the American Revolution, now operated by the National Park Service. The palmetto-log fort that repelled the British fleet is gone, but buildings and earthworks dating from 1809 convey the sense of fragility and isolation the early patriots must have felt. A 20-minute film in the Visitor Center provides an excellent introduction. It is also the burial site of the Seminole warrior Osceola who, meeting under a flag of truce, was imprisoned here in 1838.

Fort Sumter National Monument

843-883-3123.
www.nps.gov/fosu.
www.spiritlinecruises.com (for boat tour information).
Departures from a National Park Service interpretative center at 340 Concord St. by the Charleston Aquarium and Patriot's Point.
Trips usually two or three times each day, year-round, but fewer in winter months.
Admission: Adults $15; seniors $13.50; children (ages 6–11) $9.

A relaxing ferry trip, which offers splendid views of the harbor and peninsula, takes you to the place where the Civil War began. National Park Service rangers are on hand at the Fort to answer your questions; there are gun emplacements to explore, and a museum with arti-facts to help you imagine scenes of the siege, which lasted approximately two years and ended in the abandonment of the Fort by Confederate soldiers. The entire tour lasts just over two hours.

H. L. Hunley Exhibit

843-743-4865 (information); 1-877-448-6539 (to purchase tickets).
www.hunley.org.
Warren Lasch Conservation Center, 1250 Supply St., Bldg. 255, North Charleston.
Open Sat. 10–5, Sun. 12–5.
Admission $12.

The *H. L. Hunley* was the forerunner of a modern submarine, most famous for its sinking of the *Housatonic* outside Charleston Harbor, during the Civil War. Its last voyage ended in disaster; All eight men aboard died. The 40-foot submersible, powered by men pedaling a crankshaft, is undergoing restoration. Tours include a view of the conservation tank and displays of artifacts.

Patriots Point Naval and Maritime Museum

843-884-2727.
www.patriotspoint.org.
40 Patriots Point Rd., Mt. Pleasant.
Daily: 9–6:30.
Admission: Adults $15; children $8; seniors and military with ID $13; free to uniformed soldiers.

The big ones are berthed here—the aircraft carrier *Yorktown,* the World War II—sub *Clamagore,* the destroyer *Laffey,* and the cutter *Ingham*—and on self-guided tours you can see their aircraft, guns, and missiles, as well as views of how personnel lived and worked on board. The view of peninsular Charleston from the platform of the *Yorktown* is unbeatable. Snack bar and gift shop, seating areas for the rest and air you'll need: There's a lot of walking and close quarters.

Museums
Avery Research Center for African-American History and Culture
843-953-7609.
www.cofc.edu/avery.
125 Bull St.
Tours Mon. through Sat. 12–5.
Housed in one of the first schools dedicated to educating freed slaves, the center is an archive and library of printed and picture materials and objects related to the heritage of the region's African Americans. It was built by the Freedman's Bureau at the end of the Civil War to meet the needs of 1,000 eager students who had been receiving instruction from teachers sent by the American Missionary Association and other organizations. Reading room hours are Monday through Friday 10–5; Saturday 12–5.

Charleston Museum
843-722-2996.
www.charlestonmuseum.org.
360 Meeting St.
Mon. through Sat. 9–5; Sun. 1–5.
Admission: Adults $10; children $5; combination tickets to Museum and its historic properties available at a discount.

The museum, founded in 1773, is the oldest in America. This means that both the ideas that gave the collection its intellectual underpinnings and the very objects themselves, many from Charleston's oldest families, reflect more than two centuries of the city's self-consciousness. Exhibits interpreting subjects as diverse as flora and fauna, fashion, the art of silversmithing, Native American life, and plantation life, come together to provide a seamless image of a special place. The section on African American slavery—texts, artifacts, photographs, charts—is superb.

Charles Towne Landing 1670
843-852-4200.
www.charlestowne.org.
1500 Old Towne Rd. (SC 171 between I-26 and US 17).
Daily: 8:30–5, to 6 in summer months.
Admission: Adults $5; children $3.
Rental bicycles $2/hour.

Consider this 664-acre park an outdoor museum, where the lives of the Lowcountry's earliest European settlers are interpreted in several ways: in a village setting, including indentured servants' quarters; on a 17th-century replica of a typical coastal trading vessel; and in "wilderness," as found in the Animal Forest, where birds and beasts common to the area in 1670 roam in a secured habitat. A new visitor center offers expanded interpretation of first contact with the Kiawah tribe and of recent, ongoing archaeological investigations that have led to reconstruction of original fortifications.

Old Slave Mart Museum
843-958-6467.
6 Chalmers St.
Mon. through Sat. 9–5.
Admission: Adults $7; children $5.

This newly renovated museum has dramatically improved the portrait of the domestic slave economy as a driving engine that enabled Charleston's growth by putting on display previously inaccessible artifacts and manuscripts, and placing them in scholarly context. The museum is wisely divided into two sections, one focusing on the slave trade at large, which forcibly relocated some one million American-born slaves throughout the South between 1789 and 1861 and the other highlighting individual stories, letters, and documents related to African Americans, slave traders, and the physical functioning of this building and the slave market complex.

South Carolina Aquarium
843-720-1990.
www.scaquarium.org.
100 Aquarium Wharf.
Mon.–Sat. 9–5, Sun. 12–5; open till 6 daily from Apr. through Aug.
Admission: Adults $17; seniors $16; children (3–11) $10.

Set on the Cooper River, where its neighbor is a landing for the industrial port of Charleston (a port that sees more than 12 million tons of container cargo pass through each year), the new aquarium provides well-designed displays of the state's aquatic habitat, from the mountain streams of the Upcountry to Lowcountry marshes. More than 10,000 creatures reside here in the 330,000-gallon Ocean Tank, in living habitat exhibits, and in the hands-on water tables. Interpreted dive programs, where you can watch the fish being fed and learn more about them, take place at 11 AM and 1 and 3 PM daily. Kids can spot bottle-nose dolphins for themselves from the expansive deck overlooking the river—and there's always a guide to answer questions. Special exhibits on marine ecosystems around the world also featured.

Music
Charleston has a symphony orchestra and chamber groups that play regularly throughout the year, and, of course, it has **Spoleto,** which brings boys' choirs, operatic soloists, and instrumentalists to the city each May and June. The region is rich in indigenous music, too: blues, jazz, spirituals, gospel. As new audiences for these styles develop, concerts to showcase them are emerging. The **Blues Bash** in February, the **Moja Arts Festival** in September, and the **Annual Spirituals Concert** in December are some. Often, concerts of gospel music and spirituals take place in conjunction with spring and fall house tours and may be held at a historic site. You should check local newspapers for schedules or, once you arrive in Charleston, contact the organizations below for information.

Charleston Symphony Orchestra (843-723-7528; www.charlestonsymphony.com; 160 E. Bay St.) Performances under the direction of David Stahl in the Gaillard Auditorium

(77 Calhoun St.) throughout the year. Concert series might include selections from the classical repertoire, pops, and chamber works.

Lowcountry Blues Society (www.bluesbash.com) The Society's main event—The Lowcountry Blues Bash—runs for about 10 days every February and features performances at sites all over the city, from small clubs to larger theaters. Some concerts are free, others charge a modest cover, usually under $15. The shows are first rate—musicians come from Chicago, North and South Carolina, and anywhere the blues are played.

Moja Arts Festival (843-724-7305; www.mojafestival.com; 180 Meeting St.) The 16-day festival, whose name is Swahili for "one" or "unity," takes place in the fall and celebrates the African and Caribbean cultural influences on the Lowcountry. It includes many musical performances, story-telling, dance, poetry slams, and visual arts. Administered by the city's Office of Cultural Affairs.

Nightlife
Nightlife prospers in the Market Area and East Bay Street, where there are dance lounges and noisy student spots, but mellow piano bars at the Charleston Grill, the Mills House, and Charleston Chop are reliably rewarding. Farther afield, on the resort-oriented islands, you will discover the land of "shag," the original, stylized South Carolina dance set to beach music. A list of the better-known or easily accessible spots for night owls follows. Cover charges vary widely, depending on the entertainment. Check local newspaper listings when you're in town for special shows.

Charleston Chop (843-937-9300; 188 E. Bay St.) Jazz piano bar Tuesday through Saturday in this steak-and-seafood restaurant.

Charleston Grill at Charleston Place (843-571-2265; 224 King St.) Jazz trios in a sophisticated, laid-back setting.

Charlie's Little Bar (843-723-6242; 141 E. Bay St., upstairs) Favorite of the city's bright young things, but everyone's welcome.

Cumberland's (843-577-9469; 26 Cumberland St.) Band music that's live and loud.

Dunleavy's Pub (843-883-9646; 2213 Middle St., Sullivan's Island) A small place on the corner with imported beers and ales on tap. Midweek jazz piano; live bands on the weekends.

Mills House (843-577-2400; 115 Meeting St.) Two lounges, one with a piano bar where you can relax and visit. Good place to gather for an after-dinner drink. Look for Big Band tunes or jazzy guitar Thursday, Friday, and Saturday.

Music Farm (843-577-6969; www.musicfarm.com; 32 Ann St.) Where the young crowd swarms to dance and mosh.

39 Rue de Jean (843-722-8881; www.ruedejean.com; 39 John St.) A brasserie that is as lively and good-looking as its clients, and where you can eat until 1 AM. It has a neighborhood, artsy feel and excellent food. It can get noisy, but try the patio.

Spoleto
It is said that the first professional dramatic production in America of a play written here was performed in Charleston in the 18th century by a shipwrecked poet, who was washed ashore, as he put it, "full of lice, shame, poverty, nakedness and hunger."

No such description could conceivably apply to the outstanding performers who come to the city for a cultural festival that has put Charleston on the map, nationally and internationally. For 18 days at the end of spring, a time of budding oleander, fading azalea, and unapologetically fragrant magnolias, Spoleto comes to Charleston and Charleston becomes the city it has long imagined itself to be: an artistic mecca where expressions of high culture find their setting among people who believe they understand the meaning of civilized life.

Spoleto gave Charlestonians a chance to prove their claims of having shucked off their provincial preferences, and prove it they have. Emboldened by the artistic vision of Gian Carlo Menotti (who fell in love with Charleston and organized the first festival in 1977), and egged on by an indefatigable mayor, Joe Riley, Charleston's cultural and business communities have consistently—and with full attention—adapted themselves and their city to the idea that first-class art of many kinds can inhabit, enrich, and be enriched by the lively, unique qualities of this old city. Spoleto instilled new vigor, giving rise to building projects and renovations, new restaurants, and shops: It linked the pride in the Lowcountry's past to confidence in its future. It opened the doors of Charleston to the nation.

Spoleto took its name from the town in Italy where, in the 1950s, Mr. Menotti had organized another festival. Spoleto in Charleston was conceived as the counterpart to that venture, though now it stands on its own artistic direction and traditions. In any one season, it offers more than 100 scheduled events, including premieres of opera and dance as well as dozens of chamber music, choral, jazz, and orchestral performances. Performances take place indoors and out—in parks, plantation gardens, amphitheaters, and auditoriums.

If that's not enough, the regular Spoleto events are augmented by some 600 **Piccolo Spoleto** performances (often free), organized by the city's Office of Cultural Affairs (843-724-7305; www.piccolospoleto; 180 Meeting St., Charleston, SC 29401). These events can include organ, choral, and madrigal recitals in churches; mime shows, outdoor concerts, and numerous theater productions.

There are several ways to purchase tickets to Spoleto. The first thing to do is request, by mail, telephone, or online, the festival ticket brochure and guide, a near-tabloid-size schedule of events with a pre-printed order form. Contact:

Spoleto Festival U.S.A.
P.O. Box 157
Charleston, SC 29402-0157
843-722-2764 / Fax 843-723-6383 /Box office 843-579-3100
www.spoletousa.org

If you want to order a pre-designed "ticket package," which might include a dance performance, a play, an opera, and a chamber music event spread over several days, order the brochure by mid-November or December. If you're not sure of your schedule, you can order tickets to individual events beginning in January. There is a handling charge for ticket orders. The variety and number of events can be overwhelming, but poring over the brochure and making plans offers the same pleasurable anticipation that stirs avid gardeners as they read beautiful seed catalogues. Of course, the earlier you can confirm travel arrangements and lodging, the better.

If April 1st comes and you are without tickets but want to attend to Spoleto, you can still do it. With a basic Spoleto Festival ticket brochure in hand (see above address) you may order tickets by telephone (843-579-3100) and charge them. There's a handling charge levied per ticket. In person, visit the Spoleto Office at 77 Calhoun Street, which is open from mid-April until the festival closes. You may pick up your pre-ordered tickets there.

You can even arrive without tickets, and get lucky. Tickets can be purchased up to one hour before curtain time at the venue. Chairs or standing room for sold-out performances at the Dock Street Theatre and the Garden Theater go on sale one hour before the performance.

Theater

By the middle of the 18th century, theatrical performances were well established in the cultural life of Charleston. In the antebellum years, theater was but one jewel in the crown of culture, offset by the brilliant setting provided by a society that lived for pleasure and sought it in balls, concerts, seasonal celebrations, and lavish home entertaining.

In the 20th century, it wasn't until 1927—when DuBose Heyward's novel *Porgy*, the story of a lame Charleston street vendor and his love for Bess, was adapted and performed on the Broadway stage—that drama native to Charleston came alive. Theatrical performances in the Lowcountry still reflect their indigenous stories—they are often showcased during Piccolo Spoleto—but a growing audience also supports new works from nationally known dramatists and selections from the classical repertory. The Web site www.theatre charleston.com (843-813-8578) provides comprehensive ticketing information and scheduling for 10 theatre companies.

Charleston Legends and Lore Ghost Theater (843-937-0916; www.charlestonlegendsand lore.com; 161 Church St.) Charleston's ghosts and pirates come to life, as do Gullah story-tellers in 30-minute productions staged every day. The setting is an antebellum parlor.

Charleston Stage Theatre Company (843-577-5967 or 1-800-454-7093; www.charleston stage.com) Productions at Dock Street Theatre by a residential theater group that provide special enjoyment for families, plays like *Cheaper By the Dozen* or *A Christmas Carol;* original work, children's theater, and workshops.

Dock Street Theatre (843-720-3968; 135 Church St.) This is a lovely interpretation of a Georgian-style theater, of the sort 18th-century Charlestonians may have patronized. Rebuilt during the depression within the old Planters Hotel (circa 1809) as a project of the Federal Works Progress Administration, the theater's cypress interiors, intimate box seats, and terrific acoustics make it a wonderful place to attend performances. It's the site of the immensely popular Chamber Music Series during Spoleto, and festival plays, as well as a stage for roving companies.

Footlight Players (843-722-7521; www.footlightplayers.net; 20 Queen St.) An old, estab-lished theater company dedicated to community-theater repertory in a renovated cotton warehouse in the French Quarter. Six productions each season, from August through May.

Theater 99 (843-853-6687; www.thehavenots.com; 280 Meeting St., upstairs) An improvi-sational troupe works hard for your laughs in a high-energy, informal setting, with an in-house bar.

RECREATION

While guessing what a novelist had in mind while writing is risky business, perhaps when DuBose Heyward wrote "It is always Sunday on the Sea-Islands", he was thinking that there is, in every day, a piece of Sunday here, a piece of unscheduled time to enjoy the best of your surroundings, naturally and simply, with as few complications as possible. This is the definition of recreation in the Lowcountry.

Baseball

Charleston RiverDogs (a Single-A Minor League Affiliate of the New York Yankees) plays April through August at Joe Riley, Jr. Park (843-577-3647 for tickets; www.riverdogs.com; 360 Fishburne St.) Tickets are $5–$10.

Beach Access

There are hundreds of miles of coastline between Charleston and Savannah and on the barrier islands. At many points the public can reach the coast at designated access sites. Some of these offer changing areas, restrooms, showers, and picnic tables. Others are mere paths in the sand. Some, like the beaches on pristine barrier islands, are accessible only by boat.

The beaches on this coast are flat and wide, without rocks, overlooked by dunes or maritime forest. The surf ranges from placid to roiling (the Washout at Folly Beach is considered a top surfing spot). Lifeguards are not on duty at every beach access point, and swimming may be extremely hazardous: It is not wise to swim in unmonitored areas. Walking on the dunes, picking the sea oats, and driving on the beach are forbidden.

A few suggestions follow for reaching the beach by land or water. For more detailed information about specific access points, contact www.ccprc.com or the chambers of commerce or tourism commissions listed at the end of Chapter Six, *Information*.

Sullivan's Island and **Isle of Palms** are located north of the city on US 17 and SC 703. The beach at Sullivan's is marked by walkways. You may park along the side of streets unless otherwise posted, and you will be ticketed. **Isle of Palms County Park** (843-886-3863; 1st through 14th Ave., Palm Blvd.) offers pay parking, restrooms, and changing facilities. Located to the south, off US 17 on SC 171, you can enjoy the fully outfitted **Folly Beach County Park** (843-588-2426; 1010 W. Ashley Ave.), which offers 4,000 feet of oceanfront access, lifeguards, changing rooms, showers, pay parking, and a 1,045 foot fishing pier. You may rent beach chairs and umbrellas. A bit farther south off US 17, at the gate to Kiawah Island, is **Beachwalker Park** (843-768-2395; Beachwalker Dr., Johns Island) another well-developed public beach destination with facilities, lifeguards and pay parking.

Shore Refuges

Cape Romain National Wildlife Refuge (843-928-3264; www.fws.gov.caperomain; 390 Bull Island Rd., Awendaw, SC 29429) is a 64,229-acre site managed by the U.S. Fish and Wildlife Service. The refuge consists of four parts: **Bull Island,** a 5,000-acre barrier island; **Cape Island,** a favorite spot for loggerhead turtles to nest; **Garris Landing,** the site of ferry services, and an observation pier just right for birders; and **Raccoon Key Island,** a popular spot for shelling.

Coastal Expeditions, Inc. (843-881-4582, ferry information) offers exclusive ferry service to Bull Island, weather permitting. Ticket prices $30 for adults and $15 for children under 12. From March through November, the ferry makes two round-trips daily every Tuesday, Thursday, Friday, and Saturday. From December through February there's one trip only, on Saturdays. Reservations are not required but tickets must be paid for by cash or check. No credit cards.

Another refuge is **Capers Island**—a classic, undisturbed barrier island managed by the South Carolina Department of Natural Resources. Contact them (843-953-9300; www.dnr .sc.gov/managed/heritage) for general information regarding public use restrictions, instructions for anchoring and beaching boats, and camping permits. You can get there in a sea kayak from **Coastal Expeditions, Inc.** (843-884-7684; www.coastalexpeditions.com;

514-B Mill St., Mt. Pleasant, SC 29464); or on a 40-foot boat with **Barrier Island Eco Tours** (843-886-5000; www.nature-tours.com; P.O. Box 343, Isle of Palms, SC 29421). A three-and-a-half-hour day tour led by a naturalist and marine biologist costs adults $36, children $26; a two-hour sunset cruise costs adults $30, children $22. A full day tour including guided walks, kayaking, crabbing, and surf fishing lessons is $70 for adults and $55 for kids.

Bird-Watching

The barrier islands mentioned above provide the least-disturbed habitats for birds and wildlife you're likely to find in the Lowcountry; if you're a serious birder, schedule a visit.

But even if you can't make it to the islands, you will not be disappointed in what you can find in more accessible places. Because of its location on the North American flyway and its diverse natural environment, the Lowcountry attracts scores of wading, shore-, and songbirds, some of them as unusual as the roseate spoonbill and parasitic jaeger. Wood-cocks flock in plowed fields, owls hover in roadside forests, and hawks soar over open grassland. In February, you are likely to see thousands of robins and cedar waxwings swarming in country yards, picking the cherry laurel trees clean.

Local Audubon societies, conducting the annual Christmas count, have reported over 200 types of birds, from scrub areas to shorefront. Visitor-friendly sites for birding—where you may find boardwalks, observation areas, and informational slide shows or displays—are listed under "Nature Preserves" later in this chapter.

More informal birding sites recommended by local birders include the following:

Bears Bluff, located southeast of Charleston on Wadmalaw Island (843-559-2315; www.fws.gov/southeast/bearsbluff) This 31-acre fish hatchery offers sensational viewing of common and endangered species in a lovely rural setting that's also good for picnics.

Bear Island, located south of Charleston off US 17 at Green Pond, 843-844-8957; www.dnr.sc.gov/managed/wild.) Operated by the South Carolina Department of Natural Resources, an extensive habitat characterized by old rice fields, meandering creeks and rivers, marshes, and all sorts of woodlands. Open February 1 through October 14, Monday through Saturday.

I'on Swamp, 15 miles north of Mt. Pleasant off US 17 on U.S. Forest Service Rd. 228; www.sctrails.net) Spring brings warblers—possibly even the shy Bachman's—and also resident upland birds, including red-cockaded woodpeckers, who make their homes here.

Mt. Pleasant, the area leading to the old Pitt St. Bridge. Here sightings of marbled god-wits, oystercatchers, grebes, and mergansers have been reported. Activity is best at half tide, especially in fall and winter. A spotting scope is useful.

Sullivan's Island, around the beach behind Fort Moultrie. Here, in fall and winter, you might see peeps or an occasional purple sandpiper.

US 17 by the Ashepoo and Combahee River crossings. Anhinga, rails, and gallinules nest in the remnant rice fields.

Boating

Jet Skiing

Jet Skis (a.k.a. personal watercraft and waverunners) let you navigate in the shallow creeks at a fast, noisy clip. You can rent them by the hour at the following locations. Prices from $50–$75 per hour, depending on whether you take a guided group tour or ride alone.

The City Marina (843-723-5098; www.charlestoncitymarina.com).

Sun & Ski (843-588-0033; Folly Beach).

Tidal Wave Runners (843-886-8456; Isle of Palms).

Sailing

A sailor unfamiliar with Lowcountry coastal waters will encounter dramatic tides and strong currents. If you're interested in renting a sailboat, either for a day's excursion or a sunset cruise, reserve early. It's also wise to check local conditions and discuss your plans with the rental outfitter before you go. (Some boats come with their own skippers, if you get nervous.)

Sailboats in a range of sizes are available for hire from the following:

Aqua Safaris (843-886-8133; www.aqua-safaris.com; P.O. Box 309, Isle of Palms, SC 29451).

Bohicket Boat (843-768-7294; www.bohicketboat.com;Bohicket Marina Village, Seabrook Island, SC 29455).

OSA Sailing (843-971-0700; www.osasailing.com; 24 Patriots Point Rd., Mt. Pleasant, SC 29464).

Wild Dunes Yacht Harbor (843-886-5100; P.O. Box 527, Isle of Palms, SC 29451).

If you're towing your own boat, there are dozens of landings (19 in Charleston County—most paved and with landing docks, some more rustic) where you can park your trailer and launch. Parking is free, but unmonitored. Contact the following agencies for listings or maps, which show the locations of public boat landings: **Charleston County Parks** (843-795-4386; www.ccprc.com); **South Carolina Marine Resources Division** (843-762-5000; P.O. Box 12559, Charleston, SC 29412); **Lowcountry Resort Islands and Tourism Commission** (843-717-3090 or 1-800-528-6870; www.southcarolinalowcountry.com 1 Lowcountry Lane, Yemassee, SC 29945).

Bowling

AMF Charleston Lanes (843-766-0241; 1963 Savannah Hwy.).

Ashley Lanes (843-766-9061; 1568 Sam Rittenberg Blvd.).

Camping

In the old days, a camping expedition usually involved sailing or rowing—or being sailed or rowed—in boats loaded like barges, to the uninhabited barrier islands. Upon arrival, the party would set up housekeeping at a "fish camp" for several days. These same spots would be revisited year after year, although they might consist of nothing more than driftwood chairs, a palmetto-log windbreak, and a fire pit. The tradition was rustic, the site well off the beaten track, the experience enhanced by the oft-repeated stories it generated.

Today's visitor can be a happy camper, too (but near running water, toilets, a campground store, and gnat repellent) at public campgrounds at the following sites:

Buck Hall, Francis Marion National Forest (1-877-444-6777 for reservations; www.forestcamping.com)Wambaw Ranger District, P.O. Box 106, McClellanville, SC 29458) 19 sites; hiking trails, boat ramp, fishing.

James Island County Park (843-795-9884; www.ccprc.com; 871 Riverland Dr., Charleston, SC 29412) 125 RV sites, 10 three-bedroom cottages on the marsh, primitive camping area; shuttle service to downtown Charleston, paved trails, fishing and crabbing docks, playgrounds, and picnic shelters.

Privately operated campgrounds in the area include:

Lake Aire RV Park and Campground (843-571-1271; www.lakeairerv.com; 4375 SC 162, Hollywood) One hundred sites including full hookups, primitive sites, and camper sites. Seven-acre fishing lake, swimming pool, paddleboat and canoe rental, showers, laundry, recreation area, bike, and foot trails.

Oak Plantation Campground (843-766-5936; www.oakplantationcampground.com; 3540 Savannah Hwy.) Full hookups with 15-, 30- and 50-amp. service; 100 tent sites, 150 camper sites, propane, laundry, groceries, bathrooms.

Wood Brothers Campground (843-844-2208; 8446 Ace Basin Pkwy., 37 miles south of Charleston) Wooded and open sites for RVs, campers, and tents; grocery, propane, showers, fishing pond.

Canoeing and Kayaking

Interest in these activities has exploded. Guides will lead you along miles of creeks and down rivers; adventurous instructors can teach you how to get beyond the breaking waves into the ocean. Here are some popular locations and names of outfitters.

The Edisto River, thought to be the nation's longest free-flowing black-water stream, offers calm waters and great bird and wildlife observation. As you meander along, you're likely to see great blue herons wading by the oak-lined riverbank or hummingbirds feeding at wildflowers. The trail follows an ancient waterway used by Native Americans and early settlers. **Colleton State Park** (843-538-8206; Canadys, SC; US 15, 12 miles north of Walterboro, I-95 Exit 68) and **Givhan's Ferry State Park** (843-873-0692; SC 61, 16 miles west of Summerville) are along the route. You can put in there, and also camp and picnic. For more information, contact www.southcarolinaparks.com.

The **Walterboro-Colleton Chamber of Commerce** (843-549-9595; P.O. Box 426, Walterboro, SC 29488) can assist you in renting canoes or kayaks, or securing a guide at

Kayaks ready to be launched in the shallow creeks.

certain times of the year. Their Web site, www.walterboro.org, is an excellent place to find information and trail guides for paddling in the ACE Basin (Ashepoo, Combahee and South Edisto).

Nearer Charleston, boats are available for rent at **James Island County Park** (843-795-7275; 871 Riverland Dr.), **Magnolia Gardens** (843-571-1266; 3550 Ashley River Rd.), and **Palmetto Islands County Park** (843-884-0832; 444 Needlerush Pkwy., Mt. Pleasant). The following companies offer kayak rentals, tours, and instruction. The price for rentals of kayaks, safety equipment, and basic instruction is about $65–$80 per day; $30 per half day. Tours, depending on their length, cost between $45 and $65.

Bohicket Boat: Adventure & Tour Co. (843-768-7294; www.bohicketboat.com).

Coastal Expeditions (843-884-7684; www.coastalexpeditions.com).

Nature Adventures Outfitters (1-800-673-0679; www.natureadventuresoutfitters.com).

Paddlefish Kayaking (843-330-9777; www.paddlefishkayaking.com).

Diving
If you want to actually use that diver's watch you wear for looks—thick black band, fluorescent numbers, rimmed with rings and buttons—contact these outfitters. Lowcountry creeks and rivers tend to be murky with low visibility, but offshore opportunities (and instruction) are available.

Charleston Scuba (843-763-3483; www.charlestonscuba.com).

Family Fun
The Lowcountry's long summer nights, when dusk comes as late as 9 PM, mean there's always extra time for that round of miniature golf or walk on the beach. By day, there are waterslides to offer cooling thrill rides. Here are some activities that adults and kids can enjoy together.

Blackbeard's Cove Family Fun Park (843-971-1223; www.blackbeardscove.net; 3255 SC 17 North, Mt. Pleasant.) Laser tag, go-carts, climbing wall, golf, and arcade games.

Classic Golf (843-881-3131; 1528 Ben Sawyer Blvd., Mt. Pleasant) Miniature golf landscaped and lit for night play on two courses.

Frankie's Fun Park (843-767-1376; www.frankiesfunpark.com); 5000 Ashley Phospate Rd.) Two 18-hole mini golf courses, go-cart tracks, game rooms, batting cages, and bumper boats. Open daily, 10 AM–midnight. A great reward for kids who have been sightseeing all day.

James Island County Park (843-795-7275; 871 Riverland Dr., James Island) The 50-foot climbing wall and 10-foot bouldering wall would attract older kids, while the little ones enjoy the water park with slides and fountains. Rollerblading on miles of paved trails; canoes, paddleboats, and bikes for rent.

Palmetto Islands County Park (843-884-0832; 444 Needlerush Pkwy., Mt. Pleasant) Picnic areas and shelters, walking and biking trails, marsh boardwalk and fishing sites. Bicycles, canoes, and paddleboats are available for rent. Splash Island is a water fun park with slides, pools, and chutes.

Fishing

There's always fishing in the Lowcountry, no matter the time of year, and there are as many styles and venues as there are fishermen. They include: fly-fishing in the inland flats, fishing from a pier, fishing with bait from small (15'–26') and large (up to 54') craft, fishing off an artificial reef, surf casting from the beach, trolling in the Gulf Stream. Many independent guides and charter services have Web sites to help you match your interest to their services. Visit them or call for information; there are dozens of options. Reservations and deposits are almost always required (credit cards accepted); check on cancellation and inclement weather policies.

Charter fees include equipment, instruction, fuel (sometimes extra), bait, licenses, and food or drink if applicable. For small craft, the price is generally based on two people, $50 for each additional person (size of party limited by size of boat.) Large craft may include one or two groups fishing together. Prices for charter boat rentals are from $300 for two passengers for a four-hour excursion to $450 per person for a long day of Gulf Stream adventure. If you head out on your own, an unguided powerboat costs from $30 to $80 per hour (capacity is from four to ten people), rental gear extra. You need to purchase a saltwater fishing license if you fish from a boat; not necessary for shore-based fishing or recreational harvest of crab and shrimp. Here are some charter services in the Charleston area:

Absolute Reel Screamer Charters (843-270-4464; www.charleston-fishing.com; 1027 Oceanview Rd.) Light tackle and fly-fishing charters and instruction offered all year.

Bohicket Boat (843-768-7294; www.bohicketboat.com; Bohicket Marina, Seabrook Island) Large selection of boats from 14 to 55 feet for inshore bass and trout fishing, jetty fishing, and offshore fishing for shark, mackerel, tuna, marlin. Full- and half-day trips, on your own or with a guide.

Captain Ivan's Island Charters (843-762-2020; www.captainivan.com; 805 Deckhawk Retreat) Captain Ivan Schultz. Thirty-foot, wide beam boat with 21-passenger capacity, full- and half-day excursions to offshore reefs, and sportfishing trips to the Gulf Stream (12 hours).

Carolina Clipper (843-884-2992; Shem Creek, Mt. Pleasant) Captain Billy Knight pilots a 65-foot boat with a snack bar and sundeck, fully outfitted with gear and bait for Gulf Stream trips. Beginners welcome, and he especially likes seeing youngsters catch their first fish.

Headshaker Charters (843-296-5855; www.headshakercharters.com; Mt. Pleasant.) Captain Legare Leland grew up fishing here and arranges trips in Charleston harbor and nearby estuaries to troll for redfish, trout, flounder, and other species.

Fitness Facilities and Spas

Contemporary vacationers may leave their troubles behind, but few of them forget to pack their sweats. Though physical fitness hasn't ranked high among Charleston's pastimes (below hunting, fishing, eating, drinking, visiting, snoozing), the city is accommodating. Favorite places for runners are a loop that includes King Street, the Battery and Meeting Street, the Waterfront Park, and, for the mighty, a round trip across the new James Island connector or Ravenel Bridge.

Fitness centers have machines and free weights; some offer day-rates for visitors. Your hotel concierge or bed-and-breakfast host may recommend a personal trainer. Resorts and large hotels have their own facilities or spas. Fees vary widely according to service.

Earthling Day Spa & Pilates Studio (843-722-4737; www.earthlingdayspa.com; 245 E. Bay St.).

East Shore Athletic Club (843-266-5446; www.eastshoreac.com; 80 Wentworth St.) 24-hour access at nine area locations.

Sophia Institute (843-720-8528; www.thesophiainstitute.org; 26 Society St.) Yoga drop-in and a full program of lectures and day retreats focused on spiritual healing and wellness.

Spa Adagio (843-577-2444; www.spaadagio.com; 387 King St.) Full-service day spa located in the Francis Marion Hotel.

Golf

The first golf course in America was built in Charleston, and the founding of the nation's first golf club in 1786 followed immediately. Courses here, like the great houses or gardens, are designed with natural beauty in mind, built to accommodate the environmental elements, and intended to offer a variety of surprises that keep you interested. **Charleston Golf, Inc.** (843-958-3629 or 1-800-774-4444; www.charlestongolfguide.com) is a central information and reservation service for tee times, accommodations, and discount airfares. Ask for their Golf Guide.

Fees vary according to seasonal categories, sometimes nine in all. Lowest rates are usually December. through February. Carts are required at peak playing times on many courses. For resort play, golf privileges are sometimes extended to non-resort guests: Check with your concierge or call the resort directly. Club rentals and instruction are available at all courses. Greens fees/cart rentals reflect 2008 prices and do not include tax. There are about two dozen courses that welcome day players and six that are linked to resorts. You may make tee time reservations on line. Weekday rates generally assume play Monday through Thursday only.

Public and Semiprivate Courses

Charleston Municipal Course (843-795-6517; www.charlestoncity.info; 2110 Maybank Hwy.) Par 72. 6,400 yards. Greens fees during the week start at $15 if you walk, $30 with cart rental; on weekends, $17 if you walk. Twilight rates (after 4 PM) are $8.

Charleston National (843-884-7799; www.charlestonnationalgolf.com; 1360 National Dr., Mt. Pleasant) Par 72. Range: 5,103-yard forward course to 6,975-yard champion course. Fees vary according to separate seasonal categories: $35–$59 (weekdays) and $45–$76 (weekends). Play after 5 PM starts at $25.

Coosaw Creek Country Club (843-767-8988; pro shop; www.coosawcreek.com; 8610 Dorchester Rd., North Charleston) Par 71. Range: 5,064-yard forward course to 6,593-yard champion course. Fees: $35–$59 (weekdays) and $50–$65 (weekends). An Arthur Hills design.

Crowfield Golf & Country Club (843-764-4618; 300 Hamlet Circle, Goose Creek) Par 72. Range: 4,822-yard forward course to 6,964-yard champion course. Fees: $42.50 –$52.50, including cart rental.

Dunes West (843-856-9000; www.golfduneswest.com; 3535 Wando Plantation Way, Mt. Pleasant) Par 72. Range: 5,278-yard forward course to 6,871-yard champion course. Fees: $52–$62 (weekdays) and $69–$82 (weekends). Daily after 4 PM, $40.

Legend Oaks Plantation (1-888-821-4077; www.legendoaksgolf.com; 118 Legend Oaks Way, Summerville) Par 72. Range: 4,954-yard forward course to 6,974-yard championship course. Fees: $49 (weekdays) and $59 (weekends).

The Links at Stono Ferry (843-763-1817; www.stonoferrygolf.com; 5365 Forest Oaks Dr., Hollywood) Par 72. Range: 4,928-yard forward course to 6,616-yard championship course. Fees: $64–$77 (weekdays) and $74–$87 (weekends).

Patriots Point Links (843-881-0042; www.patriotspointlinks.com; 1 Patriots Pt. Rd., Mt. Pleasant) Par 72. Range: 5,562-yard forward course to 6,856-yard championship course. Fees: $40–$50 (weekdays) and $55–$85 (weekends).

Shadowmoss Plantation Golf Club (843-556-8251 or 1-800-338-4971; www.shadowmoss golf.com; SC 61) Par 72. Range: 2,700-yard forward course to 6,701-yard championship course. Fees: $36–$42 (weekdays) and $43–$52 (weekends).

Courses at Charleston Area Resorts

If you are planning a vacation around golf, you might save yourself travel time by staying in resorts where the game is the focus. Accommodations range from deluxe hotel rooms to villas and rental homes; renting through the resort yields savings in greens fees. These resorts also have complete recreational layouts, which include swimming pools, tennis courts, and marinas. Here's a list of some well-known resort golf courses near Charleston.

Kiawah Island (1-800-654-2924; www.kiawahresort.com; One Sanctuary Beach Dr., Kiawah) Five championship courses have been carved out of Kiawah's gorgeous Sea Island landscape by the game's top designers: Pete Dye, Jack Nicklaus, Gary Player, Tom Fazio, and Clyde Johnston. **The Ocean Course** (Par 72. Range: 5,327-yard forward course to 7,371 championship course) is probably the best known: The 1991 Ryder Cup was played here, and it was cited by *Golf Digest* as the toughest resort course in the country. **Osprey Point** (Par 72. Range: 5,122-yard forward course to 6,678-yard championship course) is consistently ranked in the country's top 75 courses with a landscape that includes four lakes, a maritime forest, and creeks. **Cougar Point** (Par 72. Range: 4,944-yard forward course to 6,861-yard championship course) and **Turtle Point** (Par 72. Range: 5,285-yard forward course to 6,914-yard championship course) make good use of Kiawah's unique geography—bracketed by the Atlantic and the river. **Oak Point** (Par 72. Range: 4,671-yard forward course to 6,759-yard championship course) is part of the resort but located on nearby Haulover Creek.

Seabrook Island (843-768-5000 or 1-800-777-8660; www.seabrook.com; 130 Gardener's Circle, Seabrook Island): **Crooked Oaks** (Par 72. Range: 5,250-yard forward course to 6,832-yard championship course, designed by Robert Trent Jones, Sr.) and **Ocean Winds** (Par 72. Range: 5,524-yard forward course to 6,805-yard championship course, a Willard Byrd design) won the resort a silver medal commendation from *Golf* magazine.

Wild Dunes (1-888-778-1861; www.wilddunes.com; Isle of Palms) Tom Fazio designed both courses: **The Links** (Par 72. Range: 4,849-yard forward course to 6,722-yard championship course) offers oceanfront golf at its best, wind and water hazards notwithstanding. **The Harbor** (Par 70. Range: 4,774-yard forward course to 6,402-yard championship course) features challenging holes that are, in some cases, an island apart. Make reservations up to 90 days in advance.

Horseback Riding

The first racecourse in the Lowcountry was built near Charleston in 1735, and the South Carolina Jockey Club was founded there in 1758. Equestrian showmanship, hunting, and riding for pleasure are still popular forms of recreation.

If you want to take a trail ride during your visit, call one of the following stables to make advance arrangements. They may take you from a cypress swamp to the edge of a rice field. The prices start at about $50 per hour.

Middleton Place Equestrian Center (843-556-8137; 4290 Ashley River Rd., Charleston).

Mullet Hall Equestrian Center (843-768-5867; www.ccprc.com; 2662 Mullet Hall Rd., John's Island).

Stono Ferry Stables (843-763-0566; 5304 Stono Ferry Course, Hollywood).

Stono River Stable and Farm (843-559-0773; 2962 Hut Rd., John's Island).

Storybook Farm (843-571-2820; 1136 Bee's Ferry Rd.).

Hunting

In the Lowcountry you can hunt a variety of quarry including deer, wild turkey, dove, quail, feral hog, duck, fox, rabbit, woodcock, snipe, and clapper rail. What's more, you can do so during seasons that start as early as late summer (deer) and last through fall and winter until late spring (turkey). The Lowcountry has the longest deer season in the country and is considered the premiere spot on the East Coast to bag marsh hens.

There are six Game Management Areas in the Lowcountry; hunters at work within them are required to have a variety of licenses and permits, to abide by strict size and bag limits, obtain landowners' permission before hunting on private lands, and observe safe and ethical hunting practices in the field. For information, maps, and regulations concerning South Carolina hunting areas, contact the **Wildlife and Marine Resources Deptartment** (803-734-3888; www.dnr.sc.gov). Outdoor recreation stores that specialize in hunting also provide tips, information, and licenses.

Some of the most popular public hunting grounds in the Charleston area are located in the **Francis Marion National Forest** (843-336-3248; 2421 Witherbee Rd., Cordsville), **Webb Wildlife Management Area** (803-625-3569; www.sctrails.net; SC 1, Box 80, Garnett, SC 29922), and **Palachucola Wildlife Management Area** (843-625-2114; Garnett), and on **Bear Island** (843-844-8957; Green Pond). For hunting licenses call 1-866-714-3611. Limited hunting is also permitted in the **ACE Basin** and permits can be downloaded from their Web site, www.fws.gov/acebasin.

If you prefer a more managed hunt, consider the guiding, cleaning, and transportation services of plantations that specialize in various kinds of game hunting, according to the season. Some offer overnight accommodations. For information, contact the **Lowcountry Tourism Commission** (1-800-528-6870;www.southcarolinalowcountry.com; 1 Lowcountry Lane, Yemassee, SC 29945). The **Southeastern Wildlife Exposition** (www.sewe.com), which takes place every February in Charleston, is the region's most comprehensive gathering of fishermen, hunters, outfitters, and artists who specialize in subjects of interest to sportsmen. Display sites scattered throughout the Charleston area feature Lowcountry and Western collectibles, crafts, decoys, antiques, and posters. In addition, there are presentations and demonstrations.

Nature Preserves

Many small islands, swamps, or boggy necks nestled in the creeks and riverways of the Lowcountry offer natural camouflage and a pristine habitat to the wildlife that live or migrate there. Some are more developed than others—with boardwalks or marked trails—but none require strenuous activity or advanced knowledge for enjoyment. Handicap accommodation can be minimal outside of buildings. If you are interested in the ecology of the Lowcountry, the life cycle of the marsh, the effects of tidal flow on vegetation, and the interdependence of plant and animal life, these sites will give you a feel for the rhythms of the Lowcountry beneath the surface.

ACE Basin National Wildlife Refuge (843-889-3084; www.fws.gov/acebasin; access off US 17; take SC 174 through Adams Run and follow signs to Headquarters at Grove House, an 1828 plantation home.) A consortium of private individuals, nonprofit organizations, state, and federal agencies have joined together to preserve some 350,000 acres of diverse habitat, including several islands, at the center of the Lowcountry. It is one of the largest undeveloped estuarine sanctuaries on the East Coast. ACE takes its name from the area it embraces: the lands and waters amidst the Ashepoo, Combahee, and Edisto Rivers on both sides of St. Helena Sound, a fishery so rich and pristine it accounts for nearly 10 percent of the state's shellfish harvest. Seventeen endangered species make their home here. Bring binoculars and cameras. Open year-round, daylight to dusk; you may park and walk in. Extensive trail maps are available online.

Audubon Swamp Garden (843-571-1266 or 1-800-367-3517; www.magnoliaplantation .com; 3550 Ashley River Rd.) Sixty acres of blackwater cypress and tupelo swamp, with trails and footbridges through virgin pine forests, wild flowers, and exotic plants: This is a place that impressed John J. Audubon 150 years ago. Self-guided tour. Basic admission $13.

Caw Caw Interpretive Center (843-889-8898; www.ccprc.com; 5200 Savannah Hwy., Ravenel, 20 miles south of Charleston. Closed Mon.) You can still see the earth dikes, floodgates, and rice fields that originally marked this former plantation, now home to endangered species, songbirds, and migratory birds. There are 8 miles of trails, a swamp boardwalk, and exhibits that highlight the contributions of the African Americans who worked here long ago. A good stop if you're heading down the coast to Edisto, Beaufort, or Savannah.

Cypress Gardens (843-553-0515; 3030 Cypress Gardens Rd., Moncks Corner. I-26 west to exit 208, then to SC 52 north) Take a guided tour or paddle a flat-bottom boat yourself through an old rice plantation reserve, now a protected natural swamp garden. A succession of blooms, from the earliest camellia and narcissus to trumpet vine and azalea, brightens the shadowy cypress forest. Open 9–5 daily. Adults $10, seniors $9, children $5, under 5 free.

Francis Beidler Forest in Four Holes Swamp (843-462-2150; 336 Sanctuary Rd., Harleyville. From I-95 take I-26 east to Exit 177, then south on SC 453 to US 178. Follow signs east on US 178. From Charleston, take I-26 west to Exit 187, then south on SC 27 to US 78.) The 11,000-acre sanctuary, managed by the National Audubon Society, contains the largest remaining virgin stand of bald cypress and tupelo gum trees in the world. There's a self-guided boardwalk and Visitor Center, but the point here is to walk quietly and observe well, to absorb what you can on your own without the experience being "packaged" in any way. The boardwalks are handicapped accessible. Open 9–5 daily except Mondays. Adults $7, children $4, under 6 free.

Tennis

The City of Charleston manages 60 public courts in several locations, (and only two facilities charge a nominal fee for use: the **Charleston Tennis Center** (843-769-8258; 19 Farmfield Ave., west of Charleston) has 15 outdoor hard courts, lit for night play. The **Maybank Tennis Center** (843-406-8814; 1800 Houghton Dr., James Island.) has 11 courts, including 3 clay. Visitors should call ahead to check availability, or may reserve by paying in advance. The longest-running professional event in women's tennis, the **Family Circle Cup** (1-800-677-2293; www.familycirclecup.com), has moved to a spectacular stadium at Daniel Island. There are 13 clay courts and 4 hard, all lit and open to the public except for tournament week in April. Call the number listed above or 843-849-5300 for court times or visit www.familycircletenniscenter.com. Hourly rates are $10 for hard courts and $15 for clay.

Some Lowcountry resorts also offer playing-time for non-resort guests on a space-available basis. Fees vary depending on season and time of day. Reservations are required. Inquire about tennis packages.

Kiawah Island (843-768-2838); www.kiawahresort.com) Guests renting accommodations at the resort pay $27 per hour; non-resort guests pay $37.

Wild Dunes (843-886-6000; www.wilddunes.com; Isle of Palms).

Windsurfing/Surfing

Although the currents and tides make for tricky windsurfing conditions, the Lowcountry's warm water temperature and wide-open spaces have attracted windsurfers for years. Check local forecasts and tides before you go (843-588-2261 for McKevlin's surf report; www.lowcountrysurf.com or www.charlestoncrystalball.com for live Web cam shots of Folly Beach waves) and surf in well-known areas. Even experienced windsurfers have found themselves thrust well beyond the confines of, say, Charleston Harbor by the outgoing tide, only to find they have to wait until it turns to paddle or sail in.

Many resorts have sailboards and other equipment to rent, or provide instruction first on land, then in sheltered creeks or on a quiet stretch of beach.

Barrier Island Surf Shop (843-795-4545; 3013 Folly Rd., James Island).

McKevlin's Surf Shop (843-886-8912; www.mckevlins.com; 1101 Ocean Blvd., Isle of Palms; 843-588-2247; 8 Center St., Folly Beach).

Ocean Surf Shop (843-588-9175; 31 Center St., Folly Beach).

SHOPPING

The time has passed since the port of Charleston was small and accessible, since residents had the pleasure of observing dozens of ships along the wharves and wondering what lay in their holds. Yet such pastimes of commercial life were once commonplace. The anticipation

Antiques store on King Street.

of imports—teas, seeds, books, furniture, china, mail—and the reciprocal sending of an export, was a satisfying part of life. If the export represented the result of what plantation slavery produced, the import confirmed Charleston's view of itself as a tasteful, cultivated, wealthy society. An ordinary impulse to consume took on meaning as part of a bigger equation.

Today, the impulse is still there, as is the anticipation, but no longer down at the wharves. Now it happens in small places: in glossy boutiques, in shops in old houses, in the open air of a busy corner, in commercial buildings on ballast-stone alleys, under the handsome brick and lattice sheds that line the center of Market Street for several blocks between Meeting Street and East Bay Street. The surge in commercial rents due to Charleston's popularity has forced the relocation of several unique and modest stores, the kind of stores that set a tone for a place but don't make a big splash doing so. Seek them out on Queen Street, Church Street, and especially the upper section of King Street north of Calhoun, which has become popular with stores specializing in home décor and design (www.upperkingstreet.com).

Antiques

The period of poverty that engulfed the Lowcountry after the Civil War called for living by austere means and resourcefulness. It was not a time when renovating and redecorating were considered possible.

Some residents count this as a blessing: A lot of old houses, and all they contained, were spared the wrecker's ball. In the 1920s, many houses caught the eye of Northern decorators and curators, who either imitated their look or purchased them, literally, lock, stock, barrel, and window sash. Later, when the families who had lived in the old houses produced a generation with the means to redecorate them, the urge to adorn them in the old style prevailed. Today, antiques stores throughout the Lowcountry retail this classic look, both in original pieces and in excellent reproductions.

While taste, or a good eye, is hard to define, it seems clear that the very experience of living in Charleston has produced antiques dealers who have absorbed its lessons of enduring beauty. They seem to know what fits—whether it's a pair of simple sterling candlesticks or a stunning chest-on-chest.

A short list of some of the more distinctive antiques shops follows. If you are poking around for something in particular, or a type of thing, ask for it. It's a small world, and dealers should be able to direct you elsewhere. King Street is the traditional center of Charleston antiques stores.

A'Riga IV Antiques (843-577-3075; 204 King St.) An impressive collection of old scientific instruments and medical kits, some of which can be oddly beautiful as art objects, as well as apothecary jars and ceramic containers that were put to domestic use years ago.

Carolina Antique Maps and Prints (722-4773; www.carolinaantiqueprints.com; 91 Church St.) Deep inventory and a knowledgeable staff: early botanicals, 19th-century maps, woodblocks, and hand-colored pieces.

Charleston Antique Mall (843-769-6119; www.charlestonantiquemall.net; 4 Avondale Ave. at US 17, 10 minutes south of downtown) An interior mall with 20 vendors who sell a mixture of collectibles, antiques, and art. Fun to browse for an hour.

Chicora Antiques (843-723-1711; 102 Church St.) A special eye for decorative art from the Federal and Classical periods makes this an unusual shop—although there's plenty of mahogany and brass, too.

Dailey-Grommé (843-853-2299; www.dailey-gromme.com; 208 King St.) An amazing collection of 20th-century furniture and objects from European Art Deco to Modernist designers. Many unique or studio-made pieces.

George C. Birlant & Co. (843-722-3842; www.birlant.com; 191 King St.) In business for more than 70 years, selling brass, silver, crystal, and small and large English antiques, which they import directly. Big old-fashioned picture windows open onto the street; inside there's lots of room to walk around. Reproductions of Charleston's own cypress-and-iron "Battery Bench" available.

George C. Williams American Antiques (843-377-0290; www.georgecwilliams.com; 15 King St.) A superb collection of American antiques, especially Southern and Charleston pieces, and decorative art accessories mostly dating from before 1830. The best antique store in Charleston.

Historic Charleston Reproductions (843-723-8292; www.historiccharleston.org; 105 Broad St.) Adaptations and reproductions of 18th- and 19th-century furniture, lamps, fabric, brass, wall coverings, and accessories that once graced Charleston homes. High-quality workmanship by companies like Baker Furniture, Scalamandre, and Mottahedeh.

Moore House Antiques (843-722-8065; 150 King St.) Fine American pieces where the styles from England show through, as in Sheraton side tables, shelves of Chinese export porcelain, and oriental rugs.

Ridler Page Rare Maps (843-723-1734; 205 King St.) Antique maps in a variety of sizes, some as old as the 16th century, many hand-colored.

Terrace Oaks Antique Mall (843-795-9689; 2037 Maybank Hwy.) A short drive from Charleston, this well-known establishment houses 20 dealers who sell an amazing assortment of rugs, glassware, silver, large pieces, and accessories.

Books

Local independent book dealers know their stock, particularly as it concerns the history, literature, and art of the South, have a good relationship with their customers and know their preferences, and thus are a source of suggestions. The national chains, for their part, showcase titles relating to local topics in history, gardening, culture, and photography. There are also several shops for used books and rare and historic volumes.

Barnes & Noble (843-572-2322; 7620 Rivers Ave., Charleston); (843-556-6561; 1812 Sam Rittenberg Blvd., Charleston); (843-216-9756; 1716 Town Center Way, Mt. Pleasant) The big book retailer has established itself here with an enormous quantity of books and magazines.

Blue Bicycle Books (843-722-2666; www.bluebicyclebooks.com; 420 King St.) Used, rare, and local titles.

Book Exchange (843-556-5051; 1131 Savannah Hwy.) New and used books and collectible comics.

Charleston Rare Book Co. (843-723-3330; 66 Church St.) Specializing in Charleston and Lowcountry books, including a good nautical section.

Historic Charleston Foundation Museum Shop and Bookstore (843-724-8484; www.historiccharleston.org; 108 Meeting St.) If you want to know more about regional history and the decorative arts, preservation efforts, architecture, and related topics, stop in here. Also many volumes about historic properties here and elsewhere, as well as an excellent children's section.

Pauline Books & Media (843-577-0175; 243 King St.) A religious bookstore with Bibles and a nice selection for younger readers.

Petterson Antiques (843-723-5714; 201 King St.) If the old books and magazines that sit on carts outside the store don't attract your eye, duck in and cast your gaze to the shelves and cases within. It may take time to find a treasure, but after all, you can never get enough of the atmosphere, which is free.

Preservation Society of Charleston (843-722-4360; www.preservationsociety.org; 147 King St.) The Society's headquarters has an unhurried, old-world feeling, with many books on Charleston history, art, architecture, and culture.

Waldenbooks (843-766-5879; 2070 Sam Rittenberg Blvd.) Best-sellers, good history and military section, coffee-table collections of photographs, regional cookbooks.

Clothing

In Charleston, people still wear hats. Not just baseball caps or fedoras, but straw hats, garden-party hats, fishing caps, and velvet berets—hats with attitude. They also dress their children, boys and girls, in smockery and suits. Yet among a population that tends to sartorial conservatism, there is usually a fillip of embellishment to be found, accompanied by the natural confidence to pull it off.

Women will be especially fortunate to be shopping for clothes here. There are several comfortable boutiques (low-key, welcoming, with excellent suggestions) that offer unusual suits and separates in linen, silk, and cotton blends, in a range of styles. Given the temperate climate, this is the place to find shawls and patterned sweaters rather than tweeds and down.

The following suggestions do not list clothing stores that are part of a national chain, although those to be found in Charleston include Polo, Laura Ashley, Gap, Victoria's Secret, Saks Fifth Avenue, and Talbot's.

A. J. Davis & Co. (843-577-3088; 296 King St.) Men's clothes, plain and cheerfully sporty, and accessories.

B'ZAR (843-579-2889; www.shopbzar.com; 541 King St.) A husband-and-wife team from Brooklyn have landed here with their sneakers, street clothes, old records, and art books. Something quite offbeat for Charleston.

Ben Silver (843-577-4556; www.bensilver.com; 149 King St.) This shop is the epitome of the classic Charleston look for men and women, with lots of English hunting overtones.

Berlin's (843-722-1665; 114 King St.) Men's and women's clothes in traditional styles and top quality brands. Since 1883.

Bits of Lace (843-577-0999; www.bitsoflace.com; 302 King St.) Fine lingerie and other little fancy things for women.

Bob Ellis Shoes (843-722-2605; 332 King St.) Vast selection of fine footwear for men and women and a sales staff that keeps bringing out the boxes.

Christian Michi (843-723-0575; www.christianmichi.com; 220 King St.) For women, high fashion from top European and American designers. It's as if a small section of SoHo left Manhattan for life in the provinces. Tableware and linens, too.

Copper Penny (843-723-2999; 311 King St.) If you saw it in *Vogue* or *InStyle*, it's here, too. Up-to-the-minute fashion and accessories (even if they seem a little too edgy for Charleston).

Cousins (843-937-8002; 161 King St.) Suzy Little has developed a terrific eye in nearly 20 years of selecting women's clothing and accessories and here you can buy anything from a sweater set to a little black dress, to the best work of fresh young designers. Upscale casual.

Ellington (843-722-7999; 82 Society St.) If you're returning to office life after a break and need something unusual and spiffy, or if you don't dress up much but like to wear a finely tailored piece or luscious fabrics when you do, look here for clothes with elegant, modern lines and solid construction. For men, too.

M. Dumas & Sons (843-723-8603; www.locountry.com; 294 King St.) Even the wallpaper here is riding to hounds. An original source for what has become the "American Country" look.

RTW (843-577-9748; www.rtwcharleston.com; 186 King St.) A boutique for women who delight in gorgeous fabrics, sweaters that tumble with color, one-of-a-kind shirts, hats, scarves, and accessories, and who like to dress with a sense of individuality and esprit. A rare find in any city.

Wonderland (843-577-0079; www.wonderlandlove.com; 511 King St.) Hipster outfits for infants to age seven, and related cute baby stuff.

Worthwhile (843-723-4418; www.shopworthwhile.com; 268 King St.) This wonderful, crazy store defies easy categorization: It's ironic (could be a 5&10 for yuppies, lots of small beautiful objects for the house) but sweet (flax and linen clothes for women, goofy baby hats). Cotton sweaters, T-shirts and leggings, nightclothes.

Vendors set up in the old market sheds that date from the 19th century.   Peter Loftus

Crafts

The Lowcountry's **sea grass baskets** (www.sweetgrassbaskets.com) are a regional specialty, and if you're interested in them, you won't have far to look. The basket weavers are out every day where Meeting Street and King Street meet Broad Street and in the **Market Area**. Prices vary for items as small as keepsake decorations or as large as fanner baskets and hampers. You're welcome to watch the process, which incorporates strips of palmetto frond and pine straw with the pale grass. Other weavers sell their work at stands located north of Charleston on US 17.

American Originals (843-853-5034; 153 E. Bay St., second floor) Contemporary crafts by local and national artists whose artistry and high standards shine through in glass, pottery, jewelry, pictures, textiles, and more.

Ceramics Café (843-722-7687; 432 King St.) Just behind the Visitor Center, a paint-your-own pottery studio in which you select a piece (from dozens available), paint it with glaze, and get it fired. It's one way to see if Charleston's beauty inspires. Wine and coffee available to stimulate your imagination.

Charleston Crafts (843-723-2938; www.charlestoncrafts.org; 87 Hasell St.) Crafts and exhibits by members of this local co-op, who are considered superior in their fields, be they weavers, sculptors, or photographers.

People, Places & Quilts (843-937-9333; www.ppquilts.com; 1 Henrietta St.) Folk art, quilts and quilting supplies, patterns, and sewing notions.

Farms and Farmers' Markets
The Lowcountry growing season lasts from February to the first frost in November, with many crops being planted more than once. A visit to the outdoor market at Marion Square on Saturday mornings between April and December may yield anything from fresh basil to watermelon. Farmstands on the Sea Islands have an enormous range of produce, their own and other farmers', as well as jellies, relishes, shrimp, fruit, and baked goodies. Three near Charleston are: **Stono Farm Market** (843-559-9999; www.stonofarmmarket.com; 842 Main Rd., John's Island); **Leland Farms** (843-559-1296; 4660 Maybank Hwy., Wadmalaw Island), and **Rosebank Farms** (843-768-9139; www.rosebankfarms.com; 4445 Betsy Kerrison Pkwy., John's Island).

The **Charleston Tea Plantation** (843-559-0383; www.bigelowtea.com; 6617 Maybank Hwy., Wadmalaw Island) is unique in the nation. Open weekdays from 10–4 and Sunday 12–4. (Take US 17 to SC 171. Turn east toward Folly Beach and soon after, turn south on SC 700, Maybank Highway. The plantation is located at nearly the end of this road.)

Gifts
Eighty-Two Church (843-723-7511; www.82church.com; 471 King St.) A selection of hand-smocked dresses for girls, sunbonnets, beautiful hand-knit sets for newborns, cotton christening outfits, and seersucker playsuits. Also handmade, old-fashioned toys.

ESD (843-577-6272; www.esdcharleston.com; 314 King St.) Elizabeth Stuart has made her store and interior-design service a model of the successful blending of old and new, of tried and trendy. She sells books, glassware, funky accessories, furniture, handcrafted jewelry, and antiques—some that are as new as mid-century modern and others that date from 200 years ago.

French Hare (843-577-0451; www.frenchhare.com; 418 King St.) The focus is on French colors and fabrics, majolica, accessories for your table, and wrought-iron art.

Gallery Chuma (843-722-7568; www.gallerychuma.com; 43 John St.) A large gallery with unique gifts representing work by African Americans in many media, including original paintings, prints, wearable art, and crafts.

Queen Charlotte Antiques (843-722-9121; www.queencharlotte.com; 61 Queen St.) Quirky pieces for the garden (small enough to carry), old sconces, wooden bowls, and little accent pieces that convey the look of old Charleston.

Gourmet and Health Food Stores
Aloha Natural Foods (843-849-5521; 628 Coleman Blvd., Mt. Pleasant) Organic produce and juice bar, books, herbs, face, and body products.

Bull Street Gourmet (843-720-8992; www.bullstreetcharleston.com; 60 Bull St.) Gourmet sandwiches and gourmet-to-go picnic baskets.

Hoppin' John's (1-800-828-4412; www.hoppinjohns.com) Chef John Martin Taylor's wonderful shop is no more—he's taken it online. A marvelous selection of Lowcountry foodstuffs like his signature grits, cornmeal, and corn flour (order early, demand outpaces supply), chow chow, pickles, real hoppin' john for New Year's, and salty Virginia country ham.

Olde Colony Bakery (842-216-3232; www.oldecolonybakery.com; 1391-B Stuart Engals Blvd., Mt. Pleasant.) The source, since 1919, for benne wafers and other regional Southern treats.

Raspberry's (843-556-0076; 1331 Ashley River Rd.) Natural, unprocessed foods including grains, herbs, bulk flour, and organic produce. Vitamins and body care items, too.

Home Furnishings/Kitchenware

Charleston Cooks (843-722-1212; www.charlestoncooks.com; 194 E. Bay St.) Kitchen gadgets, cookbooks, and regional foods selected by some top Charleston chefs.

fred (843-723-5699; 237 King St.) Clean, spare design once limited to black and white and stainless steel, now more colorful: kitchen basics, cutlery, towels and racks, mechanical wonders. A great local favorite.

Indigo (843-723-2983; indigohome.com; 4 Vendue Range) Fred and Beth Moore's creative lives, interests, and tastes converge here in a selection of patterned tablecloths and painted mats, iron sculpture, handmade frames, ceramics, and little metal animals like crabs and bunnies. A spirited, joyful store.

Joggling boards are as common as tree houses in Charleston backyards.   Peter Loftus

Le Creuset (843-723-4191; 241 King St.) Famous French enameled cookware at factory prices. (The factory, and another store, is located off I-95 at Yemassee if you're heading south.)

Metropolitan Deluxe (843-722-0436; 164 Market St.) The idea of an old mercantile store, updated. Several large rooms are piled high with household goods, from the opulent (velvet upholstery, leather boxes, brass lamps, high-count cotton sheets) to the funky (wire baskets, painted benches, canvas chairs, fresh flowers).

Old Charleston Joggling Boards (843-723-4331; www.oldcharlestonjogglingboard.com; 652 King St.) You see these benches, where a long springy board rests on rocking trestles, in lots of Charleston gardens. The idea is that you bounce on the plank gently with your family and friends.

Rivendell Woodworks & Gallery (843-723-9474; www.rivendellwoodworks.com; 29 Broad St.) A rare Arts & Crafts–period design store featuring handcrafted furniture, pottery, stained glass, and Mission style reproduction lighting.

South of Market (843-723-1114; www.southofmarket.biz; 173 King St.) A collection of original and reproduction or remade pieces that are French Country in style but amazingly suited to traditionally Anglophile Charleston, such as iron tables and garden accessories, oversized striped canvas pillows, sturdy bistro plates, and glass chandeliers.

Sporting Goods and Clothing

The Bicycle Shoppe (843-722-8168; www.thebicycleshoppecharleston.com; 280 Meeting St.) Rent or buy bikes, or choose from cases full of bike hardware and gadgets.

The Charleston Angler (843-571-3899; www.thecharlestonangler.com; 654 St. Andrews Boulevard) Supplies for fly-fishing and light tackle, high-end outdoor clothing, and equipment for fishing, shrimping, and crabbing.

The Charleston Bicycle Company (843-571-1211; www.charlestonbicycleco.com; 1319 Savannah Hwy.) Specialized bikes for all riders and athletic training gear.

Fairmont Skate Shop (843-853-3107; 473 King St.) Skates, boards, and clothing.

Half-Moon Outfitters (843-853-0990; www.halfmoonoutfitters.com; 280 King St.) The most durable and fashionable outdoor wear (like Patagonia) is here, plus coats, tents, packs, camping supplies, and the best advice on local outdoor adventuring to be found in the city.

Luden's Outfitters (843-723-7829; www.ludensoutfitters.com; 78 Alexander St.) In the business of outfitting hunters, sailors, and fishermen for 140 years. All the top brands in outerwear are represented as well as some dressy ties and accessories.

The Outdoor Shoppe (843-722-0618; www.theoutdoorshoppe.com; 280 Meeting St.) Located next to Charleston's best bicycle shop, it specializes in kayaking equipment and accessories for all skill levels.

Homeowners in Savannah link their landscape to their historic architecture in a sub-tropical climate, meaning that palms, olive trees, myrtle, and fig are common plantings, even since 1841 when the house was built. Peter Loftus

3

SAVANNAH

An Old City, A Modern City

It's no secret that the preservation of the great places of the Lowcountry, including the city of Savannah, occurred less as a result of enlightened social policy than from post–Civil War impoverishment. Indeed, the many years of slow growth and stalled expectations treated Savannah as they did Charleston, and to this day the cities share similar assets including vibrant, architecturally intact, downtown historic districts; a heritage that reflects the diverse contributions of generations of residents; and a culture enriched by unique musical, religious, culinary, and artistic contributions.

Yet in subtle ways, Savannah today is a more complex and interesting *modern* city than Charleston. In the last five years in particular it's become edgier and funkier, its commercial districts enlivened by retro-looking rehabs, film festivals, and hip restaurants that would not be out of place in San Francisco. For whatever historical reasons, and they run deep, it seems to have achieved an unusual sense of detachment. For every bold statement claimed about its history or beauty, there will be lurking on the lips of someone nearby a counterclaim, a small sarcasm. (Once upon a time during the cotton boom, Savannah madly envied New York City for its commercial muscle; 170 years later the two cities share a liking for gesture and attitude.)

This trait was evident even during the Civil War. Legend has it that General W. T. Sherman spared Savannah because the city was beautiful, the women were gracious, and the parties were just what he needed at the end of his blazing "March to the Sea" campaign. He took up residence, was indeed fêted, and, in a remarkable telegraph of 1864, offered the unmolested city to President Lincoln as a Christmas gift.

Well, Savannah is still beautiful . . . and still partying. (This quality, and the world it describes, is revealed with great skill in the best book on Savannah's downtown culture, John Berendt's 1994 bestseller, *Midnight in the Garden of Good and Evil.*) The blend of reverence and hilarity, of high-mindedness and getting by, gives the city its character. In fact, as time passes, it becomes more palpable. When the local minor-league baseball team renamed itself the Sand Gnats (the top choice in a citywide poll), it chose for its slogan "Bite Me." The city literally shuts down every St. Patrick's Day to accommodate 24 hours of revelry. A power outage in 2008 after the parade stopped no one from taking their "go" cups of alcohol onto the sidewalks to keep the party alive. There's less standing on ceremony here than in Charleston, for Charleston is an iconic Southern place, a city with such a significant, unique presence in American history, that it must meet all sorts of expectations.

Savannah River

TO:
General McIntosh Blvd.

RIVER ST.

Riverfront Plaza

FACTORS WALK

TO:
U.S. 80 W.,
Hwys 17 & 21 N.

TO:
U.S. 80 E.,
forts & beach

W. BAY ST.

E. BAY ST.

City Market

W. BRYAN ST.

E. BRYAN ST.

Franklin Square

Ellis Square

W. SAINT JULIAN ST.

Johnson Square

Reynolds Square

Warren Square

E. SAINT JULIAN ST.

Washington Square

W. CONGRESS ST.

E. CONGRESS ST.

W. BROUGHTON ST.

E. BROUGHTON ST.

W. STATE ST.

E. STATE ST.

Liberty Square

Telfair Square

W. PRESIDENT ST.

Wright Square

Oglethorpe Square

Columbia Square

E. PRESIDENT ST.

Greene Square

W. YORK ST.

E. YORK ST.

HOUSTON ST.

E. BROAD ST.

W. OGLETHORPE AVE.

E. OGLETHORPE AVE.

(W. BROAD ST.)

W. HULL ST.

E. HULL ST.

Colonial Park Cemetery

Elbert Square

Civic Center

Orleans Square

W. MCDONOUGH ST.

Chippewa Square

E. MCDONOUGH ST.

Crawford Square

Visitors Center

W. PERRY ST.

E. PERRY ST.

BARNARD ST.

W. LIBERTY ST.

E. LIBERTY ST.

MARTIN LUTHER KING JR. BLVD.

MONTGOMERY ST.

W. HARRIS ST.

E. HARRIS ST.

Pulaski Square

Madison Square

Lafayette Square

Troup Square

E. MACON ST.

W. CHARLTON ST.

E. CHARLTON ST.

16

JEFFERSON ST.

TATTNALL ST.

WHITAKER ST.

BULL ST.

DRAYTON ST.

ABERCORN ST.

LINCOLN ST.

HABERSHAM ST.

PRICE ST.

W. JONES ST.

E. JONES ST.

16

W. TAYLOR ST.

E. TAYLOR ST.

Chatham Square

W. WAYNE ST.

Monterey Square

Calhoun Square

Whitefield Square

E. WAYNE ST.

W. GORDON ST.

E. GORDON ST.

W. GASTON ST.

E. GASTON ST.

W. HUNTINGDON ST.

E. HUNTINGDON ST.

Forsyth Park

N

W. HALL ST.

E. HALL ST.

Victorian District

W. GWINNET ST.

E. GWINNET ST.

0   0.25 mile

0   0.25 kilometer

W. BOLTON ST.

E. BOLTON ST.

SAVANNAH

© The Countryman Press

Sixteen miles upriver from the Atlantic Ocean, Savannah is a thriving, modern port, soon to be enhanced by a joint South Carolina/Georgia port expansion.   Peter Loftus

By the time national economic and social development did recommend change—after World War II, after a manufacturing and military base undergirded the economy, after federally mandated integration—Savannah residents with the means and interest to do so were faced with reconciling their historic cultural identity, on which they relied so deeply, with a postwar world which placed increasing value on money, mobility, and a celebration of things modern and new. The time had come to set the ongoing physical and intellectual activities associated with historic preservation, neighborhood renovation, and tourist attraction on a larger and more public stage. This they did, and in the process became what might be called curators of their own collection, a collection whose very display case—the old city—is a work of art.

Originally laid out in an orderly, compact grid, downtown Savannah retains this geography today. It is defined by 22 handsome squares that function as vest-pocket parks. They are embowered and rimmed with native flowering species, and are linked by one-way cross streets along their sides, which, in turn, feed a few broad parkways divided by banks of trees and shrubs. It is the nation's largest registered Urban Historic District, containing some 1,200 buildings of architectural and historic significance.

This layout gives Savannah the modern, urban feel of a city—but of course, it isn't a big city and the Historic District is but a section. It includes blocks of magnificent townhouses, many 19th-century places of worship, and several examples of Regency architecture popularized in this country by an Englishman, William Jay. The best way to see them and to feel the roots of American urbanism is on foot or on a carriage or trolley tour.

The restoration and adaptive reuse of private and institutional buildings continues. The Savannah College of Art and Design (SCAD; www.scad.edu) has itself redone more than 40 sites. Its students are ubiquitous and have brought a feeling of freshness—a sense that things are happening in Savannah. There's no doubt that the presence of SCAD and the publication of *Midnight in the Garden of Good and Evil* (with the Mercer House as a central character) have sparked interest in Savannah, attracted not only young people and visitors, but also offered the opportunity to become modern by believing there is, and always was, more to Savannah than its history and architecture. It is now a place where an old filling station on a main artery has become an upscale market that sells arugula. Perhaps the best case in point is the addition to the Telfair Museum, a Regency-style mansion that serves as the city's art museum. After much back and forth with preservationists, historians, residents, and city government, the architect Moshe Safdie translated into bricks and mortar, so to speak, the idea that gorgeous modern design can imbed itself and relate to the historic city without diminishing its dramatic architectural fabric, scale, or intimacy.

Savannah's popularity has led to development in several distinctive sections. **City Market** is a touristy pedestrian streetscape, with shops, galleries, and restaurants. On a sunny afternoon it will be crowded with visitors—and families with young children—eating ice cream and listening to live music. Many carriage tours originate here, and many visitors will be drinking sweet tea in one of the outdoor cafés before or after their ride. On **River Street** 19th-century brick warehouses are filled with bars, restaurants, gift shops, and the hubbub that attracts people to other American cities that have revived their tired historic real estate into festival-style marketplaces. From here, ferries zip across the Savannah River to Hutchinson Island, to the International Trade & Convention Center, and to Westin Savannah Harbor Resort. By night and on weekends, jugglers and street musicians entertain the crowds. **Broughton Street** is once again a vibrant downtown artery, anchored by a luxury hotel, where strolling means window-shopping and, especially in the evening, gourmet dining or entertainment at a renovated theatre. The residential **Victorian District** features large wooden houses faced with decorative moldings, fretwork, and porches, and many gingerbread bungalows. Entrepreneurs in smaller areas, like **Wright Square** and blocks of **Whitaker Street,** have joined together to make their address a destination for design or home and garden shops. More than ever, there are sidewalk cafés where students, locals, and visitors sip lattes and watch the world go by.

As in Charleston, visitors are given the privilege to feel like residents: Nothing is frozen in amber. There is still motion in and around the most awesome architectural icons: people going to work, to school, home to lunch, to the market, just visiting.

The ways in which Savannah chose to survive have served it well. It has withstood General Sherman, Forrest Gump, and "The Book," as they call Berendt's work. Relishing its contradictions as it does, it faces the future with an extraordinary cultural and historic landscape, and a population with the sass and ginger pop to really enjoy it.

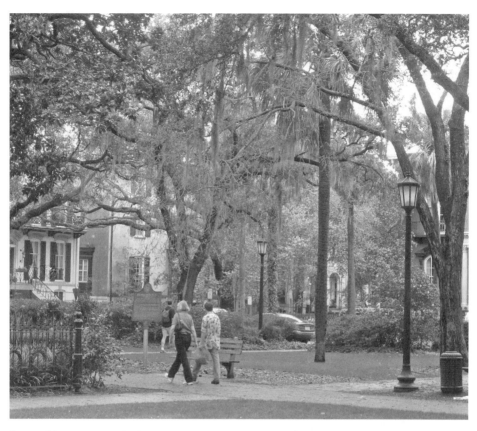

Savannah's squares, a result of enlightened urban planning, allow for shortcuts and places of rest in a congested city, as well as superb views of houses on every side. Peter Loftus

Getting There

Savannah/Hilton Head International Airport (www.savannahairport.com) is the gateway, with some 40 stops each day from East Coast and midwestern cities on AirTran, American Eagle, Continental Express, Delta, Northwest, United, and US Airways. Flights often stop in Charlotte, North Carolina, or Atlanta, but direct service is expanding. Rental cars from all major agencies are available at the airport, as are courtesy shuttles if you are staying at a big hotel. If you are staying elsewhere, ask the proprietor for advice or select a cab service at the airport. Expect to pay $20–$25 to Savannah. **Greyhound** (1-800-231-2222; www.greyhound.com) serves Savannah regularly with departures and arrivals from around the country at its downtown depot. **Amtrak** (1-800-872-7245; www.amtrak.com) offers regular daily service on the East Coast line, although the station, located between the airport and the Historic District, is a $7 cab ride away from downtown Savannah. By car, I-95 is just 10 miles from the Historic District, with an exit at I-16 that goes directly into town. Savannah is 252 miles from Atlanta, 105 miles from Charleston, 195 miles from Charlotte, 140 miles from Jacksonville, and 467 miles from Knoxville.

Lodging

Savannah and its Sea Island neighbor, Tybee Island, offer a range of accommodations, from upscale inns to funky beach villas. Tybee is closer to Savannah than Charleston's beach areas are to that city (about 20 minutes by car), and unlike Savannah's other nearby resort islands, Tybee is not a gated community.

Like Charleston, Savannah had its tradition of providing guest accommodations in city mansions whose owners had rooms to spare. As more visitors came to the area, "tourist homes" and "guest houses" sprang up to serve the mainly Northern clientele who flocked in springtime to see Savannah's gardens and experience its faded charm. The only thing you'll find faded in Savannah today is a shirt that's been left out in the sun too long. Splendid inns—some of which are listed below—have emerged, as old houses have been renovated and cityscapes renewed. Lodging has also extended to loft-like accommodations in buildings on the river.

The caveats invoked in Chapter Two, *Charleston*, hold true here: Reservations are recommended, especially in the "high season" of spring, when a two-night's minimum stay is the usual practice; cancellation policies and room deposits are standard; and smoking takes place outside if it is allowed at all on the property. Access for handicapped persons can be problematic. The larger hotels can be relied on to offer it, but it is not always available in the smaller inns or luxury hotels. Carriage houses with ground-floor access are often a good bet. Don't hesitate to ask about these and other restrictions, including whether or not children are welcome and, critically, at or under what age. This is quite important to the historic bed-and breakfast market, where families may be welcomed in renovated carriage houses on the property but not in the main house where there's an abundance of breakable china. Wi-Fi and internet data ports are reliably offered at the larger hotels. If you're on a working vacation and need access, check ahead at the smaller inns. The **Savannah Area Convention & Visitors Bureau** (1-877-728-2662; www.savannahvisit.com) provides information and links, as does www.historicinnsofsavannah.com. The Web site www.bandbofsavannah.com offers a view of six luxury sites.

The same range of rates applies in Savannah as in other Lowcountry places. They are:

Inexpensive	Up to $80
Moderate	$80 to $140
Expensive	$140 to $200
Very Expensive	$200 and up

These rates do not include room taxes or special service charges that might apply during your stay. Ask about AAA, AARP, and other discounts.

Credit Cards
AE—American Express
D—Discover Card
DC—Diner's Club
MC—MasterCard
V—Visa

Hotels and Larger Inns

Hampton Inn Historic District
912-231-9700 or 1-800-576-4945.
www.savannahlodging.com.
201 E. Bay St., Savannah, GA 31412.
Price: Moderate.
Credit Cards: AE, D, MC, V.
Handicap Access: Some.

Heart-pine flooring, Savannah gray bricks, a rooftop pool, and an atmosphere that is both cozy and simple, take the chain-hotel feeling off this renovated brick low-rise. Located across Bay St. from the riverfront, it's convenient and welcoming to families.

Hilton Savannah De Soto
912-232-9000 or 1-800-426-8483.
www.desotohilton.com.

15 E. Liberty St., Savannah, GA 31412.
Price: Expensive.
Credit Cards: AE, D, MC, V.
Handicap Access: Yes.

A wonderful location in the heart of the Historic District, a short walk to the riverfront. Some of the 246 rooms have private balconies, most have great views of Savannah's splendid squares. Pool and health club. At the high end of comfort and friendliness for a big, downtown hotel.

Hyatt Regency Savannah

912-238-1234 or 1-800-233-1234.
www.savannahhyatt.com.
2 W. Bay St., Savannah, GA 31412.
Price: Expensive to Very Expensive.
Credit Cards: AE, D, MC, V.
Handicap Access: Yes.

A 351-room hotel, with the trademark Hyatt atrium lobby and glass elevators, towers over the riverfront with an unparalleled view of the ship, ferry, and tugboat traffic. There's an indoor pool and shopping arcade, and you're steps away from busy River Street. This is the best location for River Boat excursions, the ferry to Hutchinson Island, or the day-trip ferry to Daufuskie Island and Hilton Head. Renovated in 2006.

The Marshall House

912-644-7896 or 1-800-589-6304.
www.marshallhouse.com.
123 E. Broughton St., Savannah, GA 31401.
Price: Expensive to Very Expensive.
Credit Cards: AE, D, MC, V.
Handicap Access: Some rooms.

This thoroughly renovated hotel, with its trademark ironwork balconies, opened again in 1999, nearly 150 years after it was built in bustling, downtown antebellum Savannah. Broughton Street is bustling again with theaters, upscale restaurants, and shopping, a definite plus, but it can be noisy to stay here. Its bar draws a local crowd; sometimes jazz combos perform Thursday through Saturday. There are 68 rooms, some suites among them with separate sleeping areas. It's been modernized with all the amenities to a high-gloss sheen.

The Mulberry Inn

912-238-1200 or 1-877-468-1200.
www.savannahlodging.com.
601 E. Bay St., Savannah, GA 31401.
Price: Expensive.
Credit Cards: AE, D, MC, V.
Handicap Access: Yes.

Right across the street from the commercial riverfront, this 145-room inn (including suites with wet bars) blends the close attention and formal period décor found in smaller inns with the full services of a hotel. Informal piano concerts set the tone for afternoon tea, and complimentary hors d'oeuvres are served. There's an outdoor pool and heated rooftop Jacuzzi. Special package rates are often available. Children under 18 sleep free in their parents' room.

Westin Savannah Harbor Golf Resort & Spa

912-201-2000 or 1-800-937-8461.
www.westinsavannah.com.
One Resort Dr., Savannah, GA 31421.
Price: Expensive to Very Expensive.
Credit Cards: AE, D, MC, V.
Handicap Access: Yes.

A full-service luxury resort complex located on Hutchinson Island, 90 seconds by water taxi across the Savannah River from the Historic District or a brief car trip over the Talmadge Bridge. From here the views of Savannah and the river traffic are stunning, especially from the 55 Club Level rooms, some of which feature balconies. It's a huge place (16 stories, 403 guest rooms) that was intended to impress with it size and modern art, and it does, although it's more likely you'll stay here as part of a high-end convention. There's an elaborate spa, fitness center, four tennis courts, a par-72 golf course, clubhouse, marina, two pools, bar, grill room, and restaurant.

Luxury Inns

Ballastone Inn

912-236-1484 or 1-800-822-4553.
www.ballastone.com.
14 E. Oglethorpe Ave., Savannah, GA 31401.
Price: Expensive to Very Expensive.
Credit Cards: AE, MC, V.
Handicap Access: Limited.

At Christmas, the Ballastone Inn looks like a scene out of Dickens—holly, magnolia leaves, native mistletoe, and garlands of smilax carry its grand front parlor back in time to 1838 when this townhouse was built and English taste influenced the city. The décor echoes this high-style period in rich colors (like chocolate-toned walls), drapes, and furnishings, but is updated for comfort. There are 17 rooms, including three deluxe suites—many of them with Jacuzzis and fireplaces, and a courtyard you may not want to leave. A handsome full-service bar on the first floor is a wonderful amenity, one of the coziest nooks in the city. A full Southern breakfast, afternoon tea, and hors d'oeuvres are included.

East Bay Inn

912-238-1225 or 1-800-500-1225.
www.eastbayinn.com.
225 E. Bay St., Savannah, GA 31401.
Price: Expensive.
Credit Cards: AE, D, MC, V.
Handicap Access: Yes.

Originally a circa-1853 cotton warehouse, there are now 28 guest rooms, each furnished with queen-sized four-poster beds, reproduction antiques, and coffeemakers. A modestly appointed place, it sits at a great location, across the street from the busy retail and nightlife hub of River Street. Pets and children are welcome. Large tour groups often book here.

Eliza Thompson House

912-236-3620 or 1-800-348-9378.
www.elizathompsonhouse.com.
5 W. Jones St., Savannah, GA 31401.
Price: Expensive to Very Expensive.
Credit Cards: AE, MC, V.
Handicap Access: Limited.

This 25-room inn gives off a sense of family warmth amidst beautiful old objects. It was one of Savannah's first luxury inns, and honestly it may have been outclassed in luxury, but it maintains its sense of hospitality. Its spacious courtyard and fountain, and its location (on a brick-paved street embowered by oaks and lined with iron-balconied townhouses), still fulfill the expectations of visitors who come in search of the cities of the "Old South." Many extras like breakfast in the courtyard, evening wine, coffee, and desserts.

Forsyth Park Inn

912-233-6800 or 1-866-670-6800.
www.forsythparkinn.com.
102 W. Hall St., Savannah, GA 31401.
Price: Expensive.
Credit Cards: AE, D, MC, V.

A modest, quiet place with 11 rooms, including a courtyard cottage that can

Fountain, Forsyth Park.

accommodate up to four, this inn might best be used for a romantic weekend getaway for a busy couple. The main house is a Victorian-era mansion with inlaid hardwood floors and furnished with period antiques, reproductions, and four-poster beds. The baby grand piano in the entrance hall seems right in scale with the tall ceilings and long windows.

The Gastonian

912-232-2869 or 1-800-322-6603.
www.gastonian.com.
220 E. Gaston St., Savannah, GA 31401.
Price: Very Expensive.
Credit Cards: AE, D, MC, V.
Handicap Access: Some.

This Regency/Italianate residence complex dating from 1868 has lost little of its imposing feel. Period-appropriate décor and muted colors take a visitor back to the post–Civil War era when "the Old South" was becoming "the New South." Each of the 17 suites has a gas fireplace; many have four-poster beds and some have Jacuzzi tubs or Japanese soak tubs. The side garden has been restored to its fragrant, secret self. Local people often reserve months in advance for special occasions. The Carriage House suite, with its own balcony and kitchen, is a favorite for honeymooners. Full Southern breakfast.

Hamilton-Turner Inn

912-233-1833 or 1-888-448-8849.
www.hamilton-turnerinn.com.
330 Abercorn St., Savannah, GA 31401.
Price: Expensive to Very Expensive.
Credit Cards: All major.
Handicap Access: One room.

Home of the eccentric "Mandy" in John Berendt's book, *Midnight in the Garden of Good and Evil,* this 10,000-square-foot house is a must-see for fans of the book. Even on its own, it's an amazing place, built in the Second Empire style in 1873, totally renovated in 1998 by a local family, and furnished with Empire, Eastlake, and Renaissance Revival antiques. The four-story house and carriage house contain 18 rooms and suites, many with private balconies, whirlpools, and fireplaces. Full breakfast and pre-dinner treats are served in a grand dining room.

The Kehoe House

912-232-1020 or 1-800-820-1020.
www.kehoehouse.com.
123 Habersham St., Savannah, GA 31401.
Price: Very Expensive.
Credit Cards: All major.
Handicap Access: Elevator to all rooms.

This restored Victorian mansion has had several lives; this is its grandest. There are 13 guest rooms (many with private balconies) and several opulent public rooms adorned with huge urns of fresh flowers in the main building, and three additional rooms in the townhouse across the courtyard. Everything here is scaled to fin-de-siècle oversize: the ceiling moldings, the valances, the draperies, the armoires, the library tables, even the banisters and paneling. Not a corner's been cut in refurbishing or services. Full breakfast and early-evening appetizers bookend the day.

Magnolia Place Inn

912-236-7674 or 1-800-238-7674.
www.magnoliaplaceinn.com.
503 Whitaker St., Savannah, GA 31401.
Price: Expensive to Very Expensive.
Credit Cards: AE, MC, V.

For many years, praise has been heaped on this inn from those who enjoy its carefully appointed décor, including many lovely Oriental objects and fabrics, and because the rooms are not overstuffed. Housed in a late-19th century building, it faces Forsyth Park, which offers a view and sense of restfulness in addition to being a great place to take a morning run. There are 13 rooms in the main house. Behind the inn are two two-story rowhouses, each with two bedrooms upstairs, a better option for couples traveling together or families with kids.

Mansion on Forsyth Park

912-238-5158 or 888-711-5114.
www.mansiononforsythpark.com.
700 Drayton St., Savannah, GA 31401.
Price: Very Expensive.
Credit Cards: AE, D, MC, V.

After the initial tourist rush in the mid-80s that put Savannah on the map, the lodging business stabilized, working with a successful formula of history and chocolate-on-the-pillow hospitality. As the industry matured, some of the quainter B&Bs faded and continuing renovations downtown proved the luxury market was healthy. The Mansion is the epitome of luxury. It may be over the top even for Savannah—a tricked-out car among the classics. It's not about a touch here, a touch there, a nice oil painting, or a fondly told Civil War story/myth. This is serious deluxe business, with 126 rooms, a massive gallery with hundreds of paintings and sculptures, a spa, a cooking school, and an excellent 150-seat restaurant (700 Drayton) composed of six dining rooms. Showmanship and glamour: It's rocking Savannah's world.

Smaller Accommodations and Offbeat Lodgings

These are alternatives to the full-blown, fancy places. Rates are Moderate to Expensive. They can be a budget choice, or an option for extended families or friends traveling together.

Bed & Breakfast Inn (912-238-0518 or 1-888-238-0518; www.savannahbnb.com; 117 W. Gordon St.) A mid-1850s townhouse at Chatham Square, closer to Forsyth Park than the river, but in an old neighborhood and an inn that has been around for years with many fans.

Joan's on Jones Bed and Breakfast (912-234-3863 or 1-888-989-9806; 17 W. Jones St.) Good location on one of Savannah's prettiest streets; two suites; children and some pets welcome.

Park Avenue Manor (912-233-0352; www.parkavenuemanor.com; 107 & 109 W. Park Ave.) Four rooms with private baths in an owner-occupied 1897-built bed-and-breakfast on the southwest corner of Forsyth Park, the leading edge of the Victorian District. On the froufrou side of décor but much loved by lots of repeat visitors for 10 years. No pets; children older than 16 only.

Thunderbird Inn (912-232-2661 or 866-324-2661; www.thethunderbirdinn.com; 611 W. Oglethorpe Ave.) Renovated to its retro best. If you're a hipster from Williamsburg (NY) or SoMa (SF) this is for you. Downtown.

Resorts and Rentals—Tybee Island

Savannah's beach is Tybee Island, a very informal place, the opposite of a gated resort. It has been for years a retreat from the city where you can take off your shoes and have your neighbors over for a beer, perhaps before lunch. While there are some new luxury homes, it's mostly houses raised up high, with latticed skirts hiding the pilings, and a deck out back. The beach is broad and public, with a pier and plenty of access points. There are shops for beachwear and boogie boards, two excellent restaurants, some fine B&Bs, oceanfront hotels that are not glitzy, and a campground and RV park. It's also the best place to get on the water in a kayak. (See the Recreation section of this chapter.) Condo complexes and inexpensive motels are typical lodgings but some other options are listed here.

Contact the Tybee Visitor Center (1-800-868-2322; www.tybeevisit.com) for more ideas.

Dunes Inn and Suites

912-786-4591 or 1-888-678-0763.
www.dunesinn.com.
1409 Butler Ave., Tybee Island, GA 31328.
Price: Expensive.
Credit Cards: AE, D, DC, MC, V.
Handicap Access: Yes.

An upscale version of a chain hotel. Some of the 53 rooms have kitchenettes, some have king-sized beds and Jacuzzis. It's simple, clean, close to the beach, and has a swimming pool.

Hunter House Inn

912-786-7515.
www.hunterhouseinn.com.
1701 Butler Ave., Tybee Island, GA 31328.
Price: Moderate.
Credit Cards: AE, MC, V.

Four rooms in a circa-1910 house at the beach—sounds like an old-fashioned vacation. It's one block away from the water, 25 minutes from downtown Savannah. Four rooms, including two suites that can accommodate more than just two people. Queen-sized beds and private baths are standard. Good restaurant on site.

Outdoor Inn

404-496-4691 or 1-888-529-2542.
www.seakayakgeorgia.com.
1018 US 80, Tybee Island, GA 31328.
Price: Inexpensive to Moderate.
Credit Cards: D, MC, V.

Located next door to Sea Kayak Georgia, which offers instruction, kayak touring, and equipment, this two-story beach house overlooks the marsh. The ground floor has three rooms with a shared bath; upstairs there's a larger suite. Many guests stay here while participating in a Sea Kayak Georgia program or expedition (from beginner to advanced levels), but everyone is welcome. Tybee's two best restaurants are practically next door; it's a short car or bike ride to the beach. The staff is friendly, and they know the area's paddling waters better than anyone. Share your stories and tales of the outdoors in a common living room and porch.

17th Street Inn

912-786-0607 or 1-888-909-0607.
www.tybeeinn.com.
12 17th St., Tybee Island, GA 31328.
Price: Moderate.
Credit Cards: AE, D, MC, V.

Eight rooms with private entrances and full kitchens, with a deck for all guests and plenty of room for families. Clean, friendly, funky, less than one block from the beach. Kids accommodated with beds at modest additional cost.

Tybee Island Inn

912-786-9255.
www.tybeeislandinn.com
24 Van Horne Ave., Tybee Island, GA 31328.
Price: Moderate to Expensive.
Credit Cards: MC, V.

Once part of the Fort Screven infirmary, located one block from the beach on the quieter north end of the island (closer to Savannah) amid live oaks, palmettos, and many places to walk or jog.

Rental Agents at Tybee Island

Oceanfront Cottage Rentals (912-786-0054 or 1-800-786-5889; www.oceanfront cottage.com; 717 First St., Tybee Island, GA 31328) Listing 30 homes on the ocean or with an ocean view. Many welcome pets, and usually provide boogie boards, bikes, and beach chairs. Some with pools and hot tubs.

Tybee Island Rentals (912-786-4034 or 1-800-476-0807; www.tybeeislandrentals .com; P.O. Box 627, Tybee Island, GA 31328) Some 120 properties are available for rent by the week or month, with a two-night minimum stay. The Web site is simple and helpful.

Tybee Vacation Rentals (912-786-5853 or 1-866-359-0297; www.tybeevacationrentals.com; P.O. Box 402, Tybee Island, GA 31328) Listing 60 houses, cottages, villas, houses with pools. Pet-friendly properties. Online reservations accepted.

DINING

By the end of the American Revolution, visitors to Savannah were impressed with the abundance and variety of its foods, the sophisticated way they were prepared by slaves, and the splendid manner in which meals arrived at the table. Lavish at-home dining established itself as a mark of social position.

The art and pleasure of dining stayed home-based for many years after that, well into this century. There were few places to dine out and few reasons to do so. The culture centered around home, family, the connections of friends and neighbors, and a convivial shared history. You could conduct your business in a restaurant, but not your social life.

Savannah's many restaurants show how that has changed. Today, the city is filled with plain and fancy places to eat. The local population, including thousands of students, is eager to dine out. They have the means to do so, and visitors arrive with high culinary expectations. While there may be fewer no-frills lunch counters and cafeterias, there are plenty of informal cafés, coffee bars, and beachside bistros to take their place. Don't discount Tybee Island (see "Savannah Area") as a dining destination: It's not just fried seafood anymore.

The hours and prices of restaurants have been checked as close to the date of publication as possible, but a call ahead to confirm is always wise. The general price range we list is meant to reflect the cost of a single meal, usually dinner, featuring an appetizer, entrée, dessert, and coffee. Cocktails, beer and wine, gratuity, and tax are not included in the estimated price.

Enjoying an outdoor concert at City Market.

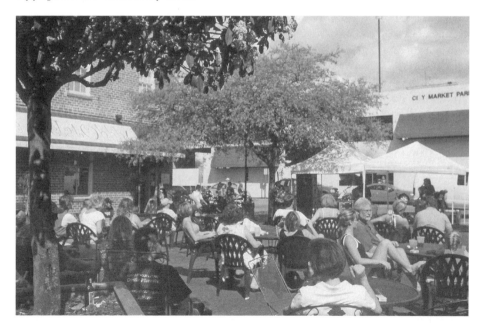

Dining Price Code

Inexpensive	Up to $10
Moderate	$10 to $30
Expensive	$30 to $50
Very Expensive	$50 or more

Credit Cards

AE—American Express
CB—Carte Blanche
D—Discover Card
DC—Diner's Club
MC—MasterCard
V—Visa

Delicatessens, sweet shops, and bakeries are listed below larger restaurants; gourmet and health-food stores are listed under "Gourmet Food" in the **Shopping** section of this chapter.

Belford's

912-233-2626.
315 W. St. Julian St.
Open: Daily.
Price: Moderate to Expensive.
Cuisine: Southern.
Serving: L, D; Sun. Brunch.
Credit Cards: AE, D, MC. V.
Reservations recommended.
Handicap Access: Yes.

Belford's opens on both sides to City Market, and has patio seating, features which make it very attractive for Sunday brunch and lunch. There's a small corner bar where you can eat in a pinch, but you'd want to be in the main dining area, one side an exposed brick wall, lots of glass windows, seating around an open grill. Steaks and seafood are the best choices, and every waiter and the carriage tour operator outside will remind you that the crab cakes have received an award. They do a great job of Lowcountry staples like greens, shrimp with smoked bacon, and crab stew.

Bistro Savannah

912-233-6266.
309 W. Congress St.
Open: Daily.
Price: Moderate to Expensive.
Cuisine: International; Seafood.
Serving: D.
Credit Cards: AE, MC, V.
Reservations recommended.
Handicap Access: Yes.

In City Market but somehow away from the noise and bustle, Bistro Savannah has a serene atmosphere enhanced by comfortable wicker chairs and soft lighting. The menu is full of fresh market specials featuring organic produce, small piquant salads, and lots of seafood that's treated with Asian sweet-and-sour pairings or robust Mediterranean spices. Extensive wine list, specializing in California vineyards. It's a foodie draw.

Casbah

912-234-6168.
wwwcasbahrestaurant.com.
118 E. Broughton St.
Open: Daily.
Price: Moderate.
Cuisine: Moroccan.
Serving: D.
Credit Cards: All major.
Reservations recommended.

A décor that calls to mind Arabian folk tales and a menu that takes North African herbs and staples like tabouli, mint, almonds, saffron, and lamb and chicken to new heights. There's even belly dancing. Perhaps unlikely in old historic Savannah, but it has found its niche. Families are welcome: It's exotic and festive.

Cha Bella

912-790-7888.
www.cha-bella.com.
102 E. Broad St.
Open: Daily.
Price: Moderate to Expensive.
Cuisine: Mediterranean.
Serving: D.
Credit Cards: AE, D, MC, V.

Organic, organic, organic. Locally produced food from sustainable farms. Very creative menu that changes every day, according to what's growing and at the fish market. Whiffs of southern Spain and Provence. Sounds too good to be true, but this exuberant, modern, restaurant has uniquely hit the tone for 21st-century Savannah with its loft-like space in a former industrial building, and its nod to the art scene, with live music some nights and weekend film screenings in the courtyard.

Clary's Café
912-233-0402.
404 Abercorn St.
Open: Daily.
Price: Inexpensive.
Cuisine: American.
Serving: B, L.
Credit Cards: AE, MC, V.
Wheelchair accessible seating.

A bacon-and-egg sandwich on wheat and coffee is a typical order at Clary's, a downtown eatery where your cup stays refilled and breakfast waffles can set you up for the day. At lunch, the Greek salad is big enough to share, or if you're hungry you might try the chicken potpie, which includes salad and a roll. Top it off with a root beer float. *Midnight in the Garden of Good and Evil* fame sent the crowds here, but the diet-busting food makes it worth the trip.

Crystal Beer Parlor
912-443-9200.
www.crystalbeerparlor.net.
301 W. Jones St.
Closed: Sun.
Price: Inexpensive to Moderate.
Cuisine: Southern.
Serving: L, D.
Credit Cards: D, MC, V.

Located at the end of one of Savannah's prettiest residential streets on the edge of the Historic District, the Crystal is a bar with leather booths and frosted mugs, and has been recently freshened up. It's not a secret—it's been written up many times—but it tends to be forgotten when it shouldn't be. Shrimp salad, fried oysters, burgers, and crab stew are popular. Live music on Fridays.

Elizabeth on 37th
912-236-5547.
www.elizabethon37th.net.
105 E. 37th St.
Open: Daily.
Price: Very Expensive.
Cuisine: American; gourmet Southern.
Serving: D.
Credit Cards: AE, MC. V.
Reservations required.

The creation of Elizabeth Terry, chef, author, and James Beard Award winner, this restaurant was one of the first in Savannah to bring seasonal products, signature flavorings, and a sense of creative possibility to mundane Southern staples like grits, grouper, and greens—and to offer them to a larger audience. It was upscale and ahead of the trend in the early 80s. Elizabeth is gone, but diners can still count on elaborate meals in the sumptuous setting of an old mansion. You'll need to drive or take a cab from downtown. Relax and enjoy the formality and the huge wine list and forget about the price. Favorites include rack of lamb encrusted with herbs, local fish, and seafood soups.

Il Pasticcio
912-231-8888.
www.ilpasticciosavannah.com.
2 E. Broughton St.
Open: Daily.
Price: Moderate to Expensive.
Cuisine: Northern Italian.
Serving: D.
Cards: AE, D, MC, V.

This is a big, Italian-style bistro plopped down in the oversized space of a former department store. The homemade stuffed pasta dishes are its signature. There are mixed grill and rotisserie specials, too. Cooks from Beaufort and Savannah come on their night off, as well as recent arrivals who miss the metro feel of cities where they used to live.

The Lady & Sons

912-233-2600.
www.ladyandsons.com.
102 W. Congress St.
Open: Daily.
Price: Moderate.
Cuisine: Country Southern.
Serving: L, D.
Credit Cards: All major.

The lunch buffet offers the full range of Southern specialties, including fried tomatoes, catfish, ribs, and shrimp grits—a smart choice if you plan to be walking and touring for the rest of the day before a late-evening meal. Paula Deen made her name on Food Network television and in cookbooks by making down-home dishes bursting with pride and flavor. The crowds at the door would make you think a rock star was eating those greens. Expect a wait, so check in and wander around City Market until your table's ready. All-you-can-eat options are available for lunch and dinner. Dinner reservations recommended.

Mrs. Wilkes' Dining Room

912-232-5997.
www.mrswilkes.com.
107 W. Jones St.
Open: Mon.–Fri.
Price: Inexpensive.
Cuisine: Southern.
Serving: L.
Credit Cards: None.
Handicap Access: Yes

This is homemade cooking served as it would be at home: the diners seated around large tables, with heaping platters of fried chicken, baskets of biscuits, and bowls of slaw, vegeta-bles, red rice, and black-eyed peas or green beans placed before them. If you've ever been grateful for the kindness of strangers, the one who gives you the last pork chop could be your friend for life. It's located in the basement of an old red-brick house; you'll recognize it by the line forming at mealtime.

The Olde Pink House

912-232-4286.
23 Abercorn St.
Open: Daily.
Price: Expensive.
Cuisine: Southern; Continental.
Serving: D.
Credit Cards: All major.

Located in an elegant 18th-century mansion designated a National Landmark, where the Declaration of Independence was read in Savannah for the first time. There's a quiet dining room upstairs, and a more lively tavern downstairs, with fireplaces roaring in winter, piano music, a welcoming bar, and a full dinner menu. This is one of the most popular places downtown to have a cocktail or relax after dinner—that is, if the diners release their tables. The seafood is recommended (a recent appetizer was sautéed shrimp with country ham and grits cake) but the entrées include fish, veal, steak, and lamb, many with a glazed sauce.

Olympia Café

912-233-3131.
5 E. River St.
Open: Daily.
Price: Inexpensive to Moderate.
Cuisine: Greek.
Serving: L, D.
Credit Cards: All major.

River Street is not a subtle stretch, with its bars and gift shops and crowds, but it's fun, and this is a reliable, inexpensive restaurant. Savannah's population of Greek descent, proud of its deep roots and civic contributions, make this a casual, friendly place. There are Mediterranean appetizers like *tzadziki* and *dolmadakia,* and gyros and kabobs, as well as traditional Greek dishes like lemon chicken and *moussaka*. If you hear servers and diners shouting "Opa," it means another order of flaming cheese appetizers was a hit.

Sapphire Grill

912-443-9962.
www.sapphiregrill.com.
110 W. Congress St.
Open: Daily.
Price: Expensive to Very Expensive.
Cuisine: American.
Serving: D.
Credit Cards: AE, MC, V.

A sophisticated, stylish restaurant on three floors serving a first-rate dinner and open late for nightcaps. Located in the City Market area, it is modern and sleek—bare hardwood floors, wooden blinds, white tablecloths, and lots of brushed metal. The bar, along one side, can get crowded and create a lot of traffic, and the restaurant tends to be noisy. Nonetheless, it's a special place. There's always an excellent choice of beef or duck, several pan-seared or grilled fish dishes, and foie gras added to any plate. Signature appetizers are shrimp, arugula salad, and fried green tomatoes with chèvre croutons. All dishes emphasize heirloom, organic, and local produce and the freshest fish and meat. The tasting menu at dinner shows off chef Christopher Nason's artistry, and it comes with a wine flight if you choose. For many it's the best Savannah restaurant.

Vinnie Van Gogo's

912-233-6394.
317 W. Bryant St.
Open: Daily.
Price: Inexpensive.
Cuisine: Pizza, Italian.

Serving: L (Sat., Sun.); D (from 4 PM)
Credit Cards: None.
Special Features: Delivery by bicycle courier to downtown area.

Calzones and thin-crust pizza by the slice or pie (14" or 18") made from dough prepared on the premises during the day, then rolled and tossed while you watch from the counter. These cooks are having fun. Toppings include healthy vegetables. Large selection of imported beers and a concoction called spodeeodee (cheap red wine, 7-Up, splash of orange soda), which sells by the glass or pitcher as fast as they can mix it up. Eat on the patio—you're surrounded by art students—and get a sense of a new population that has enlivened the old city.

SAVANNAH AREA

The Breakfast Club

912-786-5984.
1500 Butler Ave., Tybee Island.
Open: Daily (6:30 AM–1 PM).
Price: Inexpensive.
Cuisine: Southern.
Serving: B, L.
Credit Cards: MC, V.

Get a feel for the kicked-back life of Tybee here among locals sitting at booths and tables set close together in this small, unpretentious place. You might run into the shrimpers coming in or the early anglers and birders just setting out. If you want to get a jump on the day, or take a quiet walk on a deserted morning beach, this is a great place to start. On weekends, or by mid-morning, there will be a line. A classic, local experience, whether you eat the waffles or a burger.

Crab Shack at Chimney Creek

912-786-9857.
www.thecrabshack.com.
40 Estill Hammock Rd., Tybee Island (second right past Lazaretto Creek Bridge).

Open: Daily.
Price: Moderate.
Cuisine: Seafood.
Serving: L, D.
Credit Cards: MC, V.

As informal as your own back porch: wooden tables inside and out, beer in the bottle, sandy feet welcome. The food is strictly off-the-boat: raw-bar selections, fat crab served in cakes or blended with spices and cheese, and Lowcountry boil, a platter including shrimp, corn, potatoes, and sausage. Located at a bend on the creek, the view is premium Lowcountry, enjoyed from the homemade Tiki Bar or from the deck, where "Crab Shack chandeliers" (made from old baskets) light up the night. Its popularity is threatening its funkiness, but it is what it is, and it does it well. Good choice for families if you eat before the evening rush; otherwise expect a wait. No reservations.

North Beach Grill
912-786-9003.
41-A Meddin Dr. (by the Lighthouse), Tybee Island.
Open: Daily.
Price: Inexpensive to Moderate.
Cuisine: Seafood; Caribbean.
Serving: L, D.
Credit Cards: AE, MC, V.

Take an old beachside snack bar (where you could have rented surf boards and umbrellas and bought a hot dog), screen it in, add island spices and beer, and you're getting close to describing this place. It's very small, informal, and nonchalant, serving jerk chicken and pork, conch fritters, Cuban pot roast, crab with asparagus, and plantains. Success hasn't spoiled it one iota.

Bamboo Room
866-216-5795.
1106 US 80, Tybee Island.
Open: Daily.
Price: Expensive.
Cuisine: Seafood and steaks.
Serving: L, D and Sun. Brunch.
Several small rooms, upstairs, downstairs, on the porch and on the deck describe the layout; the décor is tropically bright colors offset by a dark wooden bar.

You could make a meal out of a margarita and cilantro-infused spring roll with pork and shrimp or go for blackened shellfish. Pasta and vegetarian plates, too. Music on the deck. Young, upbeat crowd and staff, with a few Margaritaville types thrown in.

FOOD PURVEYORS

Some of the places listed below should not be overlooked for lunch or brunch, although they are a welcome sight at midafternoon, after a day of touring. There are more of these very good, informal places than ever before.

Bakeries/Coffeehouses
Back In the Day Bakery (912-495-9292; www.backintheday.com; 2403 Bull St.) Located in the up-and-coming hipster neighborhood of Starland, where there are new galleries and artists' lofts, the bakery has astonishing sweets as well as wraps and sandwiches.

Ex Libris (912-525-7550; 228 Martin Luther King Jr. Blvd.) Three floors of books, art supplies, and overstuffed sofas to sit on and sip your coffee after you browse.

Firefly Café (912-234-1971; 321 Habersham St.) A neighborhood spot on Troup Square; walk a few steps down to the dining area or eat outside. Highly recommended Saturday/Sunday brunch, although lunch salads and sandwiches are exceptional. Dinner is also served, if you're tired of the formality elsewhere and simply want a good meal.

Gallery Espresso (912-233-5348; 234 Bull St.) Coffees, rum cakes, outdoor tables, and indoor art exhibits. Longtime favorite of artsy locals.

Soho South Café (912-233-1633; 12 W. Liberty St.) The bakery opens at 8 AM, but lunch starts at 11:30 and Sunday brunch at 11 AM. Inside a hip art gallery with good things to see and good people-watching. To-go menu.

Wright Square Café (912-238-1150; 21 W. York St.) The wraps at lunch are terrific (the menu also includes panini and salads) and the setting is very European, with indoor and sidewalk dining, racks of fine chocolates and coffees, comfortable chairs, and a serious attention to architectural detail, from floor to ceiling. On a square with several shops for antiques, books, upscale clothing, and home furnishings.

Candy and Ice Cream

Byrd Cookie Co. (1-800-291-2973; www.byrdcookiecompany.com; 6700 Waters Ave.) A local institution since 1924. Delicious cookies and gourmet desserts made on site. Tours available.

Kilwins Chocolates and Ice Cream (912-944-2880; www.kilwins.com; 20 E. Broughton St.) Ice cream made in the store, truffles, and fabulous chocolates.

Savannah's Candy Kitchen (912-233-8411; 225 E. River St.) The largest candy store in the South, where you can see the candies made and have some sent home.

Delis and Faster Food

Brighter Day (912-236-4703; 1102 Bull St.) A health-food store featuring a full line of natural foods, juices, and supplements as well as fresh sandwiches to go or to eat there, breads, and organic produce.

Express Café and Bakery (912-233-4683; 39 Barnard St.) An upscale Art Deco–style bakery created in the shell of a downtown storefront. Opens weekdays at 7 AM. The breads and desserts are homemade; omelets are light and fresh. Light lunches include soups and sandwiches.

Sushi Zen (912-233-1188; 41 Whitaker St.) An intimate, minimalist setting where you can get sushi, American sandwiches, and creative "lunchbox specials." Opens at 5:30 PM and stays open late on weekends.

TOURING IN THE HISTORIC DISTRICT AND BEYOND

There are so many options for tours in Savannah that you might decide whether you want to concentrate on ghosts, the Civil War, "The Book," gardens, old houses; or whether you want to go on foot, by carriage, trolley, air-conditioned bus or van; or by daylight or moonlight. Most tours last one to two hours. Reservations are strongly suggested. You can also pick up a CD/cassette and map at the Visitor Center (301 Martin Luther King Jr. Blvd.) and walk or drive at your own pace.

Some motorized tours allow you to step off and catch up with them at a later stop. Tours that are more specifically nature-oriented, or may require equipment such as a kayak or canoe, are more fully described in the **Recreation** section below. Prices range from $10 to $25 for adults, from $5 to $12 for children. Here are some ideas; check the Web sites for more information:

By Motor
Freedom Trail Tour (912-232-7477) Focuses on African American history.

Hearse Ghost Ride (912-695-1578; www.hearseghosttours.com) Yes, it's true, eight passengers ride at night in a converted hearse.

Savannah Heritage Tours (912-224-8365; www.savannahheritagetour.com).

Tours by BJ (912-233-2335; www.toursbybj.com).

By Carriage
Carriage Tours of Savannah (912-236-6756; www.savannah.com).

Historic Savannah Carriage Tours (912-443-9333 or 1-888-837-1011; www.savannah carriage.com).

Plantation Carriage (912-201-0001).

By Trolley
Oglethorpe Trolley Tours (912-233-8380; www.oglethorpetours.com).

Old Savannah Tours (912-234-8128 or 1-800-517-9007; www.oldsavannahtours.com).

Old Town Trolley Tours (912-233-0083; www.trolleytours.com).

The prices for cotton negotiated at the Cotton Exchange determined Savannah's prosperity.   Peter Loftus

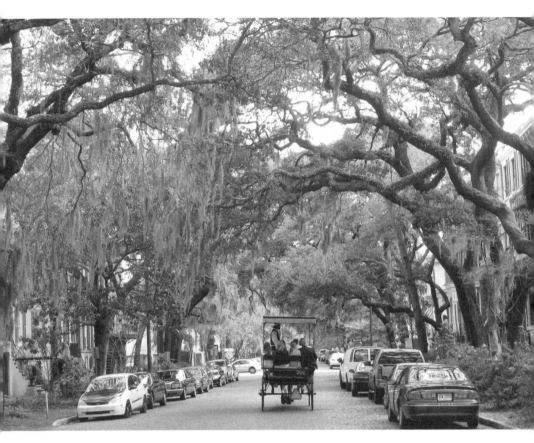

A guided carriage ride lets you soak up the ambience, history, and architecture at a 19th-century pace.
Peter Loftus

By Foot

Architectural Tours of Savannah (912-604-6354; www.architecturalsavannah.com).

Ghost Talk, Ghost Walk (912-233-3896 or 1-800-563-3896; www.savannahgeorgia.com).

GreenFeet Walkabouts (912-713-7792; www.greenfeetwalkabouts.com).

Savannah Haunted History Tours (912-604-3007; www.ghostsavannah.com).

Savannah Walks (912-238-9255 or 1-888-728-9255; www.savannahwalks.com).

See Savannah Walking Tours (912-234-3571; www.seesavannah.com).

By Boat

Bull River Marina Dolphin Watch (910-897-7300; www.bullrivermarina.com).

Dolphin Magic Tours (1-800-721-1240; www.dolphin-magic.com).

Riverboat Cruises (912-232-6404 or 1-800-786-6404; www.savannahriverboat.com).

Sea Kayak Georgia (912-786-8732; www.seakayakgeorgia.com).

CULTURE

Architecture

Appreciating architecture in Savannah is a little like being a parent: You can read about it, you can hear it described fully and well, you can understand why people do it, and you can give it a rational and historic context. But you haven't begun to feel its power until you face it for yourself, four-square, on a lazy walk in the city.

It is not necessary to arrive and hit the ground running. Whether or not you visit every historic house and church, or mentally catalogue its interior detailing, is not that important. You can buy an exquisite book for that (see Chapter Six, *Information,* for suggestions, or visit a bookstore listed under **Shopping** in this chapter). What's special about this region is that you can experience architecture in drifts, in vistas, as a harmonious whole that came into being as a response to the natural conditions of climate and the calculated ones of prevailing fashions.

Further, the very settings of these manmade gems foster appreciation for their scale and for the surviving scale of the environment around them. This you can experience only by being there.

Savannah's architectural inventory includes Federal-period mansions and townhouses; buildings designed by William Jay, the Regency-period architect who delighted in fancy scrollwork and a freehand imposition of Greek motifs; grand antebellum homes; and a whole district of Victorian homes (made of both wood and masonry). Whatever their specific style, the older buildings downtown share a formal and restrained design that makes a cohesive whole. Their colors come from a muted palette of grays, greens, and tans, and the end result is that they resonate with the geometry of Savannah's squares.

A good place to start is the **Savannah Visitor Center** (301 Martin Luther King Jr. Blvd.; www.savannahvisit.com; open daily), where you can join a tour or get an overview of the city's history.

Local people appreciate your interest and are generally welcoming, but since all but a few of the historic homes are privately owned, remember that while photographing is fine, entering gardens or climbing front stairs is not. For such closer looks, visit the house museums where well-briefed and accommodating docents can answer your questions. In addition, there are annual tours of private homes and gardens, sponsored by local preservation organizations or churches. They usually take place in March, last all day, and range in price from $15 to $40. For information, contact the **Savannah Tour of Homes and Gardens** (912-234-8054; www.savannahtourofhomes.org) or **The Garden Club of Savannah** (912-961-4805; www.gcofsavnogstour.org) about its **Annual NOGS Tour** (gardens "North of Gaston St.").

Film

(See also Theater entries below—several local venues offer both live and film events.)

Carmike Cinemas (912-353-8683; 511 Stephenson Ave.).

Regal Cinema 6 (912-352-3533; 1100 Eisenhower Dr.).

Trademark Cinema (912-355-5000; 1915 E. Victory Dr.).

Galleries

The Savannah College of Art and Design has greatly raised the profile of the city as an arts

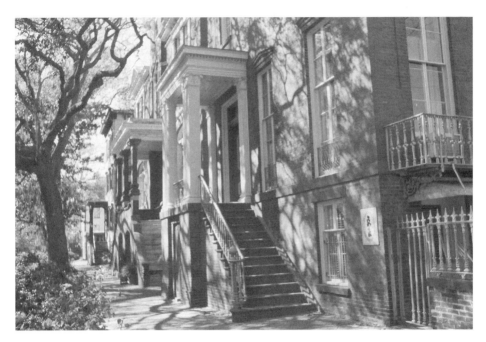

Late afternoon shadows in Savannah.

center. Frequently changing exhibitions of work are on display in college buildings throughout the city. Find schedules at www.scad.edu or call 912-525-4950. A glance at *Connect Savannah* (www.connectsavannah.com), a free weekly, will turn up undiscovered or short-run shows. Here are some places to look at art—it may or may not be for sale.

Beach Institute (912-234-8000; 502 E. Harris St.) Established in 1865 by the American Missionary Association to educate the newly freed slaves of Savannah, the Beach continues to be an African American cultural center, which features exhibits of arts and crafts. Of special interest is the collection of hand-carved wooden sculptures, including likenesses of presidents, by acclaimed folk artist and Savannah barber Ulysses Davis. Open Tuesday through Saturday 12–5. Admission is $4.

Chroma Gallery (912-232-2787; www.chromaartgallery.com; 31 Barnard St.) Contemporary art, glass, and sculpture, with new artists represented frequently. See Web site for schedule.

Desot O Row Gallery (912-236-4421; www.desotorow.com; 2427 De Soto Ave.) A non-profit gallery and performance venue for local artists, many of whom have been affiliated with the Savannah College of Art and Design.

Ellis Gallery (912-234-3537 or 1-800-752-4865; www.rayellis.com; 205 W. Congress St.) Paintings, watercolors, bronzes, and prints of golf and traditional maritime scenes by Ray Ellis, perhaps the best known of Lowcountry artists. Also, books of his work and notecards.

John Tucker Fine Arts (912-231-8161; 5 W. Charlton St.). This handsome gallery on Madison Square features several shows each year of established artists whose work sometimes reflects Southern themes.

Pei Ling Chan Garden for the Arts (322 Martin Luther King Jr. Blvd., at W. Harris St.) This walled garden, with individual sections reflecting African American, English, French, and Asian cultures, is the backdrop for sculpture exhibits. There is a small amphitheater used during theatrical productions. A nice place in the thick of downtown to have a quiet moment.

Sandfly Gallery (912-231-2300; www.sandflygallery.com; 407 Whitaker St.) Located along a stretch of design and art-oriented shops, with an emphasis on fine expressions of Lowcountry scenes, from realistic to abstract, in pottery, photographs, and paintings.

shopSCAD (912-525-5180; shopscadonline.com; 340 Bull St.) A gallery of the Savannah College of Art and Design, featuring work by students, faculty, and occasional guests each month. It has expanded into a terrific shop.

Historic Homes, Gardens & Religious Sites

A distinguishing quality of longtime Lowcountry residents is that they are, to slightly alter the words of the Rolling Stones, "practiced in the art of perception"; that is, they know how to see and how to honor, over the generations, what they see. In Savannah, this means that historic sites—be they mansions, gardens, forts, or houses of worship—are cared for in a personal way. A site is valued not just because it is important and beautiful (though they all are), but because it has given meaning to the community. Structures that could be classified as monuments are familiar touchstones. Such an attitude puts flesh on the bones of historic preservation talk.

And it's not just buildings that are treated well: Savannah's squares and cemeteries are testimonials to public beauty. Observing the years of care that have been lavished on Savannah's historic places—from effi-cient, Federal-style frame dwellings to vast Romantic Revival warehouses—is one pleasure that will come naturally to every observant visitor.

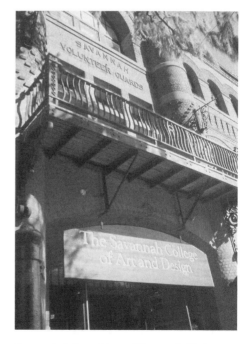

Andrew Low House

912-233-6854.
www.andrewlowhouse.com.
329 Abercorn St.
Mon. through Wed., Fri. through Sat.
10:30–4; Sun. 12–4; closed Thurs.
Admission: Adults $8; students $5.

A city house in the high style, although adapted to the rigors of Savannah's summer heat by means of jalousied rear porches. By 1849, when it was built, Savannah was in its prime: This is how the wealthy cotton merchants lived, and there is a large collection of furniture to tell their story. It was from this house that Juliette Gordon Low founded the Girl Scouts and where she died in 1927.

Savannah College of Art and Design rehabbed building.

The Gift

To His Excellency President Lincoln, Washington, D.C.: I beg to present you as a Christmas-gift the city of Savannah, with one hundred and fifty heavy guns and plenty of ammunition, also about twenty-five thousand bales of cotton.

—W. T. Sherman, Major-General. From Savannah, Dec. 22, 1864.

First African Baptist Church
912-233-6597.
23 Montgomery St.
Tours Tues. through Sat. at 11, 1, and 3.

Built in 1788 and believed to be the oldest continually active church for black worshippers in North America, and one that was built by slaves for slaves. Many original pews remain intact. It was the birthplace of the Civil Rights Movement in Savannah and a refuge on the Underground Railroad.

Green-Meldrim House
912-232-1251.
1 W. Macon St.
Tues., Thurs. through Fri. 10–3:30; Sat. 10–12:30.
Admission: Adults $7; students $3.

Used as headquarters by General W. T. Sherman during his 1864 Christmas occupation of Savannah, this Gothic Revival mansion on Madison Square was the city's most expensive house when it was built in 1850. The exterior ironwork and porches are the best example of the style in the city.

Isaiah Davenport House
912-236-8097.
www.davenportsavga.com.
324 E. State St.
Mon. through Sat. 10–4; Sun. 1–4 (last tour at 3:30).
Admission: $8.

The proposed demolition of this landmark (built circa 1820 by a master-builder from Rhode Island for his family) to salvage the brick and make way for a parking lot galvanized Savannah preservationists. That was in 1954, and the effort marked the birth of the Historic Savannah Foundation. Today it's a museum adorned with furnishings and decorative arts of the Federal period. There's a lovely garden out back and an excellent museum shop.

Juliette Gordon Low National Birthplace
912-233-4501.
10 E. Oglethorpe Ave.
Mon. through Sat. 10–4; Sun. 11–4.
Admission: Adults $8; children $7.

A Regency townhouse decorated in postbellum period style, this building commemorates the childhood of the founder of the Girl Scouts, who was born here in 1860. There's a gift shop with special things for Scouts.

King-Tisdell Cottage

912-234-8000.
www.kingtisdell.org.
514 E. Huntingdon St.
Tues. through Fri. 12–4:30; Sat. and Sun. 1–4.
Admission: Adults $3.

This charming, original Victorian cottage (circa 1896) houses a museum of the black history and culture of Savannah and the Sea Islands. Walking or driving tours on the Negro Heritage Trail, highlighting events and significant sites that pertain to black history, can be arranged in advance.

Laurel Grove—South Cemetery

912-651-6772.
At the western end of 37th St.
Daily. Tours by appointment.

The South Cemetery of Laurel Grove was dedicated in 1852 for the burial of "free persons of color" and slaves. Many of the city's most famous African Americans are buried here.

Owens-Thomas House Museum

912-233-9743.
124 Abercorn St.
Mon. 12–5; Tues. through Sat. 10–5; Sun. 1–5. Last tour at 4:30.
Admission: Adults $10; children (6–12) $4.

Designed in 1816 by Englishman William Jay and considered the best example of an urban villa in his Regency style, this house contains a collection of European and American decorative arts and has a formal garden. The Carriage House is the site of one of the few discovered slave quarters in the Historic District, and its collections offer insight into the lives of urban African American slaves.

Ralph Mark Gilbert Civil Rights Museum

912-231-8900.
460 Martin Luther King Jr. Blvd.
Mon. through Sat. 9–5.
Admission: Adults $4; children $2.

Dr. Gilbert, who died in 1956, was a leader in early efforts to gain educational, social, and political equality for African Americans in Savannah. This museum features state-of-the-art interactive exhibits focusing on the history of the Civil Rights Movement in Savannah.

Roundhouse Railroad Museum

912-651-6823.
www.chsgeorgia.org.

601 W. Harris St.
Daily 9–4.
Admission: Adults $4; students $3.50.

This National Historic Landmark is a collection of structures first built in 1838 and used as a railroad manufacturing and repair facility. Today you can see the roundhouse and turntable, a 125-foot brick smokestack, antique steam engines, diesel locomotives, and rolling stock.

Second African Baptist Church

912-233-6163.
123 Houston St.
Mon. through Fri. 10–2.

The church was established in 1802, and was the site of two historic occurrences: General W. T. Sherman's reading of the Emancipation Proclamation to the newly freed slaves and, nearly a century later, Dr. Martin Luther King's presentation of his "I Have a Dream" sermon prior to its delivery in Washington, DC.

Temple Mickve Israel

912-233-1547.
20 E. Gordon St.
Mon. through Fri. 10–12 and 2–4.

The Gothic-style synagogue was built in the 1870s, more than 100 years after the congregation was established. The museum and library house the oldest Torah in America, as well as letters, books, and historical documents.

Wormsloe Historic Site

912-353-3023.
www.gastateparks.org.
7601 Skidaway Rd., Isle of Hope.
Tues. through Sat. 9–5, Sun. 2–5:30.
Admission: Adults $4; children $2.

The tabby ruins, an avenue of oaks, and artifacts excavated from the site, are all that remain of the Colonial plantation built by Noble Jones, a physician and carpenter who came with the first settlers on the ship *Anne* and established the Georgia colony. An audio-video presentation and interpreters of Colonial life make the period vivid for visitors.

Military Museums & Sites

A strategic upriver location and an abiding sense of history that predates the American Revolution make Savannah rich in military history. The island forts and lighthouses, in particular, recall both the sense of estrangement felt by soldiers stationed there and the effort they made to create a community in an isolated setting.

Fort Jackson

912-232-3945.
www.chsgeorgia.org.
1 Fort Jackson Rd., 3 miles from downtown.

Daily 9–5.
Admission: Adults $4.25; students $3.75.

The oldest standing fort in Georgia, first established in 1809 on an earlier fortification, it was central to the Confederate network of river batteries during the Civil War. A self-guided tour takes you to military exhibits in the fort's casemates. Special military history programs enliven the fort several times each year.

Fort McAllister Historic Park

912-727-2339.
www.gastateparks.org.
3894 Fort McAllister Rd., Richmond Hill (24 miles south of Savannah on I-95).
Tues. through Sat. 9–5; Sun. 2–5.
Admission: Adults $2; children $1.

The fall of Fort McAllister, on the Ogeechee River, signaled the end of Sherman's "March to the Sea." By that time it had already outlasted other forts due to its earthen walls, which, unlike the popular masonry equivalent, could be swiftly repaired after a round of bombardment. There are self-guided tours, rangers on hand, and a good, small museum. Picnicking in the park is popular, but bring insect repellent. Biking trails and canoe/kayak rentals.

Fort Pulaski National Monument

912-786-5787.
www.nps.gov/fopu.
Cockspur Island, US 80 east, about 30 minutes from Savannah.
Daily 8:30–5; to 6:30 in summer months.
Admission: Adults $3; ages 16 and under free.

A young officer named Robert E. Lee had his first military assignment here, soon after the fort was built. It's a masterpiece of engineering, a huge and heavy brick building, surrounded by a moat, sitting on an unstable marsh. And yet during the Civil War, rifled cannons blasted holes in the masonry of such forts, and they became obsolete. Interpretive programs explain life at the fort during the Civil War, and you are free to roam its ramparts. An excellent selection of books is available at the gift shop.

Mighty Eighth Air Force Heritage Museum

912-748-8888.
www.mightyeighth.org.
175 Bourne Ave., Pooler, GA (Take I-95 exit 102 to US 80 east, then go left on Bourne Ave.).
Daily 9–5.
Admission: Adults $10; children (6–12) $6; under 6 free. Discounts for seniors and military.

Dedicated to the men and women who served in the "Mighty Eighth" (formed in Savannah in 1942) during World War II. Exhibits also track later engagements, such as Operation Desert Storm, supplemented by photos and film presentations.

Tybee Island Museum and Lighthouse/Fort Screven

912-786-5801.
www.tybeelighthouse.com.

30 Meddin Dr., Tybee Island, 18 miles east of Savannah.
Daily except Tues. 9–5:30.
Admission: Adults $6; children $5.

Located within Fort Screven, which was acquired by the federal government in 1808 and used as a post through World War II, the Museum and Lighthouse offer visitors a glimpse of life at a beach outpost over the years. The museum has an assortment of objects, Native American and Civil War weaponry, as well as illustrated newspaper accounts of the Civil War and memorabilia. A lighthouse has marked this site since 1736. Today you can climb this 19th-century version (over 150 feet tall) for a wonderful view of the river.

Museums

Oatland Island Education Center

912-898-3980.
www.oatlandisland.org.
711 Sandtown Rd.
Daily 10–4
Admission: $5.

Children will love walking the nearly 2 miles of wooded trails in this 175-acre preserve, where they can watch for animals and experience the salt marsh, forest, and wetlands habitat of the Lowcountry. Sheep, goats, ponies, and swans may cross your path; bald eagles and hawks soar overhead. There is a farmyard, too.

Savannah History Museum

912-651-6825.
www.chsgeorgia.org.

Tybee Island Lighthouse.

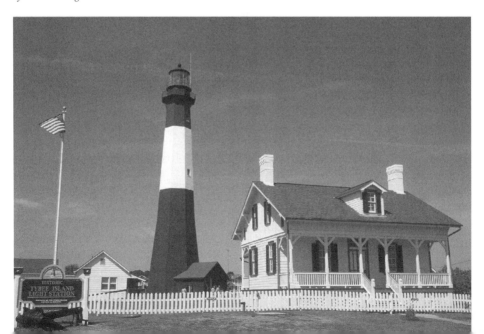

303 Martin Luther King Jr. Blvd.
Mon. through Fri. 8:30–5; Sat. and Sun. 9–5.
Admission: Adults $4; children (6–12) $3.

Audio and video presentations, displays, and objects relating to Savannah's history are housed in the old Central of Georgia railway depot train sheds, in the Visitor Center. The Black Soldier exhibit highlights the 1st South Carolina Volunteers and the 178,895 black men who fought in the Civil War.

Savannah Science Museum

912-355-6705.
4405 Paulsen St.
Tues. through Sat. 10–5; Sun. 2–5.
Admission: Adults $4.50; children $2.50.

If you are weary of house museums and want to see one of the Southeast's largest collections of amphibians and reptiles, living and dead, comprehensive collections of shells, rocks, minerals, and a wonderful pressed herbarium of indigenous plants, spend time here. There's a great planetarium, too.

Ships of the Sea Museum

912-232-1511.
www.shipsofthesea.org.
41 Martin Luther King Jr. Blvd.
Tues. through Sun. 10–5.
Admission: Adults $8; students, seniors $6.

Ship models, a magnificent dollhouse-style construction of a huge 19th-century ship, and ships-in-bottles tell the exciting story of maritime adventure, war, commerce, and exploration in the world's oceans, from the time of the Vikings forward. Located in the William Scarbrough House, a Regency jewel with a lovely garden.

Telfair Museum of Art/Jepson Center for the Arts

912-790-8800.
www.telfair.org.
121 Barnard St.
Mon. and Wed. through Sat. 10–5 (Thurs. open till 8); Sun. 12–5.
Admission: Adults $10; students $4.

Savannah's premier museum, housed in a Regency-style mansion, hosts a permanent collection of American and European Impressionist paintings, drawings, prints, and sculpture. The new building displays 20th- and 21st-century art and hosts traveling exhibitions. There's also an interactive space for kids, the ArtZeum, and a café.

University of Georgia Marine Extension Service Aquarium

912-598-2496.
30 Ocean Science Circle, Skidaway Island, 14 miles from downtown.
Mon. through Fri. 9–4; Sat. 12–5; Closed Sun.
Admission: $2.

Telfair Museum of Art.

This is a working research lab and facility, but visitors are welcome to visit the aquarium and exhibits, which depict the underwater marine and plant life of coastal Georgia. Fossils of sharks' teeth and whale skulls are prominently displayed. A self-guided visit takes about an hour. Afterward, you can picnic. From here it's but a short hop to Skidaway Island State Park (912-598-2300; see "Camping" in the **Recreation** section below) where you can walk through a maritime forest, bird-watch, and observe the teeming life of the marsh.

Music

Savannah Music Festival (912-234-3378; www.savannahmusicfestival.org) A terrific jazz, blues, classical, and world music festival that takes place for about two weeks in March and April at churches, halls, clubs, and auditoriums around the city. A mini-Spoleto that draws music aficionados from all over to the city.

Nightlife

Club One (912-232-0200; www.clubone-online.com. 1 Jefferson St.) If you're looking for Lady Chablis, who sang and carried on in the book *Midnight in the Garden of Good and Evil,* this is the spot with other performers and female impersonators nightly. Dancing on two floors.

Jazz'd (912-236-7777; www.jazzdsavannah.com; 52 Barnard St.) Located downstairs on West Broughton Street, an unlikely place for live jazz. No cover. Friday and Saturday nights, with the bonus of a tapas (small plate) bar.

Jinxed (912-236-2281; 127 W. Congress St.) Crazy punk and lots of hipsters. But some conventioneers find their way in, too.

Mercury Lounge (912-447-6954; 125 W. Congress St.) Blues and rock live, jukebox, bar, and it's open to 3 AM. Good bar food.

Planters Tavern (912-232-4286; 23 Abercorn St.) Downstairs at the Olde Pink House, a much-loved local bar with a pianist rolling through the songs we love when we're feeling sentimental and a chanteuse to match.

Theater

City Lights Theatre Company (912-234-9860; 125 E. Broughton St.) Productions in a small 75-seat theater; "Shakespeare-in-the-Park" in Washington Square in spring.

Lucas Theatre (912-525-5050; www.lucastheatre.com; 32 Abercorn St.) An old movie palace, renovated in 1998, features films, musical performances, and theatricals.

Savannah Theater Company (912-233-7764; www.savannahtheatre.com; 222 Bull St.) Seasonal productions of contemporary drama, musicals, and comedy.

SCAD's Trustees Theater (912-525-5015; www.trusteestheater.com; 206 E. Broughton St.) A former Art Deco movie house transformed by the Savannah College of Art and Design into a glittering 1,105-seat performance art hall, featuring movies, plays, and dramatic readings.

RECREATION

Baseball
The area's professional farm team is the **Savannah Sand Gnats** (912-351-9150; www.sandgnats.com; Grayson Stadium, 1401 E. Victory Dr.) When at home, they play games weeknights at 7:15 and Sundays at 3 PM. Admission is $7–$10 for adults.

Beach Access
The only beach accessible by car on Georgia's northern coast, Tybee Island lies 18 miles east of Savannah on US 80.

Ossabaw Island is a barrier island 20 miles south of Savannah and run by a nonprofit foundation. There are five campsites, and the minimum stay is two nights for groups of four or more. Transportation and fresh drinking water are available. Call 912-233-5104 for information and reservations.

Wassaw Island, located east of Savannah and Skidaway Island, can be reached by private or charter boat. It is managed by the U.S. Fish and Wildlife Service, Savannah Coastal Refuges Office (912-652-4415; www.fws.gov/wassaw; 1000 Business Center Dr., Suite 1, Savannah, GA 31405). Within its 10,000 acres, there are more than 20 miles of inland island trails and a 7-mile beach to explore.

Bird-Watching
The best spots for birding around Savannah are all part of the **Savannah National Wildlife Refuge System**, a complex of seven coastal parks that provide habitat on the beach and dunes as well as in abandoned rice fields, swamps, creeks, and estuarine systems. Explore **Tybee Island North Beach** by parking at the Tybee Island Museum (see listing above under "Military Museums & Sites" in the **Culture** section of this chapter). **Skidaway Island State Park** (912-598-2300; www.gastateparks.org; 52 Diamond Causeway, Savannah, GA 31411) is separated from the Atlantic to the east by salt marsh and to the south by Wassaw Island. This unique geography attracts a wide variety of songbirds, as well as large ospreys and bald eagles. To get there take exit 164 off I-16 west of Savannah and head south. It will become Diamond Causeway. **Harris Neck National Wildlife Refuge** (912-832-4608; www/fws.gov/harrisneck), an old World War II Army airfield, supports a large colony of wood storks and dozens of nesting wading birds. Take US 17 south to Harris Neck Rd., then travel 6.5 miles to the refuge entrance. Get a map at the Visitor Center and drive along the 4-mile Laurel Hill Wildlife Road for a good introduction to the area, which includes fresh-

water marsh, river-bottom hardwood swamp, and tidal rivers and creeks. Contact the Georgia Deptartment of Natural Resources (912-994-1438; www.dnr.state.ga.us; 116 Rum Creek Dr., Forsyth, GA 31029-6518) and ask for the pamphlet and map of Georgia's Colonial Coast Birding Trail. **Wilderness Southeast** (912-236-8115; www.wilderness southeast.org) offers all kinds of weekend birding trips near Savannah and farther afield.

Boating
Canoeing and Kayaking
If you are traveling with your own boat, access points along the Savannah River and boat landings at Isle of Hope and Skidaway Island allow you to launch into tidal creeks throughout the Savannah National Wildlife Refuge complex. For outing ideas, instruction, guided tours, maps, and expedition opportunities, **Sea Kayak Georgia** (912-786-8732 or 1-888-529-2542; www.seakayakgeorgia.com) and **Savannah Canoe and Kayak** (912-341-9502; www.savannahcanoeandkayak.com) are the experts. No experience is necessary for many trips. Trips that last three hours leave Tybee Island daily in the morning and after-noon, and longer camping expeditions are also offered. Lessons and specialized skills workshops start at $95 per person with a minimum of two participants and last three to four hours. A three-hour guided trip costs $60 per person. Daily sit-on kayak rentals cost $50 for a single, $60 for a tandem; a variety of decked models range from $60 to $130. Full-day and overnight canoe trips on the Altamaha River, including shuttle service, can also be arranged.

Alakai Outfitters (912-786-4000; 1213 US 80, Tybee Island, GA 31328).

Ogeechee Park Rentals (912-748-5996; US 80, Eden, GA).

Wilderness Southeast (912-236-8115; www.wilderness-southeast.org).

Kayak tour guide ready at the landing on Tybee Island.

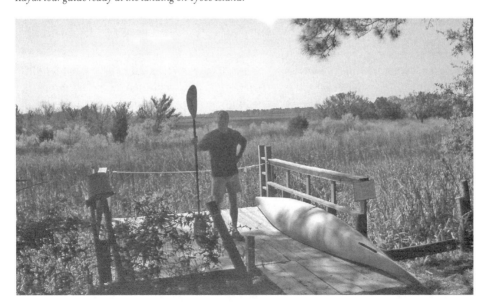

Sailing

For sailors unfamiliar with Lowcountry waters and tides, renting a sailboat or having a lesson is a good way to get acquainted with local conditions. Prices vary according to length of sail lesson or charter, and type of sail.

CompassSailing (912-441-3265; www.compasssailing.com; Bull River Marina.) Private sails for up to six people on a 38-foot Morgan 384 are $100/hour or $495 for a full seven-hour cruise.

Sail Harbor Academy (912-897-2135; 606 Wilmington Island Rd.).

Savannah Sailing Center (912-231-9996; at Lake Mayer Community Park, Montgomery Crossroad and Sallie Mood Dr.) offers lessons for $25 an hour in the calm setting of the 35-acre lake, which may be easier for a beginner to negotiate.

Bowling

AMF Bowling Lanes (912-925-0320; 115 Tibet Ave.) Open until 3 AM Monday, Friday, and Saturday.

AMF Bowling Center (912-354-5710; 2055 E. Victory Dr.).

Camping

River's End Campground and RV Park (912-786-5518 or 1-800-786-1016; www.riversendcampground.com; 915 Polk St., Tybee Island, GA 31328) 100 sites, full hookups, tent sites, and cabin rentals.

Skidaway Island State Park (912-598-2300; www.gastateparks.org; 52 Diamond Causeway, Savannah, GA 31411) A 533-acre park with 88 tent, trailer, and RV sites; laundry, pool, bathhouse, nature trail, and interpretative walks and programs.

Diving

Serious divers explore **Gray's Reef National Marine Sanctuary,** 11,000 acres of live bottom fishery (www.graysreef.noaa.gov).

Diving Locker and Ski Chalet (912-927-6603; www.divinglockerskichalet.com; 74 W. Montgomery Crossroads).

Zero Gravity Divers Depot (912-920-1155; 8602 White Bluff Rd.).

Family Fun

Island Miniature Golf (912-898-3833; www.islandminigolf.com; 7890 US 80, Whitemarsh Island) On the way to the beaches and boat landings, it includes go-karts, bumper cars, and batting cages.

Putt-Putt Golf Course (912-355-4795; www.puttputt.com; 202 Mall Blvd.) Three courses, lit for night play, open till midnight.

Fishing

The waters off Savannah provide a variety of fishing experiences. Inshore, there are fish in shallow waters and narrow creeks when the tide is right; offshore, there are bigger game fish in the Gulf Stream. Some guides specialize in the art of saltwater fly-fishing.

A good place to plan a fishing trip is at a marina, although some sporting goods stores may have recommendations (see the **Shopping** section below). Noncommercial saltwater fishing does not require a license; nonresident freshwater fishing does. Contact the Wildlife Resources Division's Savannah office (912-651-2221) for information on licenses and regulations, or talk to your guide. Licenses are available at most sporting-goods stores and bait shops.

A listing of some of the many charter boat services available follows. Most boats are fully outfitted with supplies and bait, but check in advance, especially if you have questions about bringing your favorite rod—an option for fly-fishing—or if the length of the trip requires food. Always bring sunscreen, a hat, and a windbreaker. The cost does not include gratuity for the mate(s). The 2008 prices for half-day trips (generally one to three passengers for inshore fishing, four to six for offshore fishing) started at $300. A 14-hour trip to the Gulf Stream costs about $1,200.

Bull River Marina (912-897-7300; www.bullrivermarina.com; 8005 US 80 east) Located halfway to Tybee.

Coastal River Charters (912-441-9930; www.coastalrivercharters.com) Inshore fishing and sightseeing tours of barrier islands and secluded creeks.

Lazaretto Creek Marina (912-786-5848 or 1-800-242-0166; www.tybeedolphins.com; 1 Old Hwy. 80, Tybee Island) A full-service marina offering everything from inshore trips for 6 people to Gulf Stream expeditions.

Miss Judy Charters (912-897-4921; www.missjudycharters.com; 124 Palmetto Dr., Savannah) Deep-sea fishing and trolling, Gulf Stream trips, and inshore fishing with Captain Judy Helmey.

Reel Em N (1-800-721-1240; www.reelemn.com) Up to 10 anglers fish the artificial reefs or head to the Gulf Stream.

Savannah Light Tackle Fishing Co. (912-355-32710; 1908 E. DeRenne Ave.) Fly-fishing a specialty.

Sundial Nature and Fishing Tours (912-786-9470 or 1-866-786-3283; www.sundial charters.net; 142 Pelican Dr., Tybee Island) Inshore fishing, crabbing, and net casting. Ask about the naturalist-led outings to Little Tybee and Wassaw Islands and overnight camping possibilities.

Tybee Island Charters (912-786-4801; www.fishtybee.com; P.O. Box 1762, Tybee Island) Fish inshore from a 21-foot Carolina skiff, in deeper waters aboard a 30-foot Delta Sport, or take a nature cruise.

Fitness Facilities

Coastal YMCA (912-350-5480; 6400 Habersham Pkwy.) This facility honors YMCA memberships from other parts of the country.

Downtown Athletic Club (912-236-4874; www.dacsavannah.com; 1 E. Broughton St.) A full-service health club with its own spa. Ten downtown inns and hotels offer complimentary passes.

Tybee Island YMCA (912-786-9622; 204 5th Ave. Tybee Island) A facility, open daily.

Golf

The most varied opportunities for golf exist on Hilton Head and Bluffton, about 45 minutes away depending on where you go (See Chapter Five, *Hilton Head*), but here are some local options.

Bacon Park Golf Course (912-354-2625; www.baconparkgolf.com; Shorty Cooper Dr.) Par 72. 27 holes across three layouts; 6,700 yards. Lighted driving range; putting green. Fees for 18 holes: $20–$22, plus $13–$15 cart fees.

Henderson Golf Course (912-920-4653; www.hendersongolfclub.com; 1 Henderson Dr.) Par 71. 18 holes; 6,700 yards. Five sets of tees. Lighted driving range; putting green. Fees: $39–$48. Cart included.

Savannah Inn and Country Club (912-897-1612; 612 Wilmington Island Rd.) Par 72. 18 holes; 6,876 yards. Driving range and putting green. Fees: $35–$50. Cart included.

Southbridge Golf Club (912-651-5455; www.southbridgegolf.com; 415 Southbridge Blvd.) Par 72. Rees Jones–designed 18 holes; 6,990 yards. Driving range, putting green, and a full staff of teaching pros onsite. Fees: $36–$51. Cart included.

Horseback Riding

Local stables can accommodate riders of varying skills, and it's best to call in advance to arrange lessons, trail rides, or workouts in the ring. If you can spend 50 minutes in the car, the best places to ride would be on or near Hilton Head Island, where you might arrange for a beach or country ride. Expect to pay $75 per person for 90 minutes of riding time, depending on the setting. For information on stables in the area, see www.savannahhorse .com or contact:

Norwood Stables (912-356-1387; www.norwoodstables.com; 2304 Norwood Ave.).

Hunting

As in other regions of the Lowcountry, land quarry in the Savannah area include a variety of waterfowl, turkey, and various sizes of game. Familiarize yourself with specific hunting seasons, license requirements, and bag limits by visiting an outdoor recreation store (see the **Shopping** section below) or contacting the **Game and Fish Division** of the **Georgia Department of Natural Resources** (706-557-3597; www.georgiawildlife.dnr.state.ga.us). Additional useful information can be found at www.savannah.fsw.gov, where you can download hunting and fishing brochures and permits.

Popular public hunting grounds in the greater Savannah area are located in the **Webb Wildlife Management Area** and **Palachucola Management Area** (843-625-3569; www.dnr.sc.gov), at **Turtle Island** and **Victoria Bluff** in Jasper and Beaufort Counties, and in the **Savannah National Wildlife Refuge** (912-652-4415).

Nature Preserves

Some of the most accessible, and user-friendly preserves in the Lowcountry are located within 30 minutes of Savannah. They include:

The Bamboo Farm and Coastal Gardens (912-921-5460; www.ugaextension.com; Canebrake Rd. off US 17) A 46-acre educational and research center that started more than 100 years ago when a local bamboo fancier was given three Japanese giant timber bamboo plants and cultivated them on her property. Today there are more than 100 types of plants, flowers, and trees growing here, and more than 200 species of bamboo. Open Monday through Friday 8–5, Saturday 10–5, Sunday 12–5. Free.

Harris Neck National Wildlife Refuge (912-832-4608); www.fws.gov.harrisneck; I-95 exit 67 to US 17 south, then travel approximately 1 mile to Harris Neck Rd.) The refuge entrance is 6.5 miles on the left, and signs direct you to the driving and biking trails, which wind through this 2,700-acre area of freshwater impoundments, salt marsh, forest, and field.

Pinckney Island National Wildlife Refuge (912-652-4415; www.fws.gov.pinckneyisland; US 278 at the foot of the Hilton Head bridge) A 4,053-acre complex of small islands and hammocks set in the marsh with 14 miles of trails. A good place to spend an hour walking and birding.

Savannah National Wildlife Refuge (912-652-4415); I-95 exit 5 to US 17 south; 6 miles south of Hardeeville on SC 170) The refuge consists of 25,608 acres spread across land once used for growing rice. Get a map at the Visitor Center and drive along the 5-mile Laurel Hill Wildlife road for a good introduction to an area that includes fresh water marsh, river-bottom hardwood swamp, and tidal rivers and creeks. Hiking trails (39 miles in all) are well marked, many of them following the path of the old rice dikes.

Victoria Bluff Heritage Preserve (www.dnr.sc.gov; Sawmill Creek Rd., off US 278, 3 miles from the Hilton Head bridge) This beautiful parcel of 1,000 acres on the Colleton River was long eyed for residential or industrial development, but local residents secured its protection as a passive recreation area which is open dawn to dusk daily.

Tennis
Seven city parks in and around Savannah have a total of 47 courts, and nearly all are lighted for night play. The custom at public parks is first-come, first-served. The locations are: **Bacon Park** (6262 Skidaway Rd.); **Daffin Park** (1001 E. Victory Dr.); **Forsyth Park** (Gaston St. & Drayton St.); **Lake Mayer Park** (Montgomery Crossroad & Sallie Mood Dr.); **Stell Park** (Bush Rd.); **Tybee Memorial Park** (Butler Ave.); **Wilmington Island Community Park** (Lang St. & Walthour Rd.)

SHOPPING

There's not much you can't buy in Savannah, from collard greens off a truck to a gilded armoire. There are galleries displaying the work of students from the Savannah College of Art and Design; stores with goods to dress up your house; bookstores with rare and current volumes; places to buy old prints, sea charts, and maps; and antiques stores by the dozen. In fact, antiques stores and home-furnishings stores with unusual accessories might be considered the city's specialty. The Lowcountry habit of preservation has meant that English and American antiques and accessories of an earlier day, purchased during the boom years, have remained in the old houses. Today they are trickling out to local dealers.

The region's temperate, multi-crop climate means you can buy lettuce, collards, potatoes, tomatoes, watermelons, and peaches most of the year. The man with the bags of boiled peanuts may knock at your door only in summer, but most everyone else can, and does, peddle their goods year round.

A Savannah street.

There are, too, right in the city and certainly out in the country, stores that are old and vibrant centers of community life, places of shelves that bear small quantities of many things, of dangling flypaper, squirrel nut candies, pickled eggs, moon pies, single beers, and ices. They are too modest to claim National Register status; they'll never disappear, either. Drop in for a local newspaper and a "Co' Cola."

There's particularly good strolling and shopping along Whitaker Street, Broughton Street, Abercorn Street, Wright Square, and Ellis Square. River Street is the most honky-tonk and touristy. Parking downtown can be difficult. Make use of Municipal Parking garages at City Market and Bryan Street (at Abercorn). Discount parking passes are sold at the Visitor Center, at the Bryan Street garage, and at several hotels and inns. Get an overview at www.welcome-to-savannah.com.

Antebellum Artifacts

Blatner's (912-234-1210; 347 Abercorn St.) Civil War–era military items, old bottles, glassware, and silver.

Cobblestone Lane Antiques (912-447-0504; www.cobblestone-lane-savannah.com; 230 W. Bay St.) A 10,000-square-foot restored warehouse facing the Savannah River that hosts 20 dealers and is chockablock with relics and more.

Pinch of the Past (912-232-5563; www.pinchofthepast.com; 2603 Whitaker St. at 43rd St.) Architectural fragments and vintage house parts, including antique ironwork, doorframes, columns, mantels, lighting fixtures, and hardware.

Antiques

There are antiques of probably every period and style in the city—or a dealer will find you what you want. Whether you live in a sleek, minimalist apartment or a farmhouse, you're likely to find a piece that works. A man was quoted in the paper as saying: "We love old things. It makes life easier because you don't have to like the new ones."

Alex Raskin Antiques (912-232-8205; 441 Bull St.) If the setting in the Noble-Hardee mansion on Monterey Square isn't enough to get your attention, then the inventory will. Among the big, older antiques vendors, it's a little more laid back, in that the furniture, rugs, paintings, and light fixtures simply overflow the space.

Arthur Smith Antiques (912-236-9701; 402 Bull St.) Four floors of rooms filled with antique tables, rugs, armoires, beds, and side pieces. It helps to know what you want.

Attic Antiques (912-236-4879; 224 W. Bay St.) Next door to the antiques mall at Cobblestone Lane (see above). Come here for browsing fun or if you collect very specific small items: fountain pens, buttons, advertising materials, etc.

E Storia (912-443-0202; 5 W. York St.) Art, divans, tea sets, and textiles—even old cameras.

Francis McNairy Antiques (912-232-6411; 411 Abercorn St.) Fine antiques, many of Southern origin, and many small pieces. The shop is on an intimate scale; even if you don't buy one item, you can educate yourself here.

J. D. Weed & Company (912-233-0997; www.jdweedco.com; 102 Victory Dr. West) An area native who knows just what American antiques furnished the old houses, from tea caddies and document boxes to dining tables and sideboards.

Limehouse Plantation (912-232-7212; 124 E. Jones St.) European and 20th-century American furnishings with a good selection of iron and garden ornaments and accessories. Sometimes you find nice old fabric.

Simply Silver (912-238-3652; 236 Bull St.) Most interesting is an ever-changing inventory of flatware to fill in the pieces you've lost, as well as small gift items: baby cups, fruit knives, mirrors, and frames.

V. & J. Duncan (912-232-0338; 12 E. Taylor St.) You could browse through the files and piles of prints, maps, old advertising art, and illustrations here for hours. A comprehensive, well-organized collection of fine antique material.

Books

Savannah has an unusual number of little bookstores, many specializing in certain areas. Don't overlook the small ones.

Barnes & Noble (912-353-7757; 7804 Abercorn St.) As you would expect from a mall store a thorough inventory of Savannah books and many coffee-table size volumes on architecture and related subjects.

"The Book" Gift Shop (912-233-3867; www.midnightinsavannah.com; 127 E. Gordon St.) Headquarters for *Midnight in the Garden of Good and Evil* fans, the base for tours, a mini-museum of the book that changed Savannah.

Book Lady (912-233-3628; 6 E. Liberty St.) Used and antique volumes, a longtime city business.

E. Shaver Booksellers (912-234-7257; 326 Bull St.) Right downtown and great for browsing. If some topic of Lowcountry history has captured your interest, the owners will track it down, new or used. Rooms of new and rare books, history, fiction, children's section, and excellent art books.

Ex Libris (912-525-7550; 228 Martin Luther King Jr. Blvd.) This three-story bookstore provides course books and supplies for students at the Savannah College of Art and Design, and it is also full of treasures for the avid reader. Also, art supplies and a nice café.

Clothing

There is preppy and retro fashion in Savannah, but it's still the South, after all, and there are plenty of small-scale dress shops (selling more dresses these days) that are thriving and up-to-date in their sensibility. Men's styles tend toward the casual and outdoorsy, given the weather.

Gaucho (912-232-7414; 250 Bull St. and 18 E. Broughton St.) Jewelry, leather, flowing scarves, and both rustic and romantic clothes for women, including lines from Eileen Fisher and many from new, smart designers.

Hilton Decker/Nickie Grace (912-236-6632; 11–15 W. York St.) Very up-to-date, European-styled clothes for men and women, from the little black dress to silk and linen suits.

Jezebel (912-236-4333; 25 E. River St.) Light-hearted and good-looking dresses, casual wear for women.

Kathi Rich (912-236-7424; www.kathirich.com; 2515 Abercorn St.) Very hip clothes by young designers, for women.

Terra Cotta (912-236-6150; 34 Barnard St.) Elegant, soft cottons for the bed and bath; also simply cut, stylish casual wear.

Crafts/Galleries

If you'd like to see local artists at work, drop by the City Market Art Center, a downtown art colony located upstairs (there's elevator access) at 308 and 309 W. Saint Julian St., www.savannahcitymarket.com. Other galleries worth checking out include:

Atelier Galerie (912-233-3140; www.agsavannah.com; 150 Abercorn St.) Hand-crafted jewelry by local, regional, and international artisans.

Bull St. Station (912-236-4344; www.bullst.com; 151 Bull St.) Model-railroad supplies and other accessories, kits, and tools for hobbyists of all kinds.

Friedman's Fine Art (912-234-1322; www.friedmansfineart.com; 28 W. State St.) A collection of the region's best representational artists is on exhibit here, including young, emerging, and collectible talents, but there's also fine-art framing and a large selection of antique botanical and maritime prints for sale.

Gallery 209 (912-236-4583; 209 E. River St.; www.gallery209.com.) Thirty of the region's finest artists and craftsmen show here. Their works include batik, fiber, glass, pottery, wood, paintings, and sculpture, displayed in a 19th-century cotton warehouse.

Village Craftsmen (912-236-7280; www.thevillagecraftsmen.com; 223 W. River St.) Original arts and crafts are still being created by members of this 25-year-old co-op gallery. You'll see jewelry, books, quilts, decorative painting, and more.

Walsh Mountain Ironworks (912-239-9818; 59 Wilton Lane) Specializing in locally crafted furnishings for the garden and patio, as well as functional pieces for the kitchen that blend well with both modern and antique décors.

Gifts

Cottage Shop (912-233-3820; 2422 Abercorn St.) Linens for bed and table, stationery, lamps, and crystal. The shop recently celebrated its 60th birthday: At a time of malls and chains, it may be a throwback, but it's a very gracious one.

Davenport House Museum Shop (912-236-8097; 324 E. State St.) Gifts with a Savannah theme and a Lowcountry flavor in the first house restored by the Historic Savannah Foundation.

Owens-Thomas House Museum Shop (912-233-8252; 124 Abercorn St.) A superior gift shop in a recently renovated ground-floor space with a great selection of art and architecture books, travel books, small clothing items, and prints.

Paris Market & Brocante (912-232-1500; www.the parismarket.com; 36 W. Broughton St.) Here is boutique shopping—linens, stationery, vintage posters, odd antique mirrors and garden decorations—in one of the best Savannah commercial restorations. Worth it just to browse, even if all you buy is French milled soap.

Gourmet Food

Café Mucha (912-447-0636; 202 E. Broughton St.) Gourmet coffee, bakery, a large wine selection, and gifts for the kitchen.

Hunter Horn Plantation Co. Store (912-355-1812; 7202 White Bluff Rd.) The store specializes in spiral-sliced, honey-glazed hams, but also carries baked chickens for take-out (the best in the city), and sells many varieties of salads and other deli items by the pound.

Parker's Market (912-233-1000; www.parkersav.com; 222 Drayton St.) A hip rehab downtown meets the challenge: how to take a 1930s filling station and point it in the direction of highest and best use (cool gourmet supermarket), not gasoline convenience store (but the company has those, too). Win-win. Open 24 hours, with wines and microbrews, fresh herbs and flowers, cookies and pastries baked daily, and a variety of picnic meals and take out. The corporate Web site is kind of hilarious, explaining this unlikely concept.

The Paula Deen Store (912-232-1607; www.pauladeen.com; 108 W. Congress St.) A storefront devoted to the culture and culinary empire of the Deens, including signed books and gift baskets that can be sent from Savannah.

Home Furnishings/Kitchenware

Two sections of the city have emerged as centers of home furnishing/decoration. One is the **Downtown Design District** (www.downtowndesigndistrict.com), located on Whitaker Street between Charleton and Gordon Streets, and the other is the **Starland Design District,** just south of downtown between 37th and 41st Streets, from Whitaker to Habersham. The furnishings can be sleek and modern, hand-painted, antique, or really rustic.

Arcanum (912-236-6000; 405 Whitaker St.) The designers here have a way of mixing the old with the contemporary.

Kitchens on the Square (912-236-0100; www.kitchensonthe square.com; 38 Barnard St.).

One Fish Two Fish (912-447-4600; www.onefisttwofishsavannah.com; 401 Whitaker St.) Painted chairs, benches, floor cloths, and little household accents, mixed with antiques and elegant objects.

Sporting Goods and Clothing

Most of the following stores not only have athletic equipment and accessories for sale, but they rent equipment, too. Call ahead to reserve them in advance of your stay. For bikes, you are in a hill-free land: Ask about rails-to-trails pathways to Tybee and the forts.

Bicycle Link (912-233-9401; www.bicyclelinksav.com; 408 Martin Luther King Jr. Blvd.).

Fleet Feet Sports (912-355-3527; www.fleetfeetsavannah.com; 3405 Waters Ave.).

Half Moon Outfitters (912-201-9393; www.halfmoonoutfitters.com; 15 E. Broughton St.).

Thompson's Sports Shop (912-920-0977; 8110 White Bluff Rd.

Historic cast-iron catwalks connect commercial downtown to warehouses on the Savannah River bluff. Some of them still serve as offices for cotton factories and shipping brokers. Peter Loftus

Cherry laurel and other native trees compete for sunlight with the live oaks. Peter Loftus

4

Beaufort, Edisto & Bluffton

Sea Island Gems

> A place that ever was lived in is like a fire that never goes out. It flares up, it smolders for a time, it is fanned or smothered by circumstance, but its being is intact, forever fluttering within it, the result of some original ignition. Sometimes it gives out glory, sometimes its little light must be sought out to be seen, small and tender as a candle flame, but as certain.
>
> —Eudora Welty, 1944
> (*The Eye of the Story: Selected Essays and Reviews.* Viking International, 1990)

The fields, creeks, sandy roads, and spreading marshes of the rural Lowcountry, the place where Lowcountry history began, have once again become its center of attention. All along the coast, from Charleston to Savannah, there is an increasing awareness of what the culture of the countryside, expressed in a lifetime of habits and rituals, has meant to the two great cities that bookend the region and present themselves like magnificent finished products.

Perhaps the shift in emphasis from urban to rural is simply nostalgic, spurred on by a wishful return to the basics. Perhaps it has come because coastal development is accelerating. Typical Lowcountry spaces—fields rimmed by live oaks and stands of pine—are no longer simply evocative "open space": They are potential building sites. Or maybe the mood has shifted because another shape has emerged from what was a familiar picture—like in those clever drawings, where it is sometimes the vase that appears before your eyes, and then it is the facing profiles.

The Lowcountry's alternative view, the rural view, can be seen most clearly in the areas around Beaufort—Lady's Island, St. Helena Island, and Port Royal—on Edisto Island, and in the little village of Bluffton. Before the Civil War they were as imposing, in their own small incarnations, as Charleston and Savannah: They boasted luxurious houses, profitable plantations, hundreds of slaves. Planters sent their children to be educated abroad. But all that changed one day, the day in 1861 that Federal troops arrived to occupy the Sea Islands. All at once, these self-satisfied and self-conscious towns receded from the foreground view into the rural background.

Revolutionary-era houses were generally smaller than those built later, and characterized by graceful details.
Peter Loftus

It took years for them to recover, but recover they have. Furthermore, they seem to have done so with a unique sense of the importance of celebrating both views of themselves—the part of them that was prosperous, worldly, and city-like, and the part of them that struggled for decades to make do with the essentials. It comes as no surprise that they are places where vistas, boughs, and fields are valued as much as brickwork, eaves, and intersections.

Today, rather than rely simply on one picture of themselves, these places celebrate the less apparent patterns in their composition: the landscape of "vernacular" homes of farmers and fishermen; the old market roads; the remains of a wharf; the praise houses and plantation neighborhoods; the plantation cemeteries; the creek landings and fishing holes; the "rabbit-box" stores and packing houses. The appreciation of what's plain has brought a proud recognition of how resourceful country people were.

To a visitor, this means that there is more to seek out and understand, and many more chances to do so. The most mundane memories and the most idealized ones are spilling forth from the vault of the past. Their blending is what gives the Lowcountry its dramatic, cohesive sense of place, a sense that is felt especially (if it is not immediately seen) in the rural Sea Islands.

Beaufort

Beaufort has been a small town for a long time. Spanish and French explorers came to the area 100 years before the Pilgrims landed at Plymouth Rock; they were followed, in due course, by English and Scottish settlers. The city of Beaufort is itself on Port Royal Island, one of the 65 islands that make up Beaufort County. It is the county seat. Other islands include St. Helena, Lady's, Fripp, Hilton Head, Daufuskie, Cat, Harbor, Hunting, Coosaw, Dataw, Polowana, Parris, Cane, Bray's, Lemon, and Pinckney.

Formally founded in 1711, Beaufort was a frontier settlement and trading center, attacked at times by Yemassee Indians, beset with illness, and populated by the scrupulous and unscrupulous, who made the best of the resources they had. The resources were plentiful: Beaufort's outlying lands sustained dense forests, which gave up shipbuilding timber and naval stores; vast tracts of land, suitable for raising cattle and crops like corn, potatoes, indigo, rice, and cotton; and rich marshes to feed fowl and game. The maze of waterways provided fish and shellfish in abundance.

Over time, investors spotted Beaufort and staked their claims. Settlers drifted in from Charleston and Savannah, a parish system of governance was established, and, by the time of the Revolution, Beaufort was bustling. The real boom came immediately after the war. The stability of the newly independent country, the increase in population (both slave and free), the southward migration of New England merchants and families, and, perhaps above all, the successful cultivation of highly prized long-staple Sea Island cotton and the development of the cotton gin near Savannah lit the fuse. An explosion of wealth launched Beaufort's heyday. It was a time of building houses and churches in town and developing cotton plantations and plantation households on the islands.

A visitor can see the legacies of this period throughout Beaufort. They include Palladian-inspired doorways and windows, and huge, pillared porches; ornate Adam-style carved moldings and delicately scaled gardens; churchyards filled with camellias and azalea, and towered over by steeples. Standing in Beaufort's Waterfront Park, newly renovated in 2007, it is easy to imagine a 19th-century scene come to life as dozens of schooners, bateaux, and cottonbox barges, brimming with crops, timber, mail, cotton bales, animals, passengers, produce, and the latest in English fashion and furniture, load or unload goods. There was a lot of activity, for like other societies made newly rich, Beaufort's had a taste for luxury, and indulged it.

That changed abruptly. In another time and place, the shelling of a Federal fort (in this case Fort Sumter) not far away, and the Federal response to it, might have produced a shred of hesitation as to the wisdom of the Secessionist rebellion. Not so in Beaufort: With great surprise on November 7, 1861, white residents took flight—leaving hot food on the table, the story goes—from Yankee troops who had just demolished the Confederate port defenses at Bay Point.

Thus the occupation began. Soon the grand old houses were being used as hospitals and headquarters. The area was under military command. Pickets were posted at the outskirts

---

There is something very sad about these fine deserted houses. Ours has Egyptian marble mantels, gilt cornice and centre-piece in parlor, and bath-room, with several wash-bowls set in different rooms. The force-pump is broken and all the bowls and their marble slabs smashed to get out the plated cocks.... Bureaus, commodes, and wardrobes are smashed in, as well as door panels, to get out the contents of the drawers and lockers, which I suppose contained some wine and ale, judging by the broken bottles lying about. The officers saved a good many pianos and other furniture and stored it in the jail for safe-keeping. But we kindle our fires with chips of polished mahogany, and I am writing on my knee with a piece of flower-stand across them for a table, sitting on my camp bedstead.

—Edward S. Philbrick to his wife in Brookline, MA,
Beaufort, March 9, 1862 (*from Letters From Port Royal 1862–1868*,
ed. Elizabeth Ware Pearson. Arno Press, 1969)

of town and along creeks and boat landings: Some on guard duty watched the smoke of rebel campfires across the water. Plantations were turned over to regiments who appropriated the cows, the liquor, the furniture, the wagons, and the food crops.

By April 1862, the first wave of Northern abolitionists had arrived with a mandate to live in and manage the plantations and teach the former slaves to read and write: essentially to "prepare them for freedom." Their enterprise, which was funded by private missionary societies in the North and carried out with the approval of the federal government, came to be called the Port Royal Experiment. In a sense this was an old-time Peace Corps, in which idealistic, mostly young, men and

In late February, jonquils, narcissi and camellias are plentiful. Peter Loftus

women volunteered to assist a cause they believed in under conditions of definite hardship. Their efforts had an impact on lives of freedmen that resonates today, in particular at Penn Center on St. Helena Island, still an important institution for education and empowerment.

In the years following the Civil War, promises made were usually promises broken. Some former slaves were given land; some bought tracts communally; some worked the old fields under a new owner. A nascent phosphate mining industry provided jobs for a while, but it eventually collapsed. The terrible hurricane of 1893, in which some 5,000 islanders died, soured Sea Island soil for fine cotton plants. The scourge of boll weevil in the 1920s dimmed the last hope of large-scale cotton production. For most people, living returned to subsistence-level farming and fishing. Photographs from the early 1900s and those taken even as late as 1936 by employees of the Farm Security Administration—Walker Evans and Marion Post Wolcott among them—showed islanders dressed in rags and living in shacks with matted palmetto fronds for roofs. In 1969, Beaufort County was still one of the poorest counties in the United States, the focus of a Hunger Tour by several U.S. Senators. In town, these were the years of unpaved roads and bare feet, when white people were "too poor to paint, too proud to whitewash."

As in many other parts of the South, it took the American entry into World War II to improve the economy. The United States Marines had been a presence in Beaufort since the turn of the century, and at this point their role was expanded. While not exactly prosperous, Beaufort now benefited from slow, steady growth. Commercial farming of tomatoes and other vegetables, and seafood processing, became healthy industries. By the late -1960s, with the development of resort islands like Hilton Head and Fripp, and with the first wave of retirees flocking to its shores, Beaufort's economic future was assured.

It is hard to believe that today's downtown Beaufort ever suffered reverses. The paint doesn't dare peel. It has become a destination for tourists, a second home to many, and a first home for young families who are looking for a charming small town in which to raise their children. It has been turning up on "Best Small Town" lists for years. It has even become a character in Hollywood movies: Two of native son Pat Conroy's novels have been filmed here, *The Great Santini* and *The Prince of Tides*, as well as *The Big Chill*, *Forces of Nature*, *White Squall*, and *Daughters of the Dust*. Parts of *Forrest Gump*, *Something to Talk*

Plantation houses faced their garden; shell roads led to the water.   Peter Loftus

About, and *The Jungle Book* were shot here, too. Ron and Natalie Daise's acclaimed television series for children, *Gullah Gullah Island*, was set in Beaufort and its environs, and featured many local residents in its cast.

It will take a lot more than Hollywood to turn Beaufort's head. The problems associated with regional planning and zoning, improved education, traffic and water service, land preservation, and economic development seem pressing here, as they do on the other Sea Islands. Having spent the better part of the 20th century becoming what it is today, Beaufort, it turns out, is still a work in progress.

GETTING THERE

Beaufort is 65 miles from Charleston, 45 miles from Savannah, and 30 miles from Hilton Head, and each of those locations has an airport. The easiest route by air is via the **Savannah/Hilton Head International Airport** (www.savannahairport.com), which is served by **AirTran, Continental Express, Delta, Northwest, United Express,** and **US Airways,** and all major car rental agencies. From Charleston, access Beaufort from US 17 to US 21; from Savannah (and other points north and south) via well-marked exits on I-95; from Hilton Head, via US 278 to SC 170. **Amtrak** (1-800-872-7245; www.amtrak.org) passes through Yemassee, about 30 miles north of Beaufort. One northbound and one southbound train stop each day. For cab transportation to Beaufort, contact **Yellow Cab** (843- 379-3737;), **Beaufort Cab** (843-524-4940), **Maude's Cab** (843-524-9096), and **AC Limousine** (843-986-8738). Rates are about $50, and it's best to schedule in advance. **Greyhound** (1-800-231-2222) stops in Beaufort eight times a day. Rental cars are available in Beaufort. For more detailed information, see Chapter Six, *Information*.

LODGING

The WPA Guide, *South Carolina, A Guide to the Palmetto State,* first published in 1941, indicates the presence of three hotels in Beaufort, and a number of "tourist homes" where guests could stay. Then as now, the preferred season was spring, although beginning in the 1920s, there was an informal "winter colony" of artists, playwrights, and others who liked the laid-back town. Many returned every year for an extended stay in rooms at "Tidalholm," an elegant antebellum house in the neighborhood known as "The Point."

In those days, the comings and goings of visitors were duly reported in the local paper—perhaps an indication of what made news in this sleepy town. Other seasonal arrivals included sportsmen from the north who hunted and fished in several vast private preserves, which by the 1940s claimed up to one-third of the acreage in Beaufort County.

Today, the visitor in the next room might be a painter or a fly-fisherman, a movie director scouting locations, or a honeymooning couple. It's unlikely the newspaper will pay any attention at all. There are luxury inns and several topnotch B&Bs to choose from—quite a selection for a small town—but do ask ahead about their policies regarding children as guests and their cancellation policies, which are as strict as those in the Charleston and Savannah. Smoking is generally permitted on outside porches. Wireless Internet connections are usually available. If you are visiting for a week or more, you might want to compare rates by checking the Web site www.vrbo .com which lists homes and villas for rent by owner. Be aware of exaggeration, particularly in distances to the nearest market, or to Beaufort, if the property is located on Harbor or Fripp Islands. There are bargains in these listings, though. By 2009, a new, modern inn should be ready for occupancy, promising a design sensitive to the look and scale of its historic site. The best way to keep abreast of opportunities for visitors is the Chamber of Commerce Web site: www .beaufortsc.org.

Rates

Inexpensive	Up to $80
Moderate	$80 to $140
Expensive	$140 to $200
Very Expensive	$200 and up

These rates do not include room taxes or special service charges that might apply during your stay.

Credit Cards

AE—American Express
CB—Carte Blanche
D—Discover Card
DC—Diner's Club
MC—MasterCard
V—Visa

Beaufort Inn

843-379-4667 or 1-888-522-0250.
www.beaufortinn.com.
809 Port Republic St., Beaufort, SC 29901-1257.
Price: Expensive to Very Expensive.
Credit Cards: AE, D, MC, V.
Handicap Access: Yes; full ramp, some rooms.

Trimmed in vines, and rimmed with trees and flowering shrubbery, this Victorian clapboard building with jutting bays and porches owns its busy corner. There's nothing but luxury inside, including an elevator (one of a handful in Beaufort), long hallways covered in plush carpet, chandeliers, and a vivid decorating style characterized by antiques, patterned wallpapers, draperies and soft curtains, and carefully hidden modern amenities. There are several adjoining cottages with suites; or you may rent the cottage. A new loft space increases your options. A good choice for a family or larger groups.

Beaulieu House at Cat Island and Port Royal
843-770-0303 or 1-866-814-7833.
www.beaulieuhouse.com.
3 Sheffield Court, at Island and 1103 Paris
Ave., Port Royal, SC, 29901.
Price: Expensive.
Credit Cards: All major.
Handicap Access: One room.

Vibrant Caribbean pinks and greens distin-
guish these small properties, which include
a renovated home on the main street of the
village of Port Royal, and a compound
including a main house and two cottages on
Cat Island, about a five-minute drive from
Beaufort. The Port Royal location has three
suites, and the house is within walking distance of three restaurants, cafés, and riverfront access on a public beach and fishing
pier. On Cat Island, you're next to South
Carolina National Golf Club.

Craven Street Inn
843-522-1668 or 1-888-522-0250.
1103 Craven St., Beaufort, SC 29902.
Price: Expensive.
Credit Cards: AE, MC, V.

Located right downtown, this inn offers
10 rooms, some with working fireplaces,
in the main house; a carriage house wing;
and a cottage (two of the rooms share a
private porch overlooking a garden). The
style is simple, the colors are pale and
pastel, and whether you're in the main
house or not, there are private entrances
for each room. The cottage has a living
room, kitchen, and queen-sized bed, and
is a good choice for a couple taking a long
weekend off or traveling with one or two
small children.

Cuthbert House Inn
843-521-1315 or 1-800-327-9275.
www.cuthberthouseinn.com.
1203 Bay St., Beaufort, SC 29902.
Price: Expensive to Very Expensive.
Credit Cards: AE, D, MC, V.

Handicap Access: One room.

The Cuthbert House has seen its share of
excitement, and its architecture tells the
tale. It was moved from its original site in
1810, embellished with fine Federal-period
woodcarving, served as headquarters of
Union General Rufus Saxton during the
Federal blockade and then enlarged with
Victorian additions (sun porches and bays).
Guest rooms (eight in all) include two one-
bedroom suites on the ground level (one is
wheelchair accessible) and parlor suites. Its
great site on the Beaufort River bluff makes
the full Southern breakfast, afternoon tea,
evening coffee, or simply lounging, a pleasure. Loaner bicycles are available for touring downtown.

North Street Inn
843-986-1126.
www.northstreetinn.com.
1411 North St., Beaufort, SC 29902.
Price: Moderate to Expensive.
Credit Cards: MC, V.

Three guest rooms in a restored 1910
Queen Anne home located a block from the
Beaufort River in the Historic District.
Queen beds with private baths, and a full
gourmet breakfast.

Old Point Inn
843-524-3177.
www.oldpointinn.com.
212 New St., Beaufort, SC 29902.
Price: Moderate to Expensive.
Credit Cards: AE, MC, V.

There are five guest rooms in this thoroughly renovated turn-of-the-century
Victorian, furnished with unique furniture
and artifacts collected by the owners from
years of living abroad. If you sit on the
upstairs porch, you will feel embowered,
lofted in the treetops, and very much a resident of Beaufort's "Point," one of its
Historic District neighborhoods. Each

room has a private bath and cable television; full breakfast is included. The innkeepers will arrange kayaking and golf outings, carriage tours, and they hope you'll use their bicycles to explore for yourself.

Rhett House Inn
843-524-9030 or 1-888-480-9530.
www.rhetthouseinn.com.
1009 Craven St., Beaufort, SC 29902.
Price: Expensive to Very Expensive.
Credit Cards: AE, D, MC, V.
Handicap Access: Two rooms.

This inn is the gold standard in the category. The owners left their careers in New York's fashion business to come to Beaufort, but they brought their taste and a meticulous attention to detail. They've lavished it on their ten-room inn and seven-room annex. The inn, circa 1820, is full of sunlight and breezes (only steps from the waterfront), furnished with antiques and comfortable chairs, prints, and vases of fresh flowers, flanked in the back by a garden and on the side by a courtyard fountain. Many of the rooms have fireplaces or Jacuzzi tubs; all have private baths and color televisions with cable service. The porches, upstairs and downstairs, are dreamy places to have afternoon cookies and tea, or read and rest. The rooms in the annex have private porches and entrances, minibars, and six have gas fireplaces. Full breakfast, including homemade breads and muffins, is included, and picnic baskets can be made up.

Sea Island Inn
(Best Western).
843-522-2090 or 1-800-528-1234.
1015 Bay St., Beaufort, SC 29902.
Price: Moderate.
Credit Cards: AE, CB, D, DC, MC, V.

Conveniently located on Beaufort's main street, the locally owned and operated 43-unit motel has a pool, exercise room, and outdoor patio tables. Continental breakfast is served in the lobby.

Two Suns Inn
843-522-1122 or 1-800-532-4244.
www.twosunsinn.com.
1705 Bay St., Beaufort, SC 29902.
Price: Moderate to Expensive.
Credit Cards: AE, D, DC, MC, V.
Handicap Access: One room.

Facing the Beaufort River at one of its prettiest points, just as it turns the bend and heads away from town, this former residence—now a six-room inn—dates from 1917. The room's décor reflects Victorian, Oriental, and country themes. Rates include a full breakfast.

National chain motels are well represented in Beaufort. A list of some of them follows. It's a good idea to make reservations in advance, for they are often booked by family members of the graduating classes (many each year) of "boot camp" recruits from the Parris Island Marine Corps Recruit Depot.

Best Inn (843-524-3322; 2448 Boundary St., Beaufort).

Comfort Inn (843-521-1555; 2227 Boundary St., Beaufort).

Days Inn (843-524-1551; 1660 Ribaut Rd., Beaufort).

Hampton Inn (843-986-0600; 2342 Boundary St., Beaufort).

Hilton Garden Inn (843-379-9800; 1500 Queen St., Beaufort).

Farther Afield in the Beaufort Area
Dataw Island (843-838-3838 or 1-800-848-3838; www.discoverdataw.com; One Club Rd., Dataw Island, SC 29920) Dataw is a private, 870-acre residential community with all the expected amenities, about 20 minutes from Beaufort on the way to the

beaches. It has limited accommodations, *but if you are interested in viewing sales property (homesites or homes)* you may call to make arrangements for an overnight or weekend stay.

Fripp Island Resort (843-838- 2131 or 1-800-845-4100; www.frippislandresort .com; One Tarpon Blvd., Fripp Island, SC 29920) Fripp is a private, 3,000-acre island bordered by an ocean beach about 35 minutes by car from downtown Beaufort. It's a low-key residential community with several golf courses, tennis facilities, biking trails, pools, informal restaurants, and marina. Activity programs in the summer keep children busy. Rental properties are rated in four categories, from deluxe on down, and vary in price from single family homes to townhouse units, in locations on the ocean, marsh, and internal sites. Weekly rates in the summer range from $1,700 to $5,000. Rentals through the resort enable renters to use resort facilities. If you rent properties privately, your access to resort amenities may be limited.

Harbor Island Rentals (843-838- 3535 or 1-800-553-0251; www.harborislandsc .com; 2123-B Sea Island Pkwy., Harbor Island, SC 29920) Harbor Island is a small private community with pool, tennis courts, and 3-mile beach. It has grown dramatically in the last several years: Oceanfront homes start at $3,000 for a week in summer; homes with a view of the marsh or creek from $1,850.

Palm Key (843-726- 6524 or 1-866-725-6539; www.palmkey.com; 330 Coosaw Way, Ridgeland, SC 29936) The idea at Palm Key is to enjoy the outdoor, non-oceanfront life of the Lowcountry—crabbing, fishing, kayaking, hiking, fossil-hunting, bird-watching—by slowing down and taking notice, either with a guide or on your own. No television or telephones; attractive, fully equipped cottages from $150 to $600 per night. Families welcome; pets a possibility.

DINING

As Beaufort and the Sea Islands have become popular destinations, restaurants have become more adventurous in tweaking the favorite dishes of a small town for a new audience. Thus, there will be grits and tiny creek shrimp fixed in many ways—with a spicy tasso sauce, with cheese, in soufflés, or served beside fried eggs. The same goes for greens (mustard, collard, kale, and dandelion), crops which are available fresh nearly all year long, and crab, which appears in soft shell in April, or hard shell, in soups and salads, as a stuffing or a sauce. Tomatoes are a prominent cash crop in late spring and early summer, and are widely featured at that time. (The Sea Islands have a "window" for selling tomatoes on the national market for about three weeks in May, when migrant workers and local people harvest the fields and work in the packing houses well into the night.)

Many other local dishes flourish from late March through May, before the relentless summer heat warms up the creeks and dries out the soil. These include shad roe from the Edisto River, strawberries and blueberries, kiwi fruit, and oysters. Game birds, such as dove and marsh hen, and venison, are cooler weather treats.

If you find something you especially like, look for the recipe in *Sea Island Seasons*, a cookbook published by the Beaufort County Open Land Trust, a local nonprofit land preservation group. It is available in stores, or by contacting the Trust (P.O. Box 75, Beaufort, SC 29902). Within its covers you'll find out how to make such Lowcountry specialties as Frogmore Stew (sausage, corn-on-the-cob, potatoes, and shrimp in broth); shrimp paste (a spread that retains the delicate, sweet flavor of fresh shrimp); bread-and-butter pickles; and lemon chess pie (the secret ingredient is cornmeal).

The following selections are among the better-known Beaufort restaurants; but don't neglect the smaller spots (listed below under "Cafés/Coffee Bars" and "Delis and Faster Food"), where a modest job can be done extremely well.

Dining Price Code

Inexpensive	Up to $10
Moderate	$10 to $30
Expensive	$30 to $50
Very Expensive	$50 or more

Credit Cards

AE—American Express
CB—Carte Blanche
D—Discover Card
DC—Diner's Club
MC—MasterCard
V—Visa

Bateaux

843-379-0777.
www.bateauxrestaurant.net.
610 Paris Ave., Port Royal.
Closed: Sun.
Price: Expensive to Very Expensive.
Cuisine: American.
Serving: D.
Credit Cards: All major.
Reservations highly recommended.

A stunning renovation of the brick customs house at the foot of Paris Avenue in the village of Port Royal is the setting for Bateaux, which many local people choose as Beaufort's best restaurant. The open kitchen is upstairs, and dining rooms on both floors give a feeling of relaxed sophistication. The evening light is particularly beautiful. There's an authentic commitment to using locally grown vegetables and a great variety of salad greens, which has invigorated the area's organic farmers, and you can count on fresh-caught seafood and local poultry, too. In the spirit of showcasing what's fresh, the

Local produce, St. Helena Island.

menu has an extensive selection of small plates and starters ($6–$12) that can form a meal. Entrées include steak, tuna, duck, and pork. A seafood paella, rather than a stew, uses local fish in a original way.

Breakwater

843-379-0052.
www.breakwater-restaurant.com.
205 West St.
Open: Thurs., Fri., Sat.
Price: Moderate to Expensive.
Cuisine: American.
Serving: D.
Credit Cards: MC, V.

Executive chefs Gary Lang and Elizabeth Shaw have nurtured their storefront restaurant in the last several years, given it a sleek makeover, including an attractive bar, and added tapas selections which give the menu real variety. Grilled entrées are the most popular, seasoned with spicy rubs or fruit. Located on a side street just off the bay, it's a short walk from any downtown inn. Reservations are a good idea; lots of locals come here.

11th Street Dockside

843-524-7433.
www.11thstreetdockside.com.
11th St., Port Royal.
Open: Daily.

Price: Moderate.
Cuisine: American; Seafood.
Serving: D.
Credit Cards: AE, D, MC, V.

A casual restaurant, excellent for families, right on Battery Creek, where shrimp boats tie up and the sunsets pour color in the sky. The menu offers fried, steamed, and broiled seafood specialties, as well as steak and pasta. You can work up your appetite by a visit to the town of Port Royal's marsh boardwalk and observation tower located at "The Sands," a beach to the east of the port terminal at the foot of Paris Avenue. No reservations, so expect a wait. Dinner begins at 4:30 PM.

Emily's Restaurant and Tapas Bar
843-522-1866.
www.emilysrestaurantandtapasbar.com.
906 Port Republic St.
Closed: Sun.
Price: Expensive.
Cuisine: Continental.
Serving: D.
Credit Cards: AE, D, MC, V.

At Emily's you can put together a meal from tapas items—small dishes of hot and cold appetizers, which may have light sauces or seafood stuffing. The small restaurant is narrow, dark, and cozy, attracting local business people for drinks or informal meals, as well as boaters cruising through on the Intracoastal Waterway. A busy bar scene makes it a good place for a light, late meal: tapas served to 10 PM.

Fuji
843-524-2662.
81 Sea Island Pkwy., Lady's Island.
Closed: Sun.
Price: Inexpensive.
Cuisine: Asian.
Serving: L, D.
Credit Cards: AE, MC, V.

Recently doubled in size and enhanced by the addition of a sushi bar, this drop-in favorite has grown up but retains its post-beach, pre-movie informality where a cold Kirin and quick-grilled dishes will get you on your way.

Panini's Café
843-379-0300.
www.paniniscafe.com.
926 Bay St.
Open: Daily.

Gathering and Corn-Shelling, St. Helena Island

When they go into the field to work, the women tie a bit of string or some vine round their skirts just below the hips, to shorten them, often raising them nearly to the knees; then they walk off with their heavy hoes on their shoulders, as free, strong, and graceful as possible. The prettiest sight is the corn-shelling on Mondays, when the week's allowance, a peck a hand, is given out at the corn-house by the driver. They all assemble with their baskets, which are shallow and without handles, made by themselves of the palmetto and holding from a half a peck to a bushel. The corn is given out in the ear, and they sit about or kneel on the ground, shelling it with cleared corn-cobs. Here there are four enormous logs hollowed at one end, which serve as mortars, at which two can stand with their rude pestles, which they strike up and down alternately . . . . They separate the coarse and fine parts after it is ground by shaking the grits in their baskets: the finest they call corn-flour and make hoe-cake of, but their usual food is the grits, the large portion, boiled as hominy and eaten with clabber.

— Harriet Ware (a young abolitionist and teacher from Boston, who lived and taught at Coffin Point Plantation, St. Helena Island) to her parents, May 22, 1862.
— (from Letters From Port Royal 1862–1868, ed. Elizabeth Ware Pearson. Arno Press, 1969)

Price: Moderate to Expensive.
Cuisine: Italian and Mediterranean.
Serving: L, D.
Credit Cards: AE, MC, V.

The patio overlooking the Beaufort River and its marshes recommend it; thin-crust brick oven pizzas with creative toppings are a specialty. It's an accommodating, family-friendly place where you won't go wrong with a strip steak or a bowl of pasta.

Plums

843-525-1946.
904-1/2 Bay St.
Open: Daily.
Price: Moderate to Expensive.
Cuisine: American.
Serving: L, D.
Credit Cards: D, MC, V.

Plums is still the most popular place to eat lunch in Beaufort, good food, very informal. Hot sandwiches like grilled turkey or Reubens, excellent chicken salad, and homemade soups are menu favorites; there's peanut butter and jelly for kids. A full bar serves the lively nighttime crowd that spills onto the outdoor porch, now nicely heated in chillier months.

Saltus River Grill

843-379-3474.
www.saltusrivergrill.com.
802 Bay St.
Open: Daily.
Price: Moderate to Expensive.
Cuisine: American.
Serving: D.
Credit Cards: MC, V.

Located on the Waterfront Park with a spacious outdoor deck and comfortable seating, this very attractive, upscale restaurant offers not only a new look for local restaurants (enormous space in a renovated building with a dominant bar and an urban-hip flavor) but new options, such as a full sushi bar and raw bar. Top choices include shrimp and stone-ground grits with bacon gravy or a grilled filet with upstate Clemson blue cheese. It's definitely the place for locals to see and be seen.

Sea Island Wine & Gourmet

843-524-9463.
403 Carteret St.
Closed: Sun.
Price: Moderate.
Cuisine: Continental.
Serving: L, D (Thurs., Fri., Sat.).
Credit Cards: MC, V.

A tiny dining room and some outside tables overlooking the parking lot mean that this very local, reasonably priced, hip spot is usually packed. It's Beaufort's answer to a little bistro. Dinner menus change whimsically; the lunch menu is packed with gourmet sandwiches and salads. The market features a great array of cheeses, wines, pâtés, and it does a booming business, so what you order is really fresh.

Shrimp Shack

843-838-2962.
1929 Sea Island Pkwy., St. Helena Island (about 11 miles south of Beaufort toward the beach).
Closed: Sun.
Price: Inexpensive.
Cuisine: Seafood.
Serving: L, D (until 8 PM).
Credit Cards: None.

Fresh seafood from the family dock—you can see the shrimp boats from the porch—accompanied by slaw, red rice, hush puppies, and beans. Deviled crab and shrimp burgers (ground, seasoned shrimp on a bun) are specialties. You can eat upstairs on the screened-in porch or in an adjacent gazebo. It's laid-back and local, and the hard work of the Upton family keeps the standards high. Lunch only from November through March.

Cafés /Coffee Bars

More of these casual spots are popping up in Beaufort and Port Royal; most have wireless internet and a relaxed style about surfing online and refilling your mug.

Berry Island Café (843-524-8779; www.berryislandcafe.com; One Merchant Lane, Lady's Island). The 10-minute drive across the downtown bridge to the first big intersection, and a left there, brings you to a planned community called Newpoint, which is styled in the "new urbanism" theme of clustered houses, common spaces, porches, and alleys. Berry Island is its informal gathering spot where kids come on bikes for homemade ice cream. Salads, sandwich baskets, or burgers with fries are reliably good, and breakfast is simple and unhurried.

Common Ground (843-524-2326; 102 West St. Ext.) People in the local arts world and some University types like it here; at night the porch is a sweet place to sip an espresso. Smoothies, bagels, coffee, magazines, newspapers, comfortable chairs, and a view of the river you can't beat.

Magnolia Bakery Café (843-524-1961; 703 Congress St.) A small, friendly restaurant with limited outdoor dining specializing in homemade bread and soup, desserts, and snacks. Lunch is served all day. Vegetarian-friendly, a little rare in Beaufort. Beer and wine available.

Old Towne Coffehaus (843-379-2332; 914 Paris Ave., Port Royal) A neighborhood spot that sometimes features acoustic music and iced espresso.

Palm & Moon Bagel Co. (843-379-9300; 221 Scott St.) Bagels baked in-house, good coffee, and homemade soup every day. Cheerful folks behind the counter. A great new addition to downtown.

Delis and Faster Food

Alvin Ord's Sandwich Shop (843-524-8222; 1415 Ribaut Rd., Port Royal) Long prized for its home-baked bread (French or whole wheat) and delicious sandwiches. Limited seating and very crowded at lunch, so call ahead to order. Open until 8 PM Monday through Friday, until 6 PM on Saturday.

Blackstone's Deli & Café (843-524-4330; www.blackstonescafe.com; 205 Scott St.) Best breakfast in town, and nice to sit here engrossed in the morning paper. Lunch is served until 2:30.

Maryland Fried Chicken (843-524-8766; 1100 Ribaut Rd.) Chicken and fish by the piece, box, or bucket, as well as side orders like fried okra, slaw, and beans. Drive-thru window.

Nippy's Fish (843-522-3880; 310 West St.) If you see a lunch crowd forming at the edge of a parking lot, you're here: a tiny building with outdoor tables and high stools. You order and take it away. Best bets are fried shrimp and oyster rolls for lunch, and the Friday and Saturday all-you-can-shuck-and-eat roasted oysters. Local folk musicians play on weekends.

Upper Crust (843-521-1999; 81 Sea Island Pkwy., Lady's Island) Pizza, salads, subs, beer, and wine. A slice of the super-deluxe house pie and sweet tea after a day at the beach goes a long way.

The Green in Beaufort's Point neighborhood, rimmed by antebellum homes, is protected as open space. Peter Loftus

TOURING IN THE HISTORIC DISTRICT AND BEYOND

Several companies offer narrated tours of Beaufort's Historic District and the Sea Islands. Buggy and walking tours last 45–90 minutes. Guided driving tours may last two hours. Cassettes and CDs that provide information for self-guided tours are available at the Visitor Center (843-524-3163; 2001 Boundary St..). More information can be found at the Chamber of Commerce's Web site: www.beaufortsc.org.

By Carriage: Carolina Buggy Tours (843-524-1300) and the cleverly named Southurn Rose Buggy Tours (843-524-2900; www.southurnrose.com) depart from the Downtown Marina parking lot daily from 10 AM to 5 PM. Adults $18; children $7.

On Foot: The Spirit of Old Beaufort (843-525-0459) Tours led by costumed guides leave the shop (103 West St. Ext.) Monday through Saturday at 10:30 AM and 2 and 7 PM. Adults $13; children $8. For those with difficulty walking or unable to do so, guides are available to travel in your car for an additional fee. Reservations required. Jon Sharp (843-575-5775; jonswalkinghistory.com) blends a knowledge of history with storytelling skills to make Beaufort come alive on his two-hour tours. Tours cost $20 and start at 11 AM Tuesday through Saturday and 1 PM Sunday. Reserve by phone or Web site.

On St. Helena Island: Gullah-N-Geechie Mahn Tours (843-838-7516; www.gullahngeechie tours.net) run Monday through Saturday 9:45 AM and 1:45 PM. Adults $20; children $18. Reservations required.

If you can tear yourself away from the seductions of "the built environment," you will be rewarded by views of marshes and marine life that exist in such a pristine state in only a few places in the United States. For detailed information on tours by boat—small or large—see the **Recreation** section below, specifically listings in "Boat Tours" and "Canoeing and Kayaking."

Culture

As Beaufort has grown, so have its cultural activities, both indigenous and imported. The museums and annual house tours have gained a professional thoroughness; bookstores sponsor author's signings; the University of South Carolina at Beaufort has an active exhibition and theater space and chamber-music series; many art galleries coordinate monthly walking tours. It may be enough to sit and watch the tide go out on a Friday night, but you don't have to.

For information about cultural organizations, self-guided tours of artists' studios and galleries, or upcoming events, contact: **The Arts Council of Beaufort County** (843-379-2787; www.beaufortcountyarts.com; 1111 Boundary St., Beaufort, SC, 29901). The *Lowcountry Weekly* (www.lcweekly.com) is a free newspaper with all the current cultural listings. The local newspapers of Hilton Head and Beaufort sponsor an informative Web site, including cultural listings and events at www.mylowcountry.com. Annual tours of local homes and plantations, in October and March, are sponsored by the **Historic Beaufort Foundation** (843-379-3331; www.historic-beaufort.org) and **St. Helena Episcopal Church Women** (843-524-0363; www.sthelenas1712.org).

Film

Hwy. 21 Drive-In (843-846-4500; www.hwy21drivein.com; US 21 at Parker Dr., about 2 miles north of Beaufort).

Plaza Stadium Theaters (843-524-9468; Beaufort Plaza, SC 170).

Historic Homes, Gardens and Religious Sites
Baptist Church of Beaufort
601 Charles St.

This is an 1844 Greek Revival beauty. The ceiling plasterwork and ornamented cornices seem to match—in their absolute, solid mass of decoration—the abundant self-confidence of the prosperous little town of Beaufort in its heyday.

Chapel of Ease
Land's End Rd., St. Helena Island.

The ruins of this planters' church, built in the 1740s to serve worshippers far from town, are of brick and tabby, a construction material that blends oyster shells with lime, sand, and water. The site is a wonderful place for photographs—spooky in the fog or at dawn, mellow and ageless at dusk.

John Mark Verdier House
843-379-6335.
www.historic-beaufort.org.
801 Bay St.
Mon. through Sat. 10:30–3:30.
Admission: Adults $5; children $3.

Chapel of Ease, St. Helena Island.

Penn Center, St. Helena Island.

The showcase property of the Historic Beaufort Foundation, it was built according to the Adam-influenced decoration and floor plans of the day for a local merchant around 1790. It includes a formal parlor and ballroom, ornamental fireplace friezes, carved moldings, and antiques that are original both to the family and to the period of the house.

Penn Center
843-838-2432.
www.penncenter.com.
P.O. Box 126, Martin Luther King Jr. Dr., St. Helena Island, 29920.
York W. Bailey Museum
Mon. through Sat. 11–4.
Admission: Adults $4; children $2.

Founded in 1862 by two Pennsylvania women as a school for the newly freed slaves, Penn has remained a vital institution to promote education, self-sufficiency, and cultural expression among native islanders. In the days of segregation, it was one place where blacks and whites could meet together, as they did when the Rev. Dr. Martin Luther King planned his march on Washington. The York W. Bailey Museum holds a collection of cultural artifacts, African objects, and paintings. Community sings featuring gospel choirs and spirituals, an island tradition to which visitors are welcome, take place in Frissell Hall on the third Sunday of each month from September through May at 7:30 PM. The entire campus is a National Historic Landmark.

Old Sheldon Church Ruins
Secondary Rd. 21, 1.7 miles north of the intersection of US 17 and US 21.
Beautiful brick columns, fragile arches, and sill slabs remain from a church that was burned twice, first by the British in 1779 and then by the Union Army in 1865. It's a little temple in the woods. There's a small shaded picnic area on site.

St. Helena's Episcopal Church
507 Newcastle St.
www.sthelenas1712.org.
Tues. through Fri. 10–4.; Sat. 10–1.

This church, built of brick from England in 1724, is adorned inside with graceful columns, upstairs galleries, and tall, multi-paned windows on the deep sills of which rest buckets of blossoming magnolia, daffodils, or narcissi in season. Its shaded, walled churchyard makes for a lovely stroll. See the Web site for information about tours of the church and grounds.

Tabernacle Baptist Church
907 Craven St.

A striking, white clapboard building with bell tower; in its churchyard lies the grave—and stands a fine bust—of Robert Smalls, who was born a slave, engineered a daring ship capture during the Civil War, and was later a congressman and significant figure in Beaufort's Reconstruction period.

Military Sites
National Cemetery
1601 Boundary St., Beaufort.

Created by President Lincoln in 1863 for victims of Southern battles, this 29-acre cemetery is the final resting place of some 9,000 Union soldiers and more than 100 Confederates. It is still in service.

Parris Island Museum
843-525-2951.
www.pimuseum.us.
Marine Corps Recruit Depot.
P.O. Box 190001, Parris Island, SC 29905.
Daily 10–4:30.
Admission: Free.

The museum, renovated in 2008, showcases the history and development of the area on which the famous "boot camp" stands, from its earliest settlement through contemporary recruit training. (Artifacts have been recovered from the Spanish village of Santa Elena, circa 1566; from Charlesfort, a French outpost established by Jean Ribaut in 1562; and from Fort San Marcos, circa 1576. Excavation continues at these sites, located near the depot golf course.) Exhibits of uniforms, personal items, weapons, drawings, and documents trace the history of the Marine Corps in its worldwide engagements. You can also consult Platoon Books for listings of Marines. Self-guided driving tour maps are available. If you're interested in observing morning colors or a graduation (held on Fridays), contact the Visitor Center (843-525-3650; www.mcrdpi.usmc.mil). The Visitor Center is open for extended hours during recruit graduation. Basic hours are Monday 7:30 AM–12:00 PM; Tuesday through Thursday 7:30 AM–4:30 PM; Friday 7:30 AM–3:00 PM. You may also picnic in designated areas or have an inexpensive meal at a base restaurant, including the Officer's Club. This is an active military base. At the entrance gate be prepared to show identification, vehicle registration, proof of vehicle insurance, and state your desire to visit the Museum and Visitor Center.

Museums

Beaufort Arsenal Museum

843- 379-3331.
713 Craven St.
Mon. through Sat. 10–4.
Admission: $3.

The old Beaufort Arsenal, an ochre-colored bastion with a courtyard was rebuilt in 1852. It now houses the museum, overseen by the Historic Beaufort Foundation, which has undergone a thorough renovation of both its building and collection to become a center of local history and culture.

The Lowcountry Estuarium

843-524-6600.
1402 Paris Ave., Port Royal.
www.lowcountryestuarium.org.
Fri. and Sat. 10–5.
Admission: Adults $4; children $2.

This is a place where tanks and exhibits showcase the natural marine world of the Lowcountry. Creature feedings are at 11:30 and 3.

Music

Hallelujah Singers. The group of singers under the direction of Marlena McGhee Smalls, a superior vocalist who has earned a national reputation for her singing and her acting (she was Bubba's mother in the movie *Forrest Gump*), performs throughout the year, often in a downtown church at the time of annual house tours; weekly during the summer at various sites. Contact **The Arts Council of Beaufort County** (843-379-2787; www.beaufortcount yarts.com; 1111 Boundary St., Beaufort, SC, 29901) for schedules.

Penn Center Community Sing (843-838-2432; P.O. Box 126, St. Helena Island, SC 29920) Community groups, quartets of senior citizens, gospel choirs, spur-of-the-moment vocalists, and soloists who deacon out lines of spirituals to the audience perform at 7:30 PM on the third Sunday of every month, from September through May, in Frissell Hall on the historic Penn Center campus. The popularity of the sings and the feelings of dignity and fellowship that characterize them are a moving testament to the pride of Sea Islanders in their culture and heritage. Contributions are welcome.

Nightlife

Johnson Creek Tavern (843-838-4166; 2141 Sea Island Pkwy., Harbor Island.) A no-frills beach bar about 25 minutes from town, where you'll find campers from Hunting Island State Park, young couples, and "after-party" groups who come to hear anything from bluegrass to rock.

Kathleen's (843-524-2500; 822 Bay St.) Live entertainment at lunch and dinner, on a patio overlooking the Beaufort River. At least two evenings a week there are acoustic-guitar sets.

Country roads of sand still mark many areas of the rural Lowcountry.   Peter Loftus

RECREATION

For at least 200 years, Lowcountry people have depended on the reliable bounty of land and sea. They became so accustomed to gathering and returning home with full baskets that the work of it, and the pleasure to be had in it, were easily interchanged. These days the sportsman, the naturalist, and the Sunday painter all take to the outdoors, often with equal results: going in seriousness, returning with, at the very least, a day of pleasure. Such is the natural abundance of the Lowcountry, and the dozens of opportunities to explore it— by power boat, kayak, sailboard, or bicycle; with fishing pole, crab net, paintbrush, or pup tent—that visitors still have this experience today.

Beaufort, in particular, claims the advantage over Charleston and Savannah of having its rural recreational opportunities close at hand. Informally, residents and visitors can fish or throw cast nets for shrimp at bridges off US 21 at **Cowan Creek,** from the **Waterfront Park**, and on the marsh boardwalk at **Hunting Island State Park** located off US 21, about a 30-minute drive from town. At the north end of Hunting Island is **Paradise Pier** (843-838-7437), at 1,120 feet, the state's longest. There are dozens of public boat landings within easy reach. Launching is free, and so is parking, but you're on your own—no attendants, telephones, or rest rooms. For locations, or to see about chartering your own boat, inquire at the **Downtown Marina** (843-524-4422; 1010 Bay St.), sporting goods stores, or contact the **Lowcountry Resort Islands and Tourism Commission** (1-800-528-6870; www.southcarolinalowcountry.com; P.O. Box 615, Yemassee, SC 29945). If your recreational pursuits require clothing or equipment you didn't bring with you, see the shops listed under "Sporting Goods and Clothing" in the **Shopping** section.

Perhaps the most significant resource for those who love the outdoors and savor its hidden beauty is the **ACE Basin National Wildlife Refuge**—a consolidation of some 350,000 acres of marsh, creek, and forest to the north, east, and west of Beaufort. This crescent of landscape encompasses the forested, inland shore of the Ashepoo, Combahee, and Edisto Rivers and their small tributaries, and the vastness of St. Helena Sound. And not all the activity is on the water, either: From points on dry land, birders have identified more than 250 species of resident and migratory birds. For more information contact the ACE Basin National Wildlife Refuge (843-889-3084; www.acebasin.fws.gov; 8674 Willtown Rd., Hollywood, SC 29449). To access the ACE and reach its headquarters, take SC

A beach on the edge of the ACE Basin, where the river meets the ocean.   Peter Loftus

174 from US 17, about midway between Beaufort and Charleston, continue east through Adams Run and follow the signs to Grove House. It is open year-round from daylight to dark. You may park and walk in; good maps available online. Several options for visiting the ACE Basin are listed under "Boat Tours" below.

Beach Access

Hunting Island State Park (See also entry under "Camping.") Sunrise–sunset; $4 per person. Hunting Island is eroding and as the water reclaims it, it has taken on a beautiful, wild aspect, with fallen palmettos and exposed stumps on the beach. Parking is plentiful; there are picnic areas and bathhouses, and miles to walk at the ocean's edge. Eight miles of bike paths and foot trails thread through its maritime forest. The 19th-century **Hunting Island Lighthouse** offers an expansive view of the confluence of the Atlantic Ocean and St. Helena Sound.

Bicycling

Local bicycle enthusiasts have developed cue sheets and maps for enjoyable day trips. Their efforts have led to a much greater awareness of the emerging network of linked trails from Hunting Island State Park to the ACE Basin. The trips can be from 25 to 60 miles and wind through scenic, rural areas, by Revolutionary War sites, and movie locations. An online link is at www.beaufortsc.org.

Low Country Bicycles (843-524-9585; www.lowcountrybicycles.com; 102 Sea Island Pkwy.) A shop filled with the latest mountain, cruising, high performance, and kid's bikes, maps, clothing, and accessories. The staff, owner John Feeser, and the Web site offer good touring suggestions, and helpful links, for local and longer distance rides. Bikes for adults and kids rent by the half-day ($10–$15), day, and week $50–$80. Car racks are $10–$30. Repairs on-site.

Bird-Watching

Excellent bird-watching is available about
35 minutes north of Beaufort off US 17 on
Bennett's Point Road, near the village of
Green Pond (between Beaufort and Edisto)
at the **Bear Island Wildlife Management
Area** (843-844-8957 for information;
www.carolinabirdclub.org).

Boating

Boat Tours

ACE Basin Tours (843-521-3099;
www.acebasintours.com) will take you on a
three-hour pontoon boat trip in the ACE.
The boat leaves from Coosaw Island at 10
AM Wednesdays and Saturdays, March
through November (Adults $35; children
6–12 $15.00.) Call for reservations (you can
make them online, too) and directions.
Tours may be scheduled on other days, with
a minimum 8 passengers.

*Flocks of birds gather to feed on the saltwater edge of
the ACE Basin.*   Peter Loftus

A&B Fishing and Eco Tours (843-812-2049). A local captain will guide you on a custom
trip through the marshes and rivers, or to uninhabited barrier islands. Rates are for up to
six passengers: two hours ($150); four hours ($300).

Captain Dick's River Tours (843-524-4422; www.beaufortrivertours.com) offers daily
cruises on the Beaufort River at 2 PM daily, with an additional departure at 11 AM Saturdays.
The boat leaves from the Downtown Marina (1010 Bay St.) and lasts a little more than an
hour. Adults $18, children $14. More personalized trips can also be arranged (call the
Captain directly at 843-812-2804).

Islander **Steamship** (843-524-4000) is a large vessel and a good choice for passengers
who might be nervous on the water. Seating, inside and out, for 125. Tours lasting nearly
two hours depart from the Downtown Marina most days at 2 PM, but call ahead to confirm
or check at the Marina. Adults $20; seniors/military $19; children $12.

Lowcountry Sailing (843- 662-7124) offers sailing cruises and instruction by appointment from the Port Royal Landing Marina. Typical custom cruises for four to six passengers include sunset sails or engine cruising; there's a two-hour minimum and prices start
at about $250.

River Safari (843-575-1748; www.river-safari.com) a privately guided 90-minute tour,
departs from the Port Royal Landing Marina at the foot of the McTeer bridge. Captain Bill
will accommodate your schedule: call him directly to book his 24-foot pontoon boat.
Adults $15; children $10.

Bowling

Ribaut Lanes (843-524-3111; 1140 S. Ribaut Rd.). Open daily until 10 PM.

Camping

Hunting Island State Park (843-838-2011; www.southcarolinaparks.com; 2555 Sea Island Pkwy., Hunting Island, SC 29920) on US 21, about 30 minutes from Beaufort. 193 sites, 14 cabins, nature trails, picnic sites, showers and dressing rooms, a store, water, and electrical hookups. Some sites can be reserved; some are first come, first served; one cabin is handicapped-accessible. Campsites from $19–$23; $17.50 for tents per night; cabins from $188–$291 weekends and $539–$836 for the week.

Point South KOA (843-726-5733 or 1-800-562-2948; I-95 at exit 33).

Tuc In De Wood Campground (843-838-2267; www.tuckinthewood.com; 22 Tuc In De Wood Lane, St. Helena Island, SC 29920) 74 campsites with water, electricity, and cable television connections; 65 sites with full hookups.

Canoeing and Kayaking

Trail guides and other good information about paddling in the ACE Basin and nearby rivers are available online at www.walterboro.org. (Walterboro is a small town north of Beaufort off I-95 and on the eastern edge of the ACE.) Beaufort also has a self-guided paddling trail (12.6 miles round trip) that runs along the river (www.beaufortblueways.info). You can rent single or tandem kayaks—sit-on or cockpit style—from **Higher Ground** (843-379-4327; www.highergroundofthelowcountry; 2121 Boundary St., Beaufort). Daily rates start at $40.

Beaufort Kayak Tours (843-525-0810; www.beaufortkayaktours.com) Two-hour nature tours leave from downtown and teach you the local ecology and how to cast a shrimp net. Other options include history-focused tour of peninsular Beaufort and a wildlife paddle at Hunting Island. Adults $40; children $30. Tours of the ACE basin last two or four hours, from $30 to $50 for children and $40 to $60 for adults. Call for times and reservations.

The Kayak Farm (843-838-2008; www.kayakfarm@islc.net) Guided sea kayaking in and around Hunting Island, and the ACE Basin. No experience necessary. Kayaks for rent by the full or half-day.

Outpost Moe's (843-844-2514; www.geocities.com/outpostmoe.) Located on US 17 between Charleston and Beaufort. Historically focused tours through the old rice fields can last from two to five hours ($40–$80). Kayaks can be rented ($40 per day) and delivered within 40 miles if you have a larger group (three-kayak minimum.)

Fishing

Fishing is thickly woven into the fabric of local life. Anthropologists would note its folkways: the way its residents cook, the stories they tell, the skills they wish to pass on, where they live, what kinds of politicians they elect, how they judge character, what their values are for their children. Like the myth of the Old South and Old Families, the lore of fishing confers a kind of lineage by which people know themselves. And where the Old Families might have Old Houses, people who fish have Old Cars, "fishing cars" as they are widely known—dinged-up rustbuckets that make it to the boat landing (not much farther) with the faithfulness of a hunting hound.

With still plentiful catches, pristine waterways, and lots of opportunity to get in a boat, a book written in 1856, *Carolina Sport By Land and Water* by William Elliott, can be read as a nearly modern account.

Today's enthusiast can choose freshwater or saltwater sites; fish from piers, bridges, boats, banks, or the beach; or troll an artificial offshore reef. Saltwater fly-fishing is a popular specialty. **Paradise Pier** (843-838-7437) is located on Hunting Island near Beaufort and open 24 hours. The fishing fee is $4. The catch can range from small bream, porgy, and spot—of the family commonly known as "sailor's choice"—to flounder, to big game fish like wahoo, drum, shark, and cobia. In general, the best part of the season extends from April through November, but small panfish remain active beyond those dates. You may also fish in the lagoon on Hunting Island by using light tackle with shrimp and worms for bait.

Licenses are required for freshwater fishing and for saltwater fishing under certain conditions. Most visitors interested in recreational fishing will not need one; they're not necessary for recreational shrimping or crabbing. For further information on licenses, and size and catch limits, see the **South Carolina Wildlife and Marine Resources Department** Web site (www.dnr.sc.gov).

For a comprehensive map indicating recreational fishing facilities in the Lowcountry, including marinas, boat landings, bridges and catwalks, shellfish grounds, and offshore reefs, contact the **Lowcountry Resort Islands and Tourism Commission** (1-800-528-6870; P.O. Box 615, Yemassee, SC 29945) or visit www.beaufortusa.com.

Sport-Fishing Charters

A sport-fishing charter can take you to the Gulf Stream or to any of the dozen or so artificial reefs offshore. More than 150 years ago, the first artificial reefs used in this area were approximately 6 feet high, log, hut-like structures that were sunk to attract sheepshead; today's reefs are far more elaborate affairs built of tires, concrete debris, and castoff military machinery that attract dozens of species. Given that much of the sea floor off the coast is sandy, these reefs provide the hard substrate necessary to create a "live bottom" of invertebrates, small fish, coral, crabs, and sponges. They are active feeding stations for the big fish, and experienced guides know them well. Trips of this sort generally take a full day. Trips closer to shore, in smaller boats, can be easily enjoyed by the half-day.

A listing of some of the many **charter boat services** available follows. Rods, reels, bait, and tackle are provided; lunch or snacks are usually available, but you should check in advance; boats are equipped with safety equipment and licenses; all but the smallest have heads. It is wise to bring sunscreen, windbreakers, and a towel.

Many charters will design a trip to suit your particular interest or prepare a boat for a fishing tournament. If stormy weather is forecast, call ahead to confirm that the trip is on. Also check the reservation, deposit, and cancellation policies of each charter. You'll have to plan your trip around the tides, too. The 2008 prices for half-day trips started at about $125 per person, but varied considerably depending on the type of fishing and distance traveled.

Bay Street Outfitters (843- 501-5001; www.baystreetoutfitters.com; 815 Bay St.) Visitors who are experienced in the art of fly-fishing, as well as those who are rank beginners, can find experienced guides, instruction (Redfish School one-day seminars: $200 per person), and a full line of Orvis outfits, accessories, and specialty rods here. In 2008, guided charters, including lunch, cost $350–$500 depending on how many hours were spent on the water. Licenses are not required on the charters; drinks and equipment are provided. Call ahead and see what the season has to offer.

Capt. Eddie Netherland (843-838-3782; www.fishingcapteddie1.com) Offshore and inshore trips by the day and half day on a 17-foot boat for two passengers, or a 27-foot boat for six. Charter rates begin at $440 per half-day. Trips to the Gulf and visits to remote Beaufort County islands available. Charters leave from the Fripp Island Marina. No credit cards.

Fish Beaufort (843-838-2245; www.fishbeaufort.com; St. Helena Island. Half-day inshore fishing trips start at $350 for one or two anglers; $50 for an additional angler. Sightseeing trips start at $250.

Sea Wolf VI (843-525-1174; www.seawolfcharter.com) Major Wally Phinney Jr. USA, Ret. is your guide. Deep-sea fishing, diving, cruising, by the day or half-day, aboard a 35-foot boat. Call for appointments for half-day, full-day, or Gulf excursions. Trips range from $455 to $1,510.

Fitness Facilities

Omni Health and Fitness Center (843-379-2424; www.omniofbeaufort.com; 1505 Salem Rd.) Full range of exercise equipment and programs in a new facility. Day passes available.

Ray's Gym (843-524-8351; SC 170) Complete gym, body-sculpting, Nautilus, weights, fitness machines.

YMCA of Beaufort County (843-522-9622; www.ymcaofbeaufortcounty.com; 1801 Richmond Ave., Port Royal) Pool, gym, classes. Membership in another YMCA allows guest registration.

Golf

The Lowcountry probably has more golf courses per person than any other region in the country, and more with holes offering views of the ocean or marsh, or of deer, heron, and the occasional alligator.

Whether you're a duffer or scratch golfer, there's pleasure in being on the links, either early in the morning as the heavy dew dries and the temperature rises, or late in the day as the chuck-will's-widows commence their plaintive call. Lowcountry weather allows for year-round play and (in the summer) late-afternoon starting times. The high-season months are in fall and spring, so it is wise to schedule your playing time well in advance.

On some courses carts are required at peak playing times. Special prices are often posted for midday tee-times in the height of summer. For resort play, it is usually necessary to be an overnight guest. Golf packages that include lodging are numerous, so ask about them. Club rentals and instruction are available at all courses. Greens fees/cart rentals reflect 2008 prices.

Public and Semiprivate Courses

Country Club of Beaufort at Pleasant Point (843-522-1605; 8 Barnwell Dr., Lady's Island) Russell Breeden design, 18 holes, par 72. Four sets of tees: 4,753 yards, 5,416 yards, 6,112 yards, and 6,506 yards. Greens fees including cart $40–$60.

Fripp Island (1-800- 845-4100; www.frippislandresort.com; Fripp Island) Set on the rim of the Atlantic and Fripp Inlet, Ocean Point Golf Links, par 72, is a George Cobb course, from 4,951 yards to 6,590 yards. The Ocean Creek Course, the first designed by Davis Love III, is a par 71, winding through the marshes and interior wetlands. Yardage from 4,884 to

6,629. Walking is an option at both courses. Since they lie within a gated community, you must be a resort guest or renting property of a club member to play.

Gifford's Golf (843-521-9555; 30 Grober Hill Rd., Burton) A friendly, 9-hole course with driving range and pro shop. Fees start at $8 for 9 holes.

Lady's Island Country Club (843-524-3635; www.ladysislandcc.com; 139 Francis Marion Circle, Lady's Island) Pines Course, par 72, 5,421 yards to 6,811 yards; Marsh Course, par 72, 5,192 yards to 5,929 yards. Greens fees including cart $35–$80.

Legends at Parris Island (843-228-2240; www.mccssc.com; MCRD, Parris Island) Par 72 course redesigned by Clyde Johnston in 2000, now ranked in top 10 military courses. Tees from 5,700 yards to 7,100 yards. Cart or walk, $39 for visitors.

South Carolina National Golf Club (843-524-0300; www.scnational.com; 8 Waveland Ave., Beaufort) George Cobb's last design, par 71. Four sets of tees: 4,970 yards to 6,625 yards. A British-style pub is located in the Clubhouse for lunch. Greens fees including cart $49–$80. New owners are renovating the course in 2008; expect a change in name and rates, too.

Horseback Riding

Broomfield Stables (843-521-1212), **Camelot Farms** (843-838-3938; www.camelotfarms horses.com), and **Shalimar Horse Center** (843-521-0419) welcome inquiries from visitors seeking instruction within the ring. Camelot, located on a 60-acre farm on St. Helena Island, offers beach and plantation rides that last up to two hours ($75 per rider.)

Tennis

Public courts, some of which are lit for night play, are located on Boundary Street across from the National Cemetery; on the corner of Battery Creek Road and Southside Boulevard; and in the Port Royal Park on Paris Avenue in the village of Port Royal. Free. No reservations required.

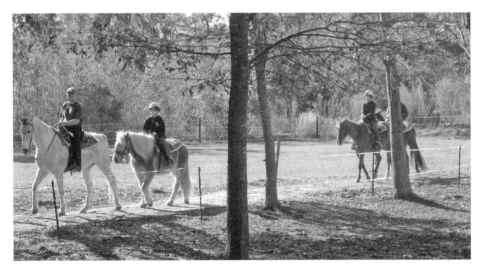

Riding on wooded trails or the beach reminds many visitors that much of the Lowcountry is still rural. Peter

Shopping

Antiques
Canup Antiques (843-524-8914; 809 Bay St.) American country furniture, tinware, white ironstone.

Der Teufelhund (843-521-9017; 13-B Marina Blvd., near Parris Island) Military books, antique gear, insignias, trunks, and other ephemera of 20th-century warfare.

Michael Rainey Antiques (843-521-4532; 702 Craven St.) A high-end collection, frequently refreshed with new purchases, largely from New England, Pennsylvania, and the south. Baskets, bureaus, benches, and paintings.

Oyster Cay Collection (843-525-6644; 917 Bay St., in the Old Bay Marketplace) Antique furniture and rugs from Indonesia, China, and elsewhere in Asia.

What's In Store (843-838-3355; 872 Sea Island Pkwy., St. Helena Island.) Large-scale furniture and vases, garden ornaments, English pine furniture.

Books/Recordings
Bay St. Trading Co. (843-524-2000; 808 Bay St.) Best-sellers, books-on-tape, excellent children's section, comprehensive local and regional history, and many fine photography books. The staff is very knowledgeable, which makes this store the best place to browse downtown.

Beaufort Bookstore (843-525-1066; Jean Ribaut Square) A large selection and wide variety of books, from best-selling fiction and nonfiction to military and Lowcountry favorites.

McIntosh Book Shoppe (843-524-1119; 919 Bay St.) New and used books on South Carolina you'll find nowhere else. Civil War albums, rare and antique volumes, as well as local writers and local history.

Candy and Ice Cream
Chocolate Tree (843-524-7980; 507 Carteret St.) A family-owned shop selling many different kinds of chocolates, truffles, and dipped fruits made right on the premises, plus candy-making accessories, gift boxes, jelly beans, cards, and gifts.

Renaissance Fine Chocolates (843-525-1328; 1001 Boundary St. at Newcastle Square) Gourmet food items like seasoned nuts and jams, but the best in stock are the handmade chocolates made from Callibaut Belgian chocolate, with no paraffin or preservatives.

Southern Sweets Ice Cream Parlor (843-379-0798; 917 Bay St., in the Old Bay Marketplace) Looks like an old-fashioned soda fountain with a long counter and serves Greenwood brand, a rich South Carolina ice cream.

Clothing
Beaufort Clothing Co. (843-524-7118; 723 Bay St.) Everything men and women need for a casual Friday or clean-cut preppy look, featuring cotton sweaters, Hawaiian shirts, pastel polos, and accessories.

Doodlebugs (843-379-3209; 802 Bay St.) Beaufort's only children's store, with charming clothes, gifts, shoes, and little extras.

Sweetgrass Ladies Apparel (843-379-3307; 707 Bay St.) Linens and light jackets, stylish but informal.

Talbot's (843-322-8040; 1029 Boundary St.) A branch of the national store with small sizes and enough to choose from if you need to get dressed up at the last minute.

Crafts

Carolina Stamper (843-522-9966; 203 Carteret St.) Rubber stamps, supplies, and lots of ideas for making stationery and artwork.

The Craftseller (843-525-6104; www. craftseller.com; 818 Bay St.) Local and regional artists' work, including jewelry, benches made of recycled wood from local buildings, fabric art, handmade paper, wind-chimes.

Sweetgrass Baskets made by local artists can be found on St. Helena Island on US 21, on the porch at the Gullah Grub restaurant, at the Red Piano Too Gallery and other roadside stands. The baskets, which incorporate palmetto frond, pine needle, and rush with the pale grass, come in many shapes and sizes, with individual variations inspired by the utilitarian shapes used in the past. They require enormous amounts of labor and skill and are useful as well as beautiful.

Galleries

For information about art walks and latest listings visit www.guildofbeaufortgalleries.com.

Art & Soul (843-379-9710; 917 Bay St., in the Old Bay Marketplace) Paintings, prints, ceramics, and textiles with a contemporary feel.

Bay Street Gallery (843-522-9210; www.baystgallery.com; 719 Bay St.) Original works by Lana Hefner including impressionistic views of marsh and woodland scenes, as well as a fine collection of Sea Island baskets, sculpture and oils by regional artists, and tiny ornaments.

Beaufort Art Association Gallery (843-379-2222; 1001 Bay St.) Original works including pottery, prints, jewelry, sculpture, photography, and acrylics by some 75 member artists. New exhibits every six weeks.

Charles Street Gallery (843-521-9054; 914 Charles St.) Original works including bronze sculpture, raku pottery, paintings, and etchings. Full-service framing and regularly scheduled gallery shows.

The Gallery (843-470-9994; www.thegallery-beaufort.com; 802 Bay St.) A wide variety of contemporary art in many media, showcased, and lit with attention to texture and detail.

Garden Studio Gallery (843-522-8911; www.sandrabaggette.com; 1908 Lenora Dr., Port Royal). Oil paintings and watercolors of flowers from Sandra Baggette's garden are stunning.

Gloria Dalvini Watercolors (843-521-0221; www.dalviniwatercolors.com; 1311 North St.) A small studio a short walk from downtown houses dozens of watercolors, and more recently, oil paintings of Lowcountry houses, gardens, and landscapes.

Four Winds Gallery (843-379-5660; 709 Bay St.) features religious and sacred art and craft from around the world.

Indigo Gallery (843-524-1036; 813 Bay St.) Limited and open editions of many of the best-known Lowcountry artists, as well as serigraphs, original art, and framing.

I. Pinckney Simons Gallery (843-379-4774; 711 Bay St.) features work in jewelry, sculpture, paintings, and more by a well-known regional artist.

Longo Gallery (843-522-8933; 103 Charles St.) Suzanne and Eric Longo, husband and wife, are proficient and playful artists. Her ideas find expression in clay and concrete sculpture; his in brightly colored, whimsical paintings (sometimes on boards or old roof tin) and found-object constructions.

LyBensons Gallery & Studio (843-525-9006; 211 Charles St.) A large, bright gallery specializing in art from Africa and from African American artists in a variety of media including verdite stone sculptures; photographs depicting the Gullah culture by Rev. Kenneth Hodges.

The Red Piano Too (843-838-2241; www.redpianotoo.com; 870 Sea Island Parkway, St. Helena Island) Located about 15 minutes from Beaufort, this gallery has an eclectic assortment of folk art and outsider art by individuals from this area and throughout the South, as well as baskets, books, jewelry, African objects, and prints. Fine framing is available.

Rhett Gallery (843-524-3339; www.rhett gallery.com; 901 Bay St.) Prints and watercolors of the Lowcountry by Nancy Ricker Rhett as well as antique first-edition prints and maps, Civil War and nautical materials, and hand-colored engravings. A companion gallery with work by her sons, also including rugs, furnishings, and hammocks, is on St. Helena Island (847-A Sea Island Pkwy.)

Red Piano Too Art Gallery, St. Helena Island.

Susan Graber Gallery (843-524-4353; www.susangraber.com; 805 London Ave., Port Royal). An accomplished portraitist, she has also been painting Lowcountry palmettos in closeup views that burst from their frames with intensity and color. Studio visits by appointment or chance.

Shipman Art Gallery (843-524-7722; 904 Bay St.) Watercolor artist Barbara Shipman offers some 100 of her paintings in collectible print editions, as well as originals. She captures the Lowcountry in both intimate and grand ways—from one crab or one blossom to an entire coastline scene.

University of South Carolina at Beaufort (843-521-4144; 901 Carteret St.) The University and The Arts Council of Beaufort County sponsor numerous shows throughout the year, from scholarly overviews to the best works of local artists.

Gifts

Beaufort Butterfly Company (843-986-0555; 928-1/2 Bay St.) Everything you'll need to attract, observe, identify, catch, and collect butterflies, as well as books about natural history and tee shirts with nature themes.

Lulu Burgess (843-524-5858; 917 Bay St.) An engaging blend of imaginative gifts such as jewelry, stationery, tableware, totes, and decorative accessories for the home. Opened by a young Beaufort native who has brought her good taste back home.

Rossignol's (843-524-2175; 817 Bay St.) Fine china patterns, silver and gold jewelry, stationery, and expensive stemware—all suitable for wedding gifts—as well as platters, picture frames, and tea towels that would make good house presents.

Verdier House Gift Shop (843-379-6335; 801 Bay St.) Located in the basement of the historic house museum, it features a collection of books, ornaments, prints, toys, and note cards with sketches of Beaufort's old homes.

Gourmet and Health Food

Cravings By the Bay (843-522-3000 or 1-800-735-3215; www.cravingsbythebay.com; 928 Bay St.) Savor Lowcountry flavors as well as memories by ordering soups, condiments, sauces, and specialty books by mail. Shrimp, oysters, clams, scallops, and soft-shell crab can be delivered overnight. Drop by for more information.

It's Only Natural (843-986-9595; 95 Factory Creek Court, Lady's Island) Just over the Beaufort bridge, a new store with organic produce, nuts and grains in bulk, and low-carb specialties.

Lowcountry Winery (843-379-3010; www.lowcountrywinery.com; 705 Bay St.) Locally made fruit wines and varietals as well as wine and picnic accessories.

Wine & Gourmet (843-524-9463; 403 Carteret St.) In addition to serving excellent sandwiches, this market carries a broad range of wine and beer; many kinds of pasta, rice, and beans; and sauces and condiments, fresh, frozen or on the shelf.

Home Furnishings/Kitchenware

The Firehouse (843-379-8810; www.thefirehousesc.com; 706 Craven St.) Both a cooking school and a high-end culinary store, with a selection of wines and cheeses, too. A recent renovation shows off beautiful brickwork and the creativity of its owners, local chefs at Breakwater.

In High Cotton (843-522-1405; 903 Bay St.) Fine linens and home furnishings.

Le Creuset Manufacturer's Outlet Store (843-589-6650; Yemassee at Exit 38 off I-95) Cast-iron cookware, utensils, pottery, and storage pieces from the French maker are available at significant discount from overstock, discontinued, and cosmetically flawed inventory.

Waterside Place (843-524-0201; 308 Charles St.) Linens and fine furnishings gathered for a custom interior design practice.

Sporting Goods and Clothing

Barefoot Bubba's (843-838-9222; www.barefootbubbas.com; 2135 Sea Island Pkwy, St. Helena Island) The latest in surf wear, surfboards, skimboards, rafts, and toys for the beach.

Bay Street Outfitters (843-524-5250; 815 Bay St.) A full line of high-end sportswear from Orvis and Barbour, as well as fishing gear, reels, binoculars, and books.

Higher Ground (843-379-4327; www.highergroundofthelowcountry.com; 2121 Boundary St.) Surfboards, kayaks, climbing gear, clothing, and camping accessories. You can rent surfboards, too.

Lowcountry Paddlesports (843-379-5292; 1109 Boundary St.) Kayaks, canoes, big kites, and all the accessories for inland and ocean water activity.

EDISTO ISLAND

Like the Sea Islands around Charleston and Beaufort, Edisto's history starts with early Native American settlements and agriculture. Later came rice, indigo, and cotton cultivation; slavery; and the occupation of Federal troops. Small farming and fishing operations have remained constant. Unlike the other Sea Islands, Edisto, while lively in the summer rental season stays quiet the rest of the time. People from Charleston and other parts of the state love it as a weekend destination for its slow pace. Development is accelerating, but local preservation groups have stayed one step ahead of the trend. If you're looking for a few days of peace and quiet, or a family reunion, enlivened by beachcombing, a good meal, a kayak or boat tour, your choice should be Edisto. A few years ago, a sickly loggerhead turtle washed up at Edisto. It was taken to Charleston where it was nursed and healed. When the time came to release it back into the ocean at Edisto Beach, more than 300 people turned up to watch, cheer, and take pictures. They found out by word of mouth. That's Edisto.

The island lies about 45 miles south of Charleston by road, and about 75 miles from Beaufort—of course far less by water. From US 17, take SC 174 (signs alert you to Edisto),

Shrimp boats at Edisto.

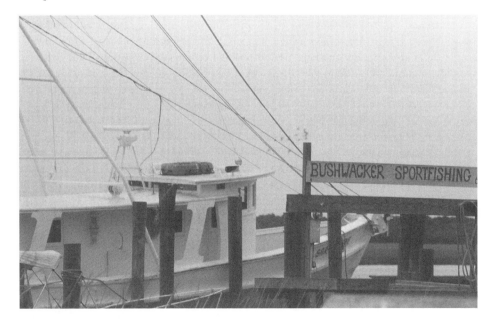

the island's main travel route. It is a two-lane road of about 20 miles from the main high-way, unlit, embowered by trees. It's a hike to travel from Charleston or Beaufort just for dinner, but fine for a day trip. Cab and car rental services are limited, so it's best to arrive there on your own. Creeks and rivers irregularly indent Edisto, so as in the past, there are roads that cross the marsh or wind through the woods in what seems to be the long way around. Original sections of the King's Highway, laid out in the early 18th century, are in use today. The main road dead-ends at the Atlantic Ocean.

For a visitor, Edisto is the least immediately knowable of the Sea Islands. What remains of its "Golden Age," the period between the Revolutionary and Civil Wars, is mostly hid-den, tucked away along secondary roads that wind through fields and patches of scrub oak, and meander by the North and South Edisto Rivers and their tributaries.

Historic sites that are listed on the National Register of Historic Places (27 so far) do include churches, but consist primarily of private plantation homes and gardens that are not open to the public. A good source of information is the **Edisto Chamber of Commerce** (843-869-3867 or 1-888-333-2781; www.edistochamber.com; P.O. Box 206, Edisto, SC 29438).

For an overview of the island's history, visit the **Edisto Island Historic Preservation Society's Museum** (843-869-1954; www.edistomuseum.org; SC 174 at Chisolm Plantation Rd.; open Tues.–Sat. 1–4 PM. Admission $4; free to children 10 and under.) Island artifacts such as baskets, clothing, farm tools, letters and documents, uniforms, and furniture are displayed in several small rooms. There are old photographs and explanatory remarks. The little gift shop sells a variety of natural history items for kids—good to use to explore and collect on their own—as well as a series of excellent reprints of booklets you're not likely to find anywhere else on your travels. They include "Edisto Island in 1808," "Indigo in America," "Gullah," and "She Came To the Island," the Edisto diary of Mary Ames, a Northern abolitionist whose account of teaching and living among the newly freed slaves during the Civil War is among the most poignant of the genre.

Since Edisto's old homes are not open to the public, one way to get inside some of them is by taking a two-and-a-half-hour tour of Edisto's churches, plantations, and other points of historic and natural interest with Edisto natives as your guides. Contact **Pink Van Tours** (843-869-1110) or **Tours of Edisto** (843-869-1984) for tour schedule—reservations are required. Adults $20; children $10. **Annual Tours of Edisto** take place the second Saturday in October. Contact the **Edisto Island Historic Preservation Society** (843-869-1954; P.O. Box 393, Edisto Island, SC 29438). Tickets generally cost $25 for adults; $8 ages 6–16.

For an education on the subject of the region's reptile life, visit the **Edisto Island Serpentarium** (843-869-1171; edistoserpentarium.com; 1374 SC 174) where more than 500 reptiles are on display in natural habitats; feeding and educational presentations occur every hour. Open in May and late August, Thursday through Saturday; June and July, Monday through Saturday Hours are 10–6. Adults $10.95; children $8.95.

One of Edisto's best places to eat is the **Old Post Office Restaurant** (843-869-2339; 1442 SC 174) a cozy place that serves lunch and dinner daily in season. This is not fried food cuisine—entrées feature steak, pork, and the best local fish and shellfish available. An affiliated and more informal restaurant is **Sunset Grille** (843-869-1010) with sunset and water views, located on Docksite Rd., by the Marina. Another is **Po Pigs Bo-B-Q** (843-869-9003; 2410 SC 174) a family-run dining room with a huge buffet and a cheerful atmosphere. It's Southern with a twist, offering curried rice with sun-dried fruit as well as country ham. The price is inexpensive to moderate. Open Thursday through Saturday 11:30

AM—9 PM., and Wednesdays from May 15 through September 15. Call both restaurants to confirm their seasonal and off-season hours. There are also pizza places, and on the docks facing St. Helena Sound, fish markets and informal restaurants.

Edisto has several art and craft galleries, with local and regional work represented informally. **With These Hands** (843-869-3509; 1444 SC 174) and **Sage Gallery** (843-869-1990; www.sagestudiogallery.com; 438 SC 174) are fine art and crafts gallieries; **Fish or Cut Bait Gallery** (843-869-2511; www.fishorcutbaitgallery.com; 142 Jungle Rd.) is a regular stop for upscale weekenders. For house and garden furnishings, prints, and fine conversation, stop by **The Crab Trap** (843-869-0226; 51 Station Court.)

For books it's the **Edisto Bookstore** (843-869-1885; www.theedistobookstore.com; 547 SC174).

Continuing across Edisto Island brings you to **Edisto Beach** (www.edistobeach.com), the curve of land that faces the Atlantic then turns to embrace the inner marsh and St. Helena Sound. It has been for years the summer destination of South Carolina families—both as day-trippers to the state park or as vacationers who stay for one or more weeks. They take up residence in the plain, raised, two-story houses that line the boulevards for about three-dozen blocks and spill across adjacent avenues. There's nothing fancy about Edisto Beach: It's informal, full of kids riding bikes (good bike lanes here, and watchful drivers), and minivans parked in the sand. A high point of the day is watching the shrimp boats come in. Plentiful beach access.

Many of these houses rent by the week, and several rental agencies list them. The market is organized by location: beachfront, second row (across the street from the beach usually with an ocean view), beach walk (easy access but on a side street), condos, and homes with docks (deep water, tidal creek, or other access, which may not be near the beach.) It is common for houses to accommodate 10—16 people—part of the charm of Edisto is its family reunion aspect—so the range of prices for a week in the summer can be from $850 to $3,700. Rental specs also include amenities like "fish cleaning sink," "hot and cold outside shower," grills, and cribs. For information contact:

Atwood Vacations (843-869-2151 or 1-800-476-0126; www.atwoodvacations.com).

Edisto Rentals (843-869-2527 or 1-800-868-5398; www.edistorealty.com).

Kapp/Lyons Co. (843-869-2516 or 1-800-945-9667; wwwkapplyons.com).

A small resort, **Fairfield Ocean Ridge/Wyndham** (843-869-4527; rentals 1-877-296-6335; www.fairfieldvacations.com; 1 King Cotton Rd., Edisto Island, SC 29438) offers rentals. Its 300-acre layout includes tennis, golf (Plantation Course; 843-869-1111) swimming, boating, and beach access. The accommodations are more rustic at the 1,255-acre **Edisto Beach State Park** (843-869-2756; www.southcarolinaparks.com; 8377 State Cabin Rd., Edisto Island, SC 29438). There's a 111-site camping area with water and electricity for tents and RVs (some are designated for handicapped visitors), a smaller section for tents only, and seven two-bedroom cabins. Restrooms near the sites offer hot showers. Nightly fees for tent sites begin at $17; full-hook ups start at $23. The cabins are furnished, heated, air-conditioned, and have access to a dock for crabbing and fishing. Nightly rates are $72–$124. Reservations are highly recommended. Call directly 1-866-345-7275 or make them online. The park includes 1.5 miles of beachfront, open marsh, a forest with nature trails, a general store, boat launching access to Big Bay Creek, and interpretive programs. The beach is a wonderful place to hunt for fossils and shark's teeth. Admission is $4 for adults; $1.50 kids.

Because of its location at the confluence of the North and South Edisto Rivers, the Atlantic, and St. Helena Sound, Edisto Beach offers probably the easiest access to the ACE Basin and all sorts of fishing, boating, and water sports. For maps and information about sightseeing and bird-watching, contact the **ACE Basin National Wildlife Refuge Headquarters** (843-889-3084; www.fws.gov; 8675 Willtown Rd., Hollywood, SC 29449) or contact the **South Carolina Department of Natural Resources** (843-844-8957; www.dnr .state.sc; 585 Donnelly Dr., Green Pond, SC 29446). A new Web site tracks things to see and do along a newly developing coastal heritage trail, and has good links: www.sc-heritage corridor.org.

If you want to tour the ACE Basin by water, stop by **Edisto Watersports & Tackle** (843-869-0663; 3702 Docksite Rd., or contact **ACE Basin Tours** (843-521-3099; www.acebasin tours.com. Captain **Ron Elliott's Edisto Island Tours** (843-869-1937) provides boat trips to offshore islands for shelling, island river tours, and inshore fishing. You may also tour by canoe and kayak with him. He is a passionate naturalist, and font of Edisto lore. Rent bikes, boats, and kayaks at **Island Bikes and Outfitters** (843-869-4444; 140 Jungle Rd.).

Bluffton

A most common mistake of visitors to Bluffton is that they make too much of the place, fret that they've missed something that was "there." An hour spent walking along its quiet streets, looking through the bramble and old fences at some of its 19th-century frame houses, visiting the church on the bluff, browsing in a few shops and art galleries, and doubling back to your parked car about does it for Bluffton.

Why bother? For one thing, the historic Bluffton village is one of the Lowcountry's last, true cul-de-sacs. There are a couple of "Historic" this-and-that signs nailed up, it is true, but what you thought it ought to have been and whether or not it ever becomes that scrubbed-up, idealized version of itself is of no concern. Tiny Bluffton has all the charm of a wonderful, barefoot kid who is not going to live up to some schoolmarm's idea of "potential."

However, it is also true that in the last five years, Bluffton has annexed so much adjacent land (in an effort to manage development) that the difference between the old, insouciant, square-mile village and the vast sprawl it now controls can be confusing. A restaurant with a Bluffton address may be located in an off-highway commercial park, not the old village. Get directions before you head out!

The most luxurious addition to greater Bluffton has been the development of **Palmetto Bluff** (843-706-6500; www.palmettobluffresort.com; 476 Mt. Pelia Rd., Bluffton, SC 29910), one of the largest and last unspoiled tracts in the area. You can dine at the inn's **River House** restaurant (843-706-6542), its luxury venue, or in a slightly less formal, though equally stylish restaurant, **Buffalo's** (843-706-6630.) Cottage accommodations run from $650–$1,100 per night in the high season of March through May and October and November. Rental houses are more expensive. Call 1-866-706-6565 for reservations or secure them online. There's a par-72 golf course for guests, as well as tennis, swimming, boating, and other resort amenities.

Visiting Bluffton

From Beaufort (about 35 minutes) follow SC 170 and continue as if you were going to Hilton Head, across the Broad River Bridge. About 8 miles ahead, exit right at the sign to Hilton Head and loop around. You are now on US 278 (William Hilton Parkway) the

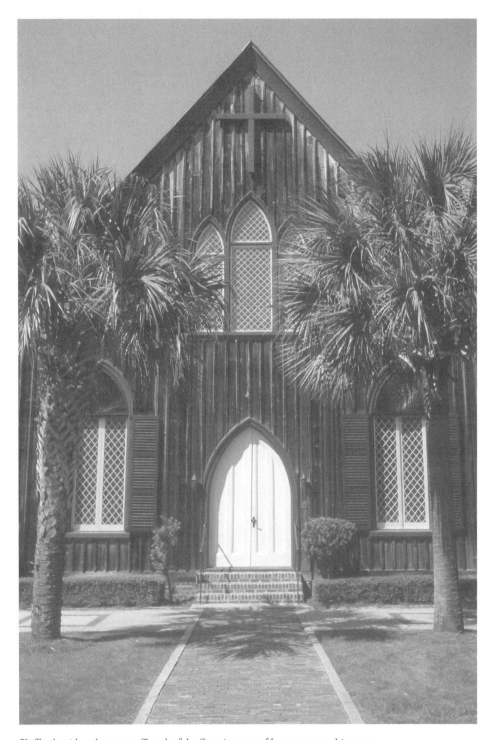

Bluffton's mid-19th-century Church of the Cross is a gem of Lowcountry architecture.

main Hilton Head road. After a couple of miles, you will see SC 46 marked as a right turn. Take it into Bluffton.

From Hilton Head (about 30 minutes) follow US 278 across the Graves Bridge and turn left on SC 46 and follow it to Boundary Street. Visitor information can be found at www.oldtownbluffton.com.

Bluffton was a summer community of island planters, and in 1863 it was nearly burned to the ground by Union troops. Ten antebellum buildings remain; another 16 or so houses were built after the Civil War. Taken together, they give a view of classic Lowcountry village life. Far from extravagant, they are nonetheless suffused with a sense of form appropriate to the landscape and to their function as seasonal dwellings belonging to families who had most likely seen better days. It is worth the trip alone to see the Church of the Cross (110 Calhoun St.) an unpainted wooden church (circa 1857) with beautiful interior detailing, original pews, and Gothic-style windows. Docents are on site Monday through Saturday, 11–2.

Start your tour of Bluffton at the town's historic center, the **Heyward House** (843-757-6293; www.heywardhouse.org; 70 Boundary St.), an 1840s Carolina farmhouse and slave cabin. It's open Monday through Friday from 10 to 3 and Saturday from 11 to 2. Tours are $5 adults; $2 students. Walking tours of the village originate here Thursdays at 9 AM or by appointment ($15 per person.) Then pick up a self-guided walking tour or biking map. Count on about two hours of wandering. Houses are marked by plaques, but not all are visible from the street. One book will help you appreciate them. It is: *No. II A Longer Short History of Bluffton, South Carolina and its Environs*, produced by the **Bluffton Historical Preservation Society** (843-757-6293; P.O. Box 742, Bluffton, SC 29910). The price is $9.95. It includes historic essays and descriptions of homes, a map, and wonderful photographs.

If you are biking, Bluffton is well situated for longer treks in rural areas. Local cyclists have created cue sheets and maps for enjoyable day trips from 25 to 60 miles that take you to historic sites and churches, remote boat landings, and some of the shooting locations for Hollywood movies. Find information online at: www.greaterblufftonpathways.org. Two bike shops will rent you equipment: **Bluffton Bike Shop** (843-706-2453; www.blufftonbicycle shop.com; 30 Plantation Park Dr.) and **Sports Addiction** (843-815-8281; www.sports addiction.us; Sheridan Park).

Bluffton (Calhoun St. in particular), has emerged as a center for working artists. Every third Friday there are street parties; gallery walks are regularly scheduled. These are just a few places to visit. **Calhoun Street Gallery** (843-757-4278; www.calhounstreetartgallery .com; 45 Calhoun St. and **Pluff Mudd** (843-757-5590; www.pluffmuddart.com; 27 Calhoun St,) feature paintings and crafts by local artists. The **Society of Bluffton Artists Gallery** (843-757-6586; www.sobagallery.com; 48 Boundary St.) includes work of 82 Lowcountry artists in a remodeled gallery space. The working studio of potter **Jacob Preston** (843-757-3084; 10 Church St. between Boundary St. and Calhoun St.) inside a converted church is open Tuesday through Saturday 10–5 or by appointment. At 69 Calhoun St. self-taught artist **Amos Hummel** exhibits his version of what locals call "the Bluffton state of mind." Outdoor sculpture consisting of remodeled bikes and motorcycles and painted furniture beckons you inside. **Fantozzi's Wrought Iron Design** (843-301-9855; 45 Calhoun St.) features functional and funky ironwork, from garden gates to candlesticks.

Bluffton's stores are no less unique. **Eggs N' Tricities** (843-757-3446; 71 Calhoun St.), which is located in an old filling station, has funky furniture outside and inside, and sells everything from 1940s era lamps and linens, to clothing and contemporary tableware.

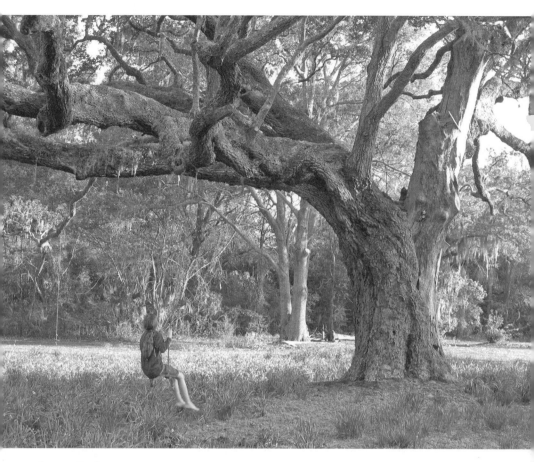

Lowcountry pleasure.   Peter Loftus

The Store (843-757-3855; 56 Calhoun St.) covers some of the same ground with similar esprit and also has wine, beer, and gourmet snacks. **Stock Farm Antiques** (843-757-8046; 1263 May River Rd.) offers prints, porcelain, silver, rugs, and furniture—some American, some English—chosen with a sense of what fits in the big new houses at the resorts as well as the real old ones. There are also several consignment shops and thrift stores in the area that offer bargains and maybe a treasure. Ask about them.

Locals take coffee breaks at **The Sippin' Cow Café** (843-757-5051; 1230 May River Rd.) or lunch at **Café Rebecca** (843-706-9693; 35 Lawton St.). Back toward "civilization" off US 278 lie two modest restaurants: **Mi Tierra** (843-757-7200; 101 Mellichamp Rd.) and **Myrtle's Bar and Grill** (843-757-6300; 32 Bruin Rd.) There are fine upscale restaurants, too: **Sigler's Rotisserie and Seafood** (843-815-5030; 12 Sheridan Circle) where roast chicken and seared meats are dinner favorites.

The Harbour Town Lighthouse at The Sea Pines Resort. Photo courtesy of the Hilton Head Island Visitor & Convention Bureau

5

HILTON HEAD

Courts, Courses, Sails & Sand

The Hilton Head Island that a visitor sees today is a far different place from what it was 40 years ago. It is the Lowcountry's boomtown, envied for its tax base, business opportunities, and recreational resources, and scrutinized as an example of the tension between planned growth and overdevelopment. Hilton Head's dynamic trajectory as a place and a resort brand has led to population increases and annexation well beyond its gated communities; to greater Bluffton, Point South, and Hardeeville. Its sometimes unenviable popularity caused a recent mayor to remark: "We're just trying to keep from getting run over."

Unlike the rest of the Lowcountry, Hilton Head is a place of condensed pleasure: In one day, a visitor can enjoy a range of activities that might have taken a week's vacation to savor in the past, had even the possibilities existed. The island is 12 miles long and 5 miles wide, shaped like a boot. It's on the Intracoastal Waterway, so there's river, ocean, and marsh access, with a mild year-round climate. Shops, tennis courts, golf courses, marinas, and restaurants prosper and proliferate. The commercial districts are discreetly screened from view, and even the busiest thoroughfare, US 278 (William Hilton Parkway), lacks neon signs. It's easy to understand why more than 1.8 million visitors come every year. Summer is the busiest time, when the year-round population of about 34,000 sees a turnover of 10,000 visitors a week.

Until 1955, when the first bridge linked Hilton Head to the mainland, the island's history resembled that of its Sea Island neighbors. First settled by planters with slaves who raised rice, indigo, and cotton on about 16 plantations, later occupied during the Civil War by Federal troops, and faced with hard times and isolation after that, the island remained rural and self-sufficient. The African American families who made up most of the island's population farmed and fished; the visitors who came were gentleman hunters, millionaires from the north. Packet steamers, sailboats, and barges supplied transportation, and more often than not, their market destination was Savannah, for Hilton Head is the southernmost area of Beaufort County.

The resort and residential development that began in earnest in the early 1960s led to the modern "plantation" layout that orders the island's geography today. Most resort activities are based in those original subdivisions, which are accessed by security gates and called private. They are: Sea Pines Plantation, Shipyard Plantation, Palmetto Dunes, Port Royal Plantation, and Hilton Head Plantation. Within and around them are the dozens of golf courses, tennis courts, and marinas that define island recreation. Stores and restau-

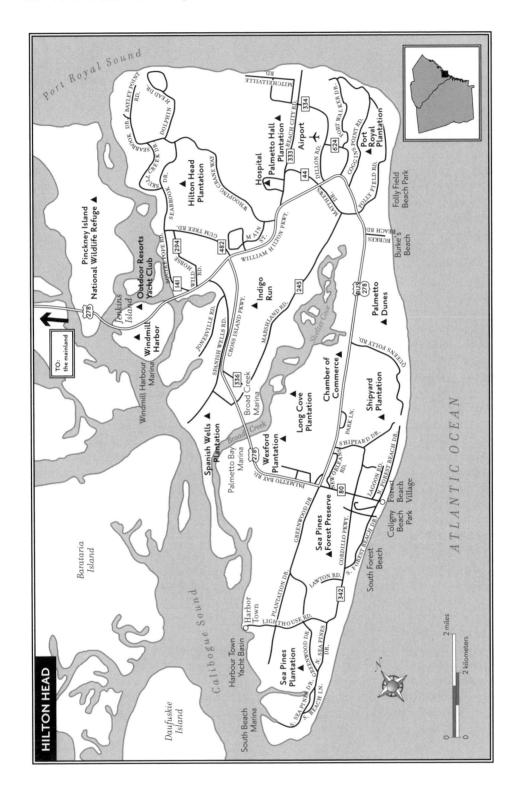

HILTON HEAD

Port Royal Sound

MITCHELLVILLE RD.

BAILEY POINT RD.

HEAD DR.

SEABROOK DR.

DOLPHIN

SKULL CREEK DR.

SEABROOK DR.

Hilton Head Plantation ▲

WHOOPING CRANE WAY

GUM TREE RD.

BEACH CITY RD.

334

333

624

PORT WALKER DR.

44

DILLON RD.

GOGGIN'S POINT RD.

Palmetto Hall Plantation ▲

Airport ✈

Hospital ▲

Port Royal Plantation ▲

FOLLY FIELD RD.

Folly Field Beach Park

Pinckney Island National Wildlife Refuge ▲

MATTHEWS DR.

BURKES BEACH RD.

Burke's Beach

SOUTH POPE RD.

141

294

WILD HORSE RD.

482

MAIN ST.

WILLIAM HILTON PKWY.

Outdoor Resorts Yacht Club ▲

Jenkins Island

278

Windmill Harbor ▲

Windmill Harbour Marina

TO: the mainland

Indigo Run ▲

245

BUS 278

Palmetto Dunes ▲

JONESVILLE RD.

CROSS ISLAND PKWY.

SPANISH WELLS RD.

MARSHLAND RD.

Shelter Cove

QUEENS FOLLY RD.

Chamber of Commerce ▲

Shipyard Plantation ▲

336

Broad Creek Marina

Spanish Wells Plantation ▲

Broad Creek

Long Cove Plantation ▲

Palmetto Bay Marina

278

Wexford Plantation ▲

PARK LN.

SHIPYARD DR.

NEW ORLEANS RD.

80

LAGOON RD.

N. FOREST BEACH RD.

Forest Beach Village

Coligny Beach Park

GREENWOOD DR.

CORDILLO PKWY.

Sea Pines Forest Preserve ▲

S. FOREST BEACH DR.

South Forest Beach

Barataria Island

PLANTATION DR.

LAWTON RD.

342

Atlantic Ocean

Calibogue Sound

Harbor Town

Harbour Town Yacht Basin

LIGHTHOUSE RD.

S. SEA PINES DR.

GREENWOOD DR.

BEACH LN.

N. SEA PINES DR.

Sea Pines Plantation ▲

South Beach Marina

Daufuskie Island

N

2 miles

2 kilometers

0

0

rants are usually gathered in mall clusters, like Shelter Cove, or in modest shopping pods, like the Village at Wexford or Coligny Plaza. Many smaller residential areas lie scattered across the island, some of them "gated" communities, others not. Because place names tend to sound alike—"cove" this and "water" that—and town regulations limit the size and shape of signs, pick up a free map.

As the island's topography has changed (much of it sculpted into golf courses), so has its population. Census figures categorize residents by race (90 percent white) and by age (some 30 percent over 60 years old). Given the fact that ongoing development has spilled over to adjacent areas, some destinations that identify themselves with the Hilton Head name might actually be located 10 miles away, in greater Bluffton. Not a deal-breaker, but you may want to call or check a Web site to factor in distances and travel time.

Growth has not blotted out the unique character of the Lowcountry; it's just led to more creative packaging, which is to a visitor's advantage. As you plan, you might want to decide what particular quality you'd like your trip to have. If you think you mostly want to play golf or tennis, you might look into options in the **Lodging** section for "stay-and-play" packages. If you're traveling with friends or family, you may want to rent a house or villa (a fully furnished unit in a condominium complex). If you decide upon a resort, you may not need a car—most resort amenities are within walking and biking distance, and you will be provided with airport transportation. For touring without a car, rent a bike and explore island-wide bike trails.

The high season starts in March, when families come on spring vacation, and continues through April, punctuated by the PGA tournament which has been played at Sea Pines since 1969; **Verizon Heritage PGA Tour** (843-671-2448; www.verizonheritage .com). May and early June tend to be quieter, before the crowds of summer, as do September and October. When the island is crowded, expect congestion and lines everywhere. Inter-island trips can take three times as long, with heavy stop-and-go traffic during morning or evening rush hour. Some of the congestion has been alleviated by the Cross Island Expressway, a new toll road that takes you from the near North End to Palmetto Bay Road.

GETTING THERE

Savannah/Hilton Head International Airport (www.savannahairport.com) and the smaller **Hilton Head Airport** (www.hiltonheadairport.com) are gateways. Flights to Hilton Head usually stop first in Charlotte, North Carolina; there are many direct flights to Savannah from cities around the country. Rental car service is available at both locations, as are courtesy shuttles if you are staying at a resort. **Low Country Adventures** (843-681-8212; www.lowcountryadventures.com) and **Palmetto Taxi** (843-683-4279; www.palmettotaxi.com) serve Hilton Head. You may make other arrangements when you arrive at a courtesy desk located in the baggage pick-up area. Call in advance to check rates and make reservations, especially if you're traveling at high season. Shared rate fares are about $40 one way. By car, take exit 8 from I-95 to US 278, the link to Hilton Head. It's about 25 minutes by car from the exit to the north end of the island and Bluffton locations. **Amtrak** (800-872-7245; www.amtrak.com) serves Savannah twice each day.

Lodging

There are more than 3,000 hotel and motel rooms and 6,000 rental units, including cottages, houses, and villas scattered across the island, from sites on or near the beach to those around golf courses, marinas, lagoons, in residential subdivisions or low-rise housing complexes, even on the main highway. Another 1,000 units are dedicated to "time-share" arrangements and may be available for rent, too. Your accommodations may be elegant or simple; offer as much or as little privacy as you wish; come with or without kitchens; lie within walking distance, or not, from the beach and recreational amenities.

Rates vary from as little as $60 per night (off-season) for an economy motel room to $6,000 per week for a luxurious oceanfront home with a swimming pool. The range reflects differences in size and location—oceanfront is premium; resort privileges add to the price—and also the time of year: Rates are obviously highest during the vacation seasons, March through April and June through mid-August. The shoulder seasons of late April and May, then September and October bring ideal golfing conditions, so prices stay high, though not at the seasonal peak. In the winter months, rates can be half what they are in the high season. Like many resort areas, Hilton Head adds an accommodations tax to lodging bills, and some establishments place a surcharge on credit-card payments. Ask for an estimate of your total bill when you are booking. Whatever accommodation you choose, inquire about special rate packages or coupons offered for restaurants, health clubs, or shops. Many hotels have discounts for golf and tennis; some have family plans, including activities for kids. In larger hotels, children often stay for free. Access to the Internet via Wi-Fi connection is widely available. In 2008, day spas represented the newest amenity at Hilton Head resorts.

The easiest way to make reservations in a hotel or motel (listed directly below) is contact by phone or Web site. To inquire about home and villa rentals, call a property management company (listed under "Vacation Property Rentals" below). Central reservation agencies can give you a sense of the whole picture, and they may be especially helpful in designing a package tailored to your specific interests. The **Hilton Head Island–Bluffton Chamber of Commerce** (843-785-3673 or 1-800-523-3373; www.hiltonheadisland.org) is a good place to start. If you're interested in camping, look into the two recreational vehicle parks listed under **Recreation,** later in this chapter. If you're staying on a boat, see "Marinas," also in the **Recreation** listings. The following rates are for one night's stay, per person, double occupancy. They do not include taxes, surcharges, or any special recreation/entertainment discounts. Prices quoted are for high season accommodations. Note that the rates for Luxury Accommodations are at least in the "Very Expensive" category: They can easily run to $260 per night. Villa and home rentals generally run from Saturday to Saturday during peak season. Three kennels provide places for your cat or dog to stay: **Brooke's Bed & Biscuit** (843-757-7387); **Evergreen Pet Lodge** (843-681-8354 or 1-866-680-8354; www.evergreenpetlodgehhi.com); and **Low Country Kennel Pet Resort and Spa** (843-681-3991; www.lowcountrykennels.com). They allow you to pick up your pet during the day, while also providing boarding, care, and grooming. Note that from Memorial Day to Labor Day pets are not permitted on the beach between 10 AM and 5 PM and at other times are required to be on a leash.

Rates

Inexpensive	Up to $80
Moderate	$80 to $140
Expensive	$140 to $200
Very Expensive	$200 and up

Credit Cards

AE—American Express
CB—Carte Blanche
D—Discover Card
DC—Diner's Club
MC—MasterCard
V—Visa

Luxury Hotels and Inns

Crowne Plaza Resort

843-842-2400 or 1-800-334-1881.
www.cphiltonhead.com.
130 Shipyard Dr., Shipyard Plantation.
Price: Very Expensive.
Credit Cards: All major.
Handicap Access: Yes.

A 340-room oceanfront luxury hotel with full concierge service, two restaurants, and a popular lounge for evening entertainment. Two pools on site, golf courses within a mile and accessed by complimentary shuttle; nearby tennis courts and a day spa, and sailing and water sports by arrangement.

Daufuskie Island Resort

843-842-2000 or 1-800-648-6778.
www.daufuskieislandresort.com.
On Daufuskie Island.
Price: Very Expensive.
Credit Cards: All major.
Handicap Access: Yes.

Though not on Hilton Head, the Daufuskie Island Resort, accessed by ferry, is modeled on its neighbor's plan (with additional privacy) that includes two golf courses, a tennis complex, an equestrian center, beach and water sports, and a new spa. Accommodations are in a main inn and in several cottages of two and four bedrooms. It's not spoiled by overdevelopment (no traffic, no crowds) and appeals to corporate clients, families, and group retreats. The island is 5 miles long by 2.5 miles wide, easy to see on an island tour.

Hilton Head Marriott Resort & Spa

843-686-8400 or 1-888-511-5086.
www.hiltonheadmarriott.com.
1 Hyatt Circle, Palmetto Dunes.
Price: Very Expensive.
Credit Cards: All major.
Handicap Access: Yes.

The largest hotel on the island, with 512 rooms, indoor pool, Olympic-sized outdoor pool, and children's pool. Health club, tennis courts, three golf courses, sailboat and bicycle rentals, and lots of beachfront. Three restaurants and a piano bar offer both formal and casual poolside dining. A children's program (for an additional fee) is available weekends year-round, daily during the summer.

Hilton Oceanfront Resort

843-842-8000 or 1-800-845-8001.
www.hiltonheadoceanfrontresort.com.
23 Ocean Lane, Palmetto Dunes.
Price: Very Expensive.
Credit Cards: All major.
Handicap Access: Yes.

A luxury, 295-room hotel that claims the largest rooms on the island—560 square feet each—with private balconies and kitchenettes. At the oceanfront setting there's an adults-only pool and a family pool, whirlpools, a fitness center, 25 tennis courts and five golf courses. Activities for kids (4–16) can be arranged for an additional charge—even at night. Restaurants and nightclubs within the complex.

Inn at Harbour Town

843-363-8100 or 1-800-732-7463.
www.seapines.com.
1 Lighthouse Lane, Sea Pines Plantation.
Price: Very Expensive.
Credit Cards: All major.
Handicap Access: Yes.

This 60-room inn is in the Harbour Town complex, a Mediterranean-style marina

Hilton Head's Main Street Inn features European-style luxury and private, decorated courtyards over a beachfront location.

village whose lighthouse is the best-recognized symbol of Hilton Head. The inn is situated just off the water, in a quieter location by the golf courses. It's more thoughtfully designed than the functional fun-and-sun architecture, or the low-slung Tahiti-roof look of Sea Pines, and its provision of service (butlers on each floor, glorious bathrooms) and serenity (a quiet library and elegant-but-casual furniture and decorations) seem to suggest another way to enjoy the resort experience: to be in it, perhaps, but not of it.

Main Street Inn
843-681-3001 or 1-800-471-3001.
www.festivaresorts.com.
2200 Main St.
Price: Expensive to Very Expensive.
Credit Cards: All major.
Handicap Access: Two rooms.

Unique on Hilton Head in that it offers the privacy of a lovely home and the services of a small European hotel, this inn has 33 luxury rooms, an outdoor lap-pool and whirlpool, lounge areas with fireplaces, and a fine restaurant where a full breakfast is included and dinner is usually sought after. The spa offers deep-cleansing facials, skin-care and hydrotherapy treatments, yoga classes, and massage. Outdoors, the Charleston-style urban gardens, with European statuary, enhance the feeling of an oasis.

Westin Hilton Head Island Resort and Spa
843-681-4000 or 1-800-937-8461.
www.westinhhi.com.
2 Grasslawn Ave., Port Royal Plantation.
Price: Very Expensive.
Credit Cards: All major.
Handicap Access: Yes.

Considered the most luxurious of the island's oceanfront resort hotels, with 412 rooms and 30 suites, plus 100 villas. The Westin is praised for its spa, Sunday brunch and upscale grill menu, the elegant decorations, rooms with balconies, and good children's program. Guests may play on three Port Royal courses and on grass, hard, and clay courts. Indoor and outdoor pools.

Smaller Hotels
Hilton Head Metropolitan Hotel
843-842-3100 or 1 800-535-3248
www.hiltonheadmetropolitan.com.
36 S. Forest Beach Dr.
Price: Expensive.
Credit Cards: All major.
Handicap Access: Yes.

This modest hotel has a good location, with beach access directly across the street. Remodeled from a Best Western.

Holiday Inn Oceanfront
843-785-5126 or 1-800-423-9897.
www.hihiltonhead.com.
1 S. Forest Beach Dr.
Price: Expensive.
Credit Cards: All major.
Handicap Facilities: Yes.

A popular public-access beach is at your
doorstep, featuring a playground, most
always a pick-up beach volleyball game, and
guaranteed people-watching from the
snack bar. Kids, who stay free, will enjoy
nearby Coligny Plaza with its touristy gift
and tee shirt shops, informal restaurants,
and movie theater. The inn tends to attract
bargain-minded international guests and
young people; it can be noisy, but has an
upbeat, friendly vibe.

Park Lane Hotel and Suites
843-686-5700 or 1-877-247-3431
www.hiltonheadparklanehotel.com.
12 Park Lane, in Central Park.
Price: Expensive to Very Expensive.
Credit Cards: All major.
Handicap Facilities: Yes.

An all-suite hotel, with rooms larger than
average and featuring a fully equipped
kitchen; some have wood-burning fireplaces. A recreation area includes basketball, volleyball and tennis courts, pool,
Jacuzzi hot tub, jogging trails, and a playground. Free shuttle to the beach.

South Beach Marina Inn
843-671-6498 or 1-800-367-3909.
www.southbeachvillage.com.
In Sea Pines Plantation.
Price: Expensive to Very Expensive.
Credit Cards: AE, D, MC, V.

Located in a New England–style marina village in Sea Pines Plantation, this 17-room
inn sits above waterfront shops and restaurants. The rooms are condominium suites
with living and dining rooms and kitch-

enettes, overlooking the courtyard or
marina. The inn has a Cape Cod feeling:
throw rugs, brass beds, and hardwood
floors. Tennis, water sports, restaurants,
and the beach close by.

Budget Choices
Each of these national chain motels of
approximately 100 rooms has a swimming
pool and is close to inexpensive restaurants
or shopping areas. They tend to be several
blocks from a beach access point.

Comfort Inn (843-842-6662 or 1-800-
522-3224; www.comfortinnhiltonhead
.com; 2 Tanglewood Dr.).

Hampton Inn (843-681-7900 or 1-800-
426-7866; www.hamptoninn.com; One
Dillon Rd.).

Beachwalk Hotel (843-842-8888 or 1-
888-843-4136; www.hiltonheadbeach
walkhotel.com; 40 Waterside Dr.).

Quality Inn (843-681-3655 or 1-800-995-
3928; www.hhqualityinn.com; US 278 at
Main Street Village).

Red Roof Inn (843-686-6808 or 1-800-
843-7663; 5 RegencyPkwy.).

Vacation Property Rentals
Most vacation rental properties are concentrated on the south end of the island in Sea
Pines Plantation, Shipyard Plantation, South
Forest Beach, and Palmetto Dunes Resort.
Several villa rental complexes are located
mid-island on or near Folly Field Beach. The
northern half of the island is geared mainly
to permanent residents; the island's other
private communities do not generally permit
short-term rental programs.

Villas and homes usually rent by the
week, but nightly rates are available. The
least expensive summer rates are about $900
per week, which can buy you a small unit
outside a plantation more than one-half
mile from the beach. In 2008, about $6,500

Hilton Head's broad beach is a 12-mile recreation area.

per week in the summer would secure an oceanfront home. From November to February, rates drop substantially.

Most rental companies manage properties in a variety of sizes, shapes, and locations. A desirable vacation rental would offer free swimming, free or discounted tennis, discounts on golf, and should be within walking distance of the beach. Some offer dining and shopping discounts, too. Before you make your final decision, you might consider where you want to be and what it is you wish to do. You need not pay premium oceanfront prices if you're going to be on the links all day.

Before you sign a rental agreement, make sure you understand policies regarding deposits, refunds in the event of cancellation, times of arrival and departure, and charges, if any, for cleaning services. If you have special needs such as handicapped-accessible rooms, or will be renting cots, cribs, bicycles, or beach chairs, alert the agent from the start. The agencies listed below are just some of many.

Adventure Inn Resort and Rentals (1-800- 845-9500; www.advinn.com) Oceanfront accommodations in efficiencies or one-, two-, and three-bedroom villas.

Beach Properties of Hilton Head (1-800-671-5155; www.beach-property.com) A variety of deluxe and non-oceanfront properties and villas, many available by the night with a four-night minimum.

Harbour Town Resorts (843-671-1400 or 1-800-541-7375; www.harbourtownresorts.com) Villa and condo rental in the marina village at Sea Pines.

Hilton Head Vacation Rentals (843-689-3010 or 1-800-232-2463; www.800beach mecom) A selection of more that 200 homes and villas in the major plantations, and on the north end of the island. Golf and tennis packages available.

Palmetto Dunes Resort (843-785-1138 or 1-866-310-6014; www.palmettodunes .com) Manages more than 400 villas and homes throughout Palmetto Dunes, including Shelter Cove Marina condominiums.

Resort Rentals of Hilton Head Island (843-686-6008 or 1-800-845-7017; www.hhivacations.com) More than 300 properties in Sea Pines and South Forest Beach.

Resort Quest Vacation Rentals (1-800-448-3412; www.resortquesthiltonhead .com) Representing some of Hilton Head's high-end properties, as well as the best in the moderate range, in five island communities.

Sea Pines Resort (1-800-732-7463; www.seapines.com) One- to six-bedroom accommodations in private homes and villas in the island's most exclusive and well-known resort.

Recreational Vehicle Parks/Camping

Hilton Head Motor Coach Resort (843-785-7699 or 1-800-722-2365; www.hilton headmotorcoachresort.com; 133Arrow Rd.) Full hookups, 401 sites, six tennis courts, pool, manmade lake, shuffleboard, horseshoes, basketball, playground, laundry, bathrooms with tubs and saunas.

Hilton Head Harbor RV Resort & Marina (843-681-3256; 1-800-845-9560; www.hiltonhadharbor.com; Jenkins Rd., north end of Hilton Head) Full hookups, 200 RV sites, bathhouses, two pools, three tennis courts, laundry, exercise room, sauna, and whirlpool.

Stoney Crest Plantation (843-757-3249; 419 May River Rd. Bluffton) Ten miles from Hilton Head, this park has 30 RV sites with full hookups as well as 10 campsites.

Reservation Services

The following services can assist you with making reservations in advance of your trip:

Hilton Head Accommodations and Golf Hotline (843-686-6662 or 1-800-444-4772; www.hiltonheadusa.com).

Hilton Head Condo Hotline (843-785-2939 or 1-800-258-5852; www.hhcondo hotline.com).

Island Visitor Center (843-341-9184 or 1-888-741-7666; www.islandvisitorcen-ter.com).

DINING AND NIGHTLIFE

The restaurants included in the listing below are just some of the 300 places to eat or relax and listen to music. There are selections in every price category. Where you go may depend on whether you're traveling with children (if you're at a resort, ask the concierge about babysitting services), your preference in music and late hours, where on the island you're staying, and your budget. Recommendations for spots you can go to after a day at the beach are also included. Fast food and moderately priced chain restaurants are well represented on Hilton Head, too.

A Web site, www.hhidining.com, provides a useful listing of restaurants by cuisine, style, and location, menus, and short-cuts to finding what you need: open on Sunday, brunch vs. lunch, specials, most crowded times, live music, etc.

The price categories are the same as described elsewhere in the guide, and represent per-person expenses estimated without tax, tip, or bar beverages. In general, dining out is more expensive on Hilton

Head than in similar restaurants elsewhere, although there are savings to be found in eating before the crowd (early-bird specials) or on a particular evening when the restaurant has an advertised special.

Dining Price Code

Inexpensive	Up to $10
Moderate	$10 to $30
Expensive	$30 to $50
Very Expensive	$50 or more

Credit Cards

AE—American Express
CB—Carte Blanche
D—Discover Card
DC—Diner's Club
MC—MasterCard
V—Visa

CQs

843-671-2779.
www.cqsrestaurant.com.
140 Lighthouse Rd.
Open: Daily.
Price: Expensive
Cuisine: Upscale Southern.
Serving: D.
Credit Cards: All major.

When Hilton Head was a lot smaller and cozier, CQs was kind of a clubhouse tucked into Sea Pines, a place that was open year-round. It still has that feel, with its murals, memorabilia, and heart-pine floors. The cuisine is much upgraded to steaks and seafood specials, and local treats like venison stew. The early seating features an inexpensive tasting menu, about $20 apiece; you can pick and choose from small-portion samplings at The Chef's Table; or select from about a dozen entrées on the dinner menu. The patio, with its tables shaded by live oaks, is popular in spring and fall. CQs is known for its comprehensive wine list, with many sold by the glass, which makes good sense if you choose the sample-menu options.

Hilton Head Diner

843-686-2400.
Open: Daily, 24 hours.
Price: Inexpensive.
Cuisine: American.
Serving: B, L, D.
Credit Cards: All major.

An update on the classic American roadside eatery. Breakfast is served all the time—but there are big sandwiches, dinner entrées (with potato, salad, and vegetable), and beer and wine available, too. Coffee refills, and desserts from the cold case.

Hudson's On the Docks

843-681-2772.
www.hudsonsonthedocks.com.
One Hudson Rd., just off Squire Pope Rd., north end of the island.
Open: Daily.
Price: Moderate.
Cuisine: Seafood.
Serving: L, D.
Credit Cards: AE, DC, MC, V.

Large, informal family restaurant, one of the first on the island, in a rustic setting overlooking the Intracoastal Waterway on the docks at Skull Creek, known for its sunsets. Plenty of seating on the deck. Entrées include fresh local seafood like crab or shrimp (fried, sautéed, boiled) and blackened or stuffed specials. No reservations—go early on a summer night or risk waiting two hours to be served.

Julep's

843-842-5857.
14 Greenwood Dr., at the Gallery of Shops.
Open: Daily.
Price: Expensive to Very Expensive.
Cuisine: Upscale Southern/Continental.
Serving: D.
Credit Cards: AE, MC, V.

In a trend made popular by New South young professionals, local foodstuffs (catfish, flounder) are tweaked and glorified, but not to an unrecognizable (or unpronounceable) state. There's always light pasta, sauced veal, beef, or fish. The setting is formal, with white tablecloths and fresh flowers; although there's a nod to children with a kid's menu. It's dressier than other spots on Hilton Head—more like East Bay Street restaurants of Charleston. Reservations recommended.

Just Pasta

843-686-3900.
One Coligny Plaza.
Open: Daily.
Price: Inexpensive to Moderate.
Cuisine: Creative pastas.
Serving: L, D.
Credit Cards: AE, D, MC, V.

Tiny, casual, made cozy by hand-painted murals, and tucked away at one end of the bustling Coligny Plaza, this is the place for a simple meal based on a dozen kinds of pasta, sauces, and additions. Specials include eggplant, shrimp scampi, and sautéed crab cakes with asparagus, sun-dried tomatoes, and pesto hollandaise over fettuccine. The breads are homemade, from its sister bakery. A short walk from the beach, which makes it a nice, pre-sunset stop.

Market Street

843-686-4976.
1 N. Forest Beach Dr.
Open: Daily.
Price: Inexpensive.
Cuisine: Mediterranean.
Serving: L, D.
Credit Cards: AE, MC, V.

If on a starry summer night you've decided to walk the beach near the Coligny Beach access point and hear Greek music, you must be nearby. Come back after your walk to enjoy informal grill food—gyros, pita wraps—or Greek specialties like *moussaka, dolmathes,* and *spanakopita.* Locals come for the homemade soups and vegetarian options.

Michael Anthony's

843-785-6272.
37 New Orleans Rd.
Closed: Sun.
Price: Expensive.
Cuisine: Italian.
Serving: D.

The kitchen elaborates on northern Italian classics like homemade gnocchi, osso buco, and veal tenderloin. Seasonal additions include game in the fall and specialty mushrooms and truffles when available. Local design firm J. Banks has made an elegant room, divided lengthwise by a curving, granite bar illuminated by pinpoint lights on one side, and a dining area accented by walls the color of terra cotta and pale wood furnishings. It feels sophisticated but not stuffy. The work of the pastry chef attracts diners for after-dinner drinks and dessert, often taken at the few booths in the bar. Very good wine list, with an unusually large selection by the glass, too. Reservations suggested.

Mi Tierra

843-342-3409.
Fairfield Square on the north end.
Open: Daily.
Price: Inexpensive to Moderate.
Cuisine: Mexican.
Serving: L, D.
Credit Cards: AE, MC, V.

Located on US 278, this unpretentious Mexican restaurant attracts locals, workers, and commuters heading for home in Beaufort or Bluffton. The parking lot can be full by 5 PM. It's as unassuming as can be: tile floor, wooden booths and tables, linens and walls in festive colors, and mostly Spanish-speaking wait staff. The food is good, the atmosphere welcoming, the portions enormous. A mariachi band performs most Mondays. Another branch is located in Bluffton.

Red Fish

843-686-3388.
www.redfishofhiltonhead.com.
8 Archer Rd.
Open: Daily
Serving: L (Mon.–Sat.), D (Mon.–Sun.)
Price: Expensive to Very Expensive.
Cuisine: Caribbean flavored with jerk
spices and grilled fruits.
Credit Cards: All major.

In the last five years Red Fish has become
the hottest new restaurant on the island
because of its creative menu of spiced
seafood (like the Cajun shrimp and lobster
burger) and steak, (although you can order
entrées simply grilled with oil and
lemon). A stunning dining room feels like
an art gallery on South Beach. The attention to its wines, and an on-site wine
market with more than 1,000 bottles from
which you may also select for your meal,
has garnered it recognition from wine
publications and the local press. Dining
indoors or out. Reservations are a good
idea.

Sage Room

843-785-5352.
sageroomhh.com.
13 Heritage Plaza.
Open: Mon.–Sat.
Price: Expensive.
Cuisine: American with fusion accents.
Serving: D.
Credit Cards: AE, MC, V.

An open kitchen and chef's "bar" (where
you can eat and watch the chef at work)
attract Hilton Head foodies. Sage is small
and comfortable, smart but not flashy,
decorated in beadboard, quiet greens, and
paintings by local artists.

Professionals from Beaufort and
Bluffton like its unpretentiousness and
excellent entrées: two cuts only of steak,
corn-fed from Nebraska; at least four
kinds of fish, some encrusted with nuts;

shrimp and pasta; classic salad of greens
with vinaigrette. A good choice before or
after the movies at Coligny Plaza, just
down the road.

Signe's Heaven Bound Bakery & Café

843-785-9118.
www.signesbakery.com.
93 Arrow Rd.
Closed: Sun.
Price: Inexpensive.
Cuisine: American.
Serving: B, L.
Credit Cards: MC, V.

Founded in 1972 by an enterprising cook,
nationally recognized many times since,
and a regular stop for returning visitors
and for residents who appreciate fresh,
healthy, food. Here are sandwiches on
whole-grain bread (which you can also
buy by the loaf), soups, many kinds of coffee cakes and muffins, fabulous pastries,
and desserts. The french toast is probably
an inch thick; the brownies and blondies
even thicker. The café and porch are modest—it's the bakery display cases that
aren't. Fruit, vegetable, and pasta salads
are great for picnics. It closes at 2 PM on
Saturday, so stock up early for Sunday
brunch.

Truffles Café

843-671-6136.
www.trufflescafe.com.
71 Lighthouse Rd., Sea Pines Center.
Open: Daily.
Price: Inexpensive to Moderate.
Cuisine: American; Continental.
Serving: L, D.
Credit Cards: All major.

Casual atmosphere, homemade soups,
huge salads, French-bread sandwiches and
wraps, quiche, fresh vegetables, and
grilled entrées. Light meals like Cuban
panini or potpie are inexpensive, and you
can order them at any time. The market is

full of gourmet items, and take-out is available. It's a cross between a fern bar and a wine bar, with a bistro menu. Truffles Grill, newly opened in 2007, serves dinner in a small, stylish setting that caters to the island's upscale professional people.

Two Eleven Park Wine Bar & Bistro
843-686-5212.
www.211parkofhilton head.com.
211 Park Plaza.
Closed: Sun.
Price: Expensive.
Cuisine: American/Southern fusion.
Serving: D.
Credit Cards: AE, D, MC, V.

A handsome checkered-floor bistro, with a mural out of Edward Hopper and décor out of Paris in the Twenties. Dozens of wines by the glass and a list two hundred deep for the table. The place may bustle at its capacity, but it feels intimate even when buzzing. A unique feature is the choice of "petite" entrée portions and a big choice of appetizers, in bistro style, but with twists like "tuna tuna tuna," a sushi offering. Rack of lamb, veal chops, and a different pasta every night.

Nightlife
The beat goes on and on at Hilton Head, especially in summer when crowds jam the dance floor or couples find quieter music in lounges or late-night eateries. Check ahead for cover charges or drink minimums. The legal drinking age is 21.

Big Bamboo (843-686-3443; Upstairs at Coligny Plaza) Late-night music and dancing from 10:30 PM Monday, Wednesday, and Friday in a pretend WW II–era South Pacific retro setting.

Eugene's Oyster Bar (843-785-9666; Palmetto Bay Marina) The bar and lounge of this marina restaurant fill up quickly, especially when musicians play weekend nights. Plates of fresh-shucked oysters (and oysters with specialty toppings) and steamed shrimp are available as early as 5 PM and last well past the sunset over Broad Creek.

Jazz Corner (843-842-8620; www.the jazzcorner.com; Village at Wexford) National and regional jazz artists perform here nightly. Check the schedule to find your favorites: Big Band, Swing, Rhythm and Blues, and Classic jazz. Shows start at 7:30.

Kingfisher (843-785-4442; Shelter Cove Harbour) Live music and dancing begins at 6 PM nightly, including Big Bands, jazz combos, and laid-back keyboardist Jim Eshleman. Bar menu or full meals (steak, pasta, seafood) served.

Quarterdeck (843-842-1999; Harbour Town) Laid-back waterfront lounge, an island classic since 1970. Late-afternoon beach music, folk-rock, steel drums outside (4–8 PM); after sunset the music rocks harder and moves inside until 12:30 AM. Open Thursday, Friday, and Saturday.

Shoreline Ballroom (843-842-0358; Hilton Head Beach and Tennis Resort, Folly Rd.) A big performing space featuring regional bands and comedy acts.

Stages (843-686-3545;25 Park Plaza) Dance club with live music.

Wild Wing Café (843-785-9464; 72 Pope Ave.) Live music daily except Tuesday and Sunday (karaoke night) from 10 PM to 1:30 AM. Happy hour specials every day.

XO Lounge (843-341-8080; Hilton Oceanfront Resort, in Palmetto Dunes) Live entertainment nightly in a swanky, recently renovated club, where champagne flights and an appetizer menu are served until late.

Touring

Here are some suggestions for exploring more of Hilton Head and the surrounding area. The towns of Bluffton and Beaufort are easy day trips. (For detailed information on these destinations, see Chapter Four, *Beaufort, Edisto & Bluffton.*) Each has a historic area of old houses, as well as shops and restaurants. Daufuskie Island is served by tour boat operators who offer cookouts and on-shore touring options. Savannah is about an hour away, and in a day you could tour the historic district, shop, have at least one meal, and be back in time for sunset over the marsh. A trip to Charleston requires a bit more time and planning, including approximately four hours by car, round-trip. For additional information on canoeing, kayaking, and eco tours, which may include dolphin-watching, see the **Recreation** section below.

Airstream Aviation (843-785-7770; Hilton Head Airport) Private charters and tours of the island, the Lowcountry, or Savannah, from $75 per person, two-person minimum.

Camelot Limousine and Tours (843-842-7777; www.camelothhi.com) On- and off-island transportation, personalized tours, maximum of six people per limousine.

Coastal Discovery Museum (843-689-6767; www.coastaldiscovery.org; 100 William Hilton Pkwy.) The Museum offers 11 tours by boat, trolley, bicycle, and on foot, suitable for all ages, including tours with historic, wildlife, marine, and landscape themes. Tours last from 90 minutes to three hours. Make reservations on their Web site.

Gullah Heritage Trail Tours (843-681-7066) Two-hour tours through 10 neighborhoods and to sites prominent in the island's African American culture.

Low Country Adventures (843-681-8212; lowcountryadventures.com) Island and off-island tours in a tour van or bus, including day trips with a guide to the historic areas of Charleston, Savannah, and Beaufort (from $55 per person).

Vagabond Cruise (843-842-7179; www.vagabondcruise.com; Harbour Town Marina, Sea Pines) Vessels take you to Savannah's River Street and pick you up four hours later. Discounted Savannah Trolley tickets sold on board. Prices $49 adults; $25 kids. A good way to avoid the driving/parking hassle and get a sense of place: why Savannah was and is such a significant port.

CULTURE

As Hilton Head has grown, so has its arts community. Check the Arts & Entertainment section of the daily newspaper, *The Island Packet* (www.islandpacket.com), for listings. The largest venue for performances is the Arts Center of Coastal Carolina (14 Shelter Cove Lane; 843-842-2787; www.artshhi.com), which features nationally touring performers, regional orchestras, dance and theater, children's theater, and gallery space. It is active all year long, and its high-quality talent attracts residents and visitors. Check its schedule for performances celebrating Gullah heritage in the Sea Islands by local gospel choirs and storytellers, the Hallelujah Singers.

Art

Hilton Head Art League (843-671-3242; www.hiltonheadartleague.org; Suite 207, Pineland Station) has shows by local artists nearly every month and features more than

800 members. (See the "Galleries" entry under **Shopping** for more art information. Also see the section on Bluffton in Chapter Four, *Beaufort, Edisto & Bluffton.*

Walter Greer Gallery (843-842-2787) Part of the Arts Center, the 2,000-square-foot space hosts a variety of local and national visual artists in monthly shows.

Film

Coligny Theatre (843-686-3500; www.colignytheatre.com; Coligny Plaza).

Northridge Ten Cinemas (843-342-3800; 435 William Hilton Pkwy.).

Park Plaza Cinemas (843-785-5001; Park Plaza).

Sea Turtle Cinemas (843-706-2888; 106 Buckwalter Pkwy., Bluffton).

Historic Sites

Several sites dating as far back as the time of Native American settlements and covering the period of the Civil War are accessible to visitors. For more information and location maps, contact Coastal Discovery Museum (see address and hours below) or contact Gullah Heritage Trail Tours (843-681-7066) for tours which include visits to praise houses and cemeteries, and to Mitchelville, the first freed Negro township in the country. The Heritage Library Foundation (843-686-6560; www.heritagelib.org) offers a unique opportunity to research families, not just sites. A microfiche database, and hundreds of books and periodicals, as well as a searchable CD-ROM database form the core of this African American research collection that places special emphasis on genealogy. Open Monday and Thursday through Saturday 9–2, but call to confirm.

Baynard Ruins The remains of a plantation house and outbuildings first constructed circa 1800 can be seen on a short, self-guided walk at the site, within Sea Pines Plantation ($5 gate fee to access Sea Pines). The ruins are made of tabby, a popular homemade Lowcountry building material that resulted from burning oyster shells (to make lime), which were then mixed with whole shells, sand, and water. This is one of few sites where you can still see it.

Coastal Discovery Museum on Hilton Head Island (843-689-6767; www.coastaldiscovery .org; 100 William Hilton Pkwy., Hilton Head Island, SC 29925) Located at the north end of the island, mile marker 1 near the bridge, Coastal Discovery is an addition to a place where so much is new. Archaeological digs have yielded a collection of artifacts relating to the island's history and culture, and these are on display, sharing exhibition space with models, dioramas, and explanatory panels on Sea Island biodiversity. Efforts to record island life through oral history interviews are ongoing; solid scholarship produced a fine four-part videotape (which is shown at the museum) documenting early habitation, the years of slavery, Reconstruction and the decades of small farming, and the fishing, oystering, and timbering industries. The gift shop offers an excellent selection of books on the Lowcountry as well as maps, field guides, and activity kits for kids. Visit their Web site for information and hour of walking tours of the marsh, the beach, and other natural areas including historic sites; marine study cruises; bird-watching; and science and nature study for children (fees vary; reservations suggested). Museum hours are Monday through Saturday 9–4:30, Sunday 11–3.

Fish Haul Plantation (off Beach City Rd.) Only the chimneys of slave dwellings remain of what was once a thriving Sea Island cotton plantation. Federal troops camped here from the time of Union occupation in November 1861.

Fort Howell (Beach City Rd.) A large earthwork built by the Union troops in 1864 to strengthen the defense of Mitchelville.

Fort Mitchel (Hilton Head Plantation) An earthwork fortification, circa 1862, constructed as part of the island's defense system.

Indian Shell Ring (Sea Pines Forest Preserve) Native Americans occupied Hilton Head and other Sea Islands some 4,000 years ago, and left their mark in huge rings and shell middens. It is thought that this site represents the refuse of oyster shells piled behind each of many huts that stood in a small circle.

Zion Chapel of Ease (William Hilton Pkwy. at Mathews Dr.) A small chapel, built circa 1786 for the convenience of worshippers who lived too far from the Episcopal Church at Beaufort, once occupied this site. The Baynard Mausoleum, circa 1846, within its cemetery is the largest antebellum structure extant on the island.

Music

Hilton Head Choral Society (843-341-3339; www.hiltonheadchoralsociety.org.) Often joined by professional soloists and members of the Hilton Head Orchestra, the choral group performs three concerts each year, usually at Christmas and in the spring.

Hilton Head Jazz Society (843-842-4457; www.hhjs.org) The group sponsors formal and informal performances at various island sites on the first Sunday of each month.

Hilton Head Orchestra (843-842-2055; hhorchestra.org) Performances of symphonic and popular music throughout the year, held in the First Presbyterian Church, 540 William Hilton Parkway.

Theater

South Carolina Repertory Company (843-342-2057; www.hiltonheadtheatre.com; 136 Beach City Rd., near the airport) The company features a diverse troupe and often collaborates with other regional companies to produce professional-quality plays, mostly for the spring season.

RECREATION

Hilton Head's reputation as a place to pursue golf, tennis, fishing, water sports, and touring, and to enjoy the beach is well deserved. The following listings offer some sense of the range of activities the island has to offer. As the town has grown, it has developed five public beach access points, with metered parking and 50 miles of pathways for bikers, in-line skaters, and runners.

Beach Access

Twelve miles of gently sloping beaches define the island's ocean edge. They can be as wide as 600 feet at low tide, providing a hard surface for fat-tired bicycles. (For tidal informa-

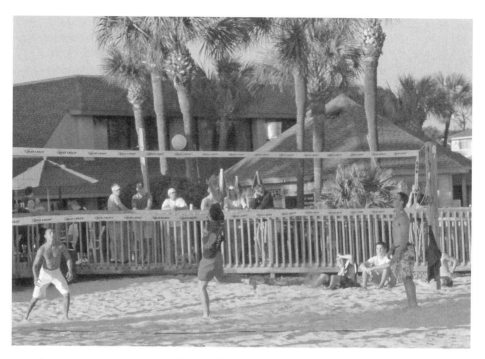

Late afternoon brings a pick-up game of beach volleyball.

tion, tune into island cable television or check *The Island Packet*.) Although most entry points to the beach are restricted—behind private resort plantation gates—the most popular public ones are: Coligny Beach Park (located at the end of Pope Ave.), Folly Field Beach Park (off Folly Field Rd.), Dreissen Beach Park (off Bradley Beach Rd.), Burkes Beach and Chaplin Community Parks (off Hwy. 278), and Alder Lane (off S. Forest Beach Dr.) All offer metered parking spaces ($.50 to $1 per hour) and Coligny and Dreissen have long-term lots. Within the plantation resorts, the beaches are accessible by marked footpaths.

On some nights (May through October), it is possible to watch the amazing loggerhead turtle, an endangered species, crawl ashore and lay its eggs in nests it digs on the beach; or to see hundreds of loggerhead hatchlings make their way back to the ocean. Volunteer groups monitor the beach and sometimes move the eggs to higher ground or protected sites, away from tides and hungry raccoons. The turtles are slow moving and docile, but chary: Do not disturb them with light, or touch the nests. Just seeing these huge creatures is magical.

Dogs are not permitted on the beach from 10 AM to 5 PM from the beginning of Memorial Day weekend through Labor Day weekend. Motor vehicles, alcohol, glass containers, and nudity are not allowed. Fishing, boating, surfing, ball-playing, and similar activities are prohibited in designated swimming areas. The beaches are patrolled by sheriff's deputies; lifeguard stations are posted.

Beach Activities
If you haven't brought your beach equipment with you, you can stock up at the **Coligny Flag and Kite Company** (843-785-5483; Coligny Plaza) or rent larger items such as boogie

boards, chairs, umbrellas, and floats on the beach. The shops at Coligny Plaza, at the end of Pope Avenue near the beach access point, offer the best selection of beach accessories on the island.

Coastal Discovery (see entry in the **Culture** section, above) offers guided walks several days per week on the island's beaches, and, on some evenings, a turtle tour to see the logger-heads nesting or hatching. Each tour lasts about 90 minutes and explains the island's ecology, flora, and fauna. Children will like learning about shells and hunting hermit crabs.

Bicycling

Bikes are easy to come by and you can expect island-wide pick-up and delivery. If you're traveling with youngsters, you'll be able to get baby-carriers, helmets, bikes with training wheels, baby "trailers" that hook on the back of bikes, and jogging strollers. Ask about in-line skate rentals, too. Local enthusiasts have created maps and cue sheets for rides of 22–60 miles that thread through rural areas. An online link is at www.hiltonhead island.org.

Public bike paths extend from the tip of North Forest Beach to the end of South Forest Beach, along Pope Avenue, and up William Hilton Parkway to Squire Pope Road, and take detours to the beach and marsh. Bike paths also thread through the plantations. At low tide, ride on the beach. Rental charges for bicycles start at $12 per day and $25 per week for a simple cruiser model. Check the following outlets:

AAA Riding Tigers (843-686-5833; www.aaaridingtigers.com).

All American Bikes (843-842-4386).

Hilton Head Bicycle Company (843-686-6888; www.hiltonheadbicycle.com).

Island Cruisers (843-785-4321).

Pedals (843-842-5522).

Bird-Watching

Hilton Head still has some very quiet places for birds to nest and feed. According to the island's Audubon Society chapter, some 200 species of birds regularly visit, and in the last 10 years, more than 350 species have been sighted. Among the most distinctive "frequent flyers" are the snowy egret, great blue heron, white ibis, and osprey. Catch a glimpse of them for yourself during daylight hours at the following sites:

Audubon Newhall Preserve (Palmetto Bay Rd., 3/4 mile from Sea Pines Circle) A 50-acre sanctuary open daily from dawn to dusk that preserves the Lowcountry environment for plants and animals. Trees and plants are labeled for self-guided walks on woodland trails, and lists of bird sightings are posted on a bulletin board at the entrance. Interpretative walks are offered in the spring and fall. To arrange a group tour call 843-842-9246.

Coastal Discovery (843-689-6767) offers guided walks in the Sea Pines Forest Preserve and has a birding exhibit on display at its museum headquarters. For nearby, off-island sites, see "Nature Preserves" in Chapter Three, *Savannah,* and in Chapter Four, *Beaufort, Edisto & Bluffton.*

Sea Pines Forest Preserve (843-842-1979; www.seapines.com; enter at Greenwood Dr. and Lawton Dr. in Sea Pines Plantation; $5 fee to enter Sea Pines Plantation) This 400-

acre site with a shell ring and old rice field offers a self-guided walking tour, which takes 1–2 hours.

Whooping Crane Conservancy (Hilton Head Plantation) features a boardwalk and self-guided nature trail.

Boating and Water Sports

For sailboat charters and bare-boat rentals, contact the companies listed below and also check the "Marina" section. If you want to nurture a wilder streak, look into waterskiing or kneeboarding, floating with a parasail, riding a waverunner, or "sledding" on a rubber tube. Some companies have special lessons/day programs for kids, so ask.

Commander Zodiac (843-671-3344; www.southbeachvillage.com; South Beach Marina) Visit the dolphins or Daufuskie Island in engine-powered rubber rafts. Small sailboats for rent, private lessons, and rides.

H2O Sports Center (843-671-4386; www.h2osportsonline.com; Harbour Town Marina, Sea Pines) Rentals for, and instruction in, parasailing, waverunning, kneeboarding, hydrosliding, waterskiing.

Island Watersports (843-671-7007; South Beach Marina; 843-689-6800) Power and sail boats for as many as 14 passengers, by the hour, half-day, or day. Guided private cruises, sailing lessons, sunset sails, parasailing. Waverunners and skis for rent.

Jarvis Creek Water Sports (843-681-9260; jarviscreekwatersports.com; 104A William Hilton Pkwy.) The hydrobikes look like sleek bicycle assemblies mounted on even sleeker rowing shells, pedal-powered by one or two people.

Coastal marinas are home to recreational and live-aboard boaters.

Palmetto Bay Parasail (843-785-7131; www.parasailhiltonhead.com; Palmetto Bay Marina.) For $65 you can rise 500 feet in the air; double parasails available; reservations required.

Palmetto Bay Water Sports (843-785-2345; www.palmettobaywatersports.com; Palmetto Bay Marina) Rentals by the hour cost about $90 for single waverunners; $85 for a 12-foot motorboat; and $15 for a single kayak.

Canoeing and Kayaking

With all of its constructed, managed, and expensive recreational sites, Hilton Head has, in its own backyard, superior low-tech, low-impact recreational options. They are found in the creek.

Today you can explore miles of Lowcountry waterways in a canoe or kayak, on your own or with a guided tour, by the half-day, the day, at sunset, by moonlight, on an overnight expedition. No experience is necessary; all safety equipment and basic instruction is provided; kids are welcome. You may end up paddling out to a sandbar, fishing, taking a birding tour, or threading through the web of coastal marshlands, pristine rivers, and nature preserves. Some outfitters offer extended programs for teens. For paddlers who feel comfortable going out on their own, day-rate rental charges start at $25 for a single, $45 for a double, and kayaks may be rented for as long as six days. Two-hour guided tours of local waters like Broad Creek, where you are likely to see lots of birds and fish in action, start at $35 per person; $17.50 for kids 12 and under; from $40 for three-hour tours. Longer tours run about $125 per person, depending on the arrangements. Customized trips and overnight camping/biking expeditions are available, just ask. Reservations suggested for tours.

Here are some outfitters who can help to get you in the water.

Awesome Expeditions Kayak (843-842-9763) Naturalist guided tours in singles and doubles depart from Shelter Cove Marina.

Cool Breeze Kayaking (843-683-4040 or 1-877-286-5154; www.coolbreezekayaking.com) Two-hour dolphin-sighting tours that embark from the Pinckney Island Wildlife Refuge or from Broad Creek.

Native Guide Tours (843-757-5411; www.nativeguidetours.com) For serious paddlers. Tours include the ACE Basin, May River, Colleton River, and sites off Hilton Head.

Outside Hilton Head (843-686-6996 or 1-800-686-6996; www.outsidehiltonhead.com) This longtime island business and outfitter offers clinics, teen camps, weekend retreats, and lessons as well as tours. Trips vary in length and season but always include two-hour and daylong excursions. Ask about special Daufuskie Island tours.

Water-Dog Outfitters (843-686-3554; www.waterdogoutfitter.com) Paddling in Broad Creek is easy enough for families and Pinckney Island challenging enough for intermediates. Bike/kayak excursions are also offered.

Cruises

Adventure Cruises (843-785-4558; www.hiltonheadisland.com; Shelter Cove Harbour) Dolphin-watch nature cruises lasting nearly two hours, evening shark trips, and sunset cruises. Adults $19; children $9.

Dolphin Adventure & Nature Cruise (843-681-2522; www.hiltonheadisland.com/dolphin tour; Broad Creek Marina) Narrated environmental tours (90 minutes) aboard the 20-passenger SS *Pelican*, a restored Navy Motor Whaler with canopy. Adults $25; children $15.

Dolphin Seafari (843-298-0661; hiltonheadisland.com/dolphinseafari; Palmetto Bay Marina) Cruises throughout the day, every day, lasting 90 minutes aboard a 24-passenger covered pontoon boat. Safe for even young kids, who will enjoy casting for crabs and pulling crab pots. Adults $20; children $15.

Flying Circus and *Pau Hana* (843-686-2582; www.hiltonheadisland.com/sailing; Palmetto Bay Marina) *Flying Circus* is a fast-moving catamaran offering two-hour daylight and sunset cruises for a maximum of six passengers. Tickets start at $30. *Pau Hana*, a larger catamaran, can carry 49 passengers. Adults $20; children $15.

Hilton Head Fireworks Tours (www.hiltonheadfireworkstours.com.) Tuesday nights in the summer, a free fireworks display lights up the sky from the Shelter Cove Marina. Visit this site for information on how to view them from the water while traveling in kayaks, small and large powerboats, and sailboats. Cruises last two hours.

Let's Go Shrimping (843-384-7833; Hudson's Seafood dock) A great experience for children to board a trawler and see firsthand the power and pull of 40-foot nets and experience a day in the life of a shrimper. During shrimping season, June through November. $30 per person, one child free with two adults.

Lowcountry Nature Tours (843-683-0187; lowcountrynaturetours.com) Another good option for children to see the dolphins and birds up close for two hours. Maximum six passengers. Call for reservations.

Stars & Stripes (843-842-7933; Harbour Town) A chance to sail on the original 12-meter America's Cup yacht, 65 feet long and powered by the wind in 2,000 square feet of sail. Call for reservations and sailing times; prices vary according to trip.

Family Fun

If you're coming with children, there are simple pleasures at hand: beachcombing, bike-riding, flying a kite, sunset concerts, weekly fireworks displays. Outside Hilton Head (843-686-6996; www.outsidehiltonhead.com) offers kayak camps for kids as young as seven, as well as teen activities. Playgrounds are located at Harbour Town (in Sea Pines; $5 admission), Shelter Cove Harbour, and the Island Recreation Center (20 Wilborn Rd. at the north end of the island). Bristol Sports Arena Skate Park is located off Arrow Rd., on the island's south end. The Rec Center features a handicapped-accessible area with a swing for wheelchairs. Check *The Island Packet* to confirm schedules or find special family-oriented events. Some of the following listings may be of help on a rainy day, or for older kids who might prefer arcades.

Adventure Cove Family Fun Center (843-842-9990; www.adventurecove.com. Folly Field Rd. and US 278) Mini-golf, batting cage, arcade, laser tag, driving range, bumper cars, and more.

Island Recreation Center (843-681-7273; www.islandreccenter.org; 20 Wilborn Rd.) A year-round activity center with camps, clinics, and sports programs organized by the day, week, and month for children, teens, and adults. Check to see if events like bike races, fishing tournaments, rollerblading races, water carnivals, or craft classes (among others) might coincide with your visit. Call ahead: Registration may be required.

Summer Concerts: In the evening, family entertainers gather large audiences for free concerts and shows. Check the local paper for listings, and plan to arrive early to secure parking. In Sea Pines Plantation (under the Liberty Oak at Harbour Town; Sea Pines gate pass $5) singers and guitarists perform nightly from 8:00 to 10:00 except Saturday. The audience sits on benches and kids are encouraged to participate. Family sing-alongs also take place Monday through Friday at Shelter Cove Harbour, and Tuesday nights there are fireworks. Various musicians, puppeteers, and clowns also turn up at Coligny Plaza (off Pope Avenue) each night to entertain families. At South Beach Marina (Sea Pines Plantation) you can enjoy music while the sun sets over the docks.

Waterfun Park (843-842-8108; 6 Tanglewood Dr.) Putt-putt golf course, three water-slides, arcade games, and a toddler's pool.

Fishing

Fishing is easy to do, but have in mind the kind of experience you're looking for. There are many options: size of the boat, length of the day, level of challenge, location, number of anglers, type of catch, and, of course, the probability of success. (All but the last can be provided.) Fly-fishing is also available. Boats are fully equipped with tackle, etc., and depart from several marinas for inshore waters, flats, artificial reefs, and the Gulf Stream. Potential catches include tarpon, marlin, and sailfish in the Gulf Stream; amberjack, shark, king mackerel, and bluefish closer to shore; and flounder, red drum, sea trout, and sheepshead in the coastal flats. Prices for four to six passengers for a half-day of fishing run from about $325 to $700. A Gulf Stream expedition (about 14 hours) starts at about $2,300 for six passengers. See www.hiltonheadfishingcharters.com for more information. Here are some suggestions.

Atlantic Fishing Charters (843-671-4534; www.harbourtown.com; Harbour Town Yacht Basin) Four boats (23 feet to 40 feet long) rigged with fish-finding equipment; fish at night for shark.

Blue Water Charters (843-671-3060; 232 S. Sea Pines Dr., South Beach Marina) Trophy fishing and taxidermy services.

Bonanza Sportfishing (843-689-5873; www.bonanzasportfishing.com; Skull Creek) Experienced professional guides take you inshore or offshore to their favorite spots.

Capt. Hook (843-785-1700; www.fishinghiltonhead.com; Shelter Cove Harbour) A good family choice for fishing: 70-foot boat with enclosed cabin and restrooms, food on board.

Lowcountry Outfitters (843-837-6100; 1533 Fording Island Rd. at Moss Creek Village, just off-island) Serious hunters and fisherman often gather and trade stories here. Guided fly-fishing and light tackle expeditions for one or two passengers on an open 18-foot boat are available. Equipment provided (or you can bring your own). Late-October through late-April you're looking for redfish and speckled trout; other times, ladyfish, spanish mackerel, jack crevalle, and bluefish. Prices for a half-day start at about $400.

Palmetto Bay Marina's Fishing Fleet (843-785-7131; Palmetto Bay Marina) Five boats and five captains can take you offshore fishing, to the Gulf Stream, or inshore to the flats. Boats' capacity from four to six passengers.

Fitness Centers/Spas

Major resorts such as the Westin and Hilton have in-house spas. Reservations are highly recommended at all locations.

Body Pilates (843-842-5562; 55 New Orleans Rd.).

Esmeralda's Pilates Studio and Muscle Therapy Center (843-785-9588; 14 New Orleans Rd.).

The European Spa (843-842-9355; www.european-spa.com; Sea Pines Circle) Two locations serving men and women, featuring aromatherapy massage, facials, and foot-and-leg massages for athletes.

Hilton Head Health Institute (843-785-3919 or 1-800-292-2440; www.hhhealth.com; 14 Valencia Rd.) A full-service spa where you can also go for extended visits to embark on a personalized program of fitness, diet, and healthier lifestyle.

Le Spa (843-363-6000; www.lespahhi.com; 71 Lighthouse Rd., Sea Pines Plantation.) A wide selection of massages is available, long and short, Shiatsu, hot rock, deep tissue, reflexology, or any combination.

The Sanctuary (843-842-5999; www.sanctuaryeurospa.com; 217 Park Plaza) A full-service spa for men and women where you can spend an hour or a day.

Seeds of Calm Spa (843-686-5525;www.seedsofcalmspa.com; 18 Executive Park Rd.) You can detoxify your body with a wrap, rejuvenate with an herbal rub, have deep massage therapy, and have a vegetarian meal brought to you.

Golf

Since the first course was built in Sea Pines Plantation in 1961, golf culture has touched every corner of life on Hilton Head; indeed it has shaped life here. Today there are some 30 courses in the Hilton Head area (on and just off the island) and more than half of them are available for public play. The remainder are for resort guests or members, located within private communities like Sea Pines and Shipyard Plantations, Palmetto Dunes Resort, and Port Royal Plantation. Golf is expensive, and Hilton Head is no different—anywhere from $95 to $250 for prime time, with the average about $125 including cart and fees. Early morning or later afternoon play costs less, as do resort packages, or packages sold by bundling brokers. Public course start at about $50. (Walking is permitted on several courses—check ahead for caddie help.) Reduced rates are available for resort guests. During the low season—winter months—prices can drop by 40 percent. For courses in and around Beaufort—within an hour's drive from Hilton Head—check Chapter Four, *Beaufort, Edisto & Bluffton.* For information and central reservations, call 1-888-465-3475; www.golfisland.com.; 1-888-445-8664; www.golfhiltonheadisland.net.

Reservations to secure tee times are essential—some courses accept reservations from non-resort guests up to 90 days in advance, others just 30 to 60 days in advance. (It gets crowded—800,000 rounds of golf are played annually at Hilton Head.) Check Web sites for advance reservation rules. Unless noted, all courses are 18 holes. Appropriate dress calls for shirts with collars for men and no blue jeans, gym shorts, or jogging shorts. At Sea Pines, nonmetal spikes are required.

If you're looking to improve your game, inquire about clinics, private instruction, and programs from one-half day to three days at **Island Golf School** (1-800-646-5376; www.island golfschools.com or **Palmetto Dunes Golf Academy** (843-785-1138; palmettodunes.com).

Hilton Head Plantation

Country Club of Hilton Head (843-681-4653; www.hiltonheadclub.com) Par 72. Range: 5,373-yard ladies course to 6,919-yard champion course. Design: Rees Jones.

Oyster Reef Golf Club (843-689-4653; www.hiltonheadgolf.net) Par: 72. Range: 5,288-yard forward course to 7,005-yard champion course. Design: Rees Jones.

Indigo Run

Golden Bear Golf Club (843-689-2200; www.goldenbear-indigorun.com) Par 72. Range: 4,974-yard course to 7,014-yard championship course. Design: Nicklaus. Fodor's *Golf Digest* four stars.

Palmetto Dunes Resort

Arthur Hills Course (1-866-310-6014; www.playpalmettodunes.com) Par 72. Range: 4,999-yard forward course to 6,651-yard champion course. Design: Arthur Hills. Fodor's *Golf Digest* four-star plus rating.

George Fazio Course (843-785-1138; www.palmettodunes.com) Named one of Fodor's *Golf Digest*'s 100 top American courses. Par 70. Range: 5,273-yard ladies course to 6,873-yard champion course. Design: George Fazio.

Robert Trent Jones (843-785-1136; www.playpalmettodunes.com) Named South Carolina's Golf Course of the year in 2003. Permanent junior tees allow young golfers to play a classic course. Par 72. Range: 2,625-yard junior to 7,005-yard champion course. Design: Robert Trent Jones/Roger Rulewich.

Palmetto Hall Plantation

Arthur Hills Course (1-866-602-7121; www.palmettohallclub.com) Par 72. Range: 4,956-yard forward course to 6,918-yard champion course. Design: Arthur Hills. Fodor's four-star rating.

Robert Cupp Course (1-866-602-7121; www.palmettohallclub.com) Par 72. Range: 5,220-yard forward course to 7,079-yard tour course. Design: Robert Cupp.

Port Royal Plantation

Barony Course (1-800-234-6318; www.hiltonheadgolf.net) Par 72. Range: 5,183-yard forward course to 6,543-yard champion course. Design: George Cobb.

Planter's Row Course (1-800-234-6318; www.hiltonheadgolf.net) Par 72. Range: 5,119-yard forward course to 6,625-yard champion course. Design: Willard Byrd.

Robber's Row Course (1-800-234-6318; www.hiltonheadgolf.net) A Pete Dye renovation of a George Cobb course near what was Fort Walker, a Civil War camp. Par 72. Range: 4,902-yard forward course to 6,675-yard champion course. Design: Cobb/Dye.

Sea Pines Plantation

Harbour Town Golf Links (843-842-8484; www.seapines.com) The Verizon Heritage is played on this course every April, rated among the top 75 in the world, among the top 50 in the U.S. Par 71. Range: 5,208-yard green course to 6,973-yard "Heritage" course. Design: Pete Dye.

Ocean Course (843-842-8484; www.seapines.com) First course on the island, redesigned in 1995 by Mark McCumber to remain challenging but still conveying an original beauty that earned it a designation as an "Audubon Cooperative Sanctuary." Par 72. Range: 5,325-yard green course to 6,906-yard "McCumber" course.

Sea Marsh Course (1-800-955-8337; www.seapines.com) Par 72. Range: 5.054-yard ladies course to 6,515-yard champion course. Design: George Cobb; redesign Pete Dye.

Shipyard Plantation
Shipyard Golf Club (1-800-234-6318; www.hiltonheadgolf.net) Par 72, 27 holes. A favorite of the senior PGA Tour. Range: 5,240-yard forward course to 6,830-yard champion course. Design: George Cobb/Willard Byrd.

Off-Island
Crescent Pointe Golf Club (843-706-2600 or 1-888-292-7778; www.crescentpointegolf .com; US 278, Bluffton) Designed for Arnie's "army." Par 71. Four tees from 5,219 yards to 6,772 yards. Design: Arnold Palmer.

Daufuskie Island Resort (1-800-648-6778; www.daufuskieislandresort.com) Two par-72 courses available to non-resort guests, accessible by private ferry. Reservations necessary, up to 60 days in advance. Bloody Point, with tees from 5,220 yards to 6,900 yards, designed by Tom Weiskopf/Jay Morrish; Melrose, with tees from 5,575 yards to 7,081 yards, was designed by Jack Nicklaus.

Eagle's Pointe Golf Club (843-757-5900 or 1-888-325-1833; www.eaglespointegolf.com; US 278, 7 miles west of Hilton Head) Designed by a five-time Heritage Classic winner. Par 71. Range: 5,210 yards to 6,782 yards. Advance reservations up to four months. Design: Davis Love III.

Executive Golf Club (843-837-6400; US 278, Bluffton, at entrance to Hilton Head National) Nine holes, par 30, lit for night play. Range: 2,360 yards to 3,330 yards. Casual dress code, beginners welcome, inexpensive.

Hidden Cypress Golf Club (843-705-4653; www.suncityhiltonheadgolf.com; Sun City/Hilton Head, Hwy. 170) Par: 72. Five tees, from 4,984 yards to 6,946 yards. Design: Mark McCumber.

Hilton Head National (843-842-5900; www.golfhiltonheadnational.com; US 278, Bluffton) Par 72, 27 holes. Range: 4,649-yard course to 6,779-yard champion course. Advance reservations up to one year. Design: Gary Player/ Bobby Weed.

Island West Golf Club (843-689-6660; www.islandgolfwest.net; US 278, Bluffton) Par 72. Range: 4,948-yard ladies course to 6,803-yard champion course. Design: Fuzzy Zoeller/Clyde Johnston.

Okatie Creek Golf Club (843-705-4653 or 1-866-705-4653; www.suncityhiltonheadgolf .com; Sun City Hilton Head, Hwy. 170). Par 72. The first of the courses at this resort designed for the over-55 crowd. Five sets of tees per hole accommodate the skilled and less-skilled golfer. Range: 4,763-yard to 6,734-yard tees. Design: Mark McCumber.

Old Carolina Golf Club (843-785-6363 or 1-888-785-7274; www.oldcarolinagolf.com; US 278, Bluffton) Par 71/72. Range: 4,725-yard ladies course to 6,805-yard champion course. Design: Clyde Johnston.

Old South Golf Links (843-785-5353 or 1-800-257-8997; www.oldsouthgolf.com; US 278, Bluffton) Par 71/72. Range: 4,776-yard ladies course to 6,772-yard champion course. Design: Clyde Johnston.

Rose Hill Golf Club (843-842-3740; www.rosehillgolf.com; Rose Hill Plantation, US 278, Bluffton) Par 36. Renovations have reconfigured the course to three nine-hole options. Range: 2,512-yard to 3,583-yard tees. A good value.

Horseback Riding

Call ahead for reservations. Small groups and families are welcome; all equipment is provided.

Happy Trails Stables (843-842-7433; Bluffton, behind Old South Golf Links) Rides in and around the golf course and forest preserve start at $25 for adults; $20 for ages 12 and under. Reservations suggested.

Lawton Stables (843-671-2586; www.lawtonstables.net; 190 Greenwood Dr., Sea Pines) Seventy-minute walking trail rides for adults and kids. Some riding experience required on trips through the 600-acre Sea Pines Forest Preserve. Prices start at $30 per person; pony rides for the younger set. Lessons (all levels) start at $35 per half-hour and include preparation of the horse.

Sandy Creek Stables (843-342-2771; 102 Jonesville Rd.) Boarding, lessons, and trail rides along the edge of the marsh and in the woods.

Sea Horse Farms (843-681-7746; 34 Mitchelville Rd.) Unique, one-hour beach rides leave four times per day except Sunday. Riders must be seven years old or older.

Marinas

The Hilton Head area has eight public marinas that offer boat rentals, transient berths, fishing charters, and services, such as dry-dock storage, launching ramps, fuel, showering facilities, ship's stores, and repair shops. Rates for berthing vary, from $1.00 to $2.50 per foot, or by week/month. Charter fishing boats, small powerboats, sailboats, and yachts as long as 150 feet are berthed side by side, offering a striking example of the many ways residents and visitors choose to enjoy the water.

Broad Creek Marina (843-681-3625; 18 Simmons Rd.) Slips accommodating boats up to 100 feet. Ship's store with boat-cleaning supplies and equipment. Charters and sightseeing, sailing instruction, and kayaking available. Low-tide draft: 15 feet.

Freeport Marina (843-785-8242; Daufuskie Island) The gateway to Daufuskie for large tour boats and the island touring headquarters. Golf-cart rental for transportation; restaurant, cookouts, gift shop, and marina store. Low-tide draft: 15 feet.

Harbour Town Yacht Basin (843-671-2704; www.harbourtown.com; Sea Pines Plantation) 85 slips accommodating boats up to 150 feet. Marina store, various types of boats for rent; tours, instruction, and cruises available. Low-tide draft: 8 feet.

Outdoor Resort Yacht Basin (843-681-3256; Jenkins Island at northern tip of Hilton Head) 101 slips, maximum boat length 70 feet. Amenities of Outdoor Resorts RV Park (see Lodging) as well as charters, waterski rentals and instruction, ship's store. Low-tide approach depth: 8 feet; 20 feet at dockside.

Palmetto Bay Marina (843-785-3910; 164 Palmetto Bay Rd.) 140 slips, maximum length 85 feet. Marina store, boat repair, fishing and sailing charters, parasailing, and youth sailing program. Low-tide draft: 20 feet.

Shelter Cove Harbour (843-842-7001; Palmetto Dunes Resort) 170 slips, maximum length 155 feet. Fish and tackle store, charters, cruises, rentals; rod and reel rental. In village-like area of shops and restaurants. Low-tide draft: 9 feet.

Skull Creek Marina (843-681-8436; Hilton Head Plantation) 180 slips, maximum length 200 feet. Sailing charters and night fishing, restaurant and lounge, courtesy bike and van transportation. Low-tide draft: 10 feet.

South Beach Marina (843-671-6699; Sea Pines Plantation) 100 wet slips, 20 dry slips, maximum length 35 feet. Tackle and bait shop, boat and motor repair, rentals, cruises, instruction, and junior sailing school. Restaurants and shops at the marina village. Approach depth at low-tide: 3 feet.

Miniature Golf

A half-dozen courses (par 40 to par 65), featuring water hazards, doglegs, and sand traps laid out in realistic settings. A great way to spend two hours. Most lit for night play. From $5.95 per adult.

Adventure Cove (843-842-9990; William Hilton Pkwy. at Folly Field Rd.).

Legendary Golf (Two locations: 843-686-3399; 900 William Hilton Pkwy. and 843-785-9214; 80 Pope Ave.).

Pirate's Island Adventure Golf (843-686-4001; William Hilton Pkwy. and Marina Side Dr.).

Waterfun Park and Mini Golf (843-842-8108; 6 Tanglewood Dr.).

Tennis

There are more than 300 tennis courts, hard, clay, and grass surfaces, on Hilton Head, spread through 19 clubs. Seven of them are open for public play: They are listed below. Call ahead for reservations—the staff may even be able to set you up with a game. Pros on site offer lessons, daily stroke clinics, and intensive camps year-round; fully stocked shops provide stringing services and sales of equipment, clothing, and accessories. Reserved court rental fees range from $18 to $25 per hour but reduced walk-on rates for midday play (12–4 PM) can be as low as $12. Free exhibitions take place at 5:30 PM Monday through Thursday and Sunday afternoons, at different clubs, on a rotating basis. Call to confirm.

Hilton Head Island Beach and Tennis Resort (843-842-0079; 40 Folly Field Rd.) 10 hard, lighted courts.

Palmetto Dunes Tennis Center (843-785-1138; www.palmettodunes.com; Palmetto Dunes Resort) 23 clay, 2 hard courts. Hard courts and eight clay courts are lighted for night play.

Port Royal Racquet Club (843-686-8803; Port Royal Resort) 10 clay, 4 hard, 2 natural grass courts. Night play available on six courts.

Sea Pines Racquet Club (843-363-4495; Sea Pines Plantation) 24 clay, 5 hard courts.

South Beach Racquet Club (843-671-2215; Sea Pines Plantation) 11 clay courts, 2 lighted.

Van der Meer Tennis Center (843-785-8388 or 1-800-845-6138; www.vdmtennis.com; DeAllyon Rd.) 28 courts: 25 hard, 3 clay. Night play available on eight courts. The center is internationally known for its rigorous teaching programs and camps for kids and pros, as well as serious players. The island's top youngsters often train here.

Van der Meer Tennis/Shipyard Racquet Club (843-686-8804; Shipyard Plantation) 20 courts: 11 clay, 9 hard. Night play on eight courts.

SHOPPING

As Hilton Head has grown, it has tried to minimize the visual impact of strip development along its major thoroughfare, US 278—the William Hilton Parkway. As a result, the small shopping centers and larger malls that have sprung up to serve 1.5 million visitors per year are destinations with parking and a mix of tenants that includes restaurants, pizza and ice-cream counters, supermarkets, and boutiques. Here are some highlights.

   Harbour Town, in Sea Pines Plantation, remains the only shopping area with a genuine village character, located around the harbor basin, clustered near the lighthouse. There's a $5 gate fee to enter Sea Pines. You can head toward Harbour Town, or pay your gate fee, park your car inside the Sea Pines Greenwood Gate, and take a free trolley (every 20 minutes) to Harbour Town. **South Beach Marina**, a Cape Cod–style village, is also in Sea Pines Plantation.

   The Mall at Shelter Cove is a more conventional shopping center, anchored by big department stores like Saks, Williams-Sonoma, Banana Republic, Ann Taylor, and Talbots. There is a food court and the mall is enclosed, making it a good rainy-day outing.

   Main Street Village (north island, just inside the entrance to Hilton Head Plantation— no gate fee) feels like a few downtown blocks in a prosperous suburb with its specialty boutiques, pubs and restaurants, and "real" stores that sell ordinary things like beer and diapers. **Village at Wexford** has the most interesting collection of stores, restaurants, and more "artsy" locales, like a gallery and a jazz club. Collections of shops around marinas at **Shelter Cove Harbour** and **Palmetto Bay Marina** support the boating and water-sport activities located there. **Coligny Plaza** is oriented toward kids and visitors, refreshingly informal, a good place to find beach toys, souvenirs, and inexpensive resort wear.

   Just off the island on US 278 are Target and other "big box" stores. At **Tanger Outlet Stores 1 & 2,** there are bargains in every category: housewares, toys, shoes, eyeglasses, children's clothing, linens, high fashion, and sportswear. Dozens of brand-name manufacturers including Coach, Brooks Brothers, J. Crew, Donna Karan, Dansk, Waterford, and Nike.

Art and Antiques

Some galleries have limited hours but welcome visitors by appointment. If you're interested in more than browsing, call ahead to check.

America Oh Yes! Folk Art Gallery (843-757-0088; www.americaohyes.com; 1536 Fording Island Rd.) More than 250 self-taught and visionary artists have work displayed here, and there are pieces for the beginning or experienced collector of folk art and art by African Americans.

Barry Honowitz Gallery (843-686-3100; Village at Wexford) Lowcountry watercolors including wildlife and golf scenes.

Decorator's Wholesale Antiques (843-681-7463; 1 Cardinal Rd.) Huge selection of stripped pine furniture, mahogany, and sports memorabilia.

De Gullah Creations Gallery & Gift Shop (843-686-5210; www.degullahcreations.com; 24 Shelter Cove Lane.) Dedicated to preserving and promoting the Sea Island Gullah culture, and recognizing its African roots, the gallery sells seagrass baskets, quilts made by islanders, original art, clothing, jewelry, and books.

The Greenery, Inc. (843-785-3848; www.thegreeneryinc.com; 960 William Hilton Pkwy.) This full-service landscape design business also has a small and ever-changing collection of antique garden statuary, containers, and accent pieces.

Guggenheim's (843-785-9580; 20 Dunnigans Alley.) Antiques and collectibles, on consignment. A place you could get lucky.

Hartough Gallery (843-671-6500; www.hartough.com) Linda Hartough, the official artist of the USGS, displays original works, lithographs, giclée prints, and golf accessories in her shop.

Hilton Head Art League Gallery (843-686-2032; Pineland Station).

Iron Fish Gallery & Studio (843-842-9448; www.ironfishart.com; 168 Benjies Point Rd., Daufuskie Island.) Chase Allen is a self-taught artist who creates metal sculptures of fish in his studio on Daufuskie, where he landed about seven years ago. A trip to his Web site might be easier than the ferry ride to Daufuskie, but if you find yourself there, well, there you are.

Moonshell Art Gallery (843-341-3339; 37 New Orleans Rd.) Varied collection of works and styles, from impressionistic Lowcountry scenes to children's portraiture with representation by many local artists.

Morris & Whiteside Galleries (843-842-4433; www.morris-whiteside.com; 807 William Hilton Pkwy. Contemporary portraits and landscapes in a realistic vein.

Red Piano Art Gallery (843-785-2318; www.redpianoartgallery.com; 220 Cordillo Pkwy.) Lowcountry landscapes, sculpture, and fine contemporary art.

Swan House Antiques (843-785-7926; 88 Arrow Rd.) Consignments make the collection eclectic and interesting: rugs, china, silver, paintings and prints, furniture.

Books and Music

Audubon Nature Store (843-785-4311; www.audubonnature.com; Village at Wexford) Field guides, children's guides on local flora and fauna.

Barnes & Noble (843-342-6690; 20 Hatton Place) The superstore for books, with many local authors and events featured each week

Heaven Sent Christian Bookstore (843-837-4727; 1540 Fording Island Rd., Bridge Center Shoppes) Inspirational literature, Bibles, children's books.

Island Bookseller (843-671-3773; Sea Pines Center) Adult and children's titles, local authors.

Paperback Exchange (843-842-5614; Village Exchange, 32 Palmetto Bay Rd.) A wide and constantly changing selection of used books. Books on tape for rent here, too.

Port Royal Bookstore (843-842-6996; Village at Wexford) Local authors, best-sellers, congenial service and recommendations.

Waldenbooks (843-785-4301; Mall at Shelter Cove) Books for beach reading, children's section, history, cooking, and coffee-table books.

Clothing

Camp Hilton Head (843-842-3666; www.camphiltonhead.com; Shelter Cove) Fun, casual beachwear embossed with unique logo of Camp Hilton Head. Find it at Harbour Town and Coligny Plaza, too.

Jamaican Me Crazy (843-785-9006; Coligny Plaza) Wacky resort wear, hip beach accessories.

Knickers (843-671-2291; Harbour Town) Classic outfits in linen, cotton, tweeds, and madras. An institution.

Loose Lucy's (843-785-8093; Coligny Plaza) A little bit of the 60s featuring tie-dye, old jeans, Indian prints, bandannas. For Phish fans and Deadheads.

Outside Hilton Head (843-686-6996; www.outsidehiltonhead.com; Plaza at Shelter Cove) Top-of-the-line durable sports clothing (Patagonia, Woolrich, Teva), footwear, and accessories. They also run camps and tours.

Porcupine (843-785-2779; The Village at Wexford) Designer sportswear for women, lingerie, excellent shoe selection, swimwear. The classiest fashion stop on the island.

S. M. Bradford–Lilly Pulitzer Shop (843-686-6161; www.forlp.com; Village at Wexford) The bright florals for women and children that are the designer's trademark, with accessories and some home goods.

Crafts

Art Café (843-785-5525; Coligny Plaza) A hands-on pottery studio, where you select an unadorned object (mug, plate, bowl, something else), choose the glazes and tools, and decorate it until it's unique. A good family project.

Harbour Town Crafts (843-671-3643; Harbour Town) Quality American handcrafts, large and small, whimsical, and functional.

Needlepoint Junction (843-842-8488 Village at Wexford) A boutique with stitchery supplies, threads, yarn, canvas, and kits.

Smith Galleries of Fine Crafts (843-842-2280; www.smithgalleries.com. Village at Wexford) More than 300 American artisans are represented in media such as glass, wood, metal, clay, and textiles.

Gifts

Creative Kitchens (843-785-8516; The Village at Wexford) An excellent kitchen and fine houseware supply store. Cooks love it; anyone who needs a bridal gift should, too.

Favors at Forsythe (843-671-7070; At Forsythe Jewelers, Sea Pines Center) MacKenzie-Childs ceramics, painted furniture, glassware, and a baby boutique.

The Goldsmith Shop (843-785-2538; www.thegoldsmithshop.com; 3 Lagoon Rd.) Gold charms of dolphins, starfish, and boats, studded with tiny jewels.

Legends Sports Gallery (843-681-4444; www.legendsportsgallery.net; Main St. Village) Old and new trading cards, autographed memorabilia, and Ted Williams signature items.

Magic Puppet (843-785-3280; Coligny Plaza) Toys, puppets, magic tricks, Playmobil sets, books.

Marina Store (843-842-7002; Shelter Cove Harbour) Everything for the sailor, including charts, boat shoes, and nautical accessories.

Gourmet and Fun Food

Chocolate Canopy (843-842-4567; www.chocolatecanopy.com; Crossroads Center, Palmetto Bay Rd.) Homemade chocolates galore.

Healthy Days Natural Food Store (843-785-7297; Coligny Plaza) Flours, herbal teas, sugar-free items.

Marley's Homemade Ice Cream (843-686-5801; Park Plaza at Greenwood Dr.) Outdoor seating; dozens of flavors and concoctions made fresh daily.

Signe's Heaven Bound Bakery (843-785-9118; 2 Bow Circle) Fresh baked breads, pastries, cakes, cookies, soups.

Truffles Market (843-671-6136; Sea Pines Center) Sandwiches, pâté, salads, breads, pastries, and wine.

Sportswear and Sports Equipment

Go Tri Sports (843-842-4786; www.gotrisports.com; Park Plaza) The island headquarters for triathletes and a fund of information about races, technique, and new products.

Lowcountry Outfitters (843-837-6100 or 1-800-935-9666; Moss Creek Village) Fly-fishing equipment, fine guns, clothing, and hunting-related gifts and many instructional videos.

Outside Hilton Head (843-686-6996, Plaza at Shelter Cove or 843-671-2643, South Beach Marina) Equipment for windsurfing, canoeing, kayaking, and camping. Patagonia, North Face clothing lines. The island standard for outdoor activity and experienced staff.

Player's World (843-842-5100; Plaza at Shelter Cove) Island's largest sporting goods store. Another branch (843-785-4653; Fresh Market Shoppes) specializes in golf equipment and accessories.

Sportline (843-686-8855; www.sportlineofhhi.com; 890 William Hilton Pkwy.) Dozens of models of tennis racquets and same-day stringing; shoes and accessories for runners and soccer players.

Sunny Daze Surf Factory (843-682-3293; www.sunnydazesurffactory; 155 William Hilton Pkwy.) Bodyboards, skimboards, surfboards, and all the accessories and apparel. Rentals and repair, too.

6

INFORMATION

Practical Matters & Seasonal Events

What follows is information to make your visit to the Lowcountry run more smoothly. It's a modest compendium of essentials—what's here and how it works—intended to make planning your trip easier and enjoying your stay simpler. The chapter covers the following topics:

Ambulance, Fire & Police	211
Area Code, Town Government & Zip Codes	212
Bibliography	213
Climate, Weather & What to Wear	219
Getting There, Getting Around	220
Handicapped Services	226
Hospitals	226
Newspapers and Magazines	227
Real Estate	228
Road Service	228
Seasonal Events in the Lowcountry	229
Tourist Information & Online Addresses	236

AMBULANCE, FIRE & POLICE

The general emergency number in the Lowcountry is 911, whether you're in Charleston, Beaufort, Hilton Head, or Savannah. Outside the cities, the counties have basic 911 service. A selected roster of other numbers, for emergencies or other business, follows:

First Call for Help (Information and referral service):
Charleston	1-800-922-2283
Beaufort/Hilton Head	843-524-4357
Savannah	912-651-7730

Poison Control:
South Carolina	1-800-922-1117 (from within SC)
Georgia	1-800-222-1222 (from within GA)

Rape Crisis Hotline:
Charleston	843-745-0144

Beaufort/Hilton Head	1-800-637-7273
Savannah	912-233-7273

Disaster/Hurricane Emergency Preparedness:

Charleston County	843-202-7400
Beaufort County	843-470-3100
Colleton County	843-549-5632
Hampton County	803-914-2150
Jasper County	843-726-7797
Chatham County	912-201-4500

State Police:

S.C. Highway Patrol:

Charleston Area	843-953-6005
Beaufort/Hilton Head	843-953-6005
Ridgeland	843-953-6005

Ga. Highway Patrol:

Savannah Area	912-754-1180

Police (non-emergency):

City of Charleston	843-720-2402
Town of Edisto Beach	843-869-2440
City of Beaufort	843-470-3003
Town of Port Royal	843-986-2220
Town of Hilton Head (sheriff)	843-470-3223
Town of Bluffton	843-757-6720
Town of Hardeeville	843-784-2233
Tybee Island	912-786-5600
City of Savannah	Dial 311 or 912-232-4141

AREA CODES, TOWN GOVERNMENT & ZIP CODES

Area Codes

The area code for the South Carolina Lowcountry is 843, with the occasional use of 803. The area code for Savannah, Georgia and its metropolitan region is 912.

Town Halls

The cities of Charleston, Beaufort, Hilton Head, and Savannah are governed by a mayor and city/town council; their outlying lands controlled by county government. The trend in government is toward consolidation of services, whereby the cities or towns and the counties they are part of share in the cost and delivery of these services.

Charleston, Beaufort, Walterboro, Ridgeland, Hampton, and Savannah are the region's county seats. For general information call:

Charleston County	843-958-4000
Beaufort County	843-470-2800
Colleton County	843-549-5221
Jasper County	843-726-7703
Hampton County	803-914-2103
Chatham County	912-652-7878

There are also smaller, scattered municipalities governed by smaller councils. For general information, contact the following town/city hall offices:

Town	Address	Telephone
Beaufort	135 Ribaut Rd., 29902	843-525-7000
Bluffton	P.O. Box 386, 29910	843-706-4500
Charleston	80 Broad St., P.O. Box 652, 29402	843-724-3729
Edisto Island	2414 Murray St., 29438	843-869-2205
Folly Beach	21 Center St., 29439	843-588-7006
Hilton Head	1 Town Center Court, 29928	843-341-4600
Isle of Palms	1207 Palm Blvd., 29451	843-886-6428
Port Royal	700 Paris Ave., 29935	843-986-2200
Ridgeland	108 E. Wilson, P.O. Drawer B, 29936	843-726-7500
Savannah	Bay St., P.O. Box 1027, 31402	912-651-6444
Tybee Island	401 Butler Ave., 31328	912-786-4573
Walterboro	42 Hampton St., P.O. Box 709, 29488	843-549-2545

BIBLIOGRAPHY

Lowcountry life, past and present, is well documented, and bookstores have ever-growing "local history" sections to prove it. Many volumes formerly out of print have been reprinted recently in response to new demand. Originals may be still found in second-hand book-stores and at all the online booksellers. Here is a suggested reading list of some classics, the books you're likely to find in residents' libraries.

These days, there are more "homegrown" histories available, courtesy of laptop publishing. Don't overlook them and the gems of local lore they contain. And, since the best part of a trip is often reliving it at home, check your local bookstore upon returning for further reading. The boxed quotes scattered throughout the text of this book are taken from books included in the list below.

The list is by no means complete: think of it as a mere guide to the shelves.

Art & Architecture

Cole, Cynthia, ed. *Historic Resources of the Lowcountry.* Yemassee, SC: Lowcountry Council of Governments, 1979, 2nd. ed. 1990. 202 pp., illus., photos, index, $29.95. The definitive four-county survey of historic houses and sites with fine historical and architectural explanation.

Dugan, Ellen, ed. *Picturing the South: 1860 to the Present.* Atlanta, GA: Chronicle Books, the High Museum of Art, 1996. 213 pp., index, $29.95. Based on a 1996 exhibit at the Photographic Galleries of the High Museum in Atlanta, the selection of pictures (from the Library of Congress Collections, private donors, historical societies, and museums) is honed to perfection and the accompanying essays (by several Southern writers of the first rank) is excellent. The book is moving without being sentimental.

Green, Jonathan. *Gullah Images: The Art of Jonathan Green.* Columbia, SC: University of South Carolina Press, 1996. Forward by Pat Conroy. 214 pp., $49.95. More than 180 gorgeous color reproductions of paintings by Jonathan Green tell the story of Sea Island life and its rituals and pleasures, as he experienced them growing up in Beaufort County, S.C.

Lane, Mills. *Architecture of the Old South: Georgia.* Savannah, GA: Beehive Press, 1986. 252 pp., photos, $75.

——*Architecture of the Old South: South Carolina.* Savannah, GA: Beehive Press, 1984. 258 pp., photos, $75. Exquisite, large format, black and white photos.

Ravenel, Beatrice St. Julian. *Architects of Charleston.* Columbia, SC: University of South Carolina Press, 1992. 338 pp., photos, index, bibliog., $19.95. First published in 1945, a detailed examination of the lives and works of the city's builders, engineers, and architects.

Rosengarten, Dale. *Row Upon Row: Sea Grass Baskets of the South Carolina Lowcountry.* Columbia, SC: McKissick Museum, 1986. 64 pp., photos, $10. A thorough and lovingly documented catalogue of a vibrant Sea Island art. It is the authoritative text on the shapes, weaving style, and uses of island baskets.

Severens, Kenneth. *Charleston Antebellum Architecture and Civic Destiny.* Knoxville, TN: University of Tennessee Press, 1988. 330 pp., photos, index, $49.95. A specialized topic explained in clear prose for the interested amateur or professional architect.

Severens, Martha R. *Charles Fraser of Charleston.* Charles L. Wyrick Jr., ed. Charleston, SC: Carolina Art Assoc., 1983. 176 pp., illus., $14.95. The subject was a miniaturist of the 19th century whose portraits of local gentry, in the collection of the Gibbes Art Gallery, are exquisite and incisive.

——*The Charleston Renaissance.* Charleston, SC: Robert M. Hicklin, Jr., Inc., 1999. 232 pp., illus., $65. A scholarly, beautifully illustrated chronicle of the artists in early 20th-century Charleston who were inspired by the city's heritage and story and expressed themselves in a variety of media.

Talbott, Page. *Classical Savannah: Fine and Decorative Arts 1800–1840.* Savannah: Telfair Museum, 1995. 320 pp., illus., $24.95. An overview of a period during which Savannah was deeply influenced by English Regency and Continental architecture and interior style.

Vlach, John Michael. *Back of the Big House: The Architecture of Plantation Slavery.* Chapel Hill, NC: University of North Carolina Press, 1993. 236 pp., illus., photos, index, $18.95. A serious, well-written, and fundamental study of the relationship of plantation "spaces"— the outbuildings, the quarters, the "Big House," the allées or avenues, fields, docks, and waterways—to the black and white people who lived there, and to each other. Numerous plantation plans are cited.

Autobiography, Biography, Diaries & Letters

Bartram, William. *Travels through North & South Carolina, Georgia, East & West Florida.* New York: Viking Penguin, 1988. 452 pp., $7.95. The account of an 18th-century trip through the Lowcountry by the famous botanist.

Chesnut, Mary Boykin. *A Diary from Dixie.* Cambridge, MA: Harvard University Press, 1980. 608 pp., $12.95. A classic account, good on Charleston society.

Daise, Ronald. *Reminiscences of a Sea Island Heritage.* Columbia, SC: Sandlapper, 1986. 103 pp., photos, $18.95. Archival black-and-white photos accompanied by text and stories of Sea Island Gullah culture. Daise and his wife, Natalie, were the creators and stars of the television series for children, *Gullah Gullah Island*, and continue to perform nationally.

Egerton, Douglas. *He Shall Go Out Free: The Lives of Denmark Vesey.* Madison, WI: Madison House, 1999. 272 pp., illus., $34.95. A complete, well-researched and well-argued account of the failed slave uprising in Charleston in 1822.

Elliott, William, & Theodore Rosengarten. *Carolina Sports by Land and Water, Including Incidents of Devil-Fishing, Wild-Cat, Deer, and Bear-Hunting, Etc.* Columbia, SC:

University of South Carolina Press, 1994. Illus., $14.95. A reprint of Elliott's 1850s original, it is still funny, easy to read, and as full of suspense as ever.

Forten, Charlotte L. *The Journal of a Free Negro in the Slave Era.* New York: W. W. Norton, 1981. 286 pp., index, $8.95. The vivid impressions of a Northern teacher who came to the Sea Islands to educate the newly freed slaves.

Georgia Writers' Project, ed. *Drums and Shadows.* Athens, GA: University of Georgia Press, 1986. $11.95. The collection of oral histories first published under the WPA program in 1940. It allows you to hear the voices of the coast.

Higginson, Thomas Wentworth. *Army Life in a Black Regiment.* New York: W. W. Norton, 1984. 279 pp., appendix, index, $6.95. Higginson, a Boston Brahmin, was the white commander of the First South Carolina Volunteers, headquartered in Beaufort, S.C. during the Civil War. Its honest, self-effacing narrative of camp life, countrysides, and skirmishes is invaluable.

Kemble, Frances Anne. *Journal of Residence on a Georgia Plantation in 1838–1839.* Athens, GA: University of Georgia Press, 1984. 488 pp., $11.95. Although the setting is the coastal Georgia plantation of the author's husband, Pierce Butler, her insights into plantation life and the culture of black female slaves make this perhaps the best account of that time.

McTeer, J. E. *High Sheriff of the Lowcountry.* Beaufort, SC: JEM Co., 1995. 101 pp., $19.70. Newly reprinted, it contains the colorful recollections of the author's days as a Lowcountry lawman and his encounters with voodoo and witch doctors, rum runners, and local scoundrels.

Olmsted, F. L. *A Journey in the Seaboard Slave States.* Westport, CT: Negro Universities Press of Greenwood Pub., 1969. Illus., index, $35.00. A reprint of the 1856 edition in which the author acutely observes the coastal region and standards of living there.

Pearson, Elizabeth Ware, ed. *Letters from Port Royal, 1862–1868.* New York: Arno Press, 1969. $14.00. In 1862, dozens of Northern abolitionists flocked to the Federally occupied area around Beaufort, S.C., to educate the newly freed slaves and manage the abandoned cotton plantations. This collection of letters by the Boston contingent is as forceful and moving a commentary on race relations and liberal expectations as exists.

Pennington, Patience. *A Woman Rice Planter.* Cambridge, MA: Belknap Press of Harvard University Press, 1961. The author was a Lowcountry native who managed her father's rice plantations after the Civil War and wrote about the experience for New York newspapers. The illustrations are by Alice Ravenel Huger Smith, a lyrical interpreter of the rural Lowcountry.

Pinkney, Roger. *The Beaufort Chronicles.* Beaufort, SC: Pluff Mud. 110 pp., $9.95. A new collection of remembrances and essays on small-town life and its simple pleasures.

Towne, Laura. *Letters and Diary Written from the Sea Islands of South Carolina, 1862–1884.* New York: American Biography Series, 1991. 310 pp., $79. Another wonderful journal of a teacher; she established Penn School, the first school for freed slaves in the United States.

Verner, Elizabeth O. *Mellowed By Time.* Charleston, SC: Tradd St. Press, 1978. $15.00. Sketches and memories of old Charleston by a distinguished artist who favored etchings, pastel, and pencil drawing.

Cultural Studies

Bluffton Historical Preservation Society. *No. II A Longer Short History of Bluffton, South Carolina and its Environs.* Bluffton, SC: Bluffton Historical Preservation Society, 1988. 49 pp., photos, $9.95. An excellent local history with photographs of classic Lowcountry cottages.

Carawan, Guy & Candy, eds. *Ain't You Got a Right to the Tree of Life? The People of John's Island, South Carolina—Their Faces, Their Words and Their Songs.* Athens, GA: University of Georgia Press, 1989. 256 pp., photos, $29.95.

Johnson, Guion G. *A Social History of the Sea Islands.* Westport, CT: Greenwood Press, 1969. 185 pp., index, bibliog., $38.50. A reprint of the 1930 edition of a series in which scholars from the University of North Carolina examined the lives, speech, culture, and folkways of Sea Island natives. Others in the series include Folk Culture on St. Helena Island by Guy B. Johnson and Black Yeomanry by T. J. Woofter, which, if you can find it, has stirring documentary photographs.

Jones-Jackson, Patricia. *When Roots Die: Endangered Traditions on the Sea Islands.* Athens, GA: University of Georgia Press, 1987. 189 pp., photos, bibliog., $19.95.

Lee, Matt and Ted. *The Lee Bros. Southern Cookbook.* New York: W. W. Norton, 2006. 589 pp., $35. The brothers relocated with their family to Charleston as preteens, and by messing around in the creeks and the kitchen, found, as they put it, that in the Lowcountry food is life. They became entrepreneurs of boiled peanuts in Manhattan—because they missed their favorite snacks—and it wasn't long before their amusing prose, goofy self-deprecation, and honest devotion to Lowcountry foodways garnered praise and fans.

Parrish, Lydia. *Slave Songs of the Georgia Sea Islands.* Athens, GA: University of Georgia Press, 1992. 252 pp., photos, musical notation, $19.95. A reprint of the 1942 original by the wife of artist Maxfield Parrish, documenting the islanders' songs from the praise house to the play yard.

Taylor, John Martin. *Hoppin' John's Lowcountry Cooking.* New York: Bantam, 1990. 345 pp., illus., $24.00.

———. *The New Southern Cook: 200 Recipes.* New York: Bantam, 1995. 287 pp., illus., $27.95. A superb follow-up to Taylor's first book, this one ranges a bit further but maintains the author's discriminating judgments and lack of pretension.

Terry, Elizabeth, with Alexis Terry. *Savannah Seasons: Food and Stories from Elizabeth on 37th.* New York: Doubleday, 1996. 340 pp., $30. Recipes and memories, written by mother and daughter, of the family's nationally acclaimed Savannah restaurant, which opened in 1980. There's a useful "source list" for ingredients available from specialty vendors by mail, too.

Vernon, Amelia Wallace. *African-Americans at Mars Bluff, South Carolina.* Columbia, SC: University of South Carolina Press, 1995. 200 pp., illus., photos, index, bibliog., $16.95. A wonderful documentary account of an African American community north of Charleston, S.C.

Welty, Eudora. *The Eye of the Story: Selected Essays and Reviews.* New York: Vintage International, 1990. 355 pp., $14.00.

Westmacott, Richard. *African-American Gardens and Yards in the Rural South.* Knoxville, TN: University of Tennessee Press, 1992. 175 pp., illus., photos, index, bibliog., $24.95. One of the most thoughtful and inspired books ever written on African American rural life (some in the Lowcountry), it focuses on several families and the way they create color, style, whimsy, and usefulness in their immediate landscape. It is part scholarlship, part oral history, and the tone is just right.

Wolfe, Michael C. *The Abundant Life Prevails: Religious Traditions of St. Helena Island.* Waco, TX: Baylor University Press, 2000. 181 pp., bibliog. and extensive chapter notes. $39.95. A tremendously thoughtful book that examines the religious traditions of St. Helena Islanders, in particular the role of Penn School and the missionary tradition.

Fiction

Berendt, John. *Midnight in the Garden of Good and Evil*. New York: Random House, 1994. 388 pp., $22.00. A wild romp in Savannah—and it's all true.

Conroy, Pat. *The Water is Wide*. New York: Bantam, 1972. 320 pp., $4.95. This was the book based on Conroy's experiences as a Beaufort County schoolteacher on isolated Daufuskie Island. His other books include *The Great Santini*, *The Prince of Tides*, and *Beach Music* and have Beaufort as their setting (even in the movie versions).

Griswold, Francis. *Sea Island Lady*. Beaufort, SC: Beaufort Book Co., reprint of the 1939 original. 964 pp., $19.95. A big, fat Southern novel set in Beaufort.

Heyward, Du Bose. *Porgy*. Charleston, SC: Tradd St. Press, 1985. 130 pp., illus., $20. A reprinting of the great tale, set in and around Charleston.

Humphreys, Josephine. *Rich in Love*. New York: Viking Penguin, 1987. 262 pp., $8.95. Set in Mount Pleasant, near Charleston, this novel (basis of the 1993 movie) captures the world view of a precocious 17-year-old girl. The author's other novels, *Dreams of Sleep* (1984) and *The Fireman's Fair* (1991), also have the Charleston area as their setting.

Naylor, Gloria R. *Mama Day*. New York: Random House, 1989. 312 pp., $9.95. A magical story set in a mythical place that nearly mirrors the Georgia/South Carolina Sea Islands.

Peterkin, Julia. *Scarlet Sister Mary*. Marietta, GA: Cherokee Press, 1991. 352 pp., $18.95. A reprint of the 1928 edition.

Powell, Padgett. *Edisto*. New York: Farrar, Strauss & Giroux, 1984. 192 pp., $11.95. A boy's coming-of-age on a Sea Island.

———. *Edisto Revisited*. New York: Henry Holt, 1996. 145 pp., $20.

Sayers, Valerie. *Due East*. New York: Doubleday, 1987. 264 pp., $15.95. The first novel in a group that chronicles life in a town like Beaufort, SC, where the author grew up. Others include *How I Got Him Back* (1989) and *Who Do You Love* (1991).

Worthington, Curtis, ed. *Literary Charleston: A Lowcountry Reader*. Charleston, SC: Wyrick & Co., 1996. 360 pp., $24.95.

History

Bridenbaugh, Carl. *Myths and Realities: Societies of the Colonial South*. New York: Atheneum, 1963. 208 pp., index, bibliog., $1.25.

Dollard, John. *Caste and Class in a Southern Town*. Madison, WI: University of Wisconsin Press, 1989. 466 pp., index, $14.50. A reissue of the 1937 work which, while not specifically about the Lowcountry, has everything to say about race relations in small towns throughout the region.

Jacoway, Elizabeth. *Yankee Missionaries in the South: The Penn School Experiment*. Baton Rouge, LA: LSU Press, 1980. 301 pp., index, bibliog.

Jones, Katharine M. *Port Royal Under Six Flags*. Indianapolis, IN: Bobbs-Merrill, 1960. 368 pp., illus., bibliog. A good general introduction to the area, with long passages quoting original documents.

Rogers, George. *Charleston in the Age of the Pinckneys*. Columbia, SC: University of South Carolina Press, 1984. 198 pp., index, $9.95. If there is one book you should read about Charleston's heyday, this is it.

Rose, Willie Lee. *Rehearsal for Reconstruction: The Port Royal Experiment*. New York: Oxford University Press, 1976. 450 pp., index, bibliog., $13.95. A beautifully written and meticulously researched account of the Northern abolitionists who went to the Sea Islands of Beaufort at the time of the Civil War. If you have a serious interest in the subject, the bibliography of this book is where you should start.

Rosen, Robert. *A Short History of Charleston.* San Francisco, CA: Lexikos, 1982. 160 pp., illus., photos, bibliog., $8.95. A popular introduction to Charleston by a native son.

Rosengarten, Theodore. *Tombee: Portrait of A Cotton Planter.* New York: McGraw, 1988. 752 pp., index, $15.00. This prize-winning book reproduces the diaries of an antebellum St. Helena Islander, Thomas B. Chaplin, and creates a context of explanation for them. This is the story—not the myth—of life on a cotton plantation, handled in vivid prose by the region's best historian.

Rowland, Lawrence, Alexander Moore, and George Rogers. *The History of Beaufort County, South Carolina: 1514–1861.* Columbia, SC: University of South Carolina Press, 1996. 480 pp., bibliog., index, maps. $39.95. The first volume of the authoritative, yet readable, history of the area that brings the Native American story into new focus and weeds out the antebellum myths about Beaufort and plantation culture.

Stampp, Kenneth. *The Peculiar Institution: Slavery in the Ante-Bellum South.* New York: Vintage, 1989. Index, $10. A classic study, first published in 1956.

Wise, Stephen R. *Gate of Hell: Campaign for Charleston Harbor, 1863.* Columbia, SC: University of South Carolina Press, 1994. 218 pp., illus., index, $29.95.

——. *Lifeline of the Confederacy: Blockade Running During the Civil War.* Columbia, SC: University of South Carolina Press, 1988. 403 pp., illus., index, $16.95.

Wood, Peter. Black Majority: *Negroes in Colonial South Carolina from 1670 through the Stono Rebellion.* New York: W. W. Norton, 1975. 384 pp., index, $9.95.

Photographic Studies

Blagden, Tom. *The Lowcountry.* Greensboro, NC: Legacy Publications, 1988. 104 pp., photos, $49.95. Views of the coastal world by an immensely talented photographer. His words of introduction, of praise for the region's natural beauty, resonate with visitors and locals alike.

——. *South Carolina's Wetland Wilderness: The ACE Basin.* Englewood, CO: Westcliffe Publishers, Inc. 1992. 110 pp., $29.95. A sumptuous study of the land and estuarine ecosystem in and around the Ashepoo, Combahee, and Edisto Rivers; much of the area is protected by federal, state, local and private organizations.

Dabbs, Edith, ed. *Face of an Island.* An album of early 20th-century photographs taken on St. Helena Island by Leigh Richmond Miner and reproduced from the glass plates. A treasure.

Ellis, Ray. *South by Southeast.* Birmingham, AL: Oxmoor House, 1983. 122 pp., $50. Watercolors of the coastal region by noted painter and Hilton Head resident.

Isley, Jane, Agnes Baldwin, and William P. Baldwin. *Plantations of the Lowcountry.* Greensboro, NC: Legacy Pub., 1987. 151 pp., $19.95. Color photographs and histories of historic homes.

McLaren, Lynn, and Gerhard Spieler. *Ebb Tide, Flood Tide.* Columbia, SC: University of South Carolina Press, 1991. 105 pp., $40. Color photographs of favorite Beaufort sites—natural and manmade.

Schultz, Constance, ed. *A South Carolina Album. 1936–1948.* Columbia, SC: University of South Carolina Press, 1992. 143 pp. A collection of photographs taken under the auspices of the Farm Security Administration, and later under the direction of its chief, Roy Stryker.

Recreation/Travel

Baldwin, William P. III. *Lowcountry Daytrips: Plantations, Gardens, and a Natural History of the Charleston Region.* Greensboro NC: Legacy Publications, 1993. 283 pp., illus., photos, index, bibliog., $18.95. The best new guide to the area, written by a Lowcountry native. It is a model of organization (with maps and mileages clearly spelled out), good design, practicality, and a writing style that lends itself to reading aloud. The book you'll lend to anyone who takes your advice and visits the Lowcountry.

Ballantine, Todd. *Tideland Treasures.* Columbia, SC: University of South Carolina Press, 1991. 218 pp., $15.95.

Federal Writers' Project Staff. *South Carolina: The WPA Guide to the Palmetto State.* Walter B. Edgar, ed. Columbia, SC: University of South Carolina Press, 1988. 514 pp., photos, index, $16.95. A reprint of the superb guide.

Georgia Conservancy. *A Guide to the Georgia Coast.* Savannah, GA: The Georgia Conservancy, 1989. 199 pp., illus., index.

Moeller, Jan and Bill Moeller. *The Intracoastal Waterway.* Camden, ME: Seven Seas Press, 1979 (updated 1991). 149 pp., $16.95.

Trask, Fred. *A Guide to Historic Beaufort.* Beaufort, SC: Historic Beaufort Foundation, 1970. 125 pp., maps, illus., photos. The definitive guide, especially good in describing walking and driving tours.

Wright, Cantey Holmes. *The Edisto Book.* Columbia, SC: MacKohn Printing, 1988. 109 pp., map, illus. Good local history.

CLIMATE, WEATHER & WHAT TO WEAR

Before spring was celebrated with house tours in Charleston and St. Patrick's Day parades in Savannah, there was just the season to rave about. Tourists came to see the blossoms and they weren't disappointed—azalea and wisteria bursting into bloom all over downtown, jasmine flowering on fence posts, dogwood and magnolia peeping out from under the shadows of live oaks in the woods. April is the Lowcountry's sunniest month.

In fact, there is something in bloom year-round in the Lowcountry, from late-summer mums to camellias to paperwhite narcissus, which scent the air at Christmas. This comes as a result of the semitropical to subtropical climate and the ever-present breezes that characterize the coastal region. There are also microclimates—as small as a yard, as wide as an acre—which make it possible to cultivate plants that are used to a warmer zone, like oranges and freesia. Rarely do days pass in succession without sunshine. The annual rainfall for the region is about 51 inches.

The winters are generally mild—maybe nine days of frost, and a half-dozen hard freezes. Spring comes early. Farmers generally break ground on February 1. In the old days, the cotton crop was finished by "lay-by time" in late August, when slaves, temporarily released from heavy field work, would tend to their cemeteries and families.

By May 1, it's hot, and that heat will penetrate every living thing through the end of September. The mean summer temperature in the Lowcountry runs between 70 degrees and 88 degrees but with the heat index and humidity figured in, it can feel much hotter. If you arrive in summer, be prepared to move slowly, wear a hat, slather on the sunscreen, and drink plenty of liquids. Even on a hazy day the sun will burn you. Take extra precautions if you're planning athletic pursuits: The tennis court is no place to be at midday. The wild cloudbursts that drench the region in summer, and the often-spectacular thunder and lightening shows that accompany them, may cool things off a bit. More likely, they'll just bring mosquitoes.

Then there are the gnats. Just when you're enjoying a creamy autumn day in the 70s, they find you. Insect repellents can be effective, as is staying out of the shade or standing in a breeze.

The seasons each bring their color, their migratory birds, their harvest of fish or shell-fish, duck or deer. And twice a year it seems as if a whole new shipment of air is carted in, too—in late October, when the marsh has turned golden and the clouds pull themselves into exquisitely defined cumuli; and again in late February, when the prevailing northeast winds of winter start to shift south and southwest.

But perhaps the best quality of Lowcountry weather is its subtlety and contradiction: the warm day in January that you were not expecting, the roaring fire in October that banishes the dampness and chill in the morning, but by late afternoon seems an inferno.

For clothing, pack more cotton shirts than you think you'll need. Take comfortable shoes for touring (high-heeled shoes are often forbidden in House Museums and on tours) and a light sweater or windbreaker. An overcoat or parka may be too much in winter; sweaters and shells work better.

The hurricane season lasts from about June to November, with most recent devastating storms having come between late August and October. If you're traveling then, make sure you are aware of evacuation routes and keep alerted to local media for hurricane watch and hurricane warning announcements. The National Weather Service (www.wchs .csc.noaa.gov) provides excellent coverage in the South Carolina and Georgia area on its Web site.

Sidewalk garden in Charleston.

GETTING THERE, GETTING AROUND

The first and most important fact about the Lowcountry is that it is mostly water. Perhaps this is why the old houses of the region's cities and towns—and the dense feeling of permanence they exude—are so venerated, above and beyond their architectural and historic status. They appear—now, as in the past—literally to triumph over their surroundings, as if daring wind, water, and the harsh storms of hurricane season to teach them the lessons of frailty.

The tides, which cast the riches of sea life toward shore and offered the first planters the possibility of harnessed power, bestowed on the Lowcountry a natural abundance of marine and bird life, and enabled the cultivation of rice. The settlements that clustered around what we know today as peninsular Charleston, flanked by the Ashley and Cooper Rivers, grew up there to take advantage of the tidal watercourses. Flat-bottomed plantation barges loaded with rice, bales of cotton, and farm produce plied the rivers and creeks to the city harbor. Throughout the Lowcountry, eight-oared bateaux, made on the plantations and navigated by slaves, clove the marsh from one plantation to another, carrying news, goods, and passengers. The Savannah River offered both protection to an English colony in the Southern wilderness, and a commercial avenue.

Quite often, what roads existed were hardly distinguishable from the water. Highways could be covered with washed-up shells, sponges, and seaweed, brought and removed by the tides each day. As time went on, people of the Lowcountry took nature one step further: They made roadbeds of oyster shell, fashioning a crown at the "center line" to facilitate drainage. These were the best roads around, and in some towns like Beaufort they were in use well into the 20th century. An unimproved road, such as you'd find—and still find today—on the Sea Islands, was plowed through fine sand, perhaps a foot deep, rutted and banked. More than one elderly Lowcountry resident can tell a tale of pushing a Model T Ford through this sand, or of watching the ice melt through the sawdust when the iceman got stuck.

Perhaps as a result of the reliance on water travel, as well as the sheer isolation of the plantations and their rural dependencies, a thickly veined series of land transportation routes never really developed in the Lowcountry. Instead there evolved a fleet of small packet steamers that made their way from island to island, picking up passengers, mail, produce, and cotton to deliver in Charleston and Savannah. And ox-drawn carts, or horses, or marsh "tackies" (diminutive horses, something like a Shetland pony) serviced them. When, in 1894, the historian Henry Adams visited St. Helena Island, he traveled first by train, then by carriage over a sand road, then on a shell road, then by foot to the ferry crossing, then over the river to board the steamer *Flora*, which carried him to his destination. These days travel is easier but there are plenty of unlit, two-lane roads flanked by drainage ditches that are major thoroughfares and require extra time and careful driving. Directions to specific areas are noted near the beginning of each chapter. The mileage charts and marina guides below are provided to give a sense of context.

The only thoroughfare by Land between Beaufort and Charleston is the 'Shell Road,' a beautiful avenue, which, about 9 miles from Beaufort, strikes a ferry across the Coosaw River. War abolished the ferry, and made the river the permanent barrier between the opposing picket lines. For 10 miles, right and left, these lines extended, marked by well-worn footpaths, following the endless windings of the stream; and they never varied until nearly the end of the war. Upon their maintenance depended our whole foothold on the Sea Islands; and upon that finally depended the whole campaign of Sherman.

—From *Army Life in a Black Regiment*
by Thomas Wentworth Higginson (New York: W. W. Norton, 1984. First published in 1869.)

By Car

Unless your visit to the Lowcountry is limited strictly to Charleston or Savannah or to a self-contained Hilton Head resort, having your own car really pays off. The Lowcountry is decentralized; a lot of space separates those "points of interest." What's more, appreciating that very space by finding yourself in it lies at the heart of the Lowcountry experience. That's where you'll find some of the region's subtle treasures: the view of a marsh at sunset, the sight of feeding pelicans as they hit the water, the faded impression of an abandoned oyster-shell road strewn with wildflowers. It is in these very open spaces, in their linked geography, that the sense of times passed and lives abundantly lived will catch up with you and shape your awareness of what the Lowcountry is all about. US 17, one of the region's oldest roads and still perhaps the most direct, threads its way from above Charleston to Savannah (and beyond) through marshes, old rice fields, and bottomland forests. Turnoffs that access the Sea Islands to the east (Kiawah, Seabrook, Edisto, Port Royal, St. Helena, Hilton Head) and the Ashley River plantations (Drayton Hall, Middleton Place, Magnolia Gardens) to the west (along SC 61) are well marked, as are historic sites, parks, and picnic grounds.

From Washington and points north: Travelers from the north can reach the Lowcountry by approaching it on I-95, which roughly parallels the coast. From there, well-marked exits direct you to downtown Charleston (via I-26), to Beaufort (via US 21), to Hilton Head (via US 278), and Savannah (via I-16). The coastal destinations beyond the big cities, such as Kiawah Island, Edisto Island, Beaufort, and Hilton Head, lie approximately 45 minutes east of I-95. Distance from Washington to Charleston: 512 miles; to Savannah: 616 miles.

From Jacksonville and points south: Like visitors from the north, drivers from the south approach on I-95 and then turn east to the coast. Distance from Jacksonville to Charleston: 241 miles; to Savannah: 139 miles.

From Asheville and points northwest: Take I-40 to I-26, then follow I-26 toward Spartanburg and Columbia. About an hour out of Columbia, you meet I-95. At that point either continue east to Charleston or turn south. Distance from Asheville to Charleston: 265 miles; to Savannah: 297 miles.

From Charlotte: Take I-77 south to I-20 at Columbia; follow I-20 for a few exits to link up with I-26 east. Distance to Charleston: 200 miles; to Savannah: 240 miles.

From Atlanta: Take I-75 to I-16. When it crosses I-95 go north for Charleston, or continue directly to Savannah. Distance to Charleston: 286 miles; to Savannah: 259 miles.

Lowcountry Access

The approximate distances and driving times to Charleston and selected cities are given in the charts below. The distance between Charleston and Savannah is 114 miles, so depending on the direction from which you are traveling, you should adjust accordingly. If you're touring within the Lowcountry, however, stopping along the way between Charleston and Savannah in places like Beaufort, Hilton Head, Bluffton, Edisto, or Walterboro, this trip easily may take a day. In general, traveling to specific Sea Island destinations located to the east of the major cities can add up to an hour to your trip.

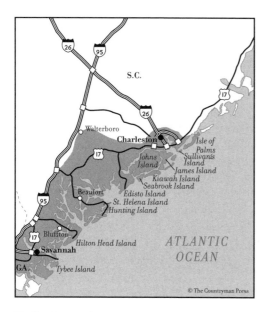

To Charleston from:

City	Miles	Hours
Atlanta	286	5
Boston	929	17
Charlotte	200	4
Chicago	906	15.5
Knoxville	395	7
Miami	590	10.5
New Orleans	784	13
New York	768	13
Washington, D.C.	512	8.5

By Bus

Greyhound (1-800-231-2222; www.greyhound.com) serves Charleston, Beaufort, and Savannah and maintains stations in those cities. It also serves points in between, but here the stops are less formal—perhaps as simple as a crossroads store. As a result, if you're planning to do a substantial amount of traveling by bus, you should consult both a detailed map and the bus schedule. Don't expect to find a taxi or rental-car stand—or even a working pay telephone—at every stop.

The service and price to Charleston and to Savannah from various points are roughly equal; in most cases the same bus goes to both cities. Travel times on longer trips may vary up to three hours, according to the number of stops and the specific route, so it's wise to ask about arrival times and whether or not it's a direct trip.

Charleston Greyhound Bus Terminal (843-744-4247; 3610 Dorchester Rd., North Charleston).

Savannah Greyhound Bus Terminal (912-232-2135; 610 W. Oglethorpe Ave).

Beaufort Greyhound Bus Terminal (843-524-4646; 3659 Trask Pkwy.).

By Train

Amtrak (1-800-872-7245; www.amtrak.com) travels the north-south corridor, making daily stops at North Charleston (843-744-8264; 4565 Gaynor Ave.), about 25 minutes from downtown; Yemassee (about 30 miles west of Beaufort); and Savannah (912-234-2611; 2611 Seaboard Coastline Dr.), about 20 minutes from downtown. Cabs are available at city depots; for Yemassee you should arrange advance transportation through a Beaufort taxi company. On the long hauls from major cities like Boston, New York, Chicago, and Miami, there are generally two trains a day, departing morning and evening and arriving either late the same day or early the following morning. Traveling by night with sleeping accommodations is a nice option for these 10- to 18-hour trips. The Web site provides detailed scheduling information and rates.

By Private Plane

If you're flying on your own, contact the following county or regional airports or services:

Beaufort County Airport	843-770-2003
East Cooper Airport Mt. Pleasant	843-884-8837
Hilton Head Airport	843-689-5400
John's Island–Charleston Executive Airport	843-559-2401
Mercury Air Center–Charleston International	843-746-7600
Savannah Aviation	912-964-1022

By Boat

The **Intracoastal Waterway** winds through creek and river, ocean and sound, from one end of the Lowcountry to the other, making for some of the most sublime cruising on the East Coast. In Charleston, Beaufort, and Hilton Head, you can dock at a marina right downtown or within walking distance of restaurants and sightseeing. Savannah's marinas are about 20 minutes from downtown. There are dozens of full-service marina options, so choose among them according to your needs, for example, if they provide repair service. If you want to make use of the charter fishing, sailing, or tour services based at marinas, see the **Recreation** section in the appropriate chapter for some ideas. If your main mode of transportation is by boat, check those listings for details on berthing facilities and services. An excellent area map—from the perspective of water—is available for $16.20 including postage, personal checks only, from **Coastal Expeditions, Inc.** (843-216-2131; www.coastal expeditions.com; 654 Serotina Court, Mt. Pleasant, SC 29464).

Touring Savannah's Historic District.

By City Transportation

Inexpensive, or free, shuttle bus service to the Historic Districts is convenient, handi-capped-accessible, and a great alternative to having to deal with a car. In Charleston, the attractive trolley-like **Downtown Area Shuttle (DASH)** (843-724-7420; www.ridecarta .com) makes regular stops along five routes in the Historic District and greater downtown area. Board at the Visitor Center (375 Meeting St.; 843-853-8000), where you can purchase your pass and park your car ($10) per day. The DASH maps and schedules are easy to follow and color-coded by route. All-day shuttle passes cost $4; a three-day pass is $9; reduced fares for adults over 55 and disabled passengers, children age six and under ride free. City buses operated by the **Charleston Area Regional Transportation Authority (CARTA)** serv-ice destinations like Kiawah Island, Isle of Palms, Sullivan's Island, and Mount Pleasant, some from the Visitor Center, some from nearby stops. Fares begin at $1. Bike racks are available at no charge on most of these routes, and take about 10 seconds to operate. For help in planning a trip outside the Historic District call CARTA (843-747-0922).

In Savannah, there's **Chatham Area Transit** (CAT) (912-233-5767; www.catchacat.org). A free shuttle bus service within the Historic District, with regular stops at the Visitor Center (912-944-0455; 301 Martin Luther King Jr. Blvd.), downtown inns and hotels, the waterfront, and many sites of interest. It connects to most bus routes, with additional fares for regional service throughout Chatham County. For $8, visitors can buy a pass that allows unlimited parking in any city lot or garage, or overtime at meters. Passes are available at most inns and hotels. Definitely worthwhile.

Handicapped Services

Most of the region's accommodations, museums, restaurants, and touring services provide access and facilities for those with special physical needs—but call ahead to confirm details: Problems remain in retrofitting the older historic buildings, and this includes some house museums and inns, for complete handicapped access. Your guides, hosts, or the Visitor Center's staff in each city will gladly assist you—several offer handicap-accessibility guides. See **Tourist Information** at the end of this chapter for addresses of city or county offices of tourism and travel. City busses and trolleys are handicapped-friendly.

Hospitals

Beaufort
Beaufort Memorial Hospital 955 Ribaut Rd.; 843-522-5200; www.bmhsc.org.

Charleston
Bon Secours St. Francis Hospital 2095 Henry Tecklenburg Dr.; 843-402-1000.

Medical University of South Carolina 171 Ashley Ave.; 843-792-2300.

Roper Hospital 316 Calhoun St.; 843-724-2000.

Trident Regional Medical Center 9330 Medical Plaza Dr.; 843-797-7000.

Veteran's Administration Medical Center 109 Bee St.; 843-577-5011.

Hilton Head
Hilton Head Medical Center and Clinics 25 Hospital Center Blvd.; 843-681-6122.

Savannah
Candler Hospital 5353 Reynolds Street; 912-819-6000.

Immediate Med 2014 E. Victory Dr.; 912-234-8466.

Memorial Medical Center 4700 Waters Ave.; 912-350-8000.

St. Joseph's Hospital 11705 Mercy Blvd.; 912-925-4100.

Late-Night Food and Fuel

The metropolitan areas of Charleston and Savannah, and the resort centers of Hilton Head, stay lit and active well after midnight—especially during the spring and summer—so finding gas or even grits should not be a problem. However, if you're traveling at night, remember that the Lowcountry is largely rural, traversed by long stretches of quiet highway. Unless you plan to gig for flounder and fry them up by the side of the road, it's best to travel with snacks or stop when you can.

Beaufort
Huddle House (food) Sea Island Pkwy. Open 24 hours.

The Pantry (grocery and fuel) 2231 S. Ribaut Rd. Open 24 hours.

CHARLESTON

King Street Station (food; beer and wine) 356 King St. Open until 2 AM.

International House of Pancakes (food) 1521 Savannah Hwy. Open 24 hours Sunday through Thursday, to midnight Friday and Saturday.

Waffle House (food) 325 Savannah Hwy.

HILTON HEAD

Hilton Head Diner (food; beer and wine) Marina Side Dr. at US 278.

Huddle House Northridge Dr. Open 24 hours.

The Pantry (grocery and fuel) US 278 and Arrow Rd. Open 24 hours.

SAVANNAH

BP Gas (grocery and fuel) 7203 Abercorn St. Open 24 hours.

Kettle Restaurant (food) 6801 Abercorn St. Open 24 hours. Wheelchair accessible.

Old Savannah Diner (food) Waters Ave. and Stephenson Ave. Opened in late 2007 to great reviews.

Waffle House (food) 7301 Abercorn St. One of several in the Savannah area, open 24 hours.

NEWSPAPERS AND MAGAZINES

BEAUFORT AND HILTON HEAD

The Beaufort Gazette (843-524-3183; www.beaufortgazette.com; P.O. Box 399, 1556 Salem Rd. 29902) Daily. Local coverage, wire-service features, and columns.

Beaufort Today (843-815-0850;www.beauforttoday.com; 52 Persimmon St., Bluffton 29910) A chatty weekly with local columnists and veteran reporters.

The Gullah Sentinel (843-982-0500; 2303 Boundary St., Beaufort 29902) A biweekly with an African American perspective, local and syndicated columnists, and provocative editorials.

The Island Packet (843-706-8100; www.islandpacket.com; 10 Buck Island Rd., Bluffton 29938) A good daily paper that has grown as the island has, with local political coverage, a variety of columnists, and wire stories.

Lowcountry Weekly (843-986-9059; www.lcweekly.com; 106 West St. Ext., Beaufort 29902) Listings, reviews, current cultural news every other week.

CHARLESTON

Charleston City Paper (843-577-5304; www.charlestoncitypaper.com; 1049 B Morrison Drive, Charleston 29403) Weekly paper, excellent listings.

Charleston Magazine (843-971-9811; www.charlestonmag.com; P.O. Box 1794, Mt. Pleasant 29465) A glossy monthly featuring stories about the city, gossip, local politics, development, and some art features. Reviews, columns, and blogs.

The Post and Courier (843-577-7111; www.postnandcourier.com; 134 Columbus St., Charleston 29403) The daily paper of Charleston.

Skirt! (843-883-3281; www.skirtmag.com; P.O. Box 806, Sullivan's Island 29482) Irreverent, fresh, funny, and good-looking, with a feminist slant. Monthly.

SAVANNAH

Connect Savannah (912-231-0250; www.connectsavannah.com; 1800 E. Victory Dr. 31404) Art and culture listings, reviews weekly.

The Herald (912-232-4505; www.savannahherald.com; 1803 Barnard St. 31401) Weekly, featuring news of the African American community.

Savannah Morning News (912-236-9511; www.savannahnews.com.; 111 W. Bay St. 31401) Daily and Sunday.

Savannah Tribune (912-233-6128; www.savannahtribune.com; 916 W. Montgomery St. 31401) Weekly, featuring news of the African American community.

REAL ESTATE

If you came to the Lowcountry and couldn't bear to leave without owning a piece, take your place in line. Practically every new resident who has settled here recently was once in your position. Even the ones who thought the Lowcountry would be their "retirement home" have quit fighting the urge and moved in early. In Beaufort County alone, the rate of building exceeds 500 units each year and the population has increased 40 percent in the last 10 years. The fastest-growing segment of the market is in traditional, single-family homes and in new "walking communities" which try to reproduce the feel of a small town. The trend for urban "in-fill" in Beaufort and Port Royal has enhanced a village look. Gated communities—glorified subdivisions, really, which may or may not be resorts—are continuing to expand in the Bluffton countryside. If you want to be on the water, be certain about rules regarding dock permits and building in the flood zones.

There are hundreds of real estate agents, many independent, some affiliated with national brokerage firms. One of them might be the proprietor of your bed and breakfast; if not, he or she will have a suggestion. For starters, you should pick up the free, widely available real-estate magazines that are published weekly throughout the Lowcountry. These will give you a general idea of what's out there and how much it costs. Gated communities usually have exclusive sales teams, offering houses or lots that come with a variety of conditions attached. Walk-ins are welcome, but if you can't find what you're looking for, ask for referrals in other towns, too.

ROAD SERVICE

Here is a list of some 24-hour towing and emergency road services.

BEAUFORT

Duke's Muffler and Auto (843-525-0155).

Gur's Wrecker Service (843-522-4285).

Port Royal Exxon (843-522-3399).

CHARLESTON
AAA Carolina Motor Club (1-800-222-4357).

Mikell Towing (843-572-9333).

HILTON HEAD
AAA Affiliate Emergency Auto (843-681-4636).

Coastal Towing (843-689-3869).

SAVANNAH
J & B 24 hour Towing (912-351-0526).

Stevens 24 hour Towing (912-351-0526).

SEASONAL EVENTS IN THE LOWCOUNTRY

The following list highlights annual events in the Lowcountry. Some of them, like outdoor concerts in a park, offer informal pleasures that you can enjoy on a whim with your family. Others, like house and garden tours, Spoleto performances, or tennis and golf tournaments, require planning. You should purchase tickets and book lodgings in advance, especially in the busy spring season. For specific information regarding dates, schedules, performance times, and admission or ticket prices (if applicable), call in advance, check online or in local media. For lodging and dining suggestions, see specific chapters.

January

CHARLESTON
Lowcountry Oyster Festival (843-577-4030; www.charlestonrestaurantassociation.com) A huge oyster roast, held on the grounds of Boone Hall Plantation in Mt. Pleasant. Games, entertainment, and contests for the whole family.

HILTON HEAD
1st Sunday Jazz (843-842-4457; www.hhjs.org; Hilton Head Jazz Society) An informal jam session held monthly at The Boardwalk, Folly Field Rd. $20.

SAVANNAH
First Friday Fireworks on the River (www.riverstreetsavannah.com) Food, crafts, and a festival atmosphere with a backdrop of pyrotechnics. Beginning in March, a First Saturday festival is added.

February

CHARLESTON
Celebration of Black History Month (www.charlestoncvb.com) Lectures, book signings, special exhibits at Drayton Hall and Caw Caw Interpretive Center, and performances trace the culture of the Lowcountry's African and African American residents.

Lowcountry Blues Bash (www.bluesbash.com) Ten days of concerts and films, many free, and often in intimate venues. The series covers every blues style including electric, acoustic, post-modern, Delta, Chicago. Tickets are usually pay-as-you-go at the venue, but some advance tickets are for sale.

Southeastern Wildlife Exposition (843-723-1748; www.sewe.com; 211 Meeting St., Charleston, SC 29401) A comprehensive, multi-site exhibition of wildlife art in various media, and presentations promoting habitat conservation and wildlife appreciation. A huge, three-day national event that draws collectors, artists, hunters, and bird-watchers. Tickets sell out early, so it's best to purchase in advance.

HILTON HEAD

Native Islander Gullah Celebration (843-689-9314; www.gullahcelebration.com) A monthlong look at island culture and its African roots, through concerts, lectures, performances by gospel choirs and choruses, storytelling, art exhibits, and tours.

SAVANNAH

Georgia Heritage Celebration (912-651-2125; www.georgiahistory.com; Historic Savannah Foundation) A 12-day celebration of the founding of Georgia and the Savannah colony which features tours, reenactments of colonial life, lectures, art exhibits, music, dance, and crafts. At various city locations.

March

BEAUFORT

Kaleidoscope: Film, Food & Fine Art (843-986-5400 or 1-800-638-3525; www.beaufort kaleidoscope.com) A new weekend festival that highlights two dozen films made by professionals and students in feature, animation, and documentary genres, selected by a competitive process. Art walks of galleries and studios, and a final gala, complement the screenings.

St. Helena's Episcopal Church Spring Tour of Homes (843-524-0363; www.sthelenas 1712.org; P.O. Box 1043, Beaufort, SC 29901) Traditionally held in March or early April, the candlelight tours are distinguished by organ concerts in the parish church, a beautiful brick structure built in 1724. The number of tickets sold can be limited by access to private homes, so it's best to reserve early.

CHARLESTON

Drayton Hall Candlelight Concert (843-766-0188; www.draytonhall.org); 3380 Ashley River Rd., Charleston, SC 29414) When this house is lit only by candles, it seems at its height of serene beauty. The concert continues the century-old tradition of piano music in the plantation house. Some years it takes place in early April.

Festival of Houses & Gardens (843-722-3405; www.historiccharleston.org; 40 E. Bay St. Charleston, SC 29401) The Historic Charleston Foundation's tours of private homes, plantations, gardens, and churches usually start toward the end of the month and last four weeks. A superbly organized event—a tradition for more than 50 years—it will enrich your understanding of the Lowcountry. Although the city may be crowded, it seems warmly accommodating, especially in the narrow streets late at night, where laughter and conversation drift from gardens and homes. Highlights are the oyster roasts and picnics at Drayton

Hall. The Charleston International Antiques Show kicks off the festival.

Alligators like to be left alone in the sun, on the golf course or in the swamp. Peter Loftus

HILTON HEAD

WineFest (Hilton Head Hospitality Assoc.; 1-800-424-3387; www.hilton headhospitalityassociation.com) A big and popular event, part of a monthlong series of activities which include musical performances and outdoor celebrations for families.

SAVANNAH

St. Patrick's Day Parade (912-233-4804; www.savannahsaintpatricksday.com; Parade Committee, P.O. Box 9224, Savannah, GA 31412) Savannah claims a substantial Irish heritage and celebrates it with abandon on this holiday. Mobs of people turn out to watch the downtown parade, which starts at 10 AM and dominates all other city activity for the day and night.

Savannah Garden and Antiques Exposition (912-236-4795; www.savannahgardenexpo .com; 321 E. York St., Savannah, GA 31401) A three-day event on the site of the 19th-century Railroad Roundhouse Museum, featuring lectures from prominent garden designers, historians, and practitioners; an open-air market with tools, antiques, and statuary; a huge plant sale; and very popular walking tours of hidden gardens. The expo benefits programs of the Historic Savannah Foundation and the Isaiah Davenport House.

Savannah Music Festival (912-234-3378; www.savannahmusicfestival.org) Fifteen days of jazz, blues, international music, and classical concerts held in the Historic District. Some 400 performances—a topnotch selection.

Savannah Tour of Homes and Gardens (912-234-8054; www.savannahtourofhomes.org) 18 Abercorn St., Savannah, GA 31401) Each day of the tour features a different neighborhood to explore at your own pace, with guides and docents on hand to answer questions. You can expect to cover about six sites, including churches and museums, in a three-hour period. Homes and gardens are not handicapped accessible.

April

CHARLESTON

Family Circle Magazine Cup Tennis Tournament (1-800-677-2293; www.familycircle cup.com. The Tennis Center at Daniel Island, Daniel Island, SC 29403) A new tennis stadium in a beautiful resort hosts this top women's professional tournament.

HILTON HEAD

Verizon Heritage PGA Tour Tournament (843-671-2448 or 1-800-234-1107; www .verizonheritage.com; 71 Lighthouse Rd., Hilton Head, SC 29928) Falling about a week after the Masters at Augusta, this premiere golf tournament brings thousands of people and the top PGA players to the Harbour Town Golf Links at Sea Pines Resort.

SAVANNAH
NOGS Tour: The Hidden Gardens of Savannah (912-961-4805; www.gcofsavannahnogs
tour.org) A small gem—usually featuring fewer than 10 walled gardens, but all treasures,
located north of Gaston St.

WALTERBORO
Colleton County Rice Festival (843-549-1079; www.scfestival-rice.com; P.O. Box 426,
Walterboro, SC 29488) Arts and crafts, cooking demonstrations, and rice-husking cele-
brate the Lowcountry's rice-growing heritage.

May

BEAUFORT
Gullah Festival (www.gullahfestival.org) Held the weekend before Memorial Day, this
event features a big outdoor market, dance performances, concerts of spiritual and gospel
music, and demonstrations of boat-building, net-tying, and other skills related to the
West African heritage of the Sea Islands. Its commercial success embraces the totality of
the African experience rather than the African American experience in the Sea Islands.

BLUFFTON
Bluffton Village Festival (843-757-3855; Bluffton Town Hall, Bluffton, SC 29910) A small,
old-fashioned street festival featuring artisans, food, and entertainment, usually held the
second Saturday of May.

CHARLESTON
Confederate Memorial Day Observance (843-722-8638; Magnolia Cemetery Trust, P.O.
Box 6214, Charleston, SC 29405) The United Daughters of the Confederacy and other
groups sponsor a program honoring the Confederate War dead. (A similar celebration
takes place in Savannah.)

Piccolo Spoleto (843-724-7305; www.piccolospoleto.com; Office of Cultural Affairs, 133
Church St., Charleston, SC 29401). The more informal aspect of Spoleto highlights
regional artists and celebrates art, music, dance, and outdoor events.

Spoleto Festival U.S.A. (843-722-2764; www.spoletousa.org; P.O. Box 157, Charleston, SC
29402) Beginning in late May and lasting for about 18 days, Spoleto brings the best of
international theater, music, art, and dance to Charleston. It's a magical time in the city.

HILTON HEAD
St. Luke's Tour of Homes and Gardens (843-785-4099; St. Luke's Episcopal Church).

SAVANNAH
Scottish Games and Highland Gathering (912-232-3945; www.savannahscottishgames
.com; P.O. Box 13435, Savannah, GA 31401) Scottish dancing, pipe bands, and traditional
games honoring Scotch heritage, usually held in mid-May.

June

COLLETON COUNTY
Edisto Riverfest (843-693-3161; www.edistoriver.org; P.O. Box 1763, Walterboro, SC
29488) Join a guided canoe and kayak flotilla as it winds down the Edisto River. Food,

entertainment, and displays of equipment featured at two state parks along the way. You can sign up for an overnight expedition or a day trip; all equipment is provided. Usually held the second weekend of the month.

HAMPTON

Hampton County Watermelon Festival (803-943-4978; Chamber of Commerce, P.O. Box 122, Hampton, SC 29924) The oldest festival in the state celebrating the county's best crop. Held at the end of the month and lasting a week, featuring seed-spitting contests, beauty queens, and a big parade.

SAVANNAH

Concerts in Johnson Square From June to August, enjoy two-hour lunchtime concerts every Wednesday and Friday, starting at 11:30 AM, in one of the city's loveliest settings.

July

Fourth of July Fireworks take place in several Lowcountry resorts as well as these locations: Brittlebank Park (Charleston), Parris Island (Beaufort), Hilton Head, Bluffton, Savannah's Riverfront, and Tybee Beach.

BEAUFORT

Beaufort County Water Festival (843-986-5400; www.beaufortsc.org; P.O. Box 910, Beaufort, SC 29901) A 10-day festival starting in mid-July that features special events each day and night: croquet, fishing, tennis, Ping-Pong, and golf tournaments, a juried art show, antiques show, kids' day, parade, and several outdoor dances. The air shows and acrobatic water-ski demonstrations are especially fun to watch.

August

HILTON HEAD

Celebrity Golf Tournament (843-842-7711; www.hhcelebritygolf.com) Held at Sea Pines, Indigo Run, and Palmetto Dunes, an island tradition that attracts movie stars, professional athletes, and media personalities to raise money for island charities.

Fishing Tournaments (Various locations) Check the "Marina" listings in the **Recreation** section Chapter Five, *Hilton Head,* to inquire about tournaments. There are many, for marlin, billfish, and other species.

September

CHARLESTON

Fall Tours of Homes and Gardens (843-722-4630 or 1-800-968-8175; www.preservation society.org; The Preservation Society, 147 King St., Charleston, SC 29402) More than one dozen different candlelight walking tours of private homes and gardens are offered over a period of about four weeks from mid-September through mid-October by the city's oldest preservation organization. Lectures and small concerts are also scheduled.

Moja Arts Festival (843-724-7305; www.mojafestival.com; Office of Cultural Affairs, 133 Church St., Charleston, SC 29401) A celebration of the African American and Caribbean heritage in the Charleston area. The influence on Southern culture is traced through music, dance, art, food, stage performances, and more.

Hardeeville

Catfish Festival (803-784-3606; Chamber of Commerce, P.O. Box 307, Hardeeville, SC 29927) Family entertainment, boat races on the Savannah River, and of course, catfish, are the focus of this festival, which takes place the third weekend in September.

Hilton Head Island

Autumn Arts Weekend (843-785-3673; www.hiltonheadisland.org; Chamber of Commerce, P.O. Box 5647, Hilton Head Island, SC 29938) Gallery tours and evening musical events open the fall season.

Savannah

Savannah Jazz Festival (912-232-2222; www.coastal-jazz.org; Coastal Jazz Association, P.O. Box 8004, Savannah, GA 31412) All styles of blues and jazz played for 10 days throughout the city.

October

Beaufort

Historic Beaufort Foundation Fall Tour of Homes (843-379-3331; www.historic-beaufort .org; P.O. Box 11, Beaufort, SC 29901) A weekend of candlelight and daytime tours of homes and gardens in and around Beaufort; the final day often features tours of outlying plantations, such as the rarely seen Auldbrass designed by Frank Lloyd Wright and meticulously restored inside and out.

Bluffton

Historic Bluffton Arts & Seafood Festival (843-757-2583; www.blufftonartsandseafood festival.com) A weeklong fair showcasing local and regional arts and crafts, historical exhibits and tours, and steaming fresh fish and shellfish.

Edisto Island

Edisto Historic Preservation Society Tour of Homes (843-869-1954; P.O. 206, Edisto Island, SC 29438) Daylong tour of homes which are not usually open to the public and not often visible from public roads.

Ridgeland

Gopher Hill Festival (843-726-8126; P.O. Box 1267, Ridgeland, SC 29936) A one-day celebration with arts and crafts, music, and food. The Ridgeland area was long known as Gopher Hill, named for the gopher tortoise, a species that lives a protected life in the sand hills of Jasper County.

Savannah

Savannah Film and Video Festival (912-651-6417; www.scad.edu; P.O. Box 3146, Savannah, GA 31406) Several days of screenings and lectures sponsored by the Savannah College of Art and Design.

November

Charleston

Holiday Festival of Lights (843-795-7275; www.holidayfestivaloflights.com; James Island

County Park) See more than 100,000 holiday lights strung in the park, a dazzling display in a place that rarely knows a white Christmas. Family entertainment and special events scheduled through Christmas.

Plantation Days (843-556-6020; www.middletonplace.org; Middleton Place, SC 61, Charleston SC 29414) The spirit of harvest days on a Lowcountry plantation is recreated through activities such as blacksmithing, wool dying and spinning, candle-making, and pottery. Traditional music and crafts, too, in the stable yards and green at Middleton Place.

ST. HELENA ISLAND

Heritage Days (843-838-2432; www.penncenter.com; Penn Center, P.O. Box 126, St. Helena Island, SC 29920) Held the second weekend in November on the historic Penn Center campus, Heritage Days celebrates Sea Island culture in its many forms. Thursday there is a special community sing; Friday there are lectures and presentations followed by an old-fashioned fish fry with musical entertainment; on Saturday, a parade and performances which include Gullah games and storytelling, dance, music, and demonstrations of traditional Sea Island crafts such as basket-making, net-weaving, and boat-building.

December

BEAUFORT

Christmas at the Verdier House (843-379-6335; 801 Bay St., Beaufort, SC 29902) The late 18th-century planter's home is decorated during Christmas week as it might have been during holidays of long ago.

Night on the Town (843-525-6644) Join in an informal, local street party as the downtown merchants welcome patrons to partake of holiday snacks and libations. There are decorations everywhere; jazz musicians, carolers, and even Santa make special appearances. An evening of small-town fun.

BLUFFTON

Christmas Parade (843-757-3855).

CHARLESTON

Christmas in Charleston (1-800-774-0006; www.christmasincharleston.com; P.O. Box 975, Charleston, SC 29402) The season brings special tours and holiday events such as a parade of boats strung with lights and open-air marketplaces. Many restaurants and hotels offer holiday specials, too.

SAVANNAH

Christmas in Savannah (1-877-728-2662; www.savannahsouthernlights.com; Convention & Visitors Bureau, P.O. Box 1628, Savannah, GA 31402-1628) All month long, Savannah comes alive with special holiday events: tours, performances, 19th-century style holiday presentations in old homes, crafts shows, and celebrations at the beach and on the river.

Tourist Information & Online Addresses

Here is a listing of the organizations in the Lowcountry that cater to visitors' needs. You may benefit from them during your stay or when you're planning. In many cases, booklets, videos, and pamphlets are available at a nominal charge; general information is free.

Fishing and Hunting Regulations

Licenses, permits, and wildlife stamps, whichever apply, must be in your possession while in the field or on the water. They may be purchased at tackle shops, sporting goods shops, and from the state. Check for links on the site to maps of boat landings and public hunting preserves.

Georgia Department of Natural Resources Game and Fish Division Route 2, Box 219-R, Richmond Hill, GA 31324; 912-651-2221. www.georgiawildlife.dnr.state.ga.us.

S.C. Department of Natural Resources P.O. Box 167, Columbia 29202; 843-734-3888; www.dnr.state.sc.us.

Visitor Information

Charleston Area Convention & Visitors Bureau 423 King St.,Charleston, SC 29402; 843-853-8000 or 1-800-774-0006; fax 843-853-0444; www.charlestoncvb.com. The Visitor Center is located at 375 Meeting St.

Edisto Island Chamber of Commerce P.O. Box 206, Edisto Island, SC 29438; 843-869-3867 or 1-888-333-2781; www.edistochamber.com. Offices located at 430 Hwy. 174, Edisto Island.

Greater Beaufort Chamber of Commerce P.O. Box 910, Beaufort, SC 29901-0910; 843-524-3163 or 1-800-638-3525; www.beaufortsc.org. A new, well-designed welcome center is located at 2001 Boundary St.

Hilton Head Island–Bluffton Chamber of Commerce P.O. Box 5647, Hilton Head Island, SC 29938; 843-785-3673 or 1-800-523-3373; www.hiltonheadisland.org. The Welcome Center and Museum is located on William Hilton Parkway, just beyond the foot of the bridge on the right.

Lowcountry and Resort Islands Tourism Commission P.O. Box 615, Yemassee, SC 29945; 843-717-3090 or 1-800-528-6870; www.southcarolinalowcountry.com. The Visitor's Center and Museum is located off I-95 at Exit 33 and US 17.

The Savannah Area Convention & Visitors Bureau P.O. Box 1628, Savannah GA 31402-1628; 912-944-0456 or 1-800-444-2427; www.savannahvisit.com. The Visitor Center is located at 301 Martin Luther King Jr. Blvd. Its number is 912-944-0455.

S.C. Department of Parks, Recreation, and Tourism 1205 Pendleton St., Columbia, SC 29201; www.discoversouthcarolinacom.

If Time Is Short

The Lowcountry divides easily into three parts: the major cities (Charleston and Savannah), the more rural areas (Beaufort, Edisto, Bluffton, and the Sea Islands), and the beach resorts (on Hilton Head Island, Kiawah, Isle of Palms, or others). Concentrating on one of these locales can make for a spectacular, relaxing, and brief, visit.

Each place has its special qualities: Refer to individual chapter openings for a sense of them. In general, the resorts are self-enclosed and limited in terms of history, culture, and sightseeing, yet their on-site recreational resources are exemplary and their use may determine your schedule. Beaufort or Edisto is a lower-keyed destination, where beach-combing and modest shopping might wrap around a day's worth of walking, biking, kayak-ing, or sightseeing. Each place has a superb restaurant. The cities, of course, are full of opportunities for touring and shopping. (A car is not necessary for a weekend trip to either city, although helpful if you want to explore the countryside or visit both Charleston and Savannah, a schedule that really requires four nights.)

I have tried throughout this book to present lots of options with as much impartiality as I could, with explanations to back up my choices so as to make it easier for you to make yours. Of course I have left things out: restaurants, hotels, tours, shops. Sometimes I did this on purpose for reasons of uneven quality or a changed market, and sometimes because my revisions, though regular, can lag behind the dynamic growth of the Lowcountry. What follows here, then, is the biased opinion of one who has lived in the Lowcountry for 30 years, who has visited every place covered in this book many times and is still not bored.

In Charleston

Governor's House Inn (843-720-2070; www.governorshouse.com; 117 Broad St.) is located in the Historic District, and waking up there makes you feel as if you're a native. It's an especially good choice for two couples who might want to stay in the carriage house. My favorite large hotel is the **Harbour View Inn** (843-853-8439; www.harbourviewcharleston .com; 2 Vendue Range), located on the river and adjacent to the Waterfront Park, a won-derful place for a morning run or a late-night stroll. These inns will be booked months in advance during the annual **Spoleto Festival** (843-722-2764; www.spoletousa.org), a series of music, dance, and theatre performances, and art exhibits that occurs in late spring.

The house museums and military sites that are most evocative are the **Heyward-Washington House** (843-722-2996; www.charlestonmuseum.com; 87 Church St.), built in 1772 and representing the height of colonial living; the **Nathaniel Russell House** (843-724-8481; www.historiccharleston.org; 51 Meeting St.), completed in 1808 with its gar-dens and free-flying spiral staircase; and the **Joseph Manigault House** (843-723-2926; www.charlestonmuseum.com; 350 Meeting St.), designed in 1803 by a native son and a marvelous example of adapting European taste for the Lowcountry elite. Slightly farther afield on SC 61 are two nationally recognized historic sites: **Middleton Place** (843-556-6020; www.middletonplace.org), where the oldest landscaped gardens in America were laid out in 1741; and **Drayton Hall** (843-729-2600; www.draytonhall.org), an 18th-century Georgian home which is a magnificent, unfurnished example of the Palladian style. Military history buffs should visit **Fort Sumter National Monument** (800-789-3678; www.fortsumtertours.com), where the Civil War began.

Popular shops among locals are along **King Street,** from Broad Street to six blocks north of Calhoun (housewares, antiques, and clothing); **Queen Street** (boutiques and art galleries); and **Church Street** (art galleries and antiques stores). **G&M** (843-577-9797; 96 Broad St.) is a place for a quick bite, **Hominy Grill** (843-937-0930;www.hominygrill.com; 207 Rutledge Ave.) for breakfast or lunch, **Il Cortile De Re** (843-853-1888; 193 A King St.) for a simple lunch downtown. For an ethnic dinner (rare in Charleston) try **Basil** (843-724-3490; 460 King St.), which serves Thai cuisine to a hip local crowd. Or try the award-winning **Peninsula Grill** (843-723-0700; www.peninsulagrill.com; 112 N. Market St.) and

Touring Savannah's Historic District.

McCrady's (843-577-0025; www.mccradysrestaurant.com; 2 Unity Alley) with one of the loveliest, quietest bars in town.

IN SAVANNAH

The Gastonian (912-232-2869 or 1-800-322-6603; www.gastonian.com; 220 E. Gaston St.) is a sumptuous luxury inn, and **The Thunderbird Inn** (866-324-2661; www.thunder birdinn.com; 611 W. Oglethorpe) is the retrohip alternative. Historic sites of architectural and military interest include: the **Green-Meldrim House** (912-233-3845; Madison Square), where General Sherman lived during the occupation of the city; the **Owens-Thomas House** (912-233-9743; www.telfair.org; 124 Abercorn St.), a Regency-style urban villa designed by William Jay in 1816; and **Fort Pulaski** (912-786-5787; www.nps.gov/fopu; US 80) a masonry fort that was, in 1847, state-of-the-art, and now is a great place for a picnic. Established in 1865, the **Beach Institute** (912-234-8000; 502 E. Harris St.) includes a permanent display of folk-art sculpture that celebrates the talent of Ulysses Davis and other African American artists.

Antiques stores proliferate downtown on **Bull Street, Abercorn Street,** and **Whitaker Street;** there are more touristy spots in **City Market** and **River Street**. Locals eat breakfast at **Clary's** (912-233-0402; 404 Abercorn St., Tybee). The best fancy restaurant is **Sapphire Grill** (912-443-9962; www.sapphiregrill.com; 110 W. Congress St.).

IN BEAUFORT AND THE SEA ISLANDS:

The Rhett House Inn (843-524-9030; www.rhetthouseinn.com; 1009 Craven St., Beaufort) is the most gracious inn outside the cities. The innkeepers may arrange kayak and bicycle outings, prepare picnics, and suggest day trips. **Hunting Island State Park** (843-838-2011 campground office; www.huntingisland.com) has cabins and camping. For a quick sandwich in downtown Beaufort, head for **Plums** (843-525-1946; 904-1/2 Bay St.), but for a fancy dinner that will equal anything in Charleston or Savannah choose **Bateaux** (843-379-0777; www.bateaux restaurant.net; Paris Ave., Port Royal) or **Breakwater** (843-379-0052; www.break water-restaurant.com; 205 West St., Beaufort.

On Edisto Island, **The Old Post Office** (843-869-2339; SC 174) is the best place for dinner; **Po Pigs Bo-B-Que** (843-869-9003; 2410 SC 174) for lunch. **Edisto Beach State Park** (843-869-4430) is fun for shelling, and rental cabins are available.

End of the day in the Lowcountry. Peter Loftus

For a sense of history, visit the **John Mark Verdier House** (843-379-6335; 801 Bay St.), the home of a wealthy 19th-century Beaufort merchant; **Penn Center** (843-838-2432; St. Helena Island), the nation's first school for freed slaves; and the **Edisto Island Museum** (843-869-1954; Edisto Island), which reveals the history of the island, from the time of Native Americans to the present. The **Museum** at the **Marine Corps Recruit Depot** at **Parris Island** (843-525-2951) features the history of the Marines and the Corps' training.

Beaufort's **Bay Street**, and the narrow streets that lead off it, have a classic main street feeling: plate-glass display windows, awnings, and family-run stores. On St. Helena, **Red Piano Too** (843-838-2241; US 21 at The Corner), an art gallery and store, is a good place to see native and outsider art and understand how those traditions both inspire and reflect today's island culture.

General Index

A

AAA Affiliate EmPeergency Auto, 229
AAA Carolina Motor Club, 229
AAA Riding Tigers, 196
A&B Fishing and Eco Tours, 162
Absolute Reel Screamer Charters, 84
ACE Basin National Wildlife Refuge, 88, 161, 174
ACE Basin Tours, 162, 174
Adventure Cove, 199, 205
Adventure Cruises, 198
Adventure Inn Resort and Rentals, 186
African-American history. *See* history, social
Aiken-Rhett House, 66
air tours, Hilton Head, 192
air travel: to Beaufort, 146; to Charleston, 40; to
    Hilton Head, 181; private planes, 224; to Savannah,
    103
A. J. Davis & Co., 93
Alakai Outfitters, 130
Alex Raskin Antiques, 135
A Limousine, 146
All American Bikes, 196
Aloha Natural Foods, 95
Alvin Ord's Sandwich Shop, 154
America Oh Yes! Folk Art Gallery, 206
American Cinema Grill, 64
American Originals, 94
American Revolution, 28–30, 44
AMF Bowling Center/AMF Lanes, 131
AMF Charleston Lanes, 81
Amos Hummel studio, 171–74
Amtrak. *See* train travel
Andolini's, 59
Andrew Low House, 121
Annual Tours of Edisto, 172
Anson, 51
Ansonborough Inn, 44
antiques: Beaufort area, 167, 176; Charleston area,
    90–91; Hilton Head, 206–7; Savannah area, 135–36
Aqua Safaris, 81
aquariums: Charleston, 75; Savannah, 127–28
Arcanum, 138
Architectural Tours of Savannah, 118
architecture, 24–25, 30, 33; Charleston area, 62;
    Savannah area, 119
area codes, 212
A'Riga IV Antiques, 91
Art & Soul, 168
Art Café, 208
art galleries: Beaufort area, 168–69, 176; Charleston
    area, 64–65; Edisto Island, 173; Hilton Head,
    192–93, 206–7; Savannah area, 119–21
Arthur Hills Course, 202
Arthur Smith Antiques, 135

Arts Council of Beaufort County, 156
Ashley Lanes, 81
Atelier Galerie, 137
Atlantic Fishing Charters, 200
Attic Antiques, 135
Atwood Vacations, 173
Audubon Nature Store, 207
Audubon Newhall Preserve, 196
Audubon Swamp Garden, 88
Avery Research Center for African-American History
    and Culture, 74
Awesome Expeditions Kayak, 198

B

Back In the Day Bakery, 115
Bacon Park, 134
Bacon Park Golf Course, 133
bakeries: Beaufort area, 154; Charleston area, 58, 96;
    Savannah area, 115–16
Baker's Café, 58
Ballastone Inn, 106
ballet, 63
Bamboo Farm and Coastal Gardens, 133–34
Bamboo Room, 115
Baptist Church of Beaufort, 156
Barefoot Bubba's, 170
Barnes & Noble: Charleston, 92; Hilton Head, 207;
    Savannah, 136
Barnwell, "Tuscarora Jack", 22
Barony Course, 202
Barrier Island Eco Tours, 80
Barrier Island Surf Shop, 89
barrier islands, 20–21
Barry Honowitz Gallery, 206
Bartram, William, 18, 19, 21
baseball: Charleston, 79; Savannah, 129
Basil, 51–52, 237
Bateaux, 151, 239
Battery Carriage House Inn, 44
Bay St. Trading Co., 167
Bay Street Gallery, 168
Bay Street Outfitters, 164–65, 171
Baynard Ruins, 193
beach access: Beaufort area, 161; Charleston area, 79;
    Edisto Island, 173; Hilton Head, 194–95; Savannah
    area, 129
Beach Institute, 120, 238
Beach Properties of Hilton Head, 186
Beachwalk Hotel, 185
Beachwalker Park, 79
Beachwalker Rentals, 50
Bear Island bird-watching site, 80
Bear Island Wildlife Management Area, 162
Bears Bluff bird-watching site, 80

Beaufort area (including Edisto and Bluffton), 173; Bluffton, 174–77; dining, 150–53, 172, 177; Edisto Island, 171–74; emergency phone numbers, 211–12; food purveyors, 177; general information, 141–43; history, 27, 34, 143–46; hospitals, medical care, 226; late-night food and fuel, 226; map, 142; newspapers and magazines, 227; recreational activities, 160–66, 173; road service, 228–29; seasonal events, 229–35; shopping, 167–71, 173, 176–77, 239; tours, 155, 172; traveling to, 146, 171–72, 222–25; visitor information, 160, 164, 172, 236

Beaufort Arsenal Museum, 159
Beaufort Art Association Gallery, 168
Beaufort Bookstore, 167
Beaufort Butterfly Company, 170
Beaufort Cab, 146
Beaufort Clothing Co., 167
Beaufort County Airport, 224
Beaufort County information, 212
Beaufort Gazette, The, 227
Beaufort Inn, 147
Beaufort Kayak Tours, 163
Beaufort Memorial Hospital, 226
Beaufort Today, 227
Beaulieu House at Cat Island and Port Royal, 148
Bed & Breakfast Inn, 108
bed & breakfasts. *See* lodging
Belford's, 111
Ben Silver, 93
Berlin's, 93
Berry Island Café, 154
Best Inn, Beaufort, 149
bibliography, books about the Lowcountry, 213–19
Bicycle Link, 139
Bicycle Shoppe, The, 61, 97
bicycling: Beaufort area, 161, 174, 176; Charleston area, 61–62; Hilton Head, 192, 196
Big Bamboo, 191
Bike The Bridge, 61
bird-watching: Beaufort area, 161, 174; Charleston area, 80; Hilton Head, 196
bird-watching site, 129–30
Bistro Savannah, 111
Bits of Lace, 93
Blackbeard's Cove Family Fun Park, 83
Blackstone's Deli & Café, 154
Blatner's, 135
Blue Bicycle Books, 92
Blue Water Charters, 200
Bluffton. *See also* Beaufort area: general information, 174, 213; traveling to, 174–76
Bluffton Bike Shop, 176
Bluffton Historical Preservation Society, 176
boat rentals. *See* boating; fishing charters
boat tours, cruises: Beaufort area, 162, 174; Charleston area, 61; Hilton Head, 198–99; Savannah area, 118
boating: Beaufort area, 162, 164–65; Charleston area,

80–81, 84; general information, 220–21, 224; Hilton Head, 197, 200, 204–5; Savannah area, 130–31
Bob Ellis Shoes, 93
Body Pilates, 201
Bohicket Boat, 81, 83–84
Bon Secours St. Francis Hospital, 226
Bonanza Sportfishing, 200
Book Exchange, 92
"Book, The" Gift Shop, 136
Book Lady, 136
bookstores, music stores: Beaufort area, 167; Charleston area, 92; Edisto Island, 173; Hilton Head, 207; Savannah area, 136
Boone Hall Plantation, 66
Bowen's Island Restaurant, 57–58
bowling: Beaufort area, 162; Charleston area, 81; Savannah area, 131
BP Gas, 227
Breakfast Club, The, 114
Breakwater, 151, 239
Brighter Day, 116
Broad Creek Marina, 204
Broad Street Guest House, 47
Broomfield Stables, 166
Buck Hall, Francis Marion National Forest, 81
Buffalo's, 174
Bull River Marina, 118, 132
Bull St. Station, 137
Bull Street Gourmet, 95
bus service, local, 225
bus service, national: to Beaufort area, 146, 224; to Charleston area, 40, 224; general information, 223–24; to Savannah area, 103, 224
bus tours: Charleston area, 60–61; Hilton Head, 192
Byrd Cookie Co., 116
B'ZAR, 93

C

Café Café, 58
Café Mucha, 138
Café Rebecca, 177
Calhoun, John C., 33
Calhoun Street Gallery, 176
Camelot Farms, 166
Camelot Limousine and Tours, 192
Camp Hilton Head, 208
camping and RV parks: Beaufort area, 163; Charleston area, 81–82; Hilton Head, 187; Savannah area, 131
Candler Hospital, 226
candy: Beaufort area, 167; Charleston area, 58–59; Hilton Head, 209; Savannah area, 116
canoeing. *See* kayaking, canoeing
Canup Antiques, 167
Cape Romain National Wildlife Refuge, 79
Capers Island wildlife refuge, 79
Capt. Eddie Netherland, 165
Capt. Hook, 200
Captain Dick's River Tours, 162

Captain Ivan's Island Charters, 84
Carmike Cinemas, Savannah, 119
Carmike James Island, 64
Carolina, 23
Carolina Antique Maps and Prints, 91
Carolina Buggy Tours, 155
Carolina Clipper, 84
Carolina Galleries, 64
Carolina Polo & Carriage Co., 62
Carolina Stamper, 168
Carriage Tours of Savannah, 117
carriages, horse-drawn. *See* horse-drawn carriage
    tours
Carroll Realty, 50
Casbah, 111
Caw Caw Interpretive Center, 88
Ceramics Café, 94
Cha Bella, 111–12
chambers of commerce, 236
Chapel of Ease, 156
Charles Street Gallery, 168
Charles Town/Charlestown, 23–27. *See also* Charleston
    area
Charles Towne Landing 1670, 24, 74–75
Charleston Angler, The, 97
Charleston Antique Mall, 91
Charleston Area Convention & Visitors Bureau, 236
Charleston area (including Sea Islands): architecture,
    33; Charles Towne Landing, 24; cultural attractions,
    62–78; dining, 50–58; emergency phone numbers,
    211–12; food purveyors, 58–59; general information,
    37–39; history, 22–27, 30, 33; hospitals, medical
    care, 226; late-night food and fuel, 227; local trans-
    portation, 225; lodging, 40–50; map, 38; museums,
    30, 34; newspapers and magazines, 227–28; recre-
    ational activities, 78–80; road service, 229; seasonal
    events, 229–35; shopping, 89–97, 237; tours, 59–62;
    town offices, 213; traveling to, 40, 222–25; visitor
    information, 236
Charleston Area Regional Transportation Authority
    (CARTA), 225
Charleston Ballet Theatre, 63
Charleston Bicycle Company, TRhe, 97
Charleston Chocolates, 58
Charleston City Paper, 227
Charleston Cooks, 96
Charleston County information, 212
Charleston County Parks, 81
Charleston Crafts, 95
Charleston Film Festival, 64
Charleston Fine Art Dealers Association, 64
Charleston Grill, 52
Charleston International Airport, 40
Charleston Legends and Lore Ghost Theater, 78
Charleston Magazine, 227
Charleston Municipal Course, 85
Charleston Museum, 30, 74
Charleston National golf course, 85

Charleston on the Beach, 48
Charleston Place, 42–43
Charleston Rare Book Co., 92
Charleston Renaissance Gallery, The, 64
Charleston RiverDogs baseball, 79
Charleston Scuba, 83
Charleston Stage Theatre Company, 78
Charleston Symphony Orchestra, 75–76
Charleston Tea Plantation, 95
Charleston Tours, Inc., 61
Charleston Walks, 62
charters, fishing: Beaufort area, 164–65; Charleston
    area, 84; Hilton Head, 200; Savannah area, 131, 132
Chatham Area Transit (CAT), Savannah, 225
Chatham County information, 212
Chesnut, Mary Boykin, 33
Chicora Antiques, 91
children, activities for, 199–200; Charleston area, 83;
    Hilton Head, 205; Savannah area, 131
Chocolate Canopy, 209
Chocolate Tree, 167
Christian Michi, 93
Chroma Gallery, 120
cinema. *See* film, cinema
Circa 1886, 52
Citadel Mall 6, 64
Citadel Museum, The, 72
City Lights Theatre Company, 128
City Marina, The, 80
Civil War, 32–34, 73
Civil War artifacts, Savannah, 135
Civil War Walking Tour, 62
Clary's Café, 112
Classic Golf, 83
climate, 219–20
clothing stores: Beaufort area, 167–68; Charleston
    area, 92–93; Hilton Head, 208, 209; Savannah area,
    136–37
Club One, 128
Coastal Discovery Museum on Hilton Head Island,
    192–93
Coastal Discovery tours, 194–96
Coastal Expeditions, Inc., 79–80, 83, 224
Coastal River Charters, 132
Coastal Towing, 229
Coastal YMCA, 132
Cobblestone Lane Antiques, 135
coffeehouses: Beaufort area, 154, 177; Charleston area,
    58; Savannah area, 115–16
Coleman Fine Art, 64
Coligny Flag and Kite Company, 194–95
Coligny Plaza, 206
Coligny Theatre, 193
Colleton, Charles, 23
Colleton County information, 212
Colleton State Park, 82
Comfort Inn: Beaufort, 149; Hilton Head, 185
Commander Zodiac, 197

Common Ground, 154
CompassSailing, 131
Confederate Museum, The, 34, 72
Congregation Beth Elohim, 66–67
Connect Savannah, 120
Connect Savannah, 228
Conroy, Pat, 35
Cool Breeze Kayaking, 198
Coosaw Creek Country Club, 85
Copper Penny, 93
Cottage Shop, 137
Cougar Point golf course, 86
Country Club of Beaufort at Pleasant Point, 165
Country Club of Hilton Head, 202
Cousins, 93
CQs, 188
Crab Shack at Chimney Creek, 114–15
Crab Trap, The, 173
crafts stores and galleries: Beaufort area, 168;
   Charleston area, 94–95; Edisto Island, 173; Hilton
   Head, 208; Savannah area, 137
Craftseller, The, 168
Craven Street Inn, 148
Cravings By the Bay, 170
Creative Kitchens, 208
Crescent Pointe Golf Club, 203
Crooked Oaks golf course, 86
Crowfield Golf & Country Club, 85
Crowne Plaza Resort, 183
Crystal Beer Parlor, 112
Culinary Tours of Charleston, 62
cultural attractions: Beaufort area, 156–59; Charleston
   area, 62–78; Hilton Head, 192–94; Savannah area,
   119–29
Cusabo Indians, 22–23
Cut Bait Gallery, 173
Cuthbert House Inn, 148
Cypress Gardens, 88
Cypress Lowcountry Grille, 52–53

D
Daffin Park, 134
Dailey-Grommé, 91
dance performances, ballet, 63
Dataw Island, 149–50
Daufuskie Island Resort, 183, 203
Davenport House Museum Shop, 138
Days Inn, Beaufort, 149
De Gullah Creations Gallery & Gift Shop, 207
Declaration of Independence, 29
Decorator's Wholesale Antiques, 207
delicatessens. *See* gourmet food stores, delis
Der Teufelhund, 167
Desot O Row Gallery, 120
dining: Beaufort area, 150–53, 174, 177; Charleston
   area, 50–58; Hilton Head, 187–91; Savannah area,
   110–15
disabled travelers, services for, 226

disaster/hurricane emergency preparedness informa-
   tion, 212
diving: Charleston area, 83; Savannah area, 131
Diving Locker and Ski Chalet, 131
Dock Street Theatre, 78
Doin' The Charleston, 61
Dolphin Adventure & Nature Cruise, 199
Dolphin Magic Tours, 118
Dolphin Seafari, 199
Dolphin Watch, Bull River Marina, 118
Doodlebugs, 168
Downtown Area Shuttle (DASH), Charleston, 225
Downtown Athletic Club, 132
Downtown Design District, Savannah, 138
Drayton Hall, 67, 237
driving: to Bluffton, 174–76; to Charleston, 40; to
   Edisto Island, 171–72; emergency service, 228–29;
   late-night food and fuel, 226; to the Lowcountry,
   222–23; within the Lowcountry, 223–24; Savannah
   area, 117
Duke'sMuffler and Auto, 228
Dunes Inn and Suites, 109
Dunes West golf course, 86

E
E. Shaver Booksellers, 136
E Storia, 136
Eagle's Pointe Golf Club, 203
Earthling Day Spa & Pilates Studio, 85
East Bay Inn, 106
East Cooper Airport Mt. Pleasant, 224
East Shore Athletic Club, 85
ecotours: Beaufort area, 162; Charleston area, 80;
   Hilton Head, 199
Edisto Beach State Park, 173, 239
Edisto Bookstore, 173
Edisto Chamber of Commerce, 172, 236
Edisto Island. *See also* Beaufort area: general informa-
   tion, 171; town halls, phone numbers for, 213
Edisto Island Historic Preservation Society/museum,
   172, 239
Edisto Island Serpentarium, 172
Edisto Watersports & Tackle, 174
Edmonston-Alston House, 68
Eggs N' Tricities, 171–74
1837 Bed and Breakfast, 47
Eighty-Two Church, 95
11th Street Dockside, 151–52
Eliza Thompson House, 106
Elizabeth on 37th, 112
Ellington, 93
Ellis Gallery, 120
Embassy Suites-Historic District, 43
emergency phone numbers: Beaufort area, 211–12;
   Charleston area, 211–12; Hilton Head, 211–12;
   Savannah area, 211–12
emergency road service, 228–29
Emily's Restaurant and Tapas Bar, 152

Emmanuel A. M. E. Church, 68
ESD, 95
Esmeralda's Pilates Studio and Muscle Therapy Center, 201
Eugene's Oyster Bar, 191
European settlement, 28
European Spa, The, 201
Eva Carter Gallery, 64
Evans, Walker, 34
Ex Libris, 115, 136
Exchange Building/Provost Dungeon, 68
Executive Golf Club, 203
Express Café and Bakery, 116

F
Fairfield Ocean Ridge/Wyndham, 173
Fairmont Skate Shop, 97
family activities. *See* children, activities for
Fantasia B&B, 47
Fantozzi's Wrought Iron Design, 171–74
farms and farmers markets, Charleston area, 95
fast food, take out: Beaufort area, 154; Charleston area, 59; Savannah area, 116
Favors at Forsythe, 209
film, cinema: Beaufort area, 156; Charleston area, 64; Hilton Head, 193; Savannah area, 119
Firefly Café, 115
Firehouse, The, 170
First African Baptist Church, 122
First Call for Help, emergency response, 211
Fish, 53
Fish Beaufort, 165
Fish Haul Plantation, 194
fishing: Beaufort area, 163–65; Charleston area, 84; Hilton Head, 200; regulations, 236; Savannah area, 131–32
fitness facilities and spas: Beaufort area, 165; Charleston area, 84–85; Hilton Head, 201; Savannah area, 132
Fleet Feet Sports, 139
Flying Circus, 199
Folly Beach area: dining, 57; general information, 213; lodging, 48
Folly Beach County Park, 79
food purveyors: Beaufort area, 154–55; Charleston area, 95, 95–96; Hilton Head, 209; late-night food and fuel, 226; Savannah area, 115–16
Footlight Players, 78
Forsyth Park, 134
Forsyth Park Inn, 106
Fort Howell, 194
Fort Jackson, 124–25
Fort Lamar Heritage Preserve, 72
Fort McAllister Historic Park, 125
Fort Mitchel, 194
Fort Moultrie, 72
Fort Pulaski National Monument, 125, 238
Fort San Felipe, 15

Fort Screven, 125–26
Fort Sumter National Monument, 73, 237
Four Winds Gallery, 169
4 Unity Alley, 47
Francis Beidler Forest in Four Holes Swamp, 88–89
Francis Marion Hotel, 43
Francis Marion National Forest, 87
Francis McNairy Antiques, 136
Frankie's Fun Park, 83
fred, 96
Freedom Trail Tour, 117
Freeport Marina, 204
French and Indian War, 28
French Hare, 95
French Protestant (Huguenot) Church, 68
Friedman's Fine Art, 137
Fripp Island Resort, 149–50, 165–66
fuel, late-night, 226
Fuji, 152
Fulton Five, 53
Fulton Lane Inn, 44–45

G
Gallery, The, 168
Gallery 209, 137
Gallery Chuma, 95
G&M, 237
Gallery Espresso, 116
Game and Fish Division, Georgia, 133
Garden Club of Savannah, The, 119
Garden Studio Gallery, 168
gardens. *See also* historic homes, gardens and religious sites
Gastonian, The, 107, 238
Gaucho, 137
Gaulart & Maliclet, 53
Gaye Sanders Fisher Gallery, 65
geography, 17–19
George C. Birlant & Co., 91
George C. Williams American Antiques, 91
George Fazio Course, 202
Georgia Department of Natural Resources, 133, 236
Georgia Highway Patrol, 212
Georgia poison control, 211
Ghost Talk, GhostWalk, 118
Ghosts of Charleston, 62
Gibbes Museum of Art, 63
Gifford's Golf, 166
gift stores: Beaufort area, 170; Charleston area, 95; Hilton Head, 208–9; Savannah area, 137–38
Givhan's Ferry State Park, 82
Gloria Dalvini Watercolors, 168
Go Tri Sports, 209
Golden Bear Golf Club, 202
Goldsmith Shop, The, 209
golf: Beaufort area, 165–66; Charleston area, 85–86; Hilton Head, 181, 201–4; Savannah area, 133

golf, miniature. *See* children, activities for: Hilton Head, 205

gourmet food stores, delis: Beaufort area, 154, 170; Charleston area, 95–96; Hilton Head, 209; Savannah area, 116, 138

Governor's House Inn, 45, 237

Gray's Reef National Marine Sanctuary, 131

Great Beach Vacations, 50

Greater Beaufort Chamber of Commerce, 236

Green Feet Walkabouts, 118

Greenery, Inc., The, 207

Green-Meldrim House, 34, 122, 238

Greyhound bus service. *See* bus service, national

Guggenheim's, 207

guided tours. *See* tours

Gullah Cuisine, 58

Gullah culture, 31

Gullah Heritage Trail Tours, 192

Gullah Sentinel, The, 227

Gullah Tours, 62

Gullah-N-Geechie Mahn Tours, 155

Gur's Wrecker Service, 228

gyms. *See* fitness facilities and spas

H

Häagen-Dazs, 59

Half Moon Outfitters, 139

Half-Moon Outfitters, 97

Hallelujah Singers, 159

Hamilton-Turner Inn, 107

Hampton County information, 212

Hampton Inn, Beaufort, 149

Hampton Inn Hilton Head, 185

Hampton Inn Historic District, 104

handcrafts. *See* crafts stores and galleries

handicapped services, 226

Hank's, 53–54

Happy Trails Stables, 204

Harbor golf course, The, 86

Harbor Island Rentals, 149–50

Harbour Town Crafts, 208

Harbour Town Golf Links, 202

Harbour Town Resorts, 186

Harbour Town shopping area, 206

Harbour Town Yacht Basin, 204

Harbour View Inn, 43, 237

Harris Neck National Wildlife Refuge, 129–30, 134

Hartough Gallery, 207

Hayne House, 47

Headshaker Charters, 84

health food stores: Beaufort area, 170; Charleston area, 95–96; Hilton Head, 209; Savannah area, 116

Healthy Days Natural Food Store, 209

Hearse Ghost Ride Savannah Heritage Tours, 117

Heaven Sent Christian Bookstore, 207

Henderson Golf Course, 133

Herald, The, 228

Heyward-Washington House, 69, 237

Hidden Cypress Golf Club, 203

Higginson, Thomas Wentworth, 20, 221

High Cotton, 54

Higher Ground, 171

Hilton County information, 206–9, 211–12

Hilton Decker, 137

Hilton Garden Inn, Beaufort, 149

Hilton Head: cultural attractions, 192–94; dining, 187–91; general information, 179–81; hospitals, medical care, 226; lodging, 182–87; map, 180; nightlife, 191; recreational activities, 194–206; road service, 229; seasonal events, 229–35; tours, 192; town halls, 213; traveling to, 181, 222–25; visitor information, 187, 192, 236

Hilton Head Accommodations and Golf Hotline, 187

Hilton Head Airport, 181, 224

Hilton Head Art League, 192–93

Hilton Head Art League Gallery, 207

Hilton Head Bicycle Company, 196

Hilton Head Choral Society, 194

Hilton Head Condo Hotline, 187

Hilton Head Diner, 188, 227

Hilton Head Fireworks Tours, 199

Hilton Head Health Institute, 201

Hilton Head Island–Bluffton Chamber of Commerce, 236

Hilton Head Jazz Society, 194

Hilton Head Marriott Resort & Spa, 183

Hilton Head Medical Center and Clinics, 226

Hilton Head Metropolitan Hotel, 184

Hilton Head National, 203

Hilton Head Orchestra, 194

Hilton Head Plantation, 202, 206

Hilton Head Vacation Rentals, 187

Hilton Oceanfront Resort, 183

Hilton Savannah De Soto, 104–5

Historic Beaufort Foundation tours, 156

Historic Charleston Foundation Museum Shop and Bookstore, 92

Historic Charleston Reproductions, 91

historic homes, gardens and religious sites. *See also* military sites; museums: Beaufort area, 156–58, 176; Charleston area, 65–72; Hilton Head, 193–94; Savannah area, 34, 119, 121–24

Historic Savannah Carriage Tours, 117

history: natural, 17–21; social, 21–35, 143–46, 221

H. L. Hunley Exhibit, 73

Holiday Inn Oceanfront, 185

home furnishings, kitchenware: Beaufort area, 170; Charleston area, 96; Edisto Island, 173; Hilton Head, 208; Savannah area, 138

Hominy Grill, 54, 237

Hoppin' John's, 96

horseback riding: Beaufort area, 166; Charleston area, 87; Hilton Head, 204; Savannah area, 133

horse-drawn carriage tours: Beaufort area, 155; Charleston, 62; Savannah area, 117

hospitals, 226

H_2O Sports Center, 197

Huddle House: Beaufort, 226; Hilton Head, 227

Hudson's On the Docks, 188

Hunter Horn Plantation Co. Store, 138

Hunter House Inn, 109

hunting: Charleston area, 87; regulations, 236; Savannah area, 133

Hunting Island State Park, 160, 161, 163, 238

hurricane emergency preparedness, 212

Hwy. 21 Drive-In, 156

Hyatt Regency Savannah, 105

I

ice cream: Beaufort area, 167; Charleston area, 58–59; Hilton Head, 209; Savannah area, 116

Il Cortile de Re, 54–55, 237

Il Pasticcio, 112–13

ImmediateMed, 226

In High Cotton, 170

Indian Shell Ring, 194

Indigo, 96

Indigo Gallery, 169

Indigo Run resorts, 202

Inn at Harbour Town, 183–84

Inn at Middleton Place, The, 48

Intercoastal Waterway, 224

International House of Pancakes, Charleston, 227

I'on Swamp bird-watching site, 80

I. Pinckney Simons Gallery, 169

Irish settlers, 24

Iron Fish Gallery & Studio, 207

Isaiah Davenport House, 122

Island Bikes and Outfitters, 174

Island Bookseller, 207

Island Cruisers, 196

Island Golf School, 201

Island Miniature Golf, 131

Island Packet, The, 192, 227

Island Realty, 50

Island Recreation Center, 199–200

Island Visitor Center, 187

Island Watersports, 197

Island West Golf Club, 203

Islander Steamship, 162

Isle of Palms: beach access, 79; boat rentals, 81; general information, 213; golfing, 86; lodging, 48–50; tennis, 89

Isle of Palms County Park, 79

It's Only Natural, 170

J

Jacob Preston studio, 171–74

Jamaican Me Crazy, 208

James Island County Park, 81–82, 83, 89

Jarvis Creek Water Sports, 197

Jasper County information, 212

Jazz Corner, 191

Jazz'd, 128

J&B 24 hour Towing, 229

J. D. Weed & Company, 136

Jepson Center for the Arts, 127

Jestine's Kitchen, 55

jet-skiing, 80–81

Jezebel, 137

Jinxed, 128

Joan's on Jones Bed and Breakfast, 108

John Carroll Doyle Art Gallery, 65

John Mark Verdier House, 156–57, 239

John Rutledge House Inn, 45

John Tucker Fine Arts, 120

John's Island: farmers' markets, 95; lodging, 49

John's Island–Charleston Executive Airport, 224

Johnson Creek Tavern, 159

Joseph Manigault House, 69, 237

Joseph's, 58

Juanita Greenberg's Nacho Royale, 59

Julep's, 188–89

Juliette Gordon Low National Birthplace, 122–23

Just Pasta, 189

K

Kapp/Lyons Co., 173

Kathi Rich, 137

Kathleen's, 159

Kayak Farm, The, 163

kayaking, canoeing: Beaufort area, 163; Charleston area, 79–80, 82–83; Hilton Head, 198; Savannah area, 118, 130

Kehoe House, The, 107

Kennedy's Market and Bakery, 59

Kettle Restaurant, 227

Kiawah Island: beach access, 79; dining, 57; golfing, 86; lodging, 49–50; tennis, 89

Kiawah Island Golf Resort and The Sanctuary, 49

Kickin' Chicken, The, 59

Kilwins Chocolates and Ice Cream, 116

King Charles Inn, 43

King Street Station, 227

Kingfisher, 191

King-Tisdell Cottage, 123

Kitchens on the Square, 138

kitchenware. See home furnishings, kitchenware

Knickers, 208

L

Lady & Sons, The, 113

Lady's Island Country Club, 166

Lake Aire RV Park and Campground, 81–82

Lake Mayer Park, 134

Laurel Grove–South Cemetery, 123

Lawton Stables, 204

Lazaretto Creek Marina, 132

Le Creuset Outlet Store, 97, 170

Le Spa, 201

Legend Oaks Plantation golf course, 86
Legendary Golf, 205
Legends at Parris Island, 166
Legends Sports Gallery, 209
Leland Farms, 95
Let's Go Shrimping, 199
Limehouse Plantation, 136
Links, The, 86
Links at Stono Ferry, The, 86
lodging: Beaufort area, 146–50, 173; Charleston area, 40–50; Hilton Head, 182–87; Savannah area, 104–10
Longo Gallery, 169
Loose Lucy's, 208
Low Country Adventures, 181, 192
Low Country Bicycles, 161
Lowcountry: books about, 213–19; geography, natural history, 16–21; social history, 21–35
Lowcountry and Resort Islands Tourism Commission, 236
Lowcountry Blues Society, 76
Lowcountry Estuarium, The, 159
Lowcountry Nature Tours, 199
Lowcountry Outfitters, 200, 209
Lowcountry Paddlesports, 171
Lowcountry Resort Islands and Tourism Commission, 81, 87, 160, 164
Lowcountry Sailing, 162
Lowcountry Weekly, 156, 227
Lowcountry Winery, 170
Lucas Neuhaus, 59
Lucas Theatre, 129
Luden's Outfitters, 97
Lulu Burgess, 170
LyBensons Gallery & Studio, 169

M

magazines, local, 227–28
Maggie Moo's Ice Cream and Treatery, 59
Magic Puppet, 209
Magnolia Bakery Café, 154
Magnolia Gardens, 83
Magnolia Place Inn, 107–8
Magnolia Plantation and Gardens, 69
Magnolia's Uptown/Down South, 55
Main Street Inn, 184
Main Street Village, 206
Mall at Shelter Cove, The, 206
Mansion on Forsyth Park, 108
Margaret Petterson Gallery, 65
Marina Store, 209
marinas, Hilton Head, 204–5
marine environment, 19–20
Market Street, 189
Marley's Homemade Ice Cream, 209
Marshall House, The, 105
Martin Gallery, 65
Maryland Fried Chicken, 154
Maude's Cab, 146

McCrady's, 55, 238
McIntosh Book Shoppe, 167
McKevlin's Surf Shop, 89
M. Dumas & Sons, 93
medical care, 226
Medical University of South Carolina, 226
Memorial Medical Center, 226
Mercury Air Center–Charleston International, 224
Mercury Lounge, 128
Merhaven Bed No Breakfast, 47
Metropolitan Deluxe, 97
Mi Tierra, 177, 189
Michael Anthony's, 189
Michael Rainey Antiques, 167
Middleton Place, 34, 69–70, 237
Middleton Place Equestrian Center, 87
Mighty Eighth Air Force Heritage Museum, 125
Mikell Towing, 229
military museums and sites. See also historic homes, gardens and religious sites; museums: Beaufort area, 158–59; Charleston area, 72–74; Hilton Head, 194; Savannah area, 124–26
Mills House, The, 43–44
Miss Judy Charters, 132
Moja Arts Festival, 76
Moonshell Art Gallery, 207
Moore House Antiques, 91
Morris & Whiteside Galleries, 207
Moultrie, William, 29
Mrs. Wilkes' Dining Room, 113
Mt. Pleasant, 80–81
Mulberry Inn, 105
Mullet Hall Equestrian Center, 87
museums. See also art galleries; historic homes, gardens and religious sites; military museums and sites: Beaufort area, 159; Charleston area, 30, 34, 63, 74–75; Edisto Island, 172; Hilton Head, 193–94; Savannah area, 126–28
music, live: Beaufort area, 159; Charleston area, 75–77; Hilton Head, 194
Mustard Seed, 58
Myrtle's Bar and Grill, 177

N

Nathaniel Russell House, 70, 237
National Cemetery, Beaufort, 158
national parks and forests, 81–82, 87
Native Americans. See history, social
Native Guide Tours, 198
natural history, geography, 16–21
Nature Adventures Outfitters, 83
nature preserves. See wildlife refuges, nature preserves
Needlepoint Junction, 208
newspapers, local, 227–28
Nickie Grace, 137
nightlife: Beaufort area, 159; Charleston area, 76–77; Hilton Head, 191; Savannah area, 128

Nina Liu and Friends, 65
Nippy's Fish, 154
North Beach Grill, 115
North Street Inn, 148
Northridge Ten Cinemas, 193
Northwoods Mall Cinema, 64
Norwood Stables, 133

O
Oak Plantation Campground, 81–82
Oak Point golf course, 86
Oatland Island Education Center, 126
Ocean Course, The, 86, 203
Ocean Surf Shop, 89
Ocean Winds golf course, 86
Oceanfront Cottage Rentals, 109
Off-Island, 203
Ogeechee Park Rentals, 130
Oglethorpe, James, 27
Oglethorpe Trolley Tours, 117
Okatie Creek Golf Club, 203
Old Carolina Golf Club, 203
Old Charleston Joggling Boards, 97
Old Point Inn, 148–49
Old Post Office Restaurant, 172, 239
Old Savannah Diner, 227
Old Savannah Tours, 117
Old Sheldon Church Ruins, 157
Old Slave Mart Museum, 75
Old South Carriage Co., 62
Old South Golf Links, 204
Old Town Trolley Tours, 117
Old Towne Coffehaus, 154
Olde Colony Bakery, 96
Olde Pink House, The, 113
Olde Towne Carriage Co., 62
Olympia Café, 113–14
Omni Health and Fitness Center, 165
One Fish Two Fish, 138
OSA Sailing, 81
Osprey Point golf course, 86
Ossabaw Island, 129
Outdoor Inn, 109
Outdoor Resort Yacht Basin, 204
Outdoor Shoppe, The, 97
outfitters, sports gears: Beaufort area, 163–65, 170–71,
   174; Charleston area, 83, 97. see outfitters, sports
   gear; Hilton Head, 209; Savannah area, 130, 139
Outpost Moe's, 163
Outside Hilton Head, 198, 208, 209
Owens-Thomas House Museum, 123, 138, 238
Oyster Cay Collection, 167
Oyster Reef Golf Club, 202

P
packing, what to wear, 219–20
Paddlefish Kayaking, 83

Palachucola Wildlife Management Area, 87, 133
Palm Key, 149–50
Palmetto Bay Marina, 200, 205–6
Palmetto Bay Parasail, 198
Palmetto Bay Water Sports, 198
Palmetto Bluff, 174
Palmetto Carriage Works, 62
Palmetto Dunes Golf Academy, 201
Palmetto Dunes Resort, 187, 202
Palmetto Dunes Tennis Center, 205
Palmetto Hall Plantation, 202
Palmetto Islands County Park, 83
Palmetto Taxi, 181
Palms Hotel, The, 48
Pam Harrington Exclusives, Inc., 50
Panini's Café, 152–53
Pantry, The: Beaufort, 226; Hilton Head, 227
Paperback Exchange, 207
Paradise Pier, 160, 164
Paris Market & Brocante, 138
Park Avenue Manor, 108
Park Lane Hotel and Suites, 185
Park Plaza Cinemas, 193
Parker's Market, 138
Parris Island Marine Corps Recruit Depot, 149
Parris Island Museum, 158, 239
Patriots Point Links, 86
Patriots Point Naval and Maritime Museum, 73–74
Pau Hana, 199
Paula Deen Store, The, 138
Pauline Books & Media, 92
Pedals, 196
Pei Ling Chan Garden for the Arts, 121
Peninsula Grill, 55, 237–38
Penn Center, 239
Penn Center Community Sing, 159
People, Places & Quilts, 95
Petterson Antiques, 92
Philbrick, Edward, 144
Philip Simmons Foundation, 62
Phoebe Pember House, 47
Pinch of the Past, 135
Pinckney Island National Wildlife Refuge, 134
Pink Van Tours, 172
Pirate's Island Adventure Golf, 205
pizza. *See* fast food, take out
Plantation Carriage, 117
Planters Inn, 45
Planter's Row Course, 202
Planters Tavern, 128
Player's World, 209
Plaza Stadium Theaters, 156
PluffMudd, 176
Plums, 153, 239
Po Pigs Bo-B-Q, 172, 239
Pocotaglio, 23
Point South KOA, 163
poison control, 211

police, state and local, 212
Porcupine, 208
Port Royal Bookstore, 208
Port Royal Exxon, 228
Port Royal, general information, 213
Port Royal Plantation, 202
Port Royal Racquet Club, 205
Port Royal Sound, 15
Post and Courier, The, 228
Preservation Society of Charleston, 92
private homes, lodgings in, 46–48
Putt-Putt Golf Course, 131

Q
Quality Inn, Hilton Head, 185
Quarterdeck, 191
Queen Charlotte Antiques, 95

R
Ralph Mark Gilbert Civil Rights Museum, 123
rape crisis hotlines, 211–12
Raspberry's, 96
Ray's Gym, 165
real estate, 228
recreational activities: Beaufort area, 160–66, 173;
    Charleston area, 78–80; Hilton Head, 194–206;
    Savannah area, 129–34
Red Fish, 190
Red Piano Art Gallery, 207
Red Piano Too, The, 169, 239
Red Roof Inn, Hilton Head, 185
Reel Em N, 132
Regal 6 Cinema, 119
religious sites. *See* historic homes, gardens and reli-
    gious sites
Renaissance Charleston Hotel, 44
Renaissance Fine Chocolates, 167
rental cars, 181
rental equipment. *See* outfitters, sporting gear *and*
    specific recreational activities
rental properties: Beaufort area, 150; Charleston area,
    50; Edisto, 173; Hilton Head, 185–87; Savannah area,
    109–10
reservation services. *See* lodging
Resort Quest Vacation Rentals, 187
Resort Rentals of Hilton Head Island, 187
resorts: Beaufort area, 149–50, 174; Charleston area,
    48–50, 86; Edisto Island, 173; Hilton Head, 183–84,
    186–87, 202; Tybee Island, 108–9
Rhett Gallery, 169
Rhett House Inn, 149, 238
Ribaut Lanes, 162
Ridgeland town hall, 213
Ridler Page Rare Maps, 91
Rivendell Woodworks & Gallery, 97
River House, 174
River Safari, 162

Riverboat Cruises, 118
River's End Campground and RV Park, 131
road service, emergency, 228–29
Robber's Row Course, 202
Robert Cupp Course, 202
Robert Ivey Ballet, 63
Robert Trent Jones, 202
Ron Elliott's Edisto Island Tours, 174
Roper Hospital, 226
Rose Hill Golf Club, 204
Rosebank Farms, 95
Rosen, Robert, 29–30
Rossignol's, 170
Roundhouse Railroad Museum, 123–24
RTW, 93
Russell, William Howard, 32–34
RV parks. *See* camping and RV parks

S
Saffron, 58
Sage Gallery, 173
Sage Room, 190
Sail Harbor Academy, 131
sailing: Charleston area, 81; Savannah area, 131
Saltus River Grill, 153
Sanctuary, The, 201
Sandfly Gallery, 121
Sandlapper Water Tours, 61
Sandy Creek Stables, 204
Sapphire Grill, 114, 238
Savannah Area Convention & Visitors Bureau, 236
Savannah area (including Tybee Island), 27–30; archi-
    tecture, 33; cultural attractions, 119–29; dining,
    110–15; emergency phone numbers, 211–12; food
    purveyors, 115–16; general information, 99–103;
    historic homes and sites, 34; history, 22–23, 23,
    27–28, 30, 33; hospitals, medical care, 226; late-
    night food and fuel, 227; local transportation, 225;
    lodging, 104–10; map, 100; newspapers and maga-
    zines, 228; recreational activities, 129–34; road
    service, 229; seasonal events, 229–35; shopping,
    134–39, 238; tours, 116–18; town halls, 213; traveling
    to, 103, 222–25; visitor information, 108, 119, 236
Savannah Aviation, 224
Savannah College of Art and Design, 119–20
Savannah Haunted History Tours, 118
Savannah History Museum, 126–27
Savannah Inn and Country Club, 133
Savannah Light Tackle Fishing Co., 132
Savannah Morning News, 228
Savannah National Wildlife Refuge, 129, 133, 134
Savannah Sailing Center, 131
Savannah Sand Gnats baseball, 129
Savannah Science Museum, 127
Savannah Theater Company, 129
Savannah Tour of Homes and Gardens, 119
Savannah Tribune, 228
Savannah Visitor Center, 119

Savannah Walks, 118
Savannah/Hilton Head International Airport, 40, 146, 181
Savannah's Candy Kitchen, 116
SCAD's Trustees Theater, 129
Schooner Pride tours, 61
Sea Horse Farms, 204
Sea Island Inn (Best Western), 149
Sea Island Wine & Gourmet, 153
Sea Islands, Charleston area, 48–50. *See also* Charleston area
Sea Kayak Georgia, 118
Sea Marsh Course, 203
Sea Pines Forest Preserve, 196–97
Sea Pines Plantation, 202, 206
Sea Pines Racquet Club, 205
Sea Pines Resort, 187
Sea Turtle Cinemas, 193
Sea Wolf VI, 165
Seabrook Exclusives, 50
Seabrook Island Resort, 49; boating, 81; dining, 57; golfing, 86
Seaside Inn, 48
seasonal events: Beaufort area, 159; Charleston, 75–76; Charleston area, 64; Edisto Island, 172; Hilton Head, 192, 194; listing of, by month, 229–35; Savannah area, 119
Second African Baptist Church, 124
See Savannah Walking Tours, 118
Seeds of Calm Spa, 201
Sermet's Corner, 56
17th Street Inn, 109
Shadowmoss Plantation Golf Club, 86
Shalimar Horse Center, 166
Shelter Cove Harbour, 205, 206
Sherman, W. T., 122
Shipman Art Gallery, 169
Ships of the Sea Museum, 127
Shipyard Golf Club, 203
Shipyard Plantation, 203
Shipyard Racquet Club, 206
shopping: Beaufort area, 167–71, 176–77, 239; Charleston area, 89–97, 237; Edisto Island, 173; Hilton Head, 206–9; Savannah area, 134–39, 238
shopSCAD, 121
shore refuges. *See* wildlife refuges
Shoreline Ballroom, 191
Shrimp Shack, 153
Sigler's Rotisserie and Seafood, 177
Signe's Heaven Bound Bakery, 209
Signe's Heaven Bound Bakery & Café, 190
Simply Silver, 136
Sippin' Cow Café, The, 177
Sites and Insight Tours by Al Miller, 61
Skidaway Island State Park, 129, 131
Skirt!, 228
Skull Creek Marina, 205
slavery, 30–33

S.M. Bradford–Lilly Pulitzer Shop, 208
Smalls, Robert, 33
Smith Galleries of Fine Crafts, 208
Smith-Killian Fine Art, 65
Society of Bluffton Artists Gallery, 176
Soho South Café, 116
Sophia Institute, 85
South Beach Marina, 205, 206
South Beach Racquet Club, 205
South Carolina Aquarium, 75
South Carolina Department of Natural Resources, 79, 174, 236
South Carolina Department of Parks, Recreation, and Tourism, 236
South Carolina Highway Patrol, 212
South Carolina Marine Resources Division, 81
South Carolina National Golf Club, 166
South Carolina Repertory Company, 194
South of Market, 97
Southbridge Golf Club, 133
Southeastern Wildlife Exposition, 87
Southern Sweets Ice Cream Parlor, 167
Spa Adagio, 85
spas. *See* fitness facilities and spas
Spirit of Old Beaufort, The, 155
Spiritline Harbor Tour, 61
Spoleto Festival U.S.A., 76–77, 237
sport fishing. *See* charters, fishing
Sportline, 209
Sports Addiction, 176
sports gear. *See* outfitters, sports gear
St. Helena Episcopal Church Women tours, 156
St. Helena Island, 155, 168
St. Helena's Episcopal Church, 158
St. Joseph's Hospital, 226
St. Michael's Episcopal Church, 70–71
St. Philip's Episcopal Church, 71
Stages, 191
Starland Design District, Savannah, 138
Stars & Stripes, 199
state police, 212
state/county parks and forests: Beaufort area, 160, 163, 173; Charleston area, 81–83, 87; Savannah area, 129, 131
Stell Park, 134
Stevens 24-hour Towing, 229
Stono Farm Market, 95
Stono Ferry Stables, 87
Stono River Stable and Farm, 87
Store, The, 177
Storybrook Farm, 87
Sullivan's Island, 79–80
Summer Concerts, Hilton Head, 200
Sun & Ski, 81
Sundial Nature and Fishing Tours, 132
Sunny Daze Surf Factory, 209
Sunset Grille, 172
surfing, 89

Susan Graber Gallery, 169
Sushi Zen, 116
Swan House Antiques, 207
sweetgrass baskets, 168
Sweetgrass Ladies Apparel, 168
Sylvan Gallery, The, 65

T
Tabernacle Baptist Church, 158
Talbot's, 168
Talk of the Towne, 61
Tanger Outlet Stores 1 & 2, 206
taxis: Beaufort area, 146; Hilton Head, 181, 192
Taylored Tours, 61
Telfair Museum of Art, 127
Temple Mickve Israel, 124
tennis: Beaufort area, 166; Charleston area, 89; Hilton
  Head, 205–6; Savannah area, 134
Terra Cotta, 137
Terrace Oaks Antique Mall, 91
theater: Charleston area, 26–27, 78; Hilton Head, 194;
  Savannah area, 128–29
Theater 99, 78
36 Meeting Street Bed and Breakfast, 47
Thomas Elfe Workshop, 71–72
Thomas Lamboll House, 47
Thompson's Sports Shop, 139
Thunderbird Inn, 108, 238
Tidal Wave Runners, 81
tours: Beaufort area, 155–56; Charleston, 59–62;
  Charleston area, 80; Edisto Island, 172; Hilton Head,
  192; Savannah area, 116–18
Tours by BJ, 117
Tours of Edisto, 172
town halls, 212–13
Trademark Cinema, 119
train travel: to Beaufort area, 146; to Charleston, 40; to
  Hilton Head, 181; to Savannah, 103
Trident Regional Medical Center, 226
trolley tours: Hilton Head, 192; Savannah area, 117
Truffles Café, 190–91
Truffles Market, 209
Trustees' Garden (Savannah), 28
Tuc In DeWood Campground, 163
Turtle Island, 133
Turtle Point golf course, 86
21 East Battery Bed & Breakfast, 47
27 State Street, 48
Two Eleven Park Wine Bar & Bistro, 191
Two Meeting Street Inn, 45
Two Suns Inn, 149
Tybee Island: dining, 114–15; general information,
  213; lodging, 108–10
Tybee Island Charters, 132
Tybee Island Inn, 109
Tybee Island Museum and Lighthouse, 125–26
Tybee Island North Beach, 129
Tybee Island Rentals, 109

Tybee Island YMCA, 132
Tybee Memorial Park, 134
Tybee Vacation Rentals, 110
Tybee Visitor Center, 108

U
University of Georgia Marine Extension Service
  Aquarium, 127–28
University of South Carolina at Beaufort, 169
Upper Crust, 154
US 17 bird-watching site, 80

V
V. & J. Duncan, 136
Vagabond Cruise, 192
Van der Meer Tennis Centers, 206
Verdier House Gift Shop, 170
Verizon Heritage PGA Tour, 181
Vesey, Denmark, 30
Veteran's Administration Medical Center, 226
Vickery's, 56
Victoria Bluff Heritage Preserve, 133, 134
Village at Wexford, 206
Village Craftsmen, 137
Vinnie Van Gogo's, 114
Vintage Restaurant and Wine Bar, 56
Virginia's on King, 56–57
visitor information: Beaufort area, 160, 164;
  Charleston area, 87; Edisto Island, 172; fishing and
  hunting regulations, 236; Hilton Head, 187, 192;
  Savannah area, 108, 119

W
Wadmalaw Island, 80, 95
Waffle House: Charleston, 227; Savannah, 227
Waldenbooks: Charleston, 92; Hilton Head, 208
walking tours: Beaufort area, 155; Charleston area,
  61–62; Hilton Head, 192; Savannah area, 118
Walsh Mountain Ironworks, 137
Walter Greer Gallery, 193
Walterboro, 213
Walterboro-Colleton Chamber of Commerce, 82–83
Ware, Harriet, 152
Wassaw Island, 129
Water-Dog Outfitters, 198
Waterfun Park and Mini Golf, 200, 205
Waterside Place, 170
weather information, 219–20
Webb Wildlife Management Area, 87, 133
Wells Gallery, 65
Wentworth Mansion, 45–46
Westin Hilton Head Island Resort and Spa, 184
Westin Savannah Harbor Golf Resort & Spa, 105–6
what to wear, 219–20
What's In Store, 167
Whooping Crane Conservancy, 197
Wild Dunes Resort, 49–50, 86, 89

Wild Dunes Yacht Harbor, 81
Wild Wing Café, 191
Wilderness Southeast, 130
Wildlife and Marine Resources Department, 87
wildlife refuges, nature preserves, 87; Beaufort area, 161, 174; Charleston area, 79–80, 88–89; Hilton Head, 196; Savannah area, 129–30, 133–34
windsurfing, 89
Wine & Gourmet, 170
With These Hands, 173
Wolcott, Marion Post, 34
Wonderland, 93
Wood Brothers Campground, 81–82
Woodward, Henry, 24
Wormsloe Historic Site, 124

Worthwhile, 93
Wright Square Café, 116

X
XO Lounge, 191

Y
Yellow Cab, 146
YMCA: Beaufort County, 165; Charleston, 132; Tybee Island, 132

Z
Zero Gravity Divers Depot, 131

Lodging by Price

Inexpensive:	Up to $60
Moderate:	$60 to $120
Expensive:	$120 to $200
Very Expensive:	Over $200

Beaufort Area (including Edisto and Bluffton)

Moderate
Sea Island Inn (Best Western), 149

Moderate–Expensive
North Street Inn, 148
Old Point Inn, 148
Two Suns Inn, 149

Expensive
Beaulieu House at Cat Island and Port Royal, 148
Craven Street Inn, 148

Expensive-Very Expensive
Beaufort Inn, 147
Cuthbert House Inn, 148
Rhett House Inn, 149

Charleston Area (including Sea Islands)

Moderate
1837 Bed and Breakfast, 47
Merhaven Bed No Breakfast, 47

Moderate–Expensive
Ansonborough Inn, 44
Charleston on the Beach, 48
Embassy Suites-Historic District, 43
Fantasia B&B, 47
King Charles Inn, 43
The Palms Hotel, 48
36 Meeting Street Bed and Breakfast, 47

Expensive
Battery Carriage House Inn, 44
Broad Street Guest House, 47
4 Unity Alley, 47
Hayne House, 47
Phoebe Pember House, 47
Renaissance Charleston Hotel, 44
Thomas Lamboll House, 47

Expensive–Very Expensive
Charleston Place, 42
Francis Marion Hotel, 43
Fulton Lane Inn, 44
Governor's House Inn, 45
Harbour View Inn, 43
The Inn at Middleton Place, 48
John Rutledge House Inn, 45
Kiawah Island Golf Resort and The Sanctuary, 49
Mills House, 43

Planters Inn, 45
Seabrook Island Resort, 49
27 State Street, 48
Wild Dunes Resort, 49–50

Very Expensive
21 East Battery Bed & Breakfast, 47
Two Meeting Street Inn, 45
Wentworth Mansion, 46

Hilton Head

Expensive
Hilton Head Metropolitan Hotel, 184
Holiday Inn Oceanfront, 185

Expensive–Very Expensive
Main Street Inn, 184
Park Lane Hotel and Suites, 185

Very Expensive
Crowne Plaza Resort, 183
Daufuskie Island Resort, 183
Hilton Head Marriott Resort & Spa, 183
Hilton Oceanfront Resort, 183
Inn at Harbour Town, 183
Westin Hilton Head Island Resort and Spa, 184

Savannah Area (including Tybee Island)

Inexpensive–Moderate
Outdoor Inn, 109

Moderate
Hampton Inn Historic District, 104
Hunter House Inn, 109
17th Street Inn, 109

Moderate–Expensive
Tybee Island Inn, 109

Expensive
Dunes Inn and Suites, 109
East Bay Inn, 106
Forsyth Park Inn, 106
Hilton Savannah De Soto, 104
The Mulberry Inn, 105

Expensive–Very Expensive
Ballastone Inn, 106
Eliza Thompson House, 106
Hamilton-Turner Inn, 107
Hyatt Regency Savannah, 105
Magnolia Place Inn, 107
The Marshall House, 105
Westin Savannah Harbor Golf Resort & Spa, 105

Very Expensive
The Gastonian, 107
The Kehoe House, 107
Mansion on Forsyth Park, 108

Dining by Price

Inexpensive:	Up to $15
Moderate:	$15 to $30
Expensive:	$30 to $50
Very Expensive:	Over 50

Beaufort Area (including Edisto and Bluffton)

Inexpensive
Fuji, 152
Shrimp Shack, 153

Moderate
11th Street Dockside, 151
Sea Island Wine & Gourmet, 153

Moderate–Expensive
Breakwater, 151
Panini's Café, 152
Plums, 153
Saltus River Grill, 153

Expensive
Emily's Restaurant and Tapas Bar, 152

Expensive–Very Expensive
Bateaux, 151

Charleston Area (including Sea Islands)

Inexpensive
Gullah Cuisine, 58

Inexpensive–Moderate
Bowen's Island Restaurant, 57
Gaulart & Maliclet, 53
Hominy Grill, 54
Il Cortile de Re, 54
Jestine's Kitchen, 55
Mustard Seed, 58
Vickery's, 56

Moderate
Basil, 51
Sermet's Corner, 56

Moderate–Expensive
Fish, 53
Fulton Five, 53
Hank's, 53
Magnolia's Uptown/Down South, 55
Virginia's on King, 56

Expensive
Anson, 51
Boathouse on East Bay, 52
Vintage Restaurant and Wine Bar, 56

Expensive–Very Expensive
Charleston Grill, 52
Circa 1886, 52

Cypress Lowcountry Grille, 52
High Cotton, 54
McCrady's, 55
Peninsula Grill, 55

Hilton Head

Inexpensive
Hilton Head Diner, 188
Market Street, 189
Signe's Heaven Bound Bakery & Café, 190

Inexpensive–Moderate
Just Pasta, 189
Mi Tierra, 189
Truffles Café, 190

Moderate
Hudson's On the Docks, 188

Expensive
CQs, 188
Michael Anthony's, 189
Sage Room, 190
Two Eleven Park Wine Bar & Bistro, 191

Expensive–Very Expensive
Julep's, 188
Red Fish, 190

Savannah Area (including Tybee Island)

Inexpensive
The Breakfast Club, 114
Clary's Café, 112
Mrs. Wilkes' Dining Room, 113
Vinnie Van Gogo's, 114

Inexpensive–Moderate
Crystal Beer Parlor, 112
North Beach Grill, 115
Olympia Café, 113

Moderate
Casbah, 111
Crab Shack at Chimney Creek, 114
The Lady & Sons, 113

Moderate–Expensive
Belford's, 111
Bistro Savannah, 111
Cha Bella, 111
Il Pasticcio, 112

Expensive
Bamboo Room, 115
The Olde Pink House, 113

Expensive–Very Expensive
Sapphire Grill, 114

Very Expensive
Elizabeth on 37th, 112

Dining by Cuisine

Beaufort Area (including Edisto and Bluffton)

American, New American
Bateaux, 151
Breakwater, 151
11th Street Dockside, 151
Plums, 153
Saltus River Grill, 153
Sunset Grille, 172

Asian
Fuji, 152

Continental
Emily's Restaurant and Tapas Bar, 152
Sea Island Wine & Gourmet, 153

Italian, Mediterranean
Panini's Café, 152

Seafood
11th Street Dockside, 151
Old Post Office Restaurant, 172
Shrimp Shack, 153

Southern, New Southern
Po Pigs Bo-B-Q, 172

Charleston Area (including Sea Islands)

American, New American
Anson, 51
Circa 1886, 52
Cypress Lowcountry Grille, 52
Hank's, 53
High Cotton, 54
McCrady's, 55
Mustard Seed, 58
Peninsula Grill, 55
Vickery's, 56
Vintage Restaurant and Wine Bar, 56

Asian
Cypress Lowcountry Grille, 52

Cuban
Vickery's, 56

French
Gaulart & Maliclet, 53

Italian, Northern Italian
Fulton Five, 53
Il Cortile de Re, 54

Mediterranean, North African
Sermet's Corner, 56

Seafood
Boathouse on East Bay, 52
Bowen's Island Restaurant, 57
Hank's, 53

Southern, New Southern
Charleston Grill, 52
Fish, 53
Gullah Cuisine, 58
Hominy Grill, 54
Jestine's Kitchen, 55
Magnolia's Uptown/Down South, 55
Peninsula Grill, 55
Virginia's on King, 56

Thai
Basil, 51

Hilton Head

American, New American
Hilton head Diner, 188
Sage Room, 190
Signe's Heaven Bound Bakery & Café, 190
Truffles Café, 190
Two Eleven Park Wine Bar & Bistro, 191

Caribbean
Red Fish, 190

Continental
Julep's, 188
Truffles Café, 190

Italian, Northern Italian
Just Pasta, 189
Michael Anthony's, 189

Mediterranean,
Market Street, 189

Mexican
Mi Tierra, 189

Seafood
Hudson's On the Docks, 188

Southern, New Southern
CQs, 188
Julep's, 188
Two Eleven Park Wine Bar & Bistro, 191

Savannah Area (including Tybee Island)

American, New American
Bamboo Room, 115
Clary's Café, 112
Elizabeth on 37th, 112
Sapphire Grill, 114

Caribbean
North Beach Grill, 115

Greek
Olympia Café, 113

International, Continental
Bistro Savannah, 111
The Olde Pink House, 113

Italian, Northern Italian
Il Pasticcio, 112
Vinnie Van Gogo's, 114

Mediterranean
Cha Bella, 111

Moroccan
Casbah, 111

Seafood
Bamboo Room, 115
Bistro Savannah, 111
Crab Shack at Chimney Creek, 114
North Beach Grill, 115

Southern, New Southern
Belford's, 111
The Breakfast Club, 114
Crystal Beer Parlor, 112
Elizabeth on 37th, 112
The Lady & Sons, 113
Mrs. Wilkes' Dining Room, 113
The Olde Pink House, 113